The Streets of Heaven
The Ideology of Wealth in the Apocalypse of John

I've never been to heaven, but I've been told, . . .
That the streets of heaven are paved with gold. . . .
("Swing Low, Sweet Chariot")

The Streets of Heaven

The Ideology of Wealth
in the Apocalypse of John

by
Robert M. Royalty, Jr.

MERCER UNIVERSITY PRESS
1998

ISBN 0-86554-609-6

MUP/H465

The Streets of Heaven. The Ideology of Wealth in the Apocalypse of John.
Copyright ©1998
Mercer University Press, Macon, Georgia USA

Part of the present work appeared as "The Rhetoric of Revelation"
in *The Society of Biblical Literature 1997 Seminar Papers*, 596–617,
©1997 Scholars Press, and is included here by permission.

Library of Congress Cataloging-in-Publication Data

Royalty, Robert M., Jr., 1961–
The streets of heaven :
the ideology of wealth in the Apocalypse of John /
by Robert M. Royalty, Jr.
viii+292pp. 6x9" (15x23cm.).
Includes bibliographical references and indexes.
ISBN 0-86554-609-6 (alk. paper).
1. Bible. N.T. Revelation—Criticism, interpretation, etc.
2. Wealth—Religious aspects—Christianity.
I. Title.
BS2825.6.W37R68   1998
228'.06—dc21   98-41237
CIP

Contents

Acknowledgments

This book began as my dissertation at Yale University. The project was inspired and guided by Professor Wayne A. Meeks, an inspiration and guide for all who would learn more about the early Christian communities, and by Professor Susan R. Garrett, now of Louisville Presbyterian Theological Seminary. I especially thank Professor Garrett for her energy and enthusiasm, patient encouragement, careful reading, and determined efforts to clarify my thinking and prose. I am thankful to others who have read and commented on the manuscript. All errors and inaccuracies of course remain my own.

In particular I thank Professors David L. Bartlett of Yale Divinity School, W. Martin Bloomer, now of the University of Notre Dame, and David E. Aune of Loyola University in Chicago. Volume 1 of the three-volume commentary on Revelation by Professor Aune became available only in the final stages of editing. The publication of his work marks a major stage in the history of research on the Apocalypse; it is sure to take the place of R. H. Charles's 1920 commentary as the standard work on Revelation. I thank the Interlibrary Loan staff at Green Library, Stanford University, and Dr. Cecil R. White of St. Patrick's Seminary, Menlo Park, for their assistance in obtaining research materials. I thank Marc A. Jolley, Edmon L. Rowell, Jr., and the rest of the staff of Mercer University Press for their professionalism, graciousness, and good humor.

I would also like to thank those who, often unknowingly, have contributed to or supported this project: Professors Bentley Layton and Abraham J. Malherbe of Yale University; Professor Lee A. Yearley and Dean Robert C. Gregg of Stanford University; Beverly H. Grove, the Rev. Katherine H. Lehman, and H. Gregory Snyder. I am grateful to the Episcopal Church Foundation for the support of a Graduate Fellowship from 1991 to 1994. The encouragement and support my father, Robert M. Royalty, Sr. (1933–1991), allowed me to begin graduate studies. He taught me, among many other things, the value of the intellectual life.

Above all I thank my wife, Anne Beeson Royalty, for her love and support in the midst of her own academic labors; our son, Nolen, who has helped me to keep a sense of perspective by always asking why I wanted to write a book about the Bible and why it was taking so long; and Virginia, for keeping all of us smiling. I dedicate this book to them with love.

Abbreviations

Annales (ESC)	*Annales (Economie, Sociétés, Civilisations)*, Paris, A. Colin
CQ	*Classical Quarterly*, Oxford University Press
ESAR	*An Economic Survey of Ancient Rome*, ed. Tenney Frank (4 vols.)
Iren., *Adv. Haer.*	Irenaeus, *Adverus Haereses*
Just. Mart., *Apol.*	Justin Martyr, *Apology*
Just. Mart., *Dial.*	Justin Martyr, *Dialogue with Trypho*
JWSTP	*Jewish Writings of the Second Temple Period*, ed. M. E. Stone
REL	*Revue des Etudes Latines*, Paris, Les Belles Lettres
SEHRE²	M. Rostovtzeff, *A Social and Economic History of the Roman Empire*, 2nd ed.
YCS	*Yale Classical Studies*

Other abbreviations follow the style set forth in the *Society of Biblical Literature Membership Directory and Handbook* (Decatur GA: Society of Biblical Literature, 1994) 223–40, as updated in "Instructions for Contributors," *Journal of Biblical Literature* 117/3 (Fall 1998): 555-79; and in *The Oxford Classical Dictionary*, 2nd ed., ed. N. G. L. Hammond and H. H. Scullard (Oxford: Clarendon Press/Oxford University Press, 1970) ix–xxii. Commentaries on Revelation are cited by author and page number(s); see the bibliography for commentaries cited.

Texts and Translations

Biblical translations are from the New Revised Standard Version (NRSV; ©1989 by the Division of Christian Education of the National Council of the Churches of Christ in the USA), with modifications as noted. Texts and translations for ancient Greek and Roman authors, including Josephus and Philo, are from the Loeb Classical Library, except where noted. Texts and translations used for other ancient Jewish literature have been cited in the text. See the bibliography for a complete list of primary sources, texts, and translations used.

Introduction

By the time of Jesus, all the lowest classes and mediocre people had realized that *never* would they get a chance to be kings, *never* would they go in chariots, never would they drink wine from gold vessels. Very well then—they would have their revenge by *destroying* it all. "Babylon the great is fallen, is fallen, and is become the habitation of devils."—how one hears the envy, the endless envy screeching through this song of triumph!   —D. H. Lawrence, *Apocalypse* (1931)

Money Talks

From John's opening vision of Jesus on the island of Patmos to the descent of the New Jerusalem from heaven, the book of Revelation includes an array of images of wealth and trade: heavenly beings dressed in gold; churches praised for their poverty and admonished for their independent means; control of buying and selling by Satan's minions; the fall of the wealthiest city on earth; and a heavenly city with pearly gates and streets of gold. Characters on all sides in the Apocalypse have wealth. The moral exhortation in the messages to Smyrna and Laodicea, delivered by a gold-clad Christ, turns on the issues of poverty and wealth. Images of wealth, trade, and luxury are used to characterize the harlot, city, and merchants of Babylon. Economic disaster plays a recurring role in the series of afflictions that John sees besetting the inhabitants of the earth. How would this wealth imagery have been heard or understood by a first-century audience? Would it have made any sense?

The prominence of wealth imagery in Revelation stirred readers and commentators long before D. H. Lawrence.[1] In the first two centuries after Revelation was written, chiliastic interpretation predominated. Chiliasts (from the Greek for "thousand," *chilioi*) took a literal interpretation of Rev 20:4–5 and looked forward to a thousand-year reign with Christ on earth. The word "millenarian" (from the Latin for "a thousand

---

[1] See D. H. Lawrence, *Apocalypse and the Writings on Revelation*, ed. M. Kalnins (Cambridge: Cambridge University Press, 1980) 3–24, on the circumstances of Lawrence's writing of *Apocalypse*; quotation on 144.

years," *mille anni*), is used today of people who take a literal view of this passage. Chiliastic readings in the second century CE tended toward materialistic interpretations of the millennium kingdom and the wealth described in the New Jerusalem.[2] The other prominent line of ancient interpretation, particularly in the ancient Greek East, was allegory. At the end of the second century, Clement of Alexandria chastised Christian women who took the description of the New Jerusalem in Revelation 21 as a warrant for wearing jewelry (*Paed.* 2.12, 119.1–3). Clement, in his typical manner, points out the allegorical or spiritual meaning of the passage: the brilliance of the stones signifies the brilliance of the spirit.[3] The Christian historian Eusebius of Caesarea records another debate over the imagery of wealth in Revelation that occurred in Alexandria during the third century CE, two generations after Clement.[4] Eusebius reports that Nepos, an Egyptian bishop, wrote a text called "Refutation of the Allegorists," in which he held that "the promises which had been made to the saints in the divine Scriptures should be interpreted after a more Jewish fashion (ἰουδαϊκώτερον)." In other words, Nepos took passages such as the vision of the New Jerusalem in Revelation 21–22 literally rather than allegorically. Nepos also described the millennium for the saints as a time of "bodily indulgence." Bishop Dionysius of Alexandria, in his "On Promises," attempted to refute the interpretation of Revelation by Nepos. In an excerpt of this book recorded by Eusebius, Dionysius defends allegorical interpretation and indeed the book of Revelation itself, which, he writes, had been impugned by others as unintelligible, illogical, and hardly the "unveiling" (ἀποκάλυψις) that the Greek

---

[2]See Swete, cvii–cxiii; Gerhard Maier, *Die Johannesoffenbarung und die Kirche*, WUNT 25 (Tübingen: J. C. B. Mohr [Paul Siebeck], 1981) 1–107; and Arthur W. Wainright, *Mysterious Apocalypse: Interpreting the Book of Revelation* (Nashville: Abingdon, 1993) 21–31; see also Eus. *Hist. Eccl.* 3.39.12 on Papias; Just. Mart. *Dial.* 81; Iren. *Adv. Haer.* 5.30.4; 5.33.1–35.2; Lactanius *Divinae Institutiones* 7.24; on the so-called "Alogoi," who opposed the Apocalypse and Gospel of John, see Iren. *Adv. Haer.* 3.2.9; Epiphanius *Panarion* 51.3.

[3]See Clem. *Paed.* 2.12 (119.2). For a general discussion of allegory, see David Dawson, *Allegorical Readers and Cultural Revision in Ancient Alexandria* (Berkeley, Los Angeles, and London: University of California Press, 1992). The work is a study of Philo, Clement (the *Protrepticus*, not the *Paedagogus*), and Valentinus.

[4]See Eus. *Hist. Eccl.* 7.24.1–25.5.

title promises.[5] Dionysius writes that "they" have claimed that the author of Revelation was neither an apostle nor a saint, but Cerinthus, labeled a heretic by the orthodox Christian party, who taught:

> that the kingdom of Christ would be on earth; and he dreamed that it would consist in those things which formed the object of his own desires (for he was a lover of the body and altogether carnal), in the full satisfaction of the belly and lower lusts, that is, in feasts and carousals and marriages, and (as a means, he thought, of procuring these under a better name) in festivals and sacrifices and slayings of victims.

Dionysius attempts to counter these critics with his allegorical interpretation and historical investigation into the question of authorship. It appears that the imagery of wealth in Revelation, when taken "literally," caused some heated discussion in the early church.[6]

Modern commentators, like their ancient counterparts in Alexandria, have tended to use allegorical interpretation when dealing with the heavenly wealth depicted in Revelation. These images of wealth have typically been understood in various "symbolic" senses, such as general descriptions of the glory of God, figures of joy at the eschaton, or symbols of the eternal nature of heaven.[7] The social and ideological force of the wealth imagery is fully expressed only when discussing the "mark of the Beast" in Rev 13:16 or "Babylon" in Revelation 17–18, since these passages refer to Rome rather than to God. A second approach in recent scholarship interprets the attack on Babylon in Revelation as a Marxist critique of Roman economic oppression and injustice.[8] This approach, to be discussed in more detail below, appears to be heavily influenced by the interpretation of D. H. Lawrence, who assumed that the attack on

---

[5]A significant number of early exegetes seriously questioned Revelation's authority within the emerging Christian canon; see Eus. *Hist. Eccl.* 3.25; A. C. Sundberg, Jr., "Canon of the NT," *IDBSup* 136–40.

[6]By placing "literal" in quotation marks, I am in agreement with Dawson and many others that there is no reified, true literal meaning residing in a text but that all meanings are culturally constructed; the "literal" meaning for a community is but one of many possible allegorical readings.

[7]A wide range of commentators typify this approach: Swete; Charles (although history-of-religions and source-critical issues are often primary); Caird; Mounce; Beasley-Murray; Roloff.

[8]This approach is typified by Richard Bauckham and, to a lesser extent, Adela Yarbro Collins (see chap. 1, nn. 36 and 68).

Babylon was motivated by Christian resentment of Roman wealth.[9] Norman Cohn's study of millenarian movements among the "rootless poor" of Europe in the eleventh to the sixteenth centuries also lies behind this Marxist approach.[10]

There is no reason, however, to let Revelation 18 speak for the entire narrative world of the Apocalypse; what of God's jewels and Christ's gold? Money talks, and all of Revelation should be listened to when reading for the imagery of wealth in the text, even if the idea of a wealthy God disturbs modern sensibilities. In this book, I will read for the ideology of both heaven's and Babylon's wealth by examining how the wealth imagery in Revelation supports and subverts the structures of power in the text and its social context. Wealth, in Revelation, functions to praise and to blame. The prominent wealth motifs in John's visions of Christ, heaven, and the New Jerusalem function to accentuate the power and glory of God, the Lamb, and the bride of Christ. The same images that glorify God vilify Babylon. Wealth motifs are equally prominent in the description of the harlot on the scarlet beast and the laments over the fallen city of Babylon, but in these passages the wealth motifs have a decidedly negative function. Babylon's lust for wealth and luxury epitomizes the moral depravity of the city. Intriguing similarities between heaven and Babylon's wealth further confound efforts to sort out the literary function of wealth imagery in Revelation. Babylon's merchants and sea captains trade in the same luxury goods that adorn the heavenly armies and the New Jerusalem. In both the descriptions of heaven and Babylon, wealth motifs have political associations.

Wealth imagery appears on both sides of the great conflict in Revelation between God and Satan. How can gold and jewels be both good and bad? When we add a second question, how would this language have been *heard* within the early Christian communities of Asia, the issue becomes even more complex. The plan of this book is designed to answer these questions. This introductory chapter sets out basic issues of methodology and defines the questions to be pursued. In chapters 2 and 3, we will explore the worlds of Jewish and Greco-Roman literature and culture contemporary to Revelation in order to learn how other writers and communities talked about wealth and commerce. This study of the

---

[9]See the quotation above and n. 1.

[10]Norman Cohn, *The Pursuit of the Millennium: Revolutionary Millenarians and Mystical Anarchists of the Middle Ages*, rev. ed. (Oxford: Oxford University Press, 1970).

social-historical context of the early Christian communities that read Revelation allows for effective analysis of the rhetoric and ideology of wealth in chapters 4–7.

Narrative Worlds, Social Worlds, Symbolic Universes

The first issue to be sorted out is what audience I am thinking of when I read for the ideology of wealth in the Apocalypse. A number of distinguished readers of Revelation have gone before me, from Irenaeus and Dionysius of Alexandria to D. H. Lawrence and Austin Farrer; the din of their voices can easily drown out how Revelation would have sounded in 95 CE. Nevertheless, I will try to hear how the text would have been heard in its original context. The relationship of text and context is a particularly difficult problem that has plagued twentieth-century literary criticism as well as biblical studies. Although Revelation has not been at the forefront of New Testament studies over the past 100 years, the interpretation of the book has been marked by the same theoretical divisions that have characterized Synoptic studies and, to a lesser extent, the study of Paul.[11] I will keep the issue in terms of the Apocalypse. Historical-criticism pays a great deal of attention to what is going on behind the text. This concern has been well represented in interpretations of the Apocalypse.[12] Revelation makes a number of historical claims and

---

[11]While Synoptic studies have been dominated by the relation of text and history since Schweitzer and Wrede, the notion of the Pauline epistles as narrative to be interpreted rather than history and theology to be reconstructed is relatively new. See Richard B. Hays, *The Faith of Jesus Christ: An Investigation into the Narrative Substructure of Galatians 3:1–4:11*, SBLDS 56 (Chico CA: Scholars Press, 1983) 1–36; and Norman Petersen, *Rediscovering Paul: Philemon and the Sociology of Paul's Narrative World* (Philadelphia: Fortress Press, 1985) 1–42.

[12]I am not speaking here of conservative interpretations that apply Revelation to their various contemporaneous situations, because such readings pay no attention to the text's historical context. For surveys of the history of interpretation of Revelation, see Bousset, 51–141 (102–40 on the triumph of historical-critical methodology); Boring, 47–51; and Wainright, *Mysterious Apocalypse*. The strictly historical interpretation has tended to flourish among British scholars and has had more success with Rev 2–3 and 13 than the visions in Revelation 4–22. See William M. Ramsay, *The Letters to the Seven Churches of Asia and Their Place in the Plan of the Apocalypse*, ed. Mark W. Wilson (Peabody MA: Hendrickson Publishers, 1994; orig. pub. London: Hodder & Stoughton; New York: A. C. Armstrong, 1904) and Colin J. Hemer, *The Letters to the Seven*

seems to describe political events in the first century CE. But on the other hand, Revelation spins such a fantastic narrative of visions and sevens and phantasmagorical characters that the "meaning" surely goes beyond the historical context of Asia Minor. The Apocalypse is what Umberto Eco has described as an "open work."[13] The seductive richness of the imagery and the complexity of the vision cycles lead scholars to construct equally rich and complex literary interpretations, which tend to leave the historical context behind in a search for more universal significance.[14] Structuralist theory has dominated literary analysis of Revelation for the past twenty-five years. While pure structuralism leans toward the ahistorical, the strong historical bent of biblical studies (the "old historicism") has kept most structuralist studies of Revelation firmly anchored in the historical context of the text.[15] In recent years, the fruits of poststructural theory, which can be radically ahistorical in its decon-

---

Churches of Asia in their Local Setting, JSNTSup 11 (Sheffield: JSOT Press, 1986). Hemer claims that the language of Revelation is referential, rather than performative, and that the letters have specific and concrete referents in the social historical setting.

[13]See Umberto Eco, "The Poetics of the Open Work," *The Role of the Reader: Explorations in the Semiotics of Texts* (Bloomington IN and London: Indiana University Press, 1979) 47–66.

[14]For source criticism, the intricate theories of R. H. Charles in his commentary rival those of Synoptic scholars. For Jungian and symbolic analysis, see Austin Farrer, *A Rebirth of Images: The Making of St Johns' Apocalypse* (London: Westminster, Dacre Press, 1949) and Adela Yarbro Collins, "Feminine Symbolism in the Book of Revelation," *Biblical Interpretation* 1 (1993): 21–33; for New Criticism, see Paul Minear, *I Saw a New Earth: an Introduction to the Visions of the Apocalypse* (Washington DC: Corpus Books, 1968).

[15]Important structuralist studies in the 1970s that have shaped subsequent research include John Gager, *Kingdom and Community: The Social World of Early Christianity* (Englewood Cliffs NJ: Prentice-Hall, 1975); Adela Yarbro Collins, *The Combat Myth in the Book of Revelation* (Missoula MT: Scholars Press, for the *Harvard Theological Review*, 1976); and Elisabeth Schüssler Fiorenza, "The Composition and Structure of Revelation," *CBQ* 39 (1977): 344–66 (repr.: *The Book of Revelation: Justice and Judgment*, 159-80 [Philadelphia: Fortress Press, 1984]). A recent study that has stayed within the structuralist fold is Leonard Thompson, *The Book of Revelation: Apocalypse and Empire* (New York: Oxford University Press, 1990). For discussion of the development of structuralist literary criticism from linguistics and anthropology, see Terry Eagleton, *Literary Theory: An Introduction* (Minneapolis: University of Minnesota Press, 1983) 95–116.

structionist guises, and ideological criticism, which may discuss the relation of a text to the structures of power in any historical context, have begun to be applied to Revelation.[16]

Battles rage over text and context at the MLA, to resurface a year later at the SBL, but most students and scholars of the Apocalypse are really interested in both its complicated narrative world and its function in its original setting. Historicist farmers and literary cowboys can be friends. Nevertheless, in order to begin to relate text and context, narrative world and social world, I must choose sides. In this book, my primary concern is with the early Christian communities, the historical audience of Revelation. This does not mean that I am choosing "meaning" over "significance," for I am not asserting the primacy and immutability of John's intentions when writing Revelation, nor do I assert that the way the text was heard by its original audience is normative for later readers.[17] But I have made the choice, for this study, to use this particular social embodiment as the context for reading Revelation. This exercise of listening with the ears of the early Christians is related to the turn to the reader in recent reader-response and reception theories. Of course, the construction of the "implied" or "competent" reader is another notoriously difficult problem in critical studies.[18] The tangles of intertextual allusion

---

[16]See Tina Pippin, "Eros and the End: Reading for Gender in the Apocalypse of John," *Semeia* 59 (1992): 193–210; idem., *Death and Desire: The Rhetoric of Gender in the Apocalypse of John* (Louisville: Westminster/John Knox, 1993); and Stephen D. Moore, "The Beatific Vision as a Posing Exhibition: Revelation's Hypermasculine Deity," *JSNT* 60 (1995): 27–55.

[17]On meaning and significance, see E. D. Hirsch, Jr., *Validity in Interpretation* (New Haven CT: Yale University Press, 1967); on the relationship of what a text means and what it meant, see Krister Stendhal, "Biblical Theology," *IDB* A–D:418–432; James Barr, "Biblical Theology," *IDBSup* 104–11; and Wayne A. Meeks, "A Hermeneutics of Social Embodiment," *HTR* 79 (1986): 176–86.

[18]I am borrowing from reader-response theorists, such as Umberto Eco, *The Role of the Reader*, 3–43; and Wolfgang Iser, *The Act of Reading: A Theory of Aesthetic Response* (Baltimore and London: Johns Hopkins University Press, 1978); but I would hesitate to characterize my method as reader-response criticism. My reading of Iser, however, is compatible with my use of anthropological methods, for Iser takes an explicitly functionalist model to describe the intersection of text and reading and describes in some detail the "repertoire" or culture that provides the context for the act of reading (see 68–79). But, as Eagleton has noted (*Literary Theory*, 78–80), this "repertoire" or context, as Iser employs it, presupposes a liberal humanist ideology, one quite different from the

to and echo of the Hebrew Bible in Revelation cast considerable doubt on how competent any reader of Revelation, ancient or modern, could be.[19] By considering the probable historical audience rather than the competent reader, one considers the social dimension and functions of the text rather than constructs an individual response based on modern sensibilities and ideologies. I will explore, therefore, the way the imagery of wealth in Revelation would have been heard in terms of the "webs of significance" of the culture (really, cultures) of the western Asian cities around 95 CE, attempting as best I can a "thick description" of that culture.[20] If the search for meaning among the artifacts of this ancient

---

culture of the early Christian communities. Adding the dimension of symbolic anthropology, I believe, provides the necessary corrective for Iser's ideological shortcomings.

[19]Several recent works have advanced the study of biblical allusion in Revelation: Jon Paulien, *Decoding Revelation's Trumpets: Literary Allusions and Interpretations of Revelation 8:7–12*, AUSS 11 (Berrien Springs MI: Andrews University Press, 1988); Jean-Pierre Ruiz, *Ezekiel in the Apocalypse: The Transformation of Prophetic Language in Revelation 16,17–19,10*, Europäische Hochschulschriften 23.376 (Frankfurt am Main: Peter Lang, 1989); and Jan Fekkes III, *Isaiah and Prophetic Traditions in the Book of Revelation*, JSNTSup 93 (Sheffield UK: JSOT Press, 1994). These studies offer painstaking and thorough textual analysis and formal delineation of quotations, references, and allusions. What is lacking is any critical method for evaluating the social and ideological implications of John's literary activity. Richard Hays, *Echoes of Scripture in the Letters of Paul* (New Haven and London: Yale University Press, 1989), offers a model approach for analysis of intertextuality in Paul, although the approach is essentially New Critical. (See the review of Hays by Dale Martin, *Modern Theology* 7 [1991]: 291–92.) Steve Moyise, *The Old Testament in the Book of Revelation*, JSNTSup 115 (Sheffield UK: Sheffield Academic Press, 1995), has attempted to apply Hays' method to Revelation, with attention to the nuances of intertextuality, but again without attention to social context or ideological force. The problems presented by Paul's use of the LXX and John's use of the Hebrew Bible are considerably different. While my thesis addresses the rhetoric and ideology of biblical intertextuality in Revelation, a fuller study of the issue, with attention to poststructural literary criticism, is called for.

[20]The anthropologist Clifford Geertz coined these phrases; see his essays collected in *The Interpretation of Cultures* (New York: Basic Books, Harper Torchbooks, 1973) esp. "Thick Description: Toward an Interpretive Theory of Culture," 3–30; "Religion As a Cultural System," 87–125; and "Ethos, Worldview, and the Analysis of Sacred Symbols," 126–41.

culture and these ancient communities—a search that has been compared to that of an ethnographer[21]—if this search generates new meanings for modern contexts, that is a felicitous but unsought outcome.

Choosing sides still leaves us with the problem of *how* to relate text and context. The text needs to speak first. Wealth motifs are too complex in this narrative world to begin to consider their meaning, whether for the text or its context, without considering the whole Apocalypse. Furthermore, this approach fits the self-presentation of the Apocalypse, which challenges the reader/audience with an "all-or-nothing" response; surely this is why so many critics have tried so hard to produce outlines to prove how it holds together. The narrative aspect of the genre "apocalypse" has been called to attention in two studies by John J. Collins and Adela Yarbro Collins and their SBL colleagues,[22] but only recently have narrative-critical studies of Revelation begun to appear.[23] The study of

---

[21]The analogy and method come from Wayne A. Meeks, *The First Urban Christians: The Social World of the Apostle Paul* (New Haven CT: Yale University Press, 1983) 6.

[22]John J. Collins, in the introduction to the studies collected in *Semeia* 14 (1979): 9, defines an "apocalypse" as "a genre of revelatory literature with a narrative framework, in which a revelation is mediated by an otherworldly being to a human recipient, disclosing a transcendent reality which is both temporal, insofar as it envisages eschatological salvation, and spatial, insofar as it involves another, supernatural world." In the introduction to *Semeia* 36 (1986), Adela Yarbro Collins raises the issue of the implied author as a problem for using a crisis as a distinguishing feature of the genre, thus bringing narrative criticism to bear on the interpretation of Revelation.

[23]The work of David L. Barr is most notable in this area: see "The Apocalypse as a Symbolic Transformation of the World: A Literary Analysis" *Int* 38 (1984): 39–50; "Towards an Ethical Reading of The Apocalypse: Reflections on John's Use of Power, Violence, and Misogyny," *SBLSP* 1997, 358–73; and his *Tales of the End: A Narrative Commentary on the Book of Revelation*, Storytellers Bible 1 (Santa Rosa CA: Polebridge Press, 1998). See also M. Eugene Boring, "Narrative Christology in the Apocalypse," *CBQ* 54 (1992): 702–23; and J. Ramsay Michaels, "Revelation 1.19 and the Narrative Voices of the Apocalypse" *NTS* 37 (1991): 604–20. Boring, whose article lacks a methodological discussion of narrative criticism, seems to have been influenced by both Hans Frei's theology and by New Criticism. Michaels offers Rev 1:19 as an interpretive key for the structure of the visions in Revelation. His complex solution lacks the elegance of Caird's simple interpretation of this verse, which Michaels rejects (see chap. 5, n. 2).

narrative has become a huge endeavor; again, it is best to keep the discussion framed in terms of the Apocalypse.[24] The implied author constructs norms in the text by deciding who has gold and jewels, who buys and sells, and how to characterize the narrator, Christ, the beasts, and the other players in the text.[25] The levels upon levels of narrativity in the visions of Revelation, however, are too slippery for us to find any sure footing there as we try to connect narrative and social worlds.[26] If I were to spend too much effort sorting out these multiple levels, this would turn into yet another study of the "well-wrought urn" of Revelation.

Revelation is a highly rhetorical text that tries to *do* something; it is, in fact, performative rather than referential language.[27] This is our first clue to how to relate text and context, narrative and social world, when reading Revelation. But what exactly is the text trying to do? We find a second clue when we start to ask questions about what that social world was like. Other contemporaneous texts, such as the Deutero-Pauline epistles, the letters of Pliny to Trajan, or the C. Vibius Salutaris inscrip-

---

[24]Critical studies that have informed my thinking on the subject include Erich Auerbach, *Mimesis: The Representation of Reality in Western Literature* (Princeton NJ: Princeton University Press, 1953, 1974); Wayne Booth, *The Rhetoric of Fiction*, 2nd ed. (Chicago and London: University of Chicago Press, 1961, 1983); M. M. Bakhtin, *The Dialogic Imagination* (Austin and London: University of Texas Press, 1981); Frank Kermode, *The Sense of an Ending: Studies in the Theory of Fiction* (Oxford: Oxford University Press, 1966, 1967); Hans Frei, *The Eclipse of Biblical Narrative* (New Haven: Yale University Press, 1974); Frederic R. Jameson, *The Political Unconscious: Narrative as a Socially Symbolic Act* (Ithaca NY: Cornell University Press, 1982); Hayden White, *Tropics of Discourse: Essays in Cultural Criticism* (Baltimore and London: The Johns Hopkins University Press, 1978).

[25]On implied author and different types of narrators, see Booth, *Rhetoric of Fiction*, 67–77, 151–65, 211–40.

[26]Boring's choice of four levels in "Narrative Christology" suggests the four levels of medieval allegory. His fourth level is really the narrative that he constructs from the canonized gospels and letters of Paul and is therefore an unreliable guide for our exploration of the narrative world of Revelation. Eco, *Role of the Reader*, 13–15, notes the "embarrassment" of levels in a text and therefore uses "boxes" rather than levels to avoid the notion of hierarchy when analyzing a narrative.

[27]See the discussion of propositional and pictorial language in Boring's commentary, 51–58; and the discussion of language and stylistic phrasing in Schüssler Fiorenza, 23–31.

tion in Ephesus, tell a quite different story from Revelation.[28] The "beast from the sea" and the harlot Babylon appear in other narratives as the Emperor and City of Rome; the "synagogue of Satan" is called elsewhere the synagogue of the Chosen People of God. "Chrestus" is neither the Lion/Lamb nor the Divine Warrior but merely a troublemaker who disturbs the Roman *pax*. The social world presupposed by the narrative of the Apocalypse is considerably at odds with other narratives. Which ones are correct? This raises questions of historiography that have long been debated. The attempt to show a greater or lesser degree of commensurability between the narrative world of Revelation and the "real world" of first- and second-century Asia suffers from the fallacy that there is one "correct" narrative that describes such a "real world" accurately.[29] Scholarly metanarratives, moreover, cannot pierce the layers of interpretation or obviate the point of view and ideological baggage that come with their sources:

> The issue of ideology points to the fact that there is no value-neutral mode of emplotment, explanation, or even description of any field of events, whether imaginary or real, and suggests that the very use of language itself implies or entails a specific posture before the world which is ethical, ideological, or more generally political: not only all interpretation, but also all language is politically contaminated.[30]

Some narratives may be more "real" than others in that they support or reflect the symbolic universes, the structure and processes of world construction, for large communities of people.[31] But who is to say whether Caesar really was a beast or not?

The raids by the U.S. government on the Branch Davidian compound in Waco, Texas, in February and April 1993 bring this issue into sharper focus. While many Americans might take a negative view of their

---

[28]While these are not necessarily narrative texts at first glance, as Eco notes, *Role of the Reader*, 13, "it is usually possible to transform a nonnarrative text into a narrative one."

[29]See Hayden White, "The Fictions of Factual Representation," *Tropics of Discourse*, 121–34.

[30]Ibid., 129.

[31]On the term "symbolic universe," see Peter L. Berger and Thomas Luckmann, *The Social Construction of Reality: A Treatise in the Sociology of Knowledge* (New York: Doubleday, 1966) 92–128.

government, few would go as far as the members of the Davidian church.[32] The Branch Davidians were not uninformed about events in the world "out there." But their *interpretation* of these events, based on David Koresh's interpretation of Revelation, was dramatically different from the interpretation presumed by most of American society. Here we see the intersection of a narrative world—a subnarrative at that, the seven seals in Revelation 6–8—and a social world with consequences both disastrous and unfathomable to many observers, even those who have studied Revelation or are familiar with the Bible. David Koresh convinced the members of his church that he was the Lamb who was sent to open these seals; that the first four seals had been opened; and that the raid by the Bureau of Alcohol, Tobacco and Firearms marked the opening of the fifth seal.[33] Two biblical scholars spent considerable time discussing Revelation with a member of the Davidian church and presented their own interpretation of Revelation to Koresh on a Dallas radio station. A letter from Koresh suggested that these scholars had convinced him that there must be a waiting period while he published his interpretation of the seven seals.[34] All of this took place in terms offered by the narrative world of Revelation, for it was from this text that the Branch Davidians constructed their symbolic universe and within which these scholars made their arguments. David Koresh created a crisis in the social world of the Branch Davidians in large part by his reading of Revelation.[35]

---

[32]As of the time of writing, the relation of the bombing of the Alfred P. Murrah Federal Building in Oklahoma City to apocalyptic or millenarian groups was not fully known. This 1995 attack took place on the second anniversary of the FBI raid on the Branch Davidians in Waco.

[33]See James D. Tabor and Eugene V. Gallagher, *Why Waco? Cults and the Battle for Religious Freedom in America* (Berkeley: University of California Press, 1995); and *From the Ashes: Making Sense of Waco*, ed. James R. Lewis (Lanham MD: Roman & Littlefield, 1994).

[34]This claim is made by James D. Tabor and J. Phillip Arnold, *From the Ashes*, 13–31; and James D. Tabor, "Religious Discourse and Failed Negotiations: The Dynamics of Biblical Apocalypticism in Waco," in *Armageddon in Waco*, ed. Stuart A. Wright (Chicago: University of Chicago Press, 1995) 263–81.

[35]We have considerably more social and psychological information to use in an analysis of Koresh and the Branch Davidians than in any analysis of John and the seven churches, but even so the limitations of sociological and psychological inquiry become quickly apparent. See the remarks by Larry McMurtry, "Return to Waco," *The New Republic*, 7 June 1993, 16–19.

So too the narrative world of the Apocalypse of John does not reflect a social historical situation so much as it attempts to create one. This view of the *Sitz im Leben* of the Apocalypse, now widely held, stands in contrast to the traditional view that the book was written in a situation of extreme oppression and organized persecution by the Roman authorities. The latter, more traditional view derives from the rhetoric of Revelation itself and is not necessarily consistent with the way other writers, including other ancient Christians, understood their world. To say that the rhetoric of Revelation attempts to create a crisis in the social world of its audience is slightly different from speaking of the crisis of the Apocalypse as "real or "perceived," as does Adela Yarbro Collins.[36] In essence I am saying the same thing about the social setting of the Apocalypse as Yarbro Collins, but I object to the implication in her terminology that, with more data, we could really know what was going on. All crises are perceived, as the events in Waco remind us yet again. More promising is the sociology-of-knowledge approach to the narrative world of Revelation set forth by Wayne Meeks. Meeks writes that "the general strategy of the Apocalypse is to oppose to the ordinary view of reality, as anyone might experience it in Smyrna or Laodicea, a quite different picture of the world as seen from the standpoint of heaven."[37] Leonard Thompson, also using the sociology-of-knowledge approach, has presented a full analysis of the social world as constructed by John of Patmos and other enemies of Domitian, such as Suetonius and Pliny, and the social-historical situation as he constructs it with the help of sources more friendly to Domitian.[38]

---

[36]See Adela Yarbro Collins, *Crisis and Catharsis: The Power of the Apocalypse* (Philadelphia: Westminster, 1984) 84–110. Yarbro Collins was instrumental in introducing the concepts of "real" and "perceived" crises, hitherto the province of specialists in sociological and anthropological methods, to a wider audience of students of the Apocalypse.

[37]Wayne A. Meeks, *The Moral World of the First Christians* (Philadelphia: Westminster, 1986) 143–44; see also Susan R. Garrett, "Chaos or Community? The Social World of the Book of Revelation" (master's thesis, Princeton Theological Seminary, 1983).

[38]Thompson, *The Book of Revelation*; see also Brian W. Jones, *The Emperor Domitian* (London: Routledge, 1992), supporting many of Thompson's findings; and Steven J. Friesen, *Twice Neokoros: Ephesus, Asia, and the Cult of the Flavian Imperial Family* (Leiden: Brill, 1993) 165–68. In her review of Thompson, *JBL* 110 (1991): 748–50, Yarbro Collins answers some of the charges brought against the use of "perceived crisis" theory.

Thompson's volume is a new addition to a growing consensus among scholars. To quote Thompson, "In a nutshell, the conflict and crisis in the Book of Revelation between Christian commitment and the social order derive from John's perspective on Roman society rather than from significant hostilities in the social environment."[39] The crisis of the Apocalypse is a construction that stems from the community of John and his circle of prophets.

The rhetoric of Revelation, which uses a narrative world to create a crisis in the social world of its audience, is the key to relating text and context.[40] Emphasizing the rhetorical aspect of Revelation has the advantage of using a method of criticism that is common to modern culture and to antiquity. Rhetorical theory was part of the social and intellectual climate in Asia Minor—Smyrna and Ephesus were famous centers of rhetorical training during the first and second centuries—and the "new rhetoric" has gained ascendancy in literary circles today. Rhetorical criticism is also compatible with the sociology-of-knowledge approach of Meeks and Thompson. While rhetorical theory helps us understand *that* Revelation is trying to convince its audience and *how* the text tries to do this, the sociology-of-knowledge helps us understand *what* Revelation tries to convince them. Revelation tries to restructure the symbolic universe of its audience; it tries to change how Christians see the world. The narrative world of Revelation provides a different set of symbols for understanding and organizing the social world of Asia Minor around the end of the first century CE from what one finds in other texts, such as 1 Peter or Pliny's *Epistles*. To make too sharp a contrast between the symbolic universe implied by Revelation and that inhabited by "everyone else" is, again, to fall under the spell of the rhetoric of Revelation, which tries to unite the "opposition" into one diabolical entity. Greeks, Romans, Jews, and Christians had a variety of interests,

---

[39]Thompson, *The Book of Revelation*, 175.

[40]In her 1991 commentary, Schüssler Fiorenza explores the sociopolitical and theoethical dimensions of Revelation through a rhetorical analysis of the text (15–37, 117–39). In general, the commentary downplays the "submerged alternative theological responses submerged in the text" (see 132–36). I take the competing theological-political responses within the Christian community to be the primary sociopolitical location of the text and the formative rhetorical situation for the ideology of Revelation. See the formative work in Schüssler Fiorenza's "Apocalyptic and Gnosis in Revelation and Paul" (orig. pub.: *JBL* 92 [1973]: 565–81; repub.: *Justice and Judgment*, 114–32).

a variety of myths and narratives, and a variety of ways of perceiving their social worlds. Describing life as a choice between only two sides is part of the rhetorical strategy of Revelation. Whether Revelation gave the Christians who adopted it as their guide to reality the knowledge to move with confidence in their social world is another question. But I have begun to make certain presuppositions about the social historical context of Revelation and these Christian communities and so I turn now to more careful consideration of this context.

The Social Setting of the Apocalypse

I have referred several times to the social world of the original audience of Revelation. Discussion of this social world involves certain presuppositions for the social-historical setting of the Apocalypse. Revelation was written by John of Patmos, who was neither the apostle John nor the author of the Gospel and epistles of John.[41] The widely held view that John of Patmos came to Asia from Palestine after the Jewish War of 66–73 CE seems reasonable. This hypothesis explains the use of Hebrew as well as Greek versions of the Bible; the Semitic Greek of Revelation; the imagery and importance of Temple rituals in the text; and the hatred and awe in Revelation of the Romans, whose power the author might have experienced firsthand during the war. The debate over the date of Revelation is complicated by the circular evidence for persecution of Christians, as I will discuss below, and the composite nature of the text.[42]

---

[41]Although Irenaeus attributed the Apocalypse to the apostle John, in part to strengthen its position as part of the emerging Christian canon by connecting it to an apostle, the question of authorship was settled by Dionysius of Alexandria (see Eus., *Hist. Eccl.* 7.25.7–27).

[42]Aune, lvi–lxx, provides the most comprehensive discussion of matters of dating, but perhaps also the least satisfying, since he finds evidence in the composite nature of the text for *both* Neronic (or even earlier) and Domitianic or Trajanic dating. While Aune's discussion of source-critical issues (cv–cxxxiv), which he recasts as "diachronic composition criticism," is again comprehensive and informative, his defense of source criticism as a valid method of inquiry (cvi–cix) is overly tendentious. In his discussion of intertextuality, he relies on Stephen D. Moore's conference paper, "Are the Gospels Unified Narratives?" (*SBLSP* 1987, 443–58), rather than major philosophical or critical discussions of the issue. Intertextuality for Aune seems to be the process by which the readers figure out the author's intentional allusions to other texts: see his "Intertextuality and the Genre of Apocalypse" (*SBLSP* 1991, 142–60).

This study assumes that the complete text of Revelation, as we now have it, was circulated among the Christian communities in western Asia around 95 CE, at the end of Domitian's reign.[43]

The scholarly discussion of exactly what that shape was intended to be and how it was heard in its original setting has become quite complicated. Candidates for the genre of Revelation include liturgical dialogue, apocalypse, and letter, specifically a prophetic letter.[44] When considering Revelation as a liturgical document, we must recognize that efforts to place Revelation's intriguing liturgical characteristics in any social-historical context have been unsuccessful.[45] The second candidate is the genre apocalypse. Revelation, which begins Ἀποκάλυψις Ἰησοῦ Χριστοῦ, "(The) Apocalypse of Jesus Christ," has given a name to this genre of ancient literature. Comparative studies of this genre, however, are not particularly helpful for analyzing the rhetorical strategies of Revelation nor are they descriptive of how the text would have been received by early Christian audiences.[46] It is clear that construing

---

[43]Agreeing, now, with Irenaeus, *Adv. Haer.* 5.30.3. A fairly long tradition before the final text, thirty years or more, seems almost certain. Garrow, 66–79, has dated Revelation to Titus's reign (ca. 80 CE), splitting the difference between the two main views, which would place Revelation in either Nero or Domitian's reign. I have recently argued that Colossians was written by a follower of Paul in response to the influx of apocalyptic strands of Christianity from Palestine into Asia Minor after the Jewish war with Rome in 66–70 CE; Revelation provides an important source for understanding the Colossians "errorists" (Robert M. Royalty, Jr., "Dwelling on Visions: On the Nature of the So-called 'Colossians Heresy,' " a paper presented at the annual meeting of the Society of Biblical Literature, San Francisco, November 1997). Thus I assume the activity of John and his circle of prophets in Asia well before the final version of the Apocalypse.

[44]Boring, "Narrative Christology," discusses Revelation as a "vision report" with narrative qualities. The discussion does not proceed beyond a comparison with the play-within-the-play in *Hamlet.*

[45]See Ugo Vanni, "Liturgical Dialogue as a Literary Form in the Book of Revelation," *NTS* 37 (1991): 348–72; the remarks on "The Liturgical Context" in Ruiz, *Ezekiel in the Apocalypse,* 184–89; and Thompson, *Revelation,* 52–73.

[46]See the articles in *Semeia* 14 (1979), on the genre "apocalypse"; the articles from the 1979 Upsalla Colloquium in part 2 of *Apocalypticism in the Mediterranean World and the Near East,* ed. David Hellholm (Tubingen: Mohr [Siebeck], 1983); and *Semeia* 36 (1986), on Revelation as an apocalypse. Edith McEwan Humphrey, *The Ladies and the Cities: Transformation and Apocalyptic Identity in Joseph and Aseneth, 4 Ezra, the Apocalypse, and the Shepherd of Hermas,*

Revelation as a prophetic letter offers the simplest solution, in light of the self-presentation of the text and our evidence of literary and prophetic activity in the early Christian communities.[47] One can hardly overestimate the importance of letter writing in ancient society and in the development of early Christianity.[48] Furthermore, the tradition of letter-writing among Christians was particularly strong in Asia; Paul and Ignatius bracket Revelation chronologically. John intentionally presented his visions to the churches in Asia in the form of a circular prophetic letter because this was how Christians communicated with each other in writing and because it connected his text to the Pauline tradition.[49] Furthermore, Revelation is a *prophetic* letter. The implied author presents the text as prophecy (Rev 1:3; 22:7, 18) and the narrator as a prophet (Rev 1:19; 10:1–11; 19:10; 22:8–9). The extensive rewriting of Isaiah, Jeremiah, Ezekiel, and Daniel in Revelation further supports the idea that this was intended to be heard as prophecy. John was a member, probably the leader, of a circle of prophets, who may have helped him distribute this letter of his prophetic

---

JSPSup 17 (Sheffield UK: Sheffield Academic Press, 1995) proceeds in the "spirit" of *Semeia* 14: see 13–29 for a discussion of genre. Aune, lxxxii–xcxc, provides an extensive discussion of "Revelation as an Apocalypse" that, while impressive from a literary perspecive, fails to convince me that modern scholarly models of the genre "apocalypse" offer clues to how the early Christian audience would have understood the text.

[47]The argument that Revelation should be read as a letter rather than an apocalypse has been made by Roloff, 7–8; and Martin Karrer, *Die Johannesoffenbarung als Brief: Studien zu ihre literarischen, historischen und theologischen Ort*, FRLANT 140 (Göttingen: Vandenhoeck & Ruprecht, 1986). Aune, lxxii, cites Canon Muratori 57–59 on Revelation's epistolary character, a valuable ancient perspective on the text.

[48]A helpful introduction is Stanley K. Stowers, *Letter Writing in Greco-Roman Antiquity* (Philadelphia: Westminster, 1986). The intense study of ancient letters and epistolary theory this century has focused on the letters of Paul in social and theological context. Probably the most important modern study after Adolph Deissmann's *Light from the Ancient East* (1911) was Paul Schubert, *Form and Function of the Pauline Thanksgivings* (Berlin: Alfred Töplemann, 1939), who pointed to the need for social-historical methods of study.

[49]Charles, 1:xciv and 43–46, holds that the seven "letters" were written at an earlier date and reedited for inclusion in the Apocalypse. Yarbro Collins, *Combat Myth*, 5–8, discusses the "superficial" and "secondary" nature of the epistolary framework and concludes that its function was to identify the liturgical and revelatory nature of the work. See Aune, lxxiv–lxxv.

visions.[50] Self-presentation of the text as prophecy and the narrator as a prophet can be understood as a rhetorical posture intended to increase the authority of the text among its audience, as well as evidence of prophetic activity among early Christian communities.[51]

John himself was certainly literate and well-educated in the Hebrew scriptures, judging by the complexity and richness of allusions in Revelation. He also demonstrates rhetorical skills in the presentation of his visions, although we do know whether he had any formal education in rhetoric.[52] My concern is how these two features of the text, the biblical echoes and the rhetorical overtones, would have been heard, or if indeed they *could* have been heard. John wrote to a wide audience—at least seven different churches, and perhaps all the Christians in Asia. While John and his immediate circle might have engaged in biblical study analogous to the Qumran community or the early rabbis, it is unlikely that his urban Greek audience had the scriptural knowledge to hear the allusions. It is noteworthy that modern biblical scholars disagree quite significantly over allusions in Revelation.[53] The audience would have been more knowledgeable about Greco-Roman culture, in which they

---

[50]See Schüssler Fiorenza, *Justice and Judgment*, 140–46; David E. Aune, *Prophecy in Early Christianity and the Ancient Mediterranean World* (Grand Rapids MI: Eerdmans, 1983) 189–231; and "The Prophetic Circle of John of Patmos and the Exegesis of Revelation 22.16," *JSNT* 37 (1989): 103–16. Compare Yarbro Collins, *Crisis and Catharsis*, 46, who opposes this hypothesis. See also M. Eugene Boring, *Sayings of the Risen Jesus: Christian Prophecy in the Synoptic Tradition* (Cambridge: Cambridge University Press, 1982); and Fekkes, *Isaiah and Prophetic Traditions*, 22–58.

[51]The point is well made by David E. Aune, "The Social Matrix of the Apocalypse of John," *BR* 26 (1981): 22. Fekkes, *Isaiah and Prophetic Traditions*, 289–90, defends the experiential basis of the visions. Apocalyptic as a literary rather than experiential phenomenon has been convincingly presented by Martha Himmelfarb, *Ascent to Heaven in Jewish and Christian Apocalypses* (New York and Oxford: Oxford University Press, 1993).

[52]Manfred Diefenbach, "Die 'Offenbarung des Johannes' offenbart, daß der Seher Johannes die antike Rhetoriklehre kennt," *Biblische Notizen* 73 (1994): 50–57, argues from the structure of the seven messages that the author did have knowledge of rhetorical theory.

[53]Such disagreements are used rhetorically by Paulien, *Decoding Revelation's Trumpets*, 121–54, and Fekkes, *Isaiah and Prophetic Traditions*, 59–63, as part of the argument for their proposed methods; see Moyise, *Old Testament in Revelation*, 14–22.

lived, than the Hebrew prophets, whom they may have never read. Our knowledge of this culture, of course, may be quite different from theirs, since the literary sources preserved reflect for the most part the ideas, attitudes, and social world of society's elite. But we should not assume that the audience had either too much or too little education and cultural sophistication. The most constructive and informative studies of the social level and status of early Christians have been done on the Pauline letters and churches.[54] The audience of Revelation was probably very much like the Pauline churches.[55] In fact, Revelation itself offers considerable evidence to add to the sociological and social-historical study of early Christianity, although the text has not featured prominently in these studies, just as it has not featured prominently in the history of Christian theology. To say that the audience of Revelation was like the Pauline communities is to say that the audience of Revelation was urban and was socially and culturally diverse. Paul speaks of Jews and Greeks, slaves and free, men and women (Gal 3:28). This same diversity would have been found among the seven churches to whom John writes, although we should be sure to add "freed" (as in former slaves) to "free." We can expect that this audience would have included a wide variety of educational and social levels, a fair cross section of urban society in Asia at the end of the first century.

Money Talk

The messages to Smyrna and Laodicea in Rev 2:8–11 and 3:14–22 point to one aspect of this diversity by characterizing the Smyrnans as poor and the Laodiceans as wealthy. The message to Laodicea invariably turns commentators to ancient economic histories, where they find evidence for the economic and commercial strength of Laodicea. The same commentators usually fail to mention that Smyrna was also very wealthy and vied with Ephesus for the title of the leading city of Asia; Laodicea was not

---

[54]See Gerd Theissen, *The Social Setting of Pauline Christianity*, including the introduction by John Schütz (Philadelphia: Fortress Press, 1982); Abraham J. Malherbe on "Social Level and Literary Culture," *Social Aspects of Early Christianity*, 2nd ed. (Philadelphia: Fortress, 1983) 29–59, who reports an "emerging consensus" among scholars that early Christians included a diverse social level and at times sophisticated awareness of literary culture; and Meeks, *First Urban Christians*, 51–73.

[55]So also Thompson, *Revelation*, 128–29.

in the same league as these other two cities. The rhetorical nature of the messages to Smyrna and Laodicea should cast some doubt on their value as economic data. I will discuss the problem of wealth and rhetoric in these two prophetic messages in more detail in chapter 5; here, I will discuss the methodological question of how this study relates to the task of the economic history of antiquity. Since my topic is wealth, the reader might think that this will be a study of the economic history of Asia Minor and the Roman Empire. That is not the case, as a discussion of the problems involved in the study of ancient economic history will show. An economic historian describes the question to be asked in terms of the "set of constraints" that an individual, firm, or members of a group would bring to bear on an economic problem. In the modern industrial West, there are few constraints in the way of the maximization of profits, but this was not the case in antiquity. Economic decisions in antiquity were not based on what we would now call economic factors but on a variety of social, legal, moral, and psychological factors that are no longer significant constraints in modern industrial society.[56] In other words, the task of ancient economic history is more complicated than setting out to count *sesterces*, shipments of corn, or the cost of a legion but must take into account these other factors.

Sir Moses Finley finds the "admiringly vague" notion of status to be most helpful for describing how wealth interacted with other social and moral factors in ancient society.[57] Class describes purely economic factors. In Marxist terminology, the productive system of capitalists and workers is determinative for class. Status, in contrast, describes the perceptions of honor or prestige among groups in a society.[58] We speak today of "middle-class values" or an "upper-middle-class lifestyle," but

---

[56]M. I. Finley, *The Ancient Economy*, Sather Classical Lectures 43 (Berkeley and Los Angeles: University of California Press, 1985).

[57]Ibid., 45–53; see also Meeks, *First Urban Christians*, 53–55.

[58]See Seymour Lipset, "Social Class," in *International Encyclopedia of the Social Sciences*, ed. David L. Sills (New York: MacMillan and Free Press, 1968) 15:296–316; and Meeks, *First Urban Christians*, 51–73. The Weberian model of class and status remains useful in current sociological study of religion; see, e.g., Kenneth D. Wald, Dennis E. Owen, and Samuel S. Hill, Jr., "Evangelical Politics and Status Issues," *JSSR* 28 (1989): 1–16; Alan Aldridge, "Negotiating Status: Social Scientists and Anglican Clergy," *Journal of Contemporary Ethnography* 22 (1993): 97–112; and Murray Milner, Jr., "Status and Sacredness: Worship and Salvation a Forms of Status Transformation," *JSSR* 33 (1994): 99–109.

these phrases signify more than income; they imply status as well as class. Status is based on a number of factors, such as wealth, education, heredity, authority, and ethnic group. It is as precious and limited a commodity in a society as wealth, often even more so. Wealth did not always bring status in antiquity, a point which is at the heart of this study. Roman orders, such as senators and knights (*equites*), had minimum financial requirements, but wealth, though necessary, was not sufficient for entry into these orders. High-status families in Greco-Roman society did have a great deal of wealth but they had the right kind of wealth as well. Any study of wealth and commerce in antiquity needs to take account of social and moral attitudes toward wealth and economic activity and the way these attitudes affected the perceptions of status in the society.[59]

Although modern American society respects wealth from almost any source, we retain this particular distinction between wealth and status. The well-worn phrase "nouveaux riches" describes those people who have acquired too much wealth too quickly or from the wrong sources.[60] Such *new* wealth raises a person's class but does not necessarily confer status. A person with new wealth acquired by questionable means might be able to buy a large house, but not necessarily in an established neighborhood. This person could have difficulty joining all the clubs he or she could afford. The term "status inconsistency" describes the social situation of having large variations between the various dimensions of social stratification, such as wealth and status. Examples of status inconsistency include the nouveaux riches; professionals such as teachers or clergy with high education and low income; or members of marginalized ethnic groups with high income.[61] This concept has also been applied in analysis of the diversity of the early Christian communities noted above. Meeks characterizes the members of Paul's churches as "people of high status inconsistency"; "They are upwardly mobile; their achieved status is higher

---

[59]See esp. Ramsay MacMullen, *Roman Social Relations, 50 B.C. to A.D. 284* (New Haven CT: Yale University Press, 1974) 88–111.

[60]See the op-ed column by David Frum, "Welcome, Noveaux Riches," *New York Times*, 14 August 1995 (with a reference to Petronius), showing that the phrase still has some resonance.

[61]See Gerhard E. Lenski, "Status Crystallization: A Nonvertical Dimension of Social Status," in *Sociology: The Progress of a Decade*, ed. S. M. Lipset and N. Smelser (Englewood Cliffs NJ: Prentice-Hall, 1961) 485–94, and Lipset, "Social Class," 313.

than their attributed status."[62] Discrepancies and variations between wealth and status are significant for how the wealth imagery in Revelation would have been heard.

Finley has highlighted the need to take account of constraints, such as tradition and status, when studying wealth in antiquity. The constraints on economic decisions in ancient society were considerably different from those in modern society. He cites an example from the correspondence of Pliny and Trajan, which has often been brought to bear on the social situation of the book of Revelation.[63] In *Epistles* 10.54, Pliny writes to Trajan about how to invest excess cash collected by one of the cities of Bithynia.[64] He cannot find property to buy nor anyone willing to borrow at the prevailing rate of 9 percent. Trajan rejects Pliny's idea that city councilors be compelled to borrow at a lower rate. The cash thus remained in the strongbox, earning nothing at all, a state of affairs which both the emperor and the city accepted. This is far different from the modern global economy, in which central banks and governments constantly try to control money supply and economic growth by setting interest rates. A second example cited by Finley is the complicated attitude of Cicero toward moneylending. In *De officiis* 1.150, in which Cicero discusses occupations, he lists moneylenders (*faeneratores*) as a primary example of one of the "mean" employments that are condemned because they incur "ill will." But while disparaging moneylenders as a moralist, Cicero the politician turned to them on several occasions for cash. Furthermore, other political figures such as Brutus, Cassius and Caesar lent money, often large sums, although they were not "mean" or "illiberal" moneylenders, in Cicero's eyes.[65] Cicero leaves law and politics, with which he was engaged, off his list of occupations entirely. Vast sums were acquired through military and political activity in the late Republic and early Empire but these were not considered "employments":

> To include the military and political activity that produced this kind of income among "employments" may seem logical to a modern mind; it would have been false according to ancient canons, and Cicero was perfectly correct not to mention it, as he was correct and consistent to

---

[62]Meeks, *First Urban Christians*, 73.

[63]Namely, the interrogation and punishment of Christians described in Plin. *Ep.* 96–97; see below, 35ff.

[64]Finley, *Ancient Economy*, 118.

[65]Ibid., 53–57.

distinguish moneylenders from the moneylending activity of his fellow-senators.[66]

In ancient society, there were dramatically different types of wealth, good and bad ways of earning money, "mean" and "illiberal" occupations and pursuits worthy of "free" men and women. This is a particularly important point to keep in mind when studying how the imagery of wealth appears in a prophetic letter written to Christians who were themselves of mixed and ambiguous status. These attitudes toward wealth represent the view of the aristocratic elite. While money alone brought greater status among groups in society with less wealth, the values and attitudes of the elite were transmitted down the social scale.[67]

Two recent studies of wealth in Revelation, Adela Yarbro Collins' *Crisis and Catharsis* and Richard Bauckham's "The Economic Critique of Rome in Revelation 18," fail to take account of the constraints on economic activity in antiquity.[68] Like D. H. Lawrence, these two scholars

---

[66]Ibid., 56–57.

[67]See G. E. M. de Ste. Croix, *The Class Struggle in the Ancient Greek World* (Ithaca NY: Cornell University Press, 1981) 274; and MacMullen, *Roman Social Relations*, 108–15.

[68]In addition to Yarbro Collins, *Crisis and Catharsis* (see n. 36), see idem., "The Political Perspective of the Revelation to John," *JBL* 96 (1977): 241–256; "Revelation 18: Taunt-Song or Dirge?" in *L'Apocalypse johannique et l'Apocalyptique dans le Noveau Testament*, BETL 53, ed. J. Lambrecht (Leuven: J. Duculot, 1980) 185–204; and Richard Bauckham, "The Economic Critique of Rome in Revelation 18," in *The Climax of Prophecy: Studies on the Book of Revelation* (Edinburgh: T.&T. Clark, 1993) 338–83. See also the discussion of Revelation in Richard Bauckham, *The Bible in Politics: How to Read the Bible Politically* (London: SPCK, 1989). Other studies that have discussed wealth in Revelation more peripherally include Jan Fekkes III, " 'His Bride has Prepared Herself': Revelation 19–21 and Isaian Nuptial Imagery" *JBL* 109 (1990): 269–87; and Robert H. Gundry, "The New Jerusalem: People as Place, Not Place for People," *NovT* 29 (1987): 254–64. Revelation does not feature prominently in major treatments of wealth in early Christianity. See Martin Hengel, *Property and Riches in the Early Church: Aspects of a Social History of Early Christianity* (Philadelphia: Fortress, 1974), 48–49, who goes no farther than Revelation 18 in his discussion. Other studies of wealth in early Christianity do not study Revelation; see Luke T. Johnson, *The Literary Function of Possessions in Luke-Acts*, SBLDS 39 (Missoula MT: Scholars Press, 1977); Carolyn Osiek, *Rich and Poor in the Shepherd of Hermas: An Exegetical-Social Investigation*, CBQMS 15 (Washington DC: Catholic Bibli-

focus on the destruction of Babylon (Revelation 18) in their discussion of wealth. They also ignore the wealth of heaven and the New Jerusalem, a serious methodological shortcoming which I have already discussed. Both Yarbro Collins and Bauckham rely on economic historians who recognize a fairly narrow and anachronistic set of constraints. Bauckham, for instance, focuses on the cargo list in Rev 18:12–13, which he believes has been too readily dismissed by commentators as a literary creation based on Ezekiel 27:12–24. He considers this list to be an example of "concrete history" and "concrete detail" deliberately provided by John; it is a description of the "concrete political and economic realities of the empire in [John's] time."[69] In his survey of the cargo items listed in Rev 18:12–13, he uses data from quantitative economic studies of the Roman empire. Bauckham writes: "Of particular importance will be evidence that the merchandise in question was generally seen as a feature of the newly conspicuous wealth and extravagance of the rich families of Rome in the early period of the Empire."[70] Bauckham fails, however, to draw out the social and rhetorical implications of this connection, particularly with regard to wealth and status. New, conspicuous wealth was somewhat of a social problem among rich Roman families, particularly if that wealth were in any way related to commerce.[71] To illustrate how enormous wealth did not necessarily result in high status, one need only mention Trimalchio. Trimalchio's wealth and aspects of his lifestyle could be favorably compared to a senator—in fact, he makes such a comparison himself. But, as a freedman, his status was completely different.[72]

In the course of her discussion of wealth in Revelation, Yarbro Collins, in *Crisis and Catharsis*, draws on the work of M. I. Rostovtzeff. While describing social unrest in Asia Minor, she writes that, according

---

cal Association of America, 1983); L. William Countryman, *The Rich Christian in the Church of the Early Empire: Contradictions and Accommodations* (New York and Toronto: Edwin Mellen, 1980); and Sondra Ely Wheeler, *Wealth as Peril and Obligation: The New Testament on Possessions* (Grand Rapids MI: Eerdmans, 1995).

[69]Bauckham, "Economic Critique of Rome," *Climax of Prophecy*, 351.

[70]Ibid., 351-52.

[71]On the involvement of senatorial families in commerce, see D'Arms, *Commerce and Social Standing*, 48–71, 152–59, and the discussion of merchants and commerce in chap. 3.

[72]Trimalchio is the fictional freedman-merchant in Petronius's *Satyricon*. See Finley, *Ancient Economy*, 50–51, 61; and the discussion in chap. 3.

to Rostovtzeff, "there was a continuous struggle in Asia Minor between rich and poor from the time of Vespasian to the rule of Hadrian." The "brilliant economic progress of Asia Minor in the early empire" was uneven, creating millionaires but leaving the poor discontented.[73] When analyzing the merchants and sailors depicted in Revelation 18, she writes that:

> John probably had in mind here citizens of the cities of western Asia Minor who had amassed great wealth from commerce and the transportation of goods. Mikhail Rostovtzeff speaks of a new class of wealthy provincials who made their fortunes in this way under the Flavians.[74]

What Yarbro Collins does not present is any criticism of Rostovtzeff's controversial methodology or results.[75] Rostovtzeff focused his attention on the bourgeoisie, a relatively small slice of the social and economic life of the empire.[76] His social and economic history of the Empire gave short shrift to the very rich, a small group who controlled virtually all the wealth of the Roman empire, and the poor slaves and peasants who comprised the majority of the empire's population. He underestimated the role of agriculture in the production of wealth in the ancient world and overestimated the role of commerce and manufacturing.[77] Rostovtzeff

---

[73]Collins, *Crisis and Catharsis*, 94, citing *SEHRE*[2].

[74]Collins, *Crisis and Catharsis*, 123.

[75]For reviews of Rostovtzeff's work, see A. Momigliano, "M. I. Rostovtzeff," in *Studies in Historiography* (London: Weidenfeld and Nicolson, 1966) 91–104; and John D'Arms, *Commerce and Social Standing in Ancient Rome* (Cambridge MA: Harvard University Press, 1981) 1–19.

[76]"He is not the historian of Roman and Hellenistic society as a whole. He is primarily the historian of their traders, gentlemen farmers, and professionals" (Momigliano, "Rostovtzeff," 100).

[77]Rostovtzeff's conviction that commerce produced most of the massive fortunes of antiquity has not been resolved satisfactorily. See *SEHRE*[2], 153, which is taken as the springboard for discussion both by D'Arms, *Commerce and Social Standing*, 11–13, and MacMullen, *Roman Social Relations*, 48–52. John D'Arms has taken up Rostovtzeff's call for research on the sources of wealth and has tried to show that the senatorial order in the early Empire did in fact engage in commerce by means of freedmen, although with inconclusive results. D'Arms attempts to show that there was a link between the Roman senatorial aristocracy and the "commercial class" and that this link was reconcilable with aristocratic values. Peter Garnsey, in a critical review of *Commerce and Social Standing* (*CPh* 79 [1984]: 85–88), wonders if D'Arms has not overstated the evidence and

conceived of the "struggle between rich and poor" that Yarbro Collins
mentions as a struggle between the peasants and the bourgeoisie
culminating in an army of peasants destroying the Roman state in the
third century CE.[78] For Rostovtzeff, the difference between the ancient and
modern economy was quantitative rather than qualitative. Yarbro Collins,
following Rostovtzeff, misses the qualitative differences between ancient
and modern society in her discussion of wealth in Revelation.

A second misconception of the workings of the ancient economy
appears in discussions of the messages to Laodicea and Thyatira in Revelation 2–3. Yarbro Collins is typical of many commentators on Revelation
throughout the twentieth century in maintaining that so-called "trade
guilds" were influential in the economic as well as social and religious
life of the cities.[79] This accepted social-historical notion does not agree
with recent studies of the function of *collegia* in the Roman empire.
Finley maintains, emphatically, that there was no such thing as a "guild"
in antiquity:

> Not only were there no Guildhalls in antiquity, there were no guilds, no
> matter how often the Roman *collegia* and their differently named Greek
> and Hellenistic counterparts are thus mistranslated. The *collegia* played
> an important part in the social and religious life of the lower classes,
> both free and slave; they sometimes performed benevolent functions, as
> in financing burials; they never became regulatory or protective agencies
> in their respective trades, and that, of course, was the *raison d'être* of
> the genuine guilds, medieval and modern.[80]

Finley, *Ancient Economy*, 193, cites D'Arms as a prime example of "the missing
persons argument" for speculation on evidence that does not exist. While D'Arms
has not proved what Rostovtzeff asserted by intuition, that the main source of
large fortunes was trade, he has focused attention on the diversity of economic
pursuits and the relationship of the aristocracy to their freedmen in commercial
activities.

[78]See *SEHRE²*, 423–32, 493–501. This theory has been widely critiqued; see
MacMullen, *Roman Social Relations*, 166n.79.

[79]Collins, *Crisis and Catharsis*, 132–38; Charles 1:68, 93; Lohmeyer, 27, 37;
Boring, 91–97; *IDB* R-Z:68; Beasley-Murray, 89–90; Aune, 201.

[80]Finley, *Ancient Economy*, 138. See also MacMullen, *Roman Social
Relations*, 18–19, 73–77; and Ste. Croix, *Class Struggle in the Ancient Greek
World*, 273, who cites the few isolated data for "strikes" in antiquity, such as
bakers in Ephesus refusing to bake bread because the prices were too low.

A more recent study of the *collegia* has supported Finley's position.[81] To be sure, the social and religious function of the *collegia* and their relation to the emerging Christian communities should not be underestimated. But the *collegia* were not economic organizations that existed for the protection of their members' careers or the maximization of profits. The economic power of the "guilds" and the supposed influence on the behavior of Christians, in order to maintain their livelihood, can be incorrectly read into the situation of the messages in Revelation 2–3, the infamous Rev 13:16–18, and the Apocalypse as a whole.

In surveying the attitudes toward wealth in antiquity, it is important to remember that the crucial question is not the amount of silver in the strongbox or numbers of bushels of corn on the ships, but the variety of attitudes toward wealth recorded in our sources. Richard Duncan-Jones, a preeminent historian of quantifiable economic data in antiquity, has examined all of the prices used in Petronius's *Satyricon*, Apuleius' *Metamorphoses* and Philostratus' *Apollonius of Tyana*.[82] A few prices in these novels do reflect what was actually paid; for instance, slave prices in the *Satyricon* are accurate. But for the most part, prices are either proverbial or pitched very high or very low for a comic or rhetorical effect. Duncan-Jones' study is a valuable statement by an economic historian highlighting the literary and rhetorical nature of wealth passages in ancient literature. The modern citizen of an industrialized country is an economic creature but the ancient resident of the Roman empire was not. A number of social and moral constraints affected economic activity in antiquity that have little correspondence to how economic decisions are made today. The problem is more complex than a "struggle between rich and poor."

The Crisis of the Apocalypse

I have already raised a major interpretive crux for this book; that is, the degree to which Revelation creates or reflects a particular social setting. Many readers of the Apocalypse assume that the text was written under oppression by the Roman authorities, or perhaps by the Jews. Less recog-

---

[81]Frank M. Ausbüttel, *Untersuchungen zu den Vereinen im Westen des römischen Reiches*, FAS 11 (Frankfurt: Michael Lassleben, 1982). See also Meeks, *First Urban Christians*, 31–32.

[82]*The Economy of the Roman Empire: Quantitative Studies*, 2nd ed. (Cambridge: Cambridge University Press, 1974, 1982) 238–40.

nized is the idea that diversity of teaching, belief, and practice among Christians in Asia was a "crisis" for John and his immediate circle of prophets. The harsh polemic against Babylon/Rome in Revelation can mask the simple fact that it was written by, for, and to Christians. Domitian and his counselors and the Roman governor of Asia never read it. While many have read Revelation since then as the description of a struggle between Christians and the Romans, I read it as a description of a struggle between Christians. The core issue in this struggle is who should have authority within the Christian communities—John and his prophets, or other prophets, teachers, and officials.[83] Several issues seem to have been at stake in this struggle: how to practice the Christian religion in relationship to the dominant Greco-Roman culture; philosophical speculation and the interpretation of Scripture; the role of women; and the role of prophecy within the emerging church structure. But the very presence of diversity in ethical and theological matters was a crisis for John and his circle, just as diversity of Christian thought was a problem for a proto-orthodox writer such as Irenaeus almost a century later. The crisis of the Apocalypse is a crisis of authority within Christian circles. This is the social setting that best accounts for the powerful rhetoric of Revelation and its attempt to change the symbolic universe of the audience.

There is considerable internal and external evidence for the thesis that a struggle for authority within the Christian communities provoked a crisis for John. The seven messages to the churches in Asia in Revelation 2–3 focus on two moral issues (postponing for now the discussion of wealth and poverty in the messages to Smyrna and Laodicea). The first is endurance in the face of suffering, and there is a clear suggestion in the text that all seven churches are not opening themselves fully to the trials of being a Christian as the author understands them.[84] The second moral issue is how each church has responded to other Christian groups or leaders: "apostles" (2:2); "Jews" (2:8, 3:9); the "Nicolaitans" (2:6, 15); "Balaam" (2:14); and "Jezebel" (2:20–25). The text raises the issue of authority within the Christian communities by mentioning other Christian leaders by name and then characterizing them negatively in Revelation. While commentators often combine these teachers into a unified opposition to John and his circle of prophets, there is no particular reason

---

[83]See Schüssler Fiorenza, *Justice and Judgment*, 114–32, on the Christian opponents of John and their relationship to Gnosticism.
[84]See Rev 3:1–5, 15–18; cf. Rev 1:9; 2:2, 10, 19.

to do so other than the rhetorical force of Revelation.[85] Instead, Revelation 2–3 should be seen as one of the first Christian heresiologies.

Bentley Layton describes early Christian heresiology as a polemical Christian adaptation of the genre of doxography used in Hellenistic philosophical discourse. According to Layton, Christian heresiology "purports to convey and record specific ideas from the past, [but] its real effects are to replace the original exposition of these ideas with trivialized substitutes, to conceal any relevance or interest they might have actually had, and to cause them to be forgotten."[86] Revelation lacks the doxographical elements found in later heresiologies but exhibits a number of other characteristics of the genre.[87] We can discern how other Christian leaders and teachers have been polemically characterized by John and why commentators, falling prey to the rhetoric of Revelation, have lumped these teachers into one monolithic opposition to John. A critical

---

[85]Aune, "Social Matrix," locates the struggle between John, the Nicolaitans, and "Jezebel" in the context of early Christian prophecy. He sees John fighting with "Jezebel" and the Nicolaitans over the majority centrist party of Christians in the seven churches. Aune's contention that the Nicolaitans of Ephesus and Pergamum are part of a movement sponsored by "Jezebel" of Thyatira has no supporting evidence. His labels of "conservative" and "liberal" to describe John and "Jezebel" (and her supposed allies) are anachronistic and have no historical or sociological value in the discussion. An emic analysis extending the discussion by Paul in 1 Corinthians and Romans might suggest the terms "weak" for John and "strong" for some of his opponents; a more rigorous etic analysis than Aune provides might suggest categories of social deviance, status, or some other more concrete descriptor of social location than liberal and conservative. I agree with Aune ("Social Matrix," p. 29 and n. 36) that labelling John's opponents as Gnostic by Schüssler Fiorenza, *Justice and Judgment*, 114–32, is anachronistic and does not add to our understanding of the groups mentioned in Revelation.

[86]Bentley Layton, "The Significance of Basilides in Ancient Christian Thought," *Representations* 28 (1989): 135–51; quotation on 136.

[87]Layton lists seven polemical features of Christian heresiology: "(1) sarcastic reduction of complex, nuanced bodies of teaching to a few pat sententiae—the dehumanization of alternative points of view; (2) worry about the authority of teachers with an intellectual pedigree; (3) assumption that truth has only one right expression; (4) professed dislike of originality; (5) belief that false ideas and the guilt for false thinking are transmitted by epidemic contagion; (6) insistence that rival thinkers belong to parties or *haereses*, but that oneself does not; (7) simple *logos* Christianity." Numbers 1–5 are clearly features of Revelation and number 6 is implicitly part of John's argument.

look at the pertinent passages in Revelation shows that John saw the authority of other Christian teachers and prophets in the Asian churches as a threat to his own authority. According to Rev 2:2, the Ephesian church is praised for testing "those who claim to be apostles" and for finding them to be false.[88] There is no other mention of what these apostles do or teach nor is there any evidence to connect them to the other teachers whom John opposes. In the rest of Revelation, apostles appear only in heaven (18:20) and the New Jerusalem (21:14), an implicit claim that apostolic authority exists only in the past. This claim, however, should be taken as a rhetorical technique by the author to undercut the authority of the "false" apostles active in Ephesus rather than as historical evidence of church organization at the end of the first century. The closing threat against "everyone who loves and practices falsehood" (Rev 22:15) refers back to the "false" apostles in Rev 2:2 as well as to the "false prophet" in the visions (Rev 13:11–18, 16:13, 19:20, 20:10) and adds eschatological force to the rhetoric of the message to the Ephesians.

The second Christian group opposed by John is the Nicolaitans. The messages to Ephesus and Pergamum mention the "works" (ἔργα, Rev 2:6) and "teaching" (διδαχήν, Rev 2:15) of the Nicolaitans, but include no specific references to what either of these might be. The implied author takes a strong position against their teaching and actions, as "Christ" praises the Ephesians for rejecting the Nicolaitans and warns the church in Pergamum against supporting them. Commentators frequently assume that the Nicolaitans hold to "the teaching of Balaam" (Rev 2:14); that is, permitting Christians to eat meat purchased from pagan temples, familiar to us intertextually from 1 Corinthians 8–10, and allowing the practice of fornication.[89] Commentators often base this on the Hebrew and Greek meanings of *Balaam* and *Nicolaus*, both of which mean "conqueror of the people," and the proximity of Balaam and the Nicolaitans in the message to Pergamum.[90] But the names given to these teachers in Revelation are surely as intentionally slanderous as "false apostles" and "Jezebel." Furthermore, the message to Pergamum refers to two different groups, some who hold to the teaching of Balaam and some who also hold to the teaching of the Nicolaitans. While it is possible and even likely that the "Nicolaitans" took the position of the "strong" Christians

---

[88]The language is reminiscent of *Did.* 11.3–6. Note that *Didache* 11 treats prophets and apostles together.

[89]See Aune, 191–94, "Excursus 2D: Eating Food Sacrificed to Idols."

[90]See Charles 1:64, who invents the word "Balaamites."

in Pauline circles and purchased their chops from the temple butcher, it is not clear that the so-called "Balaamites," a modern construction, are the same as the Nicolaitans in terms of their teaching. It is not even clear that "those who hold to the teaching of Balaam" are an organized group or theological school. They are only equated *morally* and *rhetorically* in Revelation. Granted, eating meat from the temples is frequently understood to be one sign of the accommodation to Greco-Roman culture that Revelation opposes. It is striking, however, that Pergamum is praised for not denying Christ's name when Antipas was killed (Rev 2:13), suggesting that some members of this community have taken a stand against the authorities even though they tolerate a variety of Christian teachers.

The seven messages in Revelation mention three different groups but only one individual opposed by John through "Christ," that is "Jezebel, who calls herself a prophetess" (προφῆτιν, Rev 2:20). We have more information about her than about the groups. The very name "Jezebel" is a slanderous allusion to Queen Jezebel (1 Kings 18–19, 2 Kings 9), calling her character and the validity of her prophecy into question. The polemic against "Jezebel" in the message to Thyatira reveals that she is a teacher as well as a prophet. Teacher (διδάσκαλος, ὁ διδασκῶν), like prophet, is included in Paul's lists of roles or offices in the church (Rom 12:7; 1 Cor 12:28). The words for teaching (διδάσκω, διδαχή) appear in Revelation only in negative contexts (2:14–15, 20, 24). John claims the title of prophet for himself but directs some of his harshest polemic against this woman in Thyatira who both teaches and prophesies.[91] Her disciples or students were called her children (Rev 2:23), as was customary in Greek culture. The implied author slanderously characterizes "Jezebel's" teaching when "Christ" calls it "the deep things [βαθέα] of Satan" (Rev 2:24). While the attribution of her teaching to Satan is polemical rhetoric, the word βαθέα suggests philosophical activity, such as the speculation that flourished in second-century Gnostic Christian circles.[92] The prohibition against literary criticism in Rev

---

[91]In his recent commentary, 203, Aune has suggested that "Jezebel" could have been a "patroness" or "hostess" (the gendered language is problematic) of a house church, despite John's characterization of "Jezebel" as a Christian teacher and prophet.

[92]So C. K. Barrett, "Gnosis and the Apocalypse of John," in *The New Testament and Gnosis. Essays in honour of Robert McL. Wilson*, ed. A. H. B. Logan and A. J. M. Wedderburn (Edinburgh: T.&T. Clark, 1983) 128. Barrett does see all of John's opponents united in opposition to him. Roman Heiligenthal, "Wer

22:18–19, perhaps directed toward allegorical interpretation, probably refers to the literary or philosophical activity of Christian teachers such as "Jezebel." "Christ" says that her teaching consists of "beguiling my servants to practice fornication and to eat food sacrificed to idols" (Rev 2:20). This is essentially the same as the description of the teaching of Balaam in Rev 2:14. "Jezebel" challenged John's authority on issues such as eating meat purchased from pagan temples by means of prophecy and teaching and therefore poses a threat. Her leadership role in Thyatira is part of the "crisis" of the Apocalypse.

The negative characterization of the prophet-teacher of Thyatira and her disciples includes an elaboration of the attribution of "fornication" or *porneia*, an attribution also included in the description of the teaching of Balaam. According to the message to Thyatira, "Jezebel" practices fornication (πορνεύω); she has refused to repent of her fornication (πορνεύω); and her students commit adultery with her (μοιχεύω).[93] The meaning of the *porn-* words in Revelation is a large topic.[94] Generally, in the New Testament, these words describe actual sexual behavior of some type. For instance, in John 8:41, the Jews, reacting to Jesus' accusation that they are *not* Abraham's children, claim that they "were not born of fornication"; that is, they were not conceived from *porneia*. In 1 Cor 5:1–8, Paul addresses a problem of *porneia* in the Corinthian community, a sexual relationship between a man and his stepmother. In the discussion of prostitutes or *pornai* in 1 Cor 6:13, the ethical issue is again *sexual* immorality. Although commentators on Revelation have taken the descriptions of the teaching of "Jezebel" and Balaam as advocating liberal sexual practices, a more convincing reading is that this language is part of the rhetorical slandering of John's

---

waren die 'Nikolaiten'? Ein Beitrag zur Theologiegeschichte des frühen Christen-tums" *ZNW* 82 (1991): 133–37, connects the "Nicolaitans" mentioned in Revelation, Ignatius and Irenaeus to the Skeptic philosophical tradition.

[93]On the dehumanizing portrayal of women in Revelation, see Susan R. Garrett, "Revelation," in *The Women's Bible Commentary*, ed. Carol A. Newsom and Sharon H. Ringe (London: SPCK; Louisville: Westminster/John Knox, 1992) 377–82; and Pippin, "Eros and the End."

[94]Revelation accounts for nineteen of the fifty-five occurrences of these words in the New Testament: πορνεία, Rev 2:21; 9:21; 14:8; 17:2, 4; 18:3; 19:2l; πορνεύω, Rev 2:14, 20; 17:2; 18:3, 9; πόρνη, Rev 17:1, 5, 15, 16; 19:2; πόρνος, Rev 21:8; 22:15. First Corinthians is second with fourteen, due to the discussion of sexual morality in 1 Cor 5–6.

opponents because ample precedent existed for using *sexual* immorality as a metaphor for idolatrous activity.[95] Such extreme rhetoric is typical of the messages; the implied author makes hyperbolic use of eschatological threats to bully the churches into accepting his views (see Rev 2:22–23, 3:5, 3:9, and 3:16). John's pornographic rhetoric directed against the prophet-teacher of Thyatira and her students and the "strong" Christians in Pergamum who purchase meat from the temples is further evidence that the "crisis" of Revelation was a crisis situation of ecclesiastical diversity which challenged the prophetic authority of the author.

Evidence of John's Christian opponents might possibly be found elsewhere in the New Testament as well as in the seven messages. The geographical references and epistolary framework in Revelation suggest familiarity or dialogue with the Pauline tradition.[96] But the attitude expressed in Revelation toward the governing authorities is dramatically different from that found in Rom 13:1–7, 1 Tim 2:1–4, Tit 3:1 and 1 Pet 2:17. Positive statements about the authorities in these four other New Testament epistles challenge the political rhetoric of Revelation. The Pastoral Epistles and 1 Peter both have Asian provenances, perhaps Ephesus. The dates for these letters are uncertain, made more so if we call the evidence for persecution of Christians in Revelation into question, since that has been used as a *terminus ad quem* for 1 Peter. There is no mention of bishops or deacons in Revelation, whereas Ephesians, the Pastoral Epistles, and the letters of Ignatius presuppose some form of a church structure that includes these officials.[97] It is clear that these other texts could well be as rhetorical as Revelation in their presentation of church order. In other words, the authority of the bishop in the Christian churches was not yet fixed. While 1 Timothy, Titus, and Ignatius present the image of an upstanding and authoritative bishop as part of their ideological agenda, the omission in Revelation could be taken as a direct appeal to members of the churches, intentionally bypassing church officials for ideological or theological reasons.[98] Furthermore, the issue of

---

[95]See further discussion in chap. 6.

[96]See Schüssler Fiorenza, *Justice and Judgment*, 85–113, who concludes that John had access to both Johannine and Pauline school traditions but was more familiar with Pauline theological traditions; see also 114–56, where further comparisons are made between Revelation and Pauline language and concepts.

[97]See 1 Tim 3:1–13, 5:17–22; Tit 1:5–9; Ign. *Magn.* 3–4; *Trall.* 2; *Smyrn* 8.

[98]On church polity revealed or concealed in Revelation 2–3, see Ulrich B. Müller, *Zur frühchristlichen Theologiegeschichte: Judenchristentum und Paulinis-*

"false" teaching and teachers is prominent in Colossians and the Pastoral Epistles. It is plausible that Col 2:16–23 was written against a community such as John of Patmos and his circle of prophets.[99] The evidence of diversity of teaching and of authority structures lends weight to my hypothesis that the crisis of Revelation is over authority within the Christian community.

The evidence that Revelation was written in a situation of oppression by the Roman authorities is much less abundant. Revelation itself mentions one actual martyr, Antipas (Rev 2:13). The idea that John was banished to Patmos by the Romans has little support.[100] The visions of martyrdom in Revelation could reflect past persecutions, such as those under Nero, or, alternately, they could represent the apocalyptic vision of John.[101] The question of why the early Christians were persecuted under Roman law has generated enormous interest during the last 100 years. The idea that Nero instituted a general imperial prosecution, the so-called *Institutum Neronianum* described by Tertullian, is no longer held among scholars.[102] The most likely hypothesis is that Christians were subject to sporadic localized oppression at the hands of Roman governors exercising

---

mus in Kleinasien an der Wende vom ersten zum zweiten Jahrhundert n. Chr. (Gütersloh: Gütersloh Verlagshaus Mohn, 1976) 27–38, who makes this suggestion; Schüssler Fiorenza, *Justice and Judgment*, 144–46, who disagrees with it; and Aune, "Social Matrix," 23–26, who finds this plausible in that John understood his role as mediator of divine revelation to transcend local issues.

[99]Motifs in Rev 1:5 and Rev 3:14 raise the possibility of intertextual references in Revelation to the Christ hymn in Col 1:15–23. The parallels are noted by NA[26] and most commentators; Charles, 1:94–95, develops the parallels between Revelation and Colossians at some length and concludes that John had direct or indirect knowledge of Colossians. Commentators such as Charles, writing within the orthodox Christian tradition, maintain that Colossians and Revelation are in theological agreement with each other, even countering similar strands of early Gnosticism. But Revelation and Colossians show important disagreements (see Royalty, "Dwelling on Visions").

[100]See Thompson, *Revelation*, 172–73.

[101]So Garrett, "Revelation," 378.

[102]See Tertullian *Apology* 5.3, 4; *Ad Nationes* 1.7; C. Callewaert, "Les persécutions contre les Chrétiens dans la politique religieuse de l'Etat romain," *Revue des questions historiques* 82 (1907): 8ff. L. H. Canfield, *The Early Persecutions of the Christians* (New York: Columbia University, 1913) 127–28, lends particular weight to Tertullian's "legal training and keen appreciation of the juristic status of Christians."

their *imperium* apart from specific legislation (*coercitio*).[103] The earliest outside evidence for persecution of the Christians by the Romans is Pliny's letter to Trajan and the emperor's rescript, ca. 112 CE, and Tacitus' *Annals*, ca. 115 CE. Schüssler Fiorenza maintains that Pliny's *Ep.* 10.96 represents the "rhetorical situation" of the Apocalypse.[104] But the evidence for this relies on the rhetoric of Revelation itself, while the interpretation of Pliny and Trajan's correspondence is by no means plain.[105] Pliny's letter shows ignorance of how to deal with Christians, suggesting not only that there was no imperial policy but also that the Roman authorities had not had to deal with Christians very often at all. Pliny brings in a statue of Trajan for the purpose of testing; the test of emperor worship was not a regular feature of his court. Trajan, in his reply to Pliny, avoids setting a fixed policy in his response and avoids mention of emperor worship.

A third option for the crisis of the Apocalypse is oppression of some Christians at the hand of the Jews.[106] The Jews referred to in Rev 2:9 and 3:9 could be Jewish Christians but are more likely Jews, showing that the relation of Christians to the synagogue was an important issue for John's prophetic community.[107] The Jewish community in Sardis was prominent and well established.[108] Jews could have participated in the social

---

[103] A variation of this theory holds that Christians were prosecuted for specific crimes under known criminal statutes (*flagitia cohaerentia*). See A. N. E. Sherwin-White, "Early Persecutions and Roman Law Again," *JTS* 3 n.s. (1952): 199–213; G. E. M. de Ste. Croix, "Why Were the Christians Persecuted?" *Past and Present* 26 (1963): 6–38; idem., "Why Were the Christians Persecuted?—A Rejoinder," *Past and Present* 27 (1964): 28–33. Ste. Croix's two essays are reprinted in *Studies in Ancient Society*, ed. M. I. Finley (London and Boston: Routledge and Kegan Paul, 1974) 210–62, with A. N. E. Sherwin-White, "Why Were the Early Christians Persecuted? An Amendment" (250–55). The debate between Sherwin-White and Ste. Croix centers on whether Christians were prosecuted for the name Christian alone and whether they were treated differently than any other religious group which posed a threat to social order.

[104] Schüssler Fiorenza, *Justice and Judgment*, 193.

[105] See Thompson, *Revelation*, 129–32.

[106] See Aune, 168–72, "Anatolian Jewish Communities and Synagogues."

[107] See further discussion in chap. 5. The definition of Judaism and delimitation of the Jewish people at the end of the first century CE was, of course, in some transition. A more precise term might be "proto-Rabbinic Diaspora Jews."

[108] See A. T. Kraabel, "Paganism and Judaism: The Sardis Evidence" in *Paganisme, Judaïsme, Christianisme: Influences et affrontements dans le monde*

ostracism of Christians and reported Christian activities to local or Roman authorities. This tension between Jews and John's community expressed in Revelation could also be related to expulsion from the synagogue.[109] The passages also show an intramural conflict with Jewish sects over the language and symbols of the people of Israel.[110] John advocates struggle against the Jews, but with only two references in Revelation, it is difficult to maintain that the relation between the Asian churches and the Jewish synagogue was *the* crisis of the Apocalypse.

Hand in hand with the common assumption that a crisis, either real or perceived, motivates the production of the Apocalypse for the Christians in Asia Minor is the widely accepted idea that this text helped alleviate that crisis. Comfort, catharsis, tastes of millennial bliss, alleviation of cognitive dissonance—scholars have used a variety of terms and models to explain how Revelation must have functioned in the early Christian communities.[111] Most of these interpretations rest upon the unspoken theological presupposition that a text included in the New Testament canon must have had a positive effect on the Christian community and needs to be so interpreted. We should not let this presupposition go unexamined. It is quite possible that Revelation provided comfort or catharsis to some Christians, such as John and his circle of prophets, or to second-century Chiliasts such as Justin, Irenaeus,

---

antique, Mélanges offerts à Marcel Simon, ed. A. Benoit, M. Philonenko, and C. Vogel (Paris: de Baccard, 1978) 13–33; and "The Diaspora Synagogue: Archaeological and Epigraphic Evidence since Sukenik," *ANRW* 2/19/1, 477–510.

[109]See Yarbro Collins, *Crisis and Catharsis*, 85–87. Thompson, *Revelation*, 173–74, rejects the notion that Jews denounced Christians before officials and sees instead in these passages John's negative attitude towards anyone with high standing in Greco-Roman culture.

[110]See Peder Borgen, "Polemic in the Book of Revelation," in *Anti-Semitism and Early Christianity: Issues of Polemic and Faith*, ed. C. A. Evans and D. A. Hagner (Minneapolis: Augsburg Fortress, 1993) 199–211; see also Friederich Wilhelm Horn, "Zwischen der Synagoge des Satans und dem neuen Jerusalem: Die christlich-jüdische Standortbestimmung in der Apokalypse des Johannes," *ZRGG* 46 (1994): 143–62.

[111]See Gager, *Kingdom and Community*, 49–57; Yarbro Collins, *Crisis and Catharsis*, 141–63; Thompson, *Revelation*, 186–97. See also David deSilva, "The Revelation to John: A Case Study in Apocalyptic Propaganda and the Maintenance of Sectarian Identity," *Sociological Analysis* 53 (1992): 375–95, who reads the Apocalypse as a call to action in protest of Roman society and values rather than comfort for those in crisis.

and Tertullian. Documented persecution of Christians increases in the second and third centuries. But other second-century Christians rejected Revelation and its status was still debated in the fourth century. Eventual acceptance of a book into the New Testament canon by no means involves an endorsement of the original message or function of the work. Revelation was a problem text in the early church and would not have been accepted in the East without the development of allegorical interpretation.[112]

On a more basic level, however, Revelation is chock full of threats and graphic descriptions of plagues, disease, and violent death. Commentators writing consciously from outside the Christian tradition have given more reign to the lurid, violent, and anxiety-producing aspects of Revelation.[113] Among Christian commentators, only feminist scholars have begun to read for the dehumanizing and misogynic aspects of Revelation and question the theological value of the text.[114] If the Apocalypse were written during a power struggle, in which the author and his community perceived themselves as a threatened minority, why should we expect to find comfort in this text? Among the complex rhetorical strategies of the Apocalypse, threats are quite prominent.[115] Whatever "comfort" the Apocalypse may have conveyed for the ancient Asian Christians is seriously qualified by these threats.

---

[112]The social function of allegory is the main concern of Dawson, *Allegorical Readers*. Supposed apostolic authorship, the thrust of Irenaeus' apology for the Apocalypse, may have helped as well, although this was no guarantee of acceptance, as the rejection of the Gospel of Peter by Serapion of Antioch illustrates (see Eus. *Hist. Eccl.* 6.12.3–6). On the early history of the interpretation of Revelation and its acceptance by the Christian churches, see Maier, *Johannesoffenbarung und die Kirche*, 1–107; and Wainright, *Mysterious Apocalypse*, 21–48.

[113]See, e.g., the introduction and essays collected in *The Revelation of St. John the Divine*, ed. Harold Bloom (New York, New Haven, and Philadelphia: Chelsea House, 1988). D. H. Lawrence, *Apocalypse*, included by Bloom and quoted above, 1, is the classic example of this.

[114]See Garrett, "Revelation"; Pippin, "Eros and the End"; and idem., *Death and Desire*. Schüssler Fiorenza, 117–39, and "Reading Revelation 17–18" (paper presented at the annual meeting of the Society of Biblical Literature, San Francisco, November 1997) attempts to reconstruct Revelation's theological value despite these aspects.

[115]See esp. the threats and descriptions of punishment at the end, which are juxtaposed with the most "comforting" passages of the Apocalypse (Rev 20:11–15; 21:8, 27; 22:11, 15, 18–19).

The evidence for the existence of a variety of groups within the Christian communities of Asia Minor in 95 CE and their ideological differences is well established. But what is more important are not the actual issues at stake between opposing groups, illuminating though these are, but that the Apocalypse was written and read in the context of these struggles and indeed written so as to influence the outcome. For this brings us back to my topic, the "ideology of wealth in the Apocalypse of John." As this subtitle suggests, this study is concerned with more than literary results. Wealth, in certain guises, was the preeminent symbol of power in antiquity. Wealth was also a major *topos* of moral exhortation and a mark of status. The language of wealth in Revelation is intrinsically connected to issues of power within the early Christian communities and their social worlds. The ideology of Revelation and the struggle for power and authority within the young churches are my main objects of study.

There is a struggle in Revelation between God and Satan; the imagery of wealth and luxury functions on both sides of this conflict. There is also considerable evidence of conflict within the Christian communities who read Revelation. The Apocalypse reflects the tensions and conflicts engendered by the theological and ideological struggles within the early Christian communities and between Christians and the dominant culture. My thesis that the imagery of wealth in Revelation has an ideological function in the context of these power struggles requires more evidence than I have presented to this point. It is not clear how the same wealth imagery can be "good" or "bad" when applied to different characters nor how the wealth imagery in the Apocalypse would have been heard in the social setting of the first audiences. My next task is to place the wealth passages in the Apocalypse in the context of the two great traditions which shaped the text of Revelation and the community of its first audience; that is, the literature and cultures of the people of Israel and Greece.

Wealth Imagery
in Ancient Jewish Literature

Introduction

The Apocalypse of John describes a wealthy God, a golden-clad Messiah, and their angelic forces destroying an opulent trading city and rewarding their true and loyal followers with a city of gold and jewels. John of Patmos was not the first prophet to see the throne of God or write about the destruction of Babylon and a restored city of Jerusalem. The Apocalypse stands in a long tradition of prophetic and revelatory Jewish literature. The visions of Revelation have their roots in the classical prophets of the Hebrew Bible and many parallels with Jewish texts from the Second Temple period and the decades after the destruction of the Temple. In order to begin to understand the wealth imagery of the Apocalypse, we must study its main source, the Hebrew scriptures. John borrowed extensively from the Bible; he borrowed characters, phrases, and images. There are hundreds of allusions to the Hebrew Bible or LXX in Revelation, although not one of them is marked by a citation formula. The actual number has become somewhat of an issue in recent studies of the use of the Hebrew Bible in Revelation.[1]

Of the five main concentrations of wealth imagery in Revelation, four draw most heavily on the Hebrew Bible: the vision of Christ on Patmos (Rev 1:12–16); the vision of the heavenly throne room (Rev 4:2–11); and the visions of the cities of Babylon and the New Jerusalem in Revelation 17–18 and 21–22 (I will cover the fifth major wealth passage, the messages to Smyrna and Laodicea in Revelation 2–3, in the next chapter). The extensive use of the Bible by the author of Revelation presents a

---

[1]See Paulien, *Decoding Revelation's Trumpets*, 100–54; and Fekkes, *Isaiah and Prophetic Traditions*, 59–63. Boring, 27, claims to have counted 500 from the margins of NA[26]. Moyise, *Old Testament in Revelation*, has rightly moved the debate beyond the actual count and subjective distinctions between allusion and echo to discussion of the hermeneutical complexity of Revelation's intertextuality.

clear opportunity for learning how the wealth imagery in the Apocalypse
would have been heard by its original audience. Early Christians in Asia
could have been familiar with the biblical passages on which these
visions are based, most of which are found in the biblical books of Isaiah,
Jeremiah, Ezekiel, and Daniel. Those listening to Revelation who were
familiar with the Bible would have been surprised or even shocked at
John's free, bold use of his biblical sources. When using biblical texts,
he concentrates wealth motifs by combining and conflating different
biblical passages to accentuate the wealth of heaven and the heavenly
forces. Even those unfamiliar with the Hebrew Bible would have been
struck by the prevalence of wealth imagery in John's compositions. Bits
and pieces of passages from the Hebrew Bible are plucked out—gold
here, jewels there—and combined in John's visions of Christ, heaven,
Babylon, and the New Jerusalem for an intensely opulent effect.
Furthermore, the prophetic texts used in Revelation emphasize *commercial* activity as a source of wealth for Babylon/Rome while avoiding such
references to heaven or the New Jerusalem. The extensive use of
prophetic sources for wealth imagery in Revelation, however, does not
mean that John has taken up every prophetic theme about wealth.
Revelation lacks the theme expressed in a major cluster of wealth
passages in the Hebrew prophets: concern for social and economic justice
and care for the poor, the widowed, and the orphaned. In order to
demonstrate these characteristics of the use of the Hebrew Bible in
Revelation, I will step through these four wealth passages, bringing in
other Jewish and Christian texts in order to illuminate these points.

The Human One

When John turns to see whose trumpet-like voice it is that has commanded him to write to the seven churches, he sees "seven golden lampstands
and in the midst of the lampstands I saw one like the Son of Man [or
Human One], clothed with a long robe and with a golden sash across his
chest" (Rev 1:12–13). The identification of Christ as "the Human One"
in Rev 1:13 is a clear allusion to Dan 7:13, the first appearance of the
Human One in Jewish literature.[2] Who exactly Daniel's Human One was

[2]Rev 1:13 reads ὅμοιον υἱὸν ἀνθρώπου; cf. Dan 7:13 כְּבַר אֱנָשׁ
(Aram.); ὡς υἱὸς ἀνθρώπου (Old Greek). As discussed by Adela Yarbro
Collins, "The Origin of the Designation of Jesus as the 'Son of Man,' " *HTR* 80
(1987): 391–407, the translation of the phrase υἱὸς ἀνθρώπου involves

meant or understood to be need not concern us, for it is clear that John interprets the Human One as Christ (see Rev 1:17–18).[3] His Asian audience would likely have had the same association, for Human One (υἱὸς ἀνθρώπου) was well established in early Christian tradition by the time of the Apocalypse as a title for Jesus, whether or not it functioned as an apocalyptic title prior to this time.[4] Furthermore, the audience of Revelation has been prepared for this allusion by another allusion to Dan 7:13 in Rev 1:7, the oracle which immediately precedes John's vision of Christ.[5] Identifying Christ in Rev 1:12–16 as the Human One of Jewish and Christian tradition creates more problems than it solves, because the tradition-history of the Human One is among the most complicated in Jewish and Christian literature.[6] Indeed, only the brave

---

gender, historical, and interpretive issues. Since the phrase functions in Revelation as a title that draws on a religious and literary tradition, I have used "Human One" as the best gender-inclusive translation that conveys the titular sense of the phrase. Thomas B. Slater, "*Homoion huion anthropou* in Rev. 1.13 and 14.14," *BT* 44 (1993) 359–60, has argued that the use of the phrase in Rev 1:13 and 14:14 is similar to the use in *Similitudes of Enoch*, and 4 Ezra 13 rather than the Gospel tradition and should be translated "like a son of man" (RSV) rather than "like the Son of Man" (NRSV). But the early Christian prophetic tradition in Rev 1:7 shows the influence of Gospel traditions on Revelation and therefore the phrase in Rev 1:13 should be read with a titular sense.

[3]See John J. Collins, *The Apocalyptic Imagination: An Introduction to the Jewish Matrix of Christianity* (New York: Crossroad, 1992) 81–83; and *Daniel*, Hermeneia (Minneapolis: Augsburg/Fortress, 1993) 304–10. Collins maintains that the Human One in Dan 7:13 is an angelic being. Alternatives are that this figure is meant to be a corporate entity (P. M. Casey, *The Son of Man: The Interpretation and Influence of Daniel 7* [London: SPCK, 1979]); or the messiah (G. R. Beasley-Murray, "The Interpretation of Daniel 7," *CBQ* 45 [1983]: 44–58).

[4]See Mark 13:26 = Matt 24:30, Luke 21:27; cf. Mark 14:62 = Matt 26:64, Luke 22:69.

[5]See the discussion in chap. 4.

[6]The long discussion shows no signs of ending. Recent work on the phrase (or title) in the Synoptics includes Adela Yarbro Collins, "Origin of the Designation of Jesus"; Douglas R. A. Hare, *The Son of Man Tradition* (Minneapolis: Fortress, 1990); Delbert Burkett, *The Son of Man in the Gospel Tradition*, JSNTSup 56 (Sheffield UK: Academic Press, 1991), who lists eight literature reviews published in English between 1959 and 1986 (p. 11); and Jonathan A. Draper, "The Development of 'the Sign of the Son of Man' in the Jesus tradi-

and the foolish would continue a discussion of the υἱος ἀνθρώπου in
Second Temple Judaism and early Christianity. But it is well worth our
while to pursue this significant but elusive character a bit further, since
the pursuit will show how the wealth motifs in Rev 1:12–16 distinguish
it from other Jewish and Christian interpretations of Dan 7:13.

Gold is the first and most prominent aspect of John's vision in Rev
1:12–16. He also describes hair white as wool, eyes like fire, and feet of
burnished bronze, and he hears a voice like many waters.[7] There are
seven stars in Christ's right hand and a double-edged sword issuing from
his mouth. This description of the Human One, including the wealth
imagery, makes John's vision stand out the tradition. Neither Dan
7:13–14, the *locus classicus* for "One like a Human Being" in the Jewish
tradition, nor any other passage dependent upon Daniel use wealth
imagery in their portrayal of the figure; in fact, they include *no* physical
descriptions of the Human One. Daniel sees "one like a human being
coming with the clouds of heaven" (Dan 7:13). Aside from the clouds,
there is no description of the Human One in Daniel 7—no clothes, lamps,
or parts of the body. The Human One in Revelation shares some physical
aspects with God, the "Ancient of Days" in Dan 7:9, who has snow-white
garments and hair like wool.[8] John thus takes motifs from a vision of
God in Daniel to describe Christ, a powerful theological reinterpretation
of Dan 7:9–14. In Daniel, the Human One is presented to the Ancient
One and receives dominion, glory, and kingship from God.[9] The Human

---

tion," *NTS* 39 (1993): 1–22. On the use of the term outside of the Synoptic
Gospels, see John J. Collins, "The Son of Man in First-Century Judaism," *NTS*
38 (1992): 448–66; Maurice Casey, "Idiom and Translation: Some Aspects of the
Son of Man Problem," *NTS* 41 (1995): 164–82; and Thomas B. Slater, "One
Like a Son of Man in First-Century CE Judaism," *NTS* 41 (1995): 183–98. John
J. Collins, *The Scepter and the Star: The Messiahs of the Dead Sea Scrolls and
Other Ancient Literature* (New York: Doubleday, 1995), in particular "The
Danielic Son of Man" (173–94), places the Danielic tradition in the context of
other Jewish messianic traditions. The Danielic tradition was a minor one in
Judaism (see 4Q246, in addition to the texts I discuss in this chapter), but the
one adopted by early Christianity.

[7]Fekkes, "Revelation 19–21 and Isaian Nuptial Imagery," 269–87, suggests
that Christ appears here as a bridegroom, but there is no evidence for this in Rev
1:12–16.

[8]See Collins, *Daniel*, 280–94, on the religiohistorical background and the
"Ancient of Days."

[9]And possibly a throne; see Collins, *Daniel*, 301. God is clearly the agent

One then receives the service of all peoples, nations, and languages, and an everlasting kingdom. There are no wealth motifs in Daniel 7.

While the association of Christ and Daniel's Human One clearly preceded the Apocalypse, as the Synoptic Gospel passages show, the physical description of the figure in Revelation is new to the Christian tradition. John's vision of the Human One in Revelation looks nothing like descriptions in the Synoptic Gospels. The reference in Mark 13:26 contains no element that is not found in Dan 7:13–14.[10] Nor do wealth motifs appear in descriptions of the Human One in 4 Ezra, a Jewish apocalypse contemporaneous to Revelation, where we find no physical description of the figure at all.[11] The Synoptic Gospels and 4 Ezra do not associate the Human One with wealth in any way.[12] In the Synoptic Gospels, the appearance of the Human One follows a period of tribulation and inaugurates the day of judgment (Mark 13:26–27 and par.; Matt 25:31). In 4 Ezra 13, the Human One is cast as a cosmic warrior.[13] There are no wealth motifs associated with the Human One in any of these passages. The absence of and even hostility to wealth motifs in the Synoptic Gospels makes the opulence of John's vision in Revelation stand out all the more.[14]

---

implied by the passive verb in 7:14. The LXX includes only ἐξουσία.

[10]See Vincent Taylor, *The Gospel according to Mark* (London: MacMillan & Co., 1952) 518; C. E. B. Cranfield, *The Gospel according to St. Mark*, CGTC (Cambridge: Cambridge University Press, 1959) 406; C. S. Mann, *Mark*, AB 27 (Garden City NY: Doubleday & Co., 1986) 531, 625.

[11]In 4 Ezra 13:3, the scribe describes a vision of "something like the figure of a man" coming "out of the heart of the sea." While the exact title is not the same as Dan 7:13, this man flies "with the clouds of heaven," making the identification sure. See Michael E. Stone, *Fourth Ezra*, Hermeneia (Minneapolis: Augsburg/Fortress, 1990) 381. The best external and internal evidence places the text between 70 CE, the destruction of the Jerusalem temple, and the end of the second century, when 4 Ezra is quoted by Clement of Alexandria. Stone (9–10, 361–65) narrows this date to the end of Domitian's reign.

[12]In Matt 19:27–30, Jesus hints at some reward for his followers, implicitly followers of ὁ υἱὸς τοῦ ἀνθρώπου.

[13]See Stone, *Fourth Ezra*, 211–12; he notes, 383, that the "melting of enemies is one of the major characteristics of God in the Hebrew Bible."

[14]See Raymond E. Brown, *The Death of the Messiah: From Gethsemane to the Grave. A Commentary on the Passion Narratives in the Four Gospels*, 2 vols. (New York: Doubleday, 1994) §21a. Brown writes, 478–79, that it is "very likely" that during Jesus' lifetime some of his followers thought him to be the

The Similitudes of Enoch (*1 Enoch* 37–71) pose a special case for our investigation.[15] As with Daniel, 4 Ezra, and the Synoptics, there are no wealth motifs in the visions of the Human One, who is also called the Elect or Chosen One (see *1 Enoch* 46:1–8; 71:12–17). The Elect One sits upon a throne of glory (*1 Enoch* 45:3, 62:3) but neither the Elect One nor the Human One have white hair, a golden belt, or any other physical descriptions in the Similitudes.[16] What distinguishes the Similitudes from

---

Messiah and made that claim to others: "One may object that the notion of Jesus as the Messiah king would not have come up in his ministry, granting his Galilean origins, the type of people he associated with, and his disinterest in wealth and power." Thomas E. Schmidt, *Hostility to Wealth in the Synoptic Gospels*, JSNTSup 15 (Sheffield UK: JSOT Press, 1987) argues that hostility to wealth in the Synoptic Gospels does not derive from social-economic conditions but is an expression of a conservative religious tradition independent of material concerns. Schmidt also dismisses sociological methods for the study of early Christianity. Schmidt's study is flawed in three primary aspects: a tendency to dismiss all social and economic factors in the study of early Christianity in favor of the history of ideas and the "state of the human heart" (164–65); the rigid attention to the canon of the Hebrew Bible as historically normative for his treatment of sources, which results in discussion of the canonical writings separately from contemporary noncanonical texts; and the problematic use of statistics and tables to determine "ethical norms" for readers and tests of "ethical and theological consistency" in texts (53).

[15]Unless otherwise noted, translations of *1 Enoch* are from Matthew Black, *The Book of Enoch or 1 Enoch: A New English Edition*, SVTP 7 (Leiden: E. J. Brill, 1985); see also the trans. by E. Isaac, *OTP* 1:5–89. The issue of the dating of the Similitudes, and whether they are Jewish or Jewish-Christian, is not central to my argument. J. T. Milik with Matthew Black, *The Books of Enoch: Aramaic Fragments from Qumrân Cave 4* (Oxford: Clarendon/Oxford University Press, 1976) 91–98, has argued that the absence of the Similitudes from the Qumran fragments leads to the conclusion that the Similitudes (or "the Second Vision") are a third-century CE Christian composition, in which the Son of Man passages are influenced by the Gospels. For a succinct refutation of Milik's thesis, see Collins, *Apocalyptic Imagination*, 142–43. See also J. C. Greenfield and M. E. Stone, "The Enochic Pentateuch and the Date of the Similitudes," *HTR* 79 (1977): 51–65. On the Human One, see Black, *Book of Enoch*, 181–89, and Collins, "Son of Man." Maurice Casey, "The Use of Term 'Son of Man' in the Similitudes of Enoch," *JSJ* 7 (1976): 11-29, argues that "Son of Man" in the Similitudes is used the way the phrase is used elsewhere in Hebrew and Aramaic, as an ordinary term for a person.

[16]See *1 Enoch* 46:2–4; 48:2; 62:2–14; 63:11; 69:26–29. There is no

other Second Temple texts is that the Human One has a clear and definite role in punishing the wealthy and the powerful.[17] *1 Enoch* 62:1–63:12 describes the judgment of the rich and the powerful by the Elect One in a manner typical of the Similitudes. The Lord gathers the "kings and the mighty and the exalted, and those who possess the earth" and commands them to gaze upon the Elect One (62:1). At the time when the Elect One has finally been revealed, they will realize the extent of their sin and beg and plead for mercy, but they will be delivered over to angels for punishment (62:10–11). In the dialogue between the wealthy and the Lord of the Spirits, "the Master of the rich" (63:2), the rich kings and landowners offer an extended apology and explanation for their behavior (*1 Enoch* 63:6–10): "Our souls are sated with ill-gotten gains, But they will not keep us from going down to the grave, from the flames of the *pit* of Sheol" (63:10). In the Similitudes, the association of the Human One with wealth is a negative association. A major function of the Human One in this text is to conquer and judge the rich and powerful kings and landowners.

The Biblical Sources of Wealth Motifs in Revelation 1:12–16

In John's vision, the Human One does not condemn wealth at all; in fact, he appears among golden lampstands, which he identifies with the seven Christian churches of Asia, and wears a long robe and belt of gold. While this description of the Human One in Rev 1:12–16 may be unique to the Jewish and Christian tradition, the elements themselves are hardly new. The Human One appears draped in Old Testament garments and surrounded by prophetic props that have been pulled from John's scriptural storehouse to produce a concentration of wealth motifs. While the Human One's title comes from Dan 7:13, several other descriptive

---

suggestion that Enoch's physical appearance changes when he becomes the Human One in *1 Enoch* 71:12–17. See Himmelfarb, *Ascent to Heaven*, 16–20, on the garments of God in *1 Enoch* 14:20, and 60–61, on *1 Enoch* 71:12–17. Isaac, *OTP* 1:50 note "s" to ch. 71, takes a minority position that Enoch does not become the Human One. Compare Black, *Book of Enoch*, 188–89; and Stone, "Apocalyptic Literature" and "Third Century."

[17]Power and wealth are integrally connected in the Similitudes that; see *1 Enoch* 46:3–8; 48:8–10; 50:1–5; 52:1–9; 53:1–7; 54:1–6; 55:1–10. Black, *Book of Enoch*, 196, discusses the identification of the "mighty" or "powerful kings," who appear in *1 Enoch* 38.5, 55.4, 62.1, 3, 6, 9, 63.1, 2, 12, and 67.8, 12, as Roman or Seleucid monarchs.

elements are borrowed from the vision of an angel in Dan 10:2–9. Since the golden belt, the bronze feet, and the voice like many waters from Dan 10:5–6 appear in Rev 1:12–16, it is possible that John interpreted Daniel 10 as a second appearance of the Human One of Dan 7:13.[18] The long robe (ποδήρη) in which Christ appears in Rev 1:13 could be a reference to the "man clothed in linen" in Ezek 9:2 (אִישׁ לָבֻשׁ בַּדִּים, ἀνὴρ ἐνδεδυκὼς ποδήρη), who acts as the Lord's scribe in the punishment of the guilty in Jerusalem. The word ποδήρη has strong wealth associations in the LXX, where it is used in Exodus 25–40 for priestly garments which are decorated with gold, gems, and fine cloths.[19] These chapters in Exodus describe the cultic articles, such as the ark, tables, lamps, tabernacle, altar, and vestments, and the luxury materials used to make them, such as gold, jewels, and fine dyed cloth (see Exod 25:3–7). These articles are designed according to a heavenly counterpart revealed to Moses on Sinai (Exod 25:9; 31:18). Finally, the seven lampstands in Rev 1:12 are pulled from the vision of a gold lampstand with seven lamps upon it in Zech 4:2. Two olive trees flank Zechariah's lampstand and supply them with oil from golden pipes (see Rev 11:4).

In the vision of Christ in Rev 1:12–16, John only uses Old Testament passages that are in fact visions. Two such passages, Ezekiel 9 and Daniel 10, are visions of heavenly beings while Zechariah 4 is a vision interpreted by an angel. There is no doubt that John has chosen these three passages intentionally, to emphasize Christ's wealth.[20] John does not turn to Old Testament passages describing kings to describe this vision of the "ruler of the kings of earth" (Rev 1:5). If John were searching only for gold with no regard for the gold's source, he might well have used 1 Kings 6–10, the lavish account of Solomon's opulent temple, palace,

---

[18]Beale, *Use of Daniel*, 160–62, finds the description "natural" and does not offer any rhetorical explanation for the conflation of several Daniel passages in Rev 1:12–16. There is no suggestion in Dan 10:5 that the angel who appears to Daniel by the Tigris is the Human One who is presented to the Ancient of Days. As we have seen, other Jewish and Christian passages dependent on Dan 7:13 do not link the Human One with the angel of Daniel 10.

[19]The Gr. ποδήρη is used in the LXX for the Heb. *ephôd* (אפוד), the *ḥōšen* (חשׁן), and the *mě 'îl* (מעיל); see Exod 25:6[7]; 28:5; 28:27 [31]; 35:9; Jos. *Ant.* 3 §§159–61.

[20]Here I am in agreement with Fekkes's main thesis, that the use of the Old Testament shows intentionality on John's part; see *Isaiah and Prophetic Traditions*, 59–103.

throne, and court (e.g., 1 Kings 10:23). These five chapters in 1 Kings contain 37 occurrences of χρυσός, gold, and cognates. There are allusions to 1 Kings 8:1–6 in Rev 11:19 and 1 Kings 8:10 in Rev 15:8 and other references to 1 Kings in Revelation.[21] John certainly knew and used 1 Kings but he is careful about the source of heaven's wealth. Solomon amassed his wealth, after all, through extensive commercial activity (1 Kings 9:26–28; 10:14–15; 10:22). In a text where two starkly opposed sides both have wealth, the wealth of heaven, in contrast to the wealth of Babylon, must remain pure of any such commercial associations.[22]

John's description of Christ is unique among other descriptions of the Human One in Second Temple Judaism and early Christianity, and yet totally derivative in its imagery. The passage is unique because no other vision outside of Revelation uses wealth imagery. But it is derivative because John has taken each wealth image in this vision from a different part of the Hebrew Bible and combined them in order to present to his audience the wealthiest Human One in Second Temple literature. The use of the Hebrew Bible in Rev 1:12–16 reveals a pattern we will find repeated in the three other main wealth passages in Revelation. First, the wealth passages of the Apocalypse contain significantly more wealth motifs than John's sources in the Hebrew Bible or parallel passages in Second Temple Jewish or early Christian literature. Often, a passage in the Apocalypse of John has extensive wealth motifs where the Jewish or Christian parallels have none. Second, the author of the Apocalypse has selected his biblical sources so as to intensify the wealth imagery in his visions.

The Throne of God

This pattern recurs in the next wealth passage based on the Hebrew Bible, the vision of the heavenly throne room in Rev 4:2–11. John's vision of

---

[21]Most notably Jezebel (1 Kings 16:31) in Rev 2:20. Rev 11:6 and 12:6 refer to the story of Elijah in the desert (1 Kings 17:1–7); Rev 13:13 to the contest between Elijah and the prophets of Baal (1 Kings 18:38). There are perhaps references to 1 Kings 22:19 in Rev 5:7, 11 and 1 Kings 22:21–23 in Rev 16:13. The index to NA[26] suggests references to 1 Kings 8:27 in Rev 21:3 and to 1 Kings 10:18 in Rev 20:11, although these connections are more tenuous.

[22]This point is developed further in chap. 3 and applied to Revelation in chap. 6.

the throne room derives much of its motifs from scriptural antecedents.[23] John's vision of heaven looks enough like other visions that an audience familiar with the Hebrew Bible would find it believable.[24] The vision also shows extensive rewriting of these scriptural sources, the effect of which is to trade upon the authority of other prophetic visions even while claiming its own authority as a new vision.[25]

The vision begins when John sees a door opening in heaven and hears the trumpet-like voice of Christ summoning him again, this time to "come up here, and I will show you what must take place after this" (Rev 4:1). John views these events from the heavenly throne room, described in Rev 4:2–11. From John's first glimpse of the throne in 4:2 to God's speech in 21:5–8, the throne is the central image of the Apocalypse.[26] Everything John describes in this vision revolves around the throne of God. God wears jewels and God's throne shines with jewels: "The one seated there looks like jasper and carnelian, and around the throne is a rainbow that looks like an emerald" (Rev 4:3). Twenty-four elders sit upon thrones around God's throne, wearing white robes and golden crowns (στεφάνους χρυσοῦς, 4:4).[27] Since Christ promises both

---

[23]See Christopher Rowland, *The Open Heaven: A Study of Apocalyptic in Judaism and Early Christianity* (New York: Crossroad, 1982) 222–26; and L. W. Hurtado, "Revelation 4–5 in the Light of Jewish Apocalyptic Analogies," *JSNT* 25 (1985): 105–24.

[24]See George W. E. Nickelsburg, *Jewish Literature between the Bible and the Mishnah: A Historical and Literary Introduction* (Philadelphia: Fortress, 1981) 53, on the throne vision in *1 Enoch* 14, which similarly trades upon traditional imagery in order to validate the authority of the revelation in *1 Enoch*.

[25]Charles, 1:106–34, analyzes the text of Rev 4:2–11 more in terms of the history of religions and conceptions current between 200 BCE and 100 CE in apocalyptic literature, citing primarily *1 Enoch* but also Daniel, *Testament of the 12 Patriarchs*, *2 Baruch*, and *4 Ezra*. The effect of this analysis is to mitigate the literary dependence upon Isaiah and Ezekiel and to explain away the reinterpretation of the biblical passages.

[26]See Caird, 22; Aune, "Roman Imperial Court," 7.

[27]The identity and source of the elders is one of the unsolved mysteries of the Apocalypse. The ancient commentary of Victorinus of Pettau maintains that the elders are heavenly representatives of the community, a view also taken by Bousset, 289–92, and Swete, 69. The knotty question is the number 24. Bousset decided that 24 represents the 12 Old Testament patriarchs combined with the 12 New Testament apostles. Charles, 1:128–33, argues against this view and, with strong emphasis on the history of religions, takes the position that they must be

crowns and thrones in the seven messages (Rev 2:10; 3:11, 21), the elders should be taken as heavenly representatives of the earthly churches. Thunder, lightning and sounds come from the throne; seven lamps burn before it; something like a sea of crystal lies in front of the throne (4:5–6). John describes four "living creatures," similar to a lion, an ox, a person, and an eagle, full of eyes and with six wings, "around the throne, and on each side of the throne" (4:6b–8).[28]

Envisioning the gods in a palace or court setting was typical of ancient Near Eastern religions and there are several examples in the Hebrew Bible.[29] The foundational text for Rev 4:2–11 is Ezek 1:4–28.[30] Ezekiel's vision of the throne-chariot influenced every apocalyptic vision of God in heaven in the Second Temple period and served as the focal text for a long-standing tradition of Jewish mysticism.[31] John takes the

---

an order of angels. In recent commentaries, they have been taken as "human symbols, heavenly counterparts of the earthly church" (Harrington, 79); angelic figures in the heavenly council (Roloff, 70; Roloff prefers 24 as signifying the 24 hours in a day, since they praise God ceaselessly); and as heavenly representatives of the church (Boring, 106).

[28]So the NRSV, which seems to follow the suggestion of Charles, 1:118, that ἐν μέσῳ τοῦ θρόνου is either a gloss or mistranslation of the Heb. in Ezek 1:5. Swete, 70–71, suggests a gyrating dance in which one of the creatures is always before the throne. The suggestion of Kraft, 98, that "throne" here means "heaven" causes more difficulties than it resolves. Robert G. Hall, "Living Creatures in the Midst of the Throne: Another Look at Revelation 4.6," *NTS* 36 (1990) 609–13, uses interpretations of the descriptions of the ark found in Exod 25:17–22; 37:6–9; *Pirque R. El.* 4; *Shir. Rab.* 3.10.4; and Jos. *Ant.* 3 §137 to explain how the creatures are actually part of the seat (see also Caird, 64; and Roloff, 71).

[29]See esp. the prophet Micaiah ben-Imlah's vision of Yahweh on his throne (1 Kings 22:19–23) and Isaiah's vision of the heavenly throne room (Isa 6:1–13), which takes place in the Jerusalem temple; see also Pss 11:4; 80; 103:19; Zech 3:1–2. On the mythological lineage of the divine council see Frank M. Cross, *Canaanite Myth and Epic* (Cambridge MA: Harvard University Press, 1973); and John Gray, *I & II Kings: A Commentary*, 2nd ed., OTL (Philadelphia: Westminster, 1970) 451–52.

[30]As noted, John also draws on Isa 6:1–13.

[31]While the experiential and psychological basis of apocalyptic visions has been argued by a number of commentators (for instance, Rowland, *Open Heaven*; C. R. A. Morray-Jones, "Transformational Mysticism in the Apocalyptic-Merkabah Tradition," *JJS* 43 [1992]: 1–31; and Stone, *Fourth Ezra*), Himmel-

essential elements of Ezekiel's vision and then makes significant changes to cast this prophetic vision as his own. The basic plot of the two throne visions is different, for Ezekiel has his on earth while John ascends to heaven.[32] John sees the throne at the outset of his vision, while Ezekiel sees the throne at the end of his. The four living creatures (Ezek 1:5–14) are major characters in Ezekiel's vision; these creatures and the wheels of the throne-chariot (Ezek 1:15–21) receive extended description. The creatures are not as important in Revelation, at least in terms of the length of the description, and there are no wheels.[33] Each creature in Ezekiel has four faces, that of a human, lion, ox, and eagle; in Revelation, each creature looks like only one of these four. The creatures in Ezekiel have four wings but in Revelation, as in Isa 6:2, they have six, and they sing the praises of God as do the seraphim in Isaiah 6.[34] There are a few wealth motifs in Ezekiel's vision: beryl on the wheels of the chariot (Ezek 1:16); crystal in the firmament above the creatures, holding back the waters of heaven (1:22); and the appearance of sapphire or lapis lazuli on the throne itself (1:26).[35] Above what appears to be the loins of

---

farb, *Ascent to Heaven*, makes a convincing case that "the apocalypses are literary documents in which the depiction of the hero's experience needs to be understood as an act of imagination, with its specifics determined by the author's manipulation of conventions, rather than as a literary representation of the author's own experiences" (98). On the Jewish mystical tradition based on Ezekiel's vision of the throne-chariot, see Gershom G. Scholem, *Jewish Gnosticism, Merkabah Mysticism, and Talmudic Tradition*, 2nd. ed. (New York: Jewish Theological Seminary, 1965); David Halperin, *The Faces of the Chariot: Early Jewish Responses to Ezekiel's Vision* (Tübingen: J. C. B. Mohr [Paul Siebeck], 1988); and C. R. A. Morray-Jones, "Paradise Revisited (2 Cor 12:1–12): The Jewish Mystical Background of Paul's Apostolate," *HTR* 86 (1993): 177–217 and 265–92.

[32]As Himmelfarb notes, *Ascent to Heaven*, 9, the significant shift of the throne vision in Jewish literature from earth to heaven begins with the ascent of Enoch in *1 Enoch* 14.

[33]Whereas the rims of the wheels in Ezek 1:18 are full of eyes, in Rev 4:6 it is the creatures who are "full of eyes in front and behind"; see Charles, 1:123–24; Beasley-Murray, 116–17.

[34]See Fekkes, *Isaiah and Prophetic Traditions*, 141–49. Fekkes sees a transition from the use of Ezekiel to Isaiah in Rev 4:8 that corresponds to a shift from the physical description of the living creatures to a description of their function.

[35]The word for beryl (שׁישׁרת, θάρσις) could also mean chrysolite; it appears only in Exod 28:20; 39:13; Ezek 1:16; 10:9; Cant 5:14; and Dan 10:6 and

God, Ezekiel sees "something like" the gleaming of *hašmal* (Heb. חַשְׁמַל,
Gr. ἤλεκτρον, Ezek 1:27; see 1:4), perhaps a type of gold or gem.[36]
These touches of wealth in Ezekiel's vision do not rival the gold, jasper,
emeralds, and other jewels John sees in his first vision of heaven in Rev
4:2–11; subsequent visions keep the opulence of heaven in the foreground
for John's audience (see Rev 5:8, 12; 8:3; 14:14; 15:6–7).

A major change from Ezekiel to Revelation is the change of the order
of description. Ezekiel describes the action as it happens: he first sees the
stormy wind from the north, then the four living creatures in the midst of
the storm, and then finally the dome of heaven and the throne of God.
John's attention, in contrast, is fixed first on the center of the scene, the
throne and God seated on the throne; he then begins to describe its
appearance and everything around the throne.[37] What is last in Ezekiel is
first in Revelation. Both the first and the last positions in a narrative are
dramatic, but the effect of John's reversal increases the prominence of
wealth motifs. Because John describes the throne first, the jewels that
surround the throne and signify the glory of God also have an emphatic
position in the vision. And whereas Ezekiel and John both see jewels
around the throne of God, Ezekiel's vision is obscured, as it were, by the
fire and "splendor" (Ezek 1:27) that surround the image. John sees
lightning coming from the throne of God and hears peals of thunder;
seven torches burn before the throne (Rev 1:5); but he has a clearer view
of the jewels that shine on God's throne.

---

cannot be precisely defined. See Zimmerli, *Ezekiel 1*, 129, and Greenberg,
Ezekiel, 47. On "crystal," see BDB, 901, s.v. II. קֶרַח (2). This can mean frost or
ice but is generally translated here as crystal, following the LXX. The LXX lacks
a word for הַנּוֹרָא, "awesome," and it is omitted by most translators. Rev 4:6
follows the LXX with κρυστάλλος; cf. *1 Enoch* 14:18. The word for firmament
or dome, רָקִיעַ, is the same used in Gen 1:6–8.

[36]The meaning of this word is unclear. The Greek word used in the LXX,
ἤλεκτρον, could mean amber, the resin, or an alloy of gold and silver ("pale
gold"). On ἤλεκτρον or amber, see Pliny *HN* 33.1, 80–81 [1, 23]. The word
may also refer to a blue stone, a gold stone, brass, or inlay work; see BDB, 365,
s.v. חַשְׁמַל; LSJ, 768, s.v. ἤλεκτρον.

[37]While there is no description of God's clothing, as there is in Isa 6:1, "one
seated upon the throne" in Rev 4:2 is more anthropomorphic than "something
that seemed like a human form" (Ezek 1:27).

Interpretations of Ezekiel 1

John's vision and the audience's expectations could have been influenced by other visions of the throne of God that reinterpret Ezekiel 1, such as we find in Daniel and *1 Enoch*. I have already discussed Dan 7:9–12, with which John was clearly familiar, in the context of my analysis of Rev 1:12–16. I noted there that Daniel's vision of the Ancient of Days and the Human One does not include any wealth imagery. The plural "thrones" in Dan 7:9 may have influenced Rev 4:4, where the elders are seated upon 24 thrones.[38] These elders in Revelation are wearing white garments, as is the Ancient of Days in Daniel. Daniel describes an immense divine council; thousands and thousands attend and serve the Ancient of Days (Dan 7:10b; cf. 1 Kings 22:19–23; Isa 6:1–13). In Revelation, John sees and hears this innumerably large group in the second part of the throne room narrative, after the Lamb takes the scroll (Rev 5:11).

The other early interpretation of Ezek 1:4–28 that may have influenced John or his audience is *1 Enoch* 14:8–25.[39] This is the first vision in the Jewish tradition in which the seer ascends to heaven. The heaven that Enoch reports on bears a definite resemblance to a temple, perhaps the Jerusalem Temple.[40] The vision of the heavenly throne room in *1 Enoch* 14:8–25 includes some wealth imagery, but it appears in a

---

[38]Aram. כרסון (= Heb. כסאות), θρόνοι. See Collins, *Daniel*, 310; *1 Enoch* 90:20; Ps 122:5; 11QShirShabb 2.1.9; Matt 19:28; Rev 20:4; Col 1:16.

[39]Milik, *Enoch*, 199, notes the influence of *1 Enoch* 14:18 on Rev 4:6 and maintains that John had a Greek copy of Enoch; cf. *1 Enoch* 22:12 and Rev 6:9–10; *1 Enoch* 86:1 and Rev 8:10; 9:1, 11; and *1 Enoch* 91:16 and Rev 21:1. The relation of Daniel 7 and *1 Enoch* 14 is debated, as a number of elements not found in Ezekiel are common to Daniel and Enoch; see Black, *Book of Enoch*, 151–52 and Collins, *Daniel*, 300. On the relation of *1 Enoch* 14 to Ezekiel, see Black, *Book of Enoch*, 147–52, and Himmelfarb, *Ascent to Heaven*, 9–28.

[40]It is central to Himmelfarb's argument that Enoch becomes equal to the angels through the process of priestly investiture, and thus that heaven is conceived of as a temple, but that this temple is based on *literary* reinterpretation of Ezekiel 1 rather than an actual physical temple; see *Ascent to Heaven*, 3–8 and 14–28. Nickelsburg, *Jewish Literature*, 53, sees Enoch as making his way through the heavenly temple to its holy of holies and placing himself in the line of prophets by using the prophetic commissioning here. Charles, *Enoch*, 34, interprets this vision as a palace rather than a temple.

paradoxical manner.[41] The temple of heaven consists of two great chambers surrounded by a protecting wall of fire.[42] In the first part of the vision, Enoch draws near to "a large house built of hailstones; and the walls of the house were like tesselated paving stones, all of snow, and its floor was of snow" (*1 Enoch* 14:10).[43] This is a house of fire and ice, in which Enoch finds no "delights" (τρυφή ζωῆς, *1 Enoch* 14:13).[44] There is no wealth or luxury in this first house. Enoch moves on to a second house, "all constructed of tongues of fire. And in every respect it excelled in glory and honour and grandeur that I am unable to describe to you its glory and grandeur" (*1 Enoch* 14:15–16). This only hints at wealth but gives no specifics; if the Second Temple were in mind here, as Josephus describes it (*J.W.* 5 §§222–23), we would have some notion of the grandeur suggested. The comparison with the first house, moreover, in which there are no earthly delights, is as paradoxical as a house that burns with fire and is cold as ice. Furthermore, Enoch, with Daniel and against Ezekiel on this point, sees no jewels on the throne of God.[45]

---

[41]See the comment by Nickelsburg, *Jewish Literature*, 53, that Enoch's "description of the heavenly temple is shot through with paradox," referring to the fire and ice, hot and cold contradictions.

[42]The Greek and Ethiopic texts differ as to whether the outer structure is a wall (so Ethiopic; see Black, *Book of Enoch* 33, 146) or a house (οἰκοδομή; see Matthew Black, ed., *Apocalypsis Henochi Graece*, PVTG 3 [Leiden: E. J. Brill, 1970] 28). Himmelfarb, *Ascent to Heaven*, 14, prefers the Greek reading in order to match a "three-chambered temple quite nicely."

[43]Compare the translation by Isaac, "a great house which was built of white marble, and inner wall(s) were like mosaics of white marble, the floor of crystal" (*OTP* 1:20). His translation appears to be influenced by the conception of wealth in heaven in Revelation. The words for "great house" (Aram. ביארב; Gk. οἶκος μέγας) do not pose much difficulty. But Isaac has supplied "white marble" and "crystal" for "snow" or "hailstones" (Aram. חלג; Gk. χιόνεος); and "mosaics of white marble" for a phrase better translated "paving stones" or perhaps "flagstones" (Aram. לוחות אבנין; Gk. λιθόπλακες). See Black, *Book of Enoch*, 147; Milik, *Enoch*, 198. Charles, *Enoch*, 33, reads "crystals."

[44]So Black, *Book of Enoch*, 33; cf. the commentary, 147; Milik, *Enoch*, 194; see also Charles, *Enoch*, 33; Sir 14:16; 44:16 and *b.Erub.* 54a.

[45]Collins, *Apocalyptic Imagination*, 34–35, compares the figure of Enoch, who is seventh in line from Adam in Genesis, to the seventh king in the Sumerian King List, Enmeduranki or Enmenduranna. In the description of Enmeduranki's enthronement, he is set upon "a large throne of gold." While Collins maintains that "Evidently the biblical seventh man emulates the

And where Ezekiel and John see crystal above or spreading out from the throne, Enoch sees "crystals of ice" (*1 Enoch* 14:18).[46] The rest of this vision of God on the heavenly throne has no wealth imagery and no further mention of glory or grandeur (*1 Enoch* 14:19–25).

A second vision of the throne of God in *1 Enoch* 18:6–8, which does not fall within the throne-chariot tradition of Ezekiel 1, deserves attention because it presents heavenly wealth in such a positive manner that it suggests some influence on John's vision of the heavenly throne room. After his vision of God in *1 Enoch* 14, Enoch is taken on an extraterrestrial journey to see the origins of the winds, stars, and thunder. In the course of this journey, Enoch sees seven mountains of precious stones (18:6–8). The seven mountains are arranged in three groups. The three mountains that lie toward the east are made of "stones of varied hues," pearl, and antimony. The three in the south are carnelians. The mountain in the middle reaches up into the heavens, "like the throne of God," and is made of emeralds and sapphires.[47] This is the most explicitly opulent vision in the Book of the Watchers.[48] Carol Newsom has suggested that the scene depicted in *1 Enoch* 17–19 can be compared to the royal practice of displaying the wealth, and thus also the strength, of the king and the kingdom (see 2 Kings 20:13).[49] This description of God's throne

---

Mesopotamian seventh king," in this way at least Enmeduranki is more of a contrast than a parallel.

[46]So Black, 33; cf. 149n. He is apparently influenced by the NEB translation of Ezek 1:22. The Greek reads ὡσεὶ κρυστάλλινον. Cf. Isaac, *OTP* 1:21, "its appearance was like crystal."

[47]The meaning of several of the words for these gems is uncertain; see Black, *Book of Enoch*, 158–59.

[48]On a subsequent journey, Enoch travels to the west beyond seven mountains of fire to view "seven magnificent mountains, each differing from the other, whose stones were priceless for their beauty " (*1 Enoch* 24:2). The vision then shifts from mountains of precious stones to a fragrant tree, which bears food to be eaten by the elect as a reward after the day of judgment (*1 Enoch* 24:4–25:6). Enoch also journeys to the east (chaps. 28–32), finding increasing agricultural delights, including seven fragrant mountains of nard, cinnamon, and pepper, until he comes to Eden itself and views the tree of righteousness there (*1 Enoch* 32:5–6).

[49]See Carol A. Newsom, "The Development of *1 Enoch* 6-19: Cosmology and Judgment," *CBQ* 42 (1980): 324. See Exodus 25–31 and 1 Kings 6–10 *passim* for displays of gold and wealth in the Hebrew cult and kingdom. On the relationship of apocalyptic eschatology to royal ideology by way of wisdom tra-

is closer to Rev 4:3 than the other passages we have seen, including Ezek 1:26–28. John sees jasper, carnelian, and emerald; Ezekiel mentions only bronze and sapphire. Enoch sees seven mountains of gems.

In Enoch's vision, the images of wealth adorning the throne of God are clearly positive.[50] But these positive associations in the Book of the Watchers are negated in the rest of *1 Enoch*. *1 Enoch* is a composite text in which the Book of the Watchers (*1 Enoch* 1–36) has been edited with a number of other texts, several of which follow the Book of the Watchers chronologically as well as narratively. The visions in the Book of the Watchers are repeated, reinterpreted, and reshaped in the later layers of the complete text.[51] We have already seen that the function of

---

ditions, see Jonathan Z. Smith, "Wisdom and Apocalyptic," in *Visionaries and their Apocalypses*, ed. Paul D. Hanson, IRT 4 (Philadelphia: Fortress; London: SPCK, 1983) 101–20.

[50]The 'Aśa'el material in *1 Enoch* 6–11, however, connects the corruption of humanity and therefore the punishment of the Watchers to the improper knowledge taught by 'Aśa'el, which includes the art of making jewelry with gold, silver, and precious stones. See George W. E. Nickelsburg, "Apocalyptic and Myth in 1 Enoch 6–11," *JBL* 96 (1977): 383–405.

[51]*First Enoch* consists of five sections: the Book of the Watchers, chaps. 1–36; the Similitudes or Parables of Enoch, chaps. 37–71, which we have already discussed in reference to the Human One (see above, n. 15); the Astronomical Book or Book of the Heavenly Luminaries, chaps. 72–82; the Dream Visions or Book of Dreams, chaps. 83–91; and the Epistle or Testament of Enoch, chaps. 92–106. The chronological order of composition of these sections differs from their literary order in *1 Enoch*. Four of the five sections, all but the Similitudes, were found at Qumran. Milik dated 4QEnastr[a] to the end of the third or begin-ning of the second century BCE (*Enoch*, 139–40) and 4QEn[a] to between 200 and 150 BCE (*Enoch*, 273). Neither of these manuscripts are autographs; therefore the composition of the Astronomical Book and Book of the Watchers can be dated to the third century BCE (see Michael E. Stone, "The Book of Enoch and Judaism in the Third Century, B.C.E.," *CBQ* 40 [1978]: 479–92). The Book of Dreams, which contains the so-called Animal Apocalypse (*1 Enoch* 85–91) and the Epistle, which includes the Apocalypse of Weeks (*1 Enoch* 93:1–10 + 91:11–17) can be dated roughly to the time of the Maccabean Revolt on internal and ex-ternal grounds. Milik's theory of a third-century CE date for the Similitudes has been soundly rejected, but the actual date is still debated (see n. 15). I operate with the assumption that the Similitudes circulated in the first century of this era, although precision on this date and even the question of whether the Similitudes are pre- or post-Christian are not crucial for my purposes here. On the redaction

the Human or Chosen One, identified in *1 Enoch* 71:14 with Enoch
himself, includes the judgment and punishment of the wealthy and
powerful. This strong polemic against the rich, the powerful and their
wealth does not include a corresponding promise of a luxurious reward
for the righteous, such as we find in Revelation 21. The reward for God's
righteous and elect ones in the Similitudes is physical—food, rest,
clothes—but hardly luxurious (*1 Enoch* 62:14–16). In a striking reinterpretation of Enoch's visions of seven mountains of jewels in the Book of
the Watchers, the Similitudes contain a vision in which the mountains of
wealth melt away. Enoch travels to the "same place" in the west and sees
six mountains of iron, copper, silver, gold, colored metal, and lead (*1
Enoch* 52:1–2). Enoch asks the angel for the meaning of this secret vision
and is told that these exist so that the Messiah might receive praise upon
the earth (52:4). The angel then explains that:

> And these mountains which your eyes have seen, the mountains of iron,
> the mountain of copper, and the mountain of silver, and the mountain
> of gold, and the mountain of soft metal, and the mountain of lead, all
> these shall be, in the presence of the Elect One, as wax before the fire,
> and like water which streams down from above. These mountains shall
> become powerless under his feet. And it shall come to pass in those
> days that they shall not be saved. Either by gold or silver, and none be
> able to escape. (*1 Enoch* 52: 6–7)

This passage provides divine confirmation that wealth will not help rich
and powerful rulers and landowners at the day of judgment. It also
reinterprets the mountains of jewels that Enoch is depicted as seeing in
1 Enoch 18, challenging the ideology in the Book of the Watchers by
reversing the association of God and wealth.

The Epistle, the final section of *1 Enoch* (*1 Enoch* 92–105), includes
a significant number of woes condemning those who have amassed
wealth and fine things, often at the expense of the poor.[52] Nickelsburg
identifies a consistent pattern in the Epistle of Enoch in which riches and
possessions are always bad, usually ill-gotten, and cause for swift judg-

---

of *1 Enoch*, see Devorah Dimant "The Biography of Enoch and the Books of
Enoch," *VT* 33 (1983): 14–29; Nickelsburg, *Jewish Literature*, 150–51.

[52]See *1 Enoch* 94:6–11; 96:4–8; 97:8–10; 98:1–3; 99:12–13; 100:6, 10–13;
103:5–104:13.

ment by God and eternal punishment.[53] The extended woe in *1 Enoch* 97:8–10 epitomizes this pattern:[54]

> Woe to you who acquire gold and silver (but) not by righteousness, and say: "We have become exceedingly rich and acquired possessions; And we have obtained everything we have wished. And now let us do whatever we desire, For we have gathered silver, and filled our storehouses, And many are the goods in our houses." But like water they will be poured out; You are deceived, for your riches shall not abide for you, But they will quickly *be taken away from you*; For you have acquired it all unjustly, And you will be delivered up to a great curse.

The portrayal of wealth and associated power in *1 Enoch* may be effectively compared to the function of wealth in Revelation. The positive use of wealth imagery to describe the throne of God in *1 Enoch* 14 and 18 parallels the description of the heavenly throne room in Revelation 4; the Book of the Watchers has no gold, as does Revelation, but Enoch sees more jewels adorning the mountains in the west than John sees on the throne of God. But the Human One in Revelation wears gold while the Human One in the Similitudes destroys wealth. And, while the woes against the rich in the Epistle of Enoch have early Christian parallels in Luke 12:16–20 and James 5:1–6, there is no such universal condemnation of wealth in Revelation. Mountains of gold melt away under the Elect One's feet in the Similitudes of Enoch. In contrast, in Revelation the bride of Christ is adorned with gold and jewels.

There are, of course, other visions of the heavenly throne room to compare to Revelation, but these do not add significantly to our understanding of the development of the use of wealth imagery from Ezekiel to Revelation.[55] John greatly expands the wealth motifs found in Ezekiel,

---

[53]See George W. E. Nickelsburg, "Riches, the Rich, and God's Judgment in 1 Enoch 92–105 and the Gospel according to Luke," *NTS* 25 (1979): 332.

[54]The parallels between *1 Enoch* 97:8–10 and Luke 12:16–20 have been discussed in detail by Sverre Aalen, "St Luke's Gospel and the Last Chapters of 1 Enoch," *NTS* 13 (1966): 1–13; and Nickelsburg, "Riches, the Rich, and God's Judgment."

[55]See *As. Mos.* 4:2; *T. Levi* 5:1–4; 4Q491 fr. 11 (called by Vermes, *Dead Sea Scrolls in English*, "The Song of Michael and the Just"; but see John Collins, *Apocalypticism and the Dead Sea Scrolls* [London: Routledge, 1997] 143–47, who argues that the fragment represents the boast of an exalted human); and 4QShirSabb. 4Q491 breaks off "No pure gold or gold of Ophir . . . ," a

multiplying the number of jewels and adding gold to his description of the throne room. While throne visions in *1 Enoch* describe God or attendants dressed in white, no other vision includes the attendants of God wearing golden crowns.[56] Indeed, no other text envisions the amount of gold in the subsequent throne room passages in Revelation (Rev 5:9; 8:3; 14:14; 15:6). Wealth imagery in *1 Enoch* 18:6–8 is the closest parallel to Revelation in terms of both extent of jewels and other motifs and the positive association of wealth and divinity. But the reinterpretation of the visions of the Book of the Watchers in the Similitudes and Epistle of Enoch challenges this ideology and reverses the positive association of God and wealth. The positive association of wealth and God in Revelation, in contrast, is one of the strongest facets of the text. God, in the Apocalypse, dwells in a wealthier heaven than any Old Testament text describes. John has concentrated wealth motifs from the Old Testament tradition in his visions of the heavenly throne room. We saw the same process in John's use of Zech 4:1–4 and Dan 10:2–9 in his depiction of the Human One in Rev 1:12–16. John concentrates wealth motifs in such a manner that any hearer/reader, knowledgeable about the Old Testament or not, would have felt the impact. This concentration of wealth motifs in the opening visions anticipates the glorious city of Jerusalem that descends from heaven as the bride of Christ in Revelation 21–22. But the new city does not descend from heaven until the evil city of Babylon has been destroyed.

---

tantalizing hint of the rejection of wealth. The throne visions in 4Q405 20 ii 21–22 and 4Q405 23 ii contain some wealth motifs, analogous to the Book of the Watchers; see esp. 4Q405 23 ii, 8–9: "In the midst of the glorious appearance of scarlet [שׁני], the colors of most holy spiritual light, they stand firm in their holy station before the [K]ing, spirits in garments of [*purest*] color in the midst of the appearance of whiteness. And this glorious spiritual substance is like fine gold work [כמעשׂי אפירים]." "Fine gold work" here literally reads "the work of Ophir," the land from which fine gold was obtained (Dan 10:5, "Uphaz," as we noted above; see also 1 Kings 9:28, Isa 13:12, Ps 45:10, Job 28:16, 1 Chr 29:4). See Carol A. Newsom, *Songs of the Sabbath Sacrifice: A Critical Edition*, HSS (Atlanta: Scholar's Press, 1985) 332–38. This passage is a fairly close parallel to Rev 4:4, but the golden crowns mentioned in inscriptions contemporary to Revelation, as discussed in chap. 3, provide a closer and more convincing parallel. The parallel may be more illuminating for Rev 1:12–16.

[56]See Ps 20:4; Wis Sol 5:16.

Babylon the Great

There are many characters cast as enemies in Revelation with names drawn from the Hebrew Bible—Jezebel and Balaam, the Beast from the Sea, the Dragon. In Rev 14:8, the audience first hears of another enemy borrowed from the scriptures and history of Israel, "Babylon the Great," when an angel announces its fall. Revelation 17–18 describes the judgment of Babylon, who appears as both a harlot and a city, in detail. When sorting out the expectations aroused by John's choice of names, we are again faced with the effects of a complicated literary tradition. Not only the name "Babylon" but also the imagery used to describe Babylon comes from the Hebrew Bible. Indeed, Revelation 18 hardly contains two consecutive words that have not been joined in similar phrasing or context by one of the Hebrew prophets. When we look more closely at the major biblical passages used in Revelation 17–18, however, we see that John's Babylon is considerably different from the city excoriated by the Hebrew prophets. This is because John draws extensively on prophetic oracles against Tyre, a city destroyed by Babylon, as well as those against Babylon itself and applies them to his construction of Babylon. Furthermore, John clearly intends Babylon to refer to Rome (Rev 17:9, 18).[57] His vision of the city's destruction thus taps into a tradition of Jewish opposition to Rome, expressed in texts such as the *Sibylline Oracles*. We are thus faced with a variety of traditions in Revelation 17–18 and a variety of expectations for descriptions of Babylon as well as attacks on Rome. To gauge the expectations of the audience, we will again look at the prophetic texts used in Revelation 17–18 and then look at contemporary texts that engage in ideological opposition to Rome.

Babylon in the Hebrew Bible

The importance of Babylon in the Hebrew Bible can hardly be overstated; Walter Brueggemann has described how "Babylon goads and challenges Israel's theological imagination . . . . in the postexilic period, it is Babylon and not Persia that continues to function as a powerful theological

---

[57]Yarbro Collins, "Political Perspective," has called the identification of Babylon in Revelation as Rome one of the victories of historical-critical scholarship. For a list of commentators who concur with this position, see idem., "Revelation 18," 185.

metaphor for Israel."[58] The major prophetic oracles against Babylon in the Hebrew Bible are in the books of Isaiah and Jeremiah.[59] John's use of these oracles is quite selective. The Hebrew prophets emphasized Babylon's military power, pride and its role in God's plan. Babylon is *the* enemy of Israel, an adversary worthy of Yahweh, and a symbol of all the nations in opposition to God's plan for history.[60] But the wealth of Babylon, so prominent in Revelation, hardly appears at all in the Hebrew Bible.

Oracles against Babylon in Isaiah make little or no mention of the city's wealth. The graphic description of the destroyed city in Isa 13:21–22 is reworked as part of Rev 18:2.[61] This first Isaian oracle against Babylon clearly presupposes that Babylon has wealth, for it is a world power, but the wealth of the city is not a major theme of the passage.[62] The second oracle against Babylon in Isaiah, the taunt-song in

---

[58]Walter Brueggemann, "At the Mercy of Babylon: A Subversive Rereading of the Empire," *JBL* 110 (1991): 3. See also R. Martin-Achard, "Esaïe 47 et la tradition prophétique sur Babylone," *Prophecy: Essays Presented to Georg Fohrer on his Sixty-Fifth Birthday*, BZAW 150, ed. J. A. Emerton (Berlin: de Gruyter, 1980) 83–105.

[59]Fekkes, *Isaiah and Prophetic Traditions*, 90, claims that there are five Babylon oracles in the Old Testament (Isa 13–14; 21:1–10; 47:1–15; Jer 25:12–38; and Jer 50–51) and that John draws on every one. His presentation of this evidence is designed to support his thesis that John's use of the Old Testament is indicative of conscious authorial strategies. Fekkes has shaped his evidence here to make this point; for instance, Isa 13:1–22 and 14:3–21 are separate oracles and Rev 17–18 does not use any passage from Isaiah 14. More importantly, as Brueggemann has shown, the notion of Babylon in the Old Testament can in no way be confined to these five passages listed by Fekkes. Brueggemann chooses Jer 42:9–17; 50:41–43; Isa 47:5–7; 1 Kgs 8:46–53; 2 Chr 36:15–21; and Dan 4:19–27.

[60]Brueggemann, "At the Mercy of Babylon," 3; Martin-Achard, "Esaïe 47," 104.

[61]The comment by Fekkes, *Isaiah and Prophetic Traditions*, 215, that the issue of the use of Isa 13:21 or 34:11, 13b–14 in Rev 18:2 "is complicated by [John's] paraphrasing style and the existence of parallel traditions," highlights the major methodological problem of analyzing Revelation in terms of the Old Testament. The magnitude of the intertextuality effectively eliminates the prophets as authoritative texts within the narrative world of Revelation.

[62]Note the use of gold for the figure in Isa 13:12 and the reference to "the gold of Ophir." The destruction of Babylon is described in 13:6–19 with the traditional imagery of the "day of the Lord" (יום יהוה, ἡ ἡμέρα κυρίου,

Isa 14:4–21, focuses on pride and oppression, rather than wealth, although it alludes to the fallen glory of Babylon (14:11, 13). This oracle is not used in Revelation 17–18.[63] The strange oracle announcing the fall of Babylon in Isa 21:1–10 conveys a strong sense of horror and doom at an event that should be a cause for rejoicing, as it was in Isa 14:4–21.[64] Isa 21:9, "Fallen, fallen is Babylon," provides part of the text for the angel who cries aloud in Rev 14:8 and 18:2. The contrast between the two cities of Isaiah 21 and Revelation 18 is quite prominent, for Isa 21:1–10 does not condemn Babylon in any way at all, nor does it mention wealth. The portrayal of the city and its punishment in Isa 47:1–15 provides an important backdrop for Babylon in Revelation. Isaiah 47 is the only Old Testament passage used in Revelation where Babylon, rather than Jerusalem or Tyre, is personified as a harlot.[65] In the Isaian passage, Babylon the "virgin daughter" becomes a stripped slave and cast-off mistress. The courtesan-city was "tender and delicate" and "a lover of pleasures" (Isa 47:1, 8), delighting in both sexual pleasure and luxury.[66] The subtlety of the wealth imagery in the Isaian passage only highlights the hyperbolic quality of the depiction of wealth in Revelation.

Isa 13:6). See Otto Kaiser, *Isaiah 13–39: A Commentary*, OTL (Philadelphia: Westminster, 1974) 15–16; Clements, *Isaiah 1–39*, 134; Martin-Achard, "Esaïe 47," 98–99; Amos 5:18–20; Isa 2:11–22.

[63]Although Fekkes, *Isaiah and Prophetic Traditions*, 186–89, calls the association between Rev 12:7–9 and Isa 14:12–15 "tenuous" and "mistaken," the Isaian passage likely influenced Revelation, along with other traditions of the fall of Satan (see also *Life of Adam and Eve [Vita]* 12–16; *1 Enoch* 9–10; 86. See esp. Yarbro Collins, *Combat Myth*, 79–85; also Kraft, 167; Roloff, 143; and the discussion of Luke 10:17–20 in Susan R. Garrett, *The Demise of the Devil: Magic and the Demonic in Luke's Writings* (Minneapolis: Augsburg Fortress, 1989) 50–54 and 135–36nn.54–60.

[64]See esp. Isa 21:3–4. On the tensions and contradictions in this passage, see Kaiser, *Isaiah 13–39*, 121–129, who concludes that the poem was composed after the destruction of Babylon in 539 BCE. Martin-Achard, "Esaïe 47," 97, attributes this poem to a contemporary of Second Isaiah rather than Isaiah.

[65]Fekkes, *Isaiah and Prophetic Traditions*, 211–212, draws attention to the use of the Tyre oracle from Isa 23:17 in Rev 17:2 as the source of the Harlot-Babylon image.

[66]"Tender and delicate," (רכה ועננה, ἁπαλὴ καὶ τρυφερά, Isa 47:1); "a lover of pleasures," (עדינה, τρυφερά, Isa 47:8); see Westermann, *Isaiah 40–66*, 190: "the terms conjure up the idea of luxury, the refinements of the court, the elegant life of carefree enjoyment."

Revelation 18 also draws on the loose collection of oracles against Babylon in Jeremiah 50–51 [27–28].[67] Rev 18:4–8 and 18:20–24, the two passages which frame the laments of the kings, merchants, and seafarers, are constituted substantially of echoes and allusions to Jeremiah.[68] As in Isaiah, so here in Jeremiah Babylon is personified as a woman, the mother of her people (Jer 50:12–14, cf. 50:43), but there is no suggestion in Jeremiah that Babylon is a harlot. The themes of luxury and opulence are absent from this long passage in Jeremiah. These two chapters consist primarily of military and agricultural images and metaphors rather than the language of wealth and luxury (e.g., Jer 50:8–11; 51:27–40). The great city, in Jeremiah, is wealthy only in the sense that all great powers have some amount of wealth. Of the three occurrences of wealth imagery in these two chapters (Jer 50:37; 51:7, and 51:13), John uses the most ostentatious image, the golden cup in Jer 51:7 (Rev 17:4).[69] The oracle of the sword in Jer 50:35–38 places Babylon's wealth in considerably different perspective than we find in Revelation 18. This oracle describes the order of destruction of Babylon: officials and sages, diviners, warriors, horses, chariots, foreign troops, then treasures (אוצרת, θησαυροί, 50:37 [27:37]), and finally a drought upon her waters.[70] Walls and fortifications, not gold or jewels, are the objects of destruction in Jeremiah 50–51.

---

[67]See also Fekkes, *Isaiah and Prophetic Traditions*, 90.

[68]The "golden cup [כוס־זהב, ποτήριον χρυσοῦν] in the Lord's hands" of Jer 51:7 [28:7] appears in Revelation as a golden cup (ποτήριον χρυσοῦν) in the hand of the harlot Babylon (Rev 17:4); see also Rev 14:8; 18:3. In Rev 18:6, the second heavenly voice uses the words of Jer 50:29 when calling for the city to receive a double portion of her own works. The cry of the second angel for the people to come out of Babylon in Rev 18:4 echoes Jer 51:45. See Charles 2:97; Jer 51:45 does not appear in the LXX of Jeremiah 27 and so this phrase in Revelation appears to be a direct translation from the Hebrew. The call to rejoice in Rev 18:20 and the figure of a stone thrown into the water as a symbol of the destruction of the city are adapted from Jer 51:48 and 51:63.

[69]Rev 17:1 may allude to Jer 51:13, but the allusion does not include "rich in many treasures" (רבת אוצרת, ἐπὶ πλήθει θησαυρῶν). See the discussion of Rev 17:1–6 in chap. 6.

[70]See Holladay, *Jeremiah* 2:420; the drought refers to irrigation canals or defensive lakes.

Tyre, Merchant of the Peoples

Military power, oppression, and pride are the prominent attributes of Babylon in the Hebrew Bible. Wealth and luxury, so conspicuous in Revelation, are minor characteristics. John uses oracles against Tyre, a city renowned for its wealth, to add connotations of luxury and especially commercial power to his reconstruction of Babylon. Tyre's status as a trading center is particularly important for the portrait of Babylon/Rome in Revelation. The words of the angel in Rev 18:3 and the bulk of Rev 18:9–19 are shaped from Ezekiel 26–27;[71] there are also allusions to the oracle against Tyre in Isa 23:1–18 in Revelation (Isa 23:17 in Rev 17:2; Isa 23:8 in Rev 18:3, 23).[72] John combines these oracles against Tyre from the Hebrew Bible with the Babylon oracles to produce a unique and remarkable composition in Revelation 17–18. The boldness of John's intertextual reinscription of Babylon in Revelation can be seen foremost in the irony that Tyre, like Jerusalem, is the object of Babylon's destruction. The beginning of the very passage in Ezekiel from which John borrows his merchants of Babylon describes how King Nebuchadrezzar brings his siege weapons and chariots against Tyre (Ezek 26:8–12). Ironically, then, John uses the lament over one of Babylon's victims to describe the destruction of *his* Babylon in Revelation.

Another significant difference between Babylon and Tyre in the Bible, in addition to being attacker and attacked, is the wealth of the two cities. The proverbial wealth of Tyre comes not from military conquest,

---

[71]The oracle against Tyre includes a third part, Ezek 28:1–10, but there are no references to this passage in Revelation 18; cf. however, Rev 17:4 and 21:19. Ruiz, *Ezekiel in the Apocalypse*, is a major study of Ezekiel and Rev 16:17–19:10. Ruiz discusses the "real transformation of prophetic language" in the Revelation passage, which combines Ezekiel 16, 23, 26–28; Daniel 7, and other texts (229). His conclusions (517–39) emphasize the unity of Rev 16:17–19:10; the importance of a consistent rereading of Ezekiel 16, 23, and 21:1–28:19 in that unity; and prophetic activity as a literary activity that invites the reader/hearer to join in the hermeneutical process of rereading and reactualization of the Jewish scriptures in a Christian setting. Like Fekkes, *Isaiah and Prophetic Traditions*, Ruiz does not consider the ideological dimension of John's subversive intertextual rewriting of the prophets to construct his own authoritative book of prophecy.

[72]This allusion is important evidence for Fekkes, *Isaiah and Prophetic Traditions*, 91, 211–212, in demonstrating the intentionality of John's authorial strategies in his use of Old Testament passages.

as did Babylon's, but from trade. Tyre is first and foremost a *commercial power*. The theme is central in the two main Tyre oracles in the Hebrew Bible, Isa 23:1–18 and Ezekiel 26–28. There is a very high concentration of the words for trade, merchant, and merchandise in these three chapters in Ezekiel.[73] Tyre's riches, merchandise, and fine houses are included in the catalogue of destruction by the Babylonian army (Ezek 26:12); this destruction causes the "princes of the sea," Tyre's allies and trading partners, to strip off their "embroidered garments" and raise a lament (קינה, *qînāh*) over the city (Ezek 26:16–18). Ezekiel 27 portrays Tyre, "merchant of the peoples on many coastlands" (Ezek 27:1), as a beautiful sailing vessel. The forerunner of the Babylonian merchants' cargo list in Rev 18:11–13 can be found in Ezek 27:12b–25a, which lists the nations that traded with Tyre, including Israel and Judah, and the merchandise that they exchanged (see also Isa 23:2–3, 8). Each trading partner has a specialty item that they exchanged in Tyre for her "goods," "merchandise," and "abundant wares."[74] But, unlike every other nation listed here, no specific items for Tyre's merchandise are given in this catalogue. It is rather the *activity* of trade that is Tyre's source of wealth.[75]

[73]Merchant or tradesperson, רֹכֵל, Ezek 27:3, 13, 15, 17, 20, 22, 22, 23, 23, 24; also in Ezek 17:4; Num 3:16; Neh 3:31, 32; 13:20; 27:3, 20, 23; merchant or wholesaler, סֹחֵר, Ezek 27:12, 15, 16, 18, 21, 21, 26; Isa 23:2, 8; also in Ezek 38:13; Gen 23:16; 37:28; Isa 47:15 [Babylon and the sorcerers]; 1 Kgs 10:28 = 1 Chr 1:16; trade or merchandise, רְכֻלָּה, Ezek 26:12; 28:5, 16, 18; plus מַרְכֹּלֶת, Ezek 27:24; סַחַר, Isa 23:3, 3, 8; also Isa 45:14; Prov 3:14, 14, 14; 31:18; סְחֹרָה, Ezek 27:15; and מַעֲרָב, Ezek 27:13, 17, 19, 25, 27, 34.

[74]The list includes silver, iron, tin, and lead from Tarshish; slaves and bronze from Javan, Tubal, and Meshech; horses and mules from Beth-togarmah; ivory and ebony from the Rhodians (Dedanites); turquoise, purple, embroidery, fine linen, coral, and rubies from Edom; grain, honey, oil, and balm from Israel and Judah; wine and wool from Damascus; iron, cassia, and sweet cane from Uzal; saddle cloths from Dedan; flocks and herds from Arabia; spices, precious stones, and gold from Sheba and Raamah; and garments, carpet, and cloth from Mesopotamia.

[75]Zimmerli, *Ezekiel 2*, 71: "To the beauty of the stately ship [a later redactor added] the fully elaborated reference to the commercial wealth and the profusion of the worldwide relationships of the city." See also Ezek 27:32–33; 28:2–6, 12–15.

Summary: Babylon and Tyre

The two cities that inspire the portrait of Babylon in Revelation carry quite different associations in the Hebrew Bible. Babylon is the great military power, the enemy of Yahweh and Israel, and the destroyer of Jerusalem. Long after its political power had disappeared, the name Babylon continued to function in Jewish literature as a metaphor for military might and as a symbol of God's control of the nations. The wealth of Babylon does appear in a few biblical texts, but rarely as commercial wealth.[76] Tyre, in contrast, a city which was destroyed by Babylon, had enormous wealth. Tyre's power came not from military might but commercial networks, trade, and ships. By drawing on these specific oracles against Babylon and Tyre in Isaiah, Jeremiah, and Ezekiel, John creates a new Babylon that combines aspects of both cities.

Jewish Opposition to Rome: The Sibylline Oracles

The attack on Babylon in Revelation is really an attack on the Roman Empire at the end of the first century CE, hence my frequent use of the term "Babylon/Rome" to keep the historical context in mind while analyzing literary imagery. Other texts used the code name "Babylon" when addressing Rome, although no other enemy of Rome weaves the prophetic texts together as John does to produce such a powerful and extended polemic against the city.[77] Aside from Revelation, early Christian

---

[76]Ezekiel calls Babylon a city of merchants and trade (Ezek 16:29, 17:4), but Ezekiel's description of Babylon agrees in large part with Isaiah's and Jeremiah's. Babylon is "the most terrible of the nations" (Ezek 28:7) and the agent of Tyre's destruction (Ezek 26:7–14). Dan 4:30, in which Nebuchadnezzar praises the glories of "Babylon the Great," is probably the source of the title in Rev 14:8, 16:19, and 18:2 (Charles 2:14; Lohmeyer, 124; Prigent, 227; Roloff, 175; Fekkes, *Isaiah and Prophetic Traditions*, 213n.55; Collins, *Daniel*, 230; Harrington, 150).

[77]See 1 Pet 5:13; 4 Ezra 3:2, 28–31; 2 Bar 11:1. The association of the name Babylon with Rome probably derives from the destruction of the Jerusalem Temple by the Roman army in 70 CE, although the Qumran pesharim interpret "Chaldeans" in the Hebrew Bible as "Kittim" (see Gen 10:4). See Harold Fuchs, *Der geistige Widerstand gegen Rom in der antiken Welt*, 2nd ed. (Berlin: de Gruyter, 1938, 1964) 20–22, 60–62, 67–74, 78–79; Fekkes, *Isaiah and Prophetic Traditions*, 89n.60. 1 Peter, 4 Ezra, and 2 Baruch do not associate Babylon/Rome with any wealth motifs. 4 Ezra frames the destruction of the Jerusalem Temple by the Romans in 70 CE in terms of the destruction of the first temple by the

texts do not advocate opposition to the empire. The narrator of 1 Peter calls Rome "Babylon" but he also exhorts Christians in Asia Minor to "accept the authority of every human institution, whether of the emperor as supreme, or of governors, as sent by him to punish those who do wrong and to praise those who do right" (1 Pet 2:13–14). The attitude toward Rome in Revelation hardly fits with early Christian texts such as 1 Peter (see also Rom 13:1–7; 1 Tim 2:1–3; Tit 3:1). We must turn to Jewish texts of the Second Temple period to find similar attacks on Rome. The tradition of theological and political opposition to foreign powers, including Rome, was well established in Jewish literature by the time the Apocalypse was written.[78] One group of texts often cited when studying Revelation 18, the *Sibylline Oracles*, is illustrative of this tradition. The polemic against Rome in books 3, 4, and 5 of the *Sibylline Oracles* and the attack on "Babylon" in Revelation are similar in terms of polemical techniques and shared interpretive conventions.[79] It has even been suggested that John himself may have brought sibylline traditions from Palestine to Asia.[80]

Ill-gained wealth is a prominent part of the attack on Rome in *Sibylline Oracles* 3. This earlier of these three sibylline books does not use the code name "Babylon" but it does contain several passages harshly attacking Rome (under the name "Rome").[81] These oracles depict the

---

Babylonians in 586 BCE; see Michael E. Stone, "Reactions to Destructions of the Second Temple: Theology, Perception and Conversion," *JSJ* 12 (1981): 195–204.

[78]Against foreign domination, see *1 Enoch* 83–91; 1 and 2 Maccabees; against Rome, see *Pss. Sol.* 1:4–2:5; 2:19–21; *Psalms of Solomon* 17, which will be discussed in more detail below; 1QpHab 3:2; 6:1–2 [cf. 6:5–6]; 4QpPsᵃ 2:9–11; 3:8–11.

[79]On the Sibyllina, see John J. Collins, *The Sibylline Oracles of Egyptian Judaism*, SBLDS 13 (Missoula MT: Scholars Press, 1974); and the translation, with introduction and critical notes, idem., *OTP* 1:317–472. The Greek text used is Johannes Geffcken, *Die Oracula Sibyllina*, GCS 8 (Leipzig: J. C. Hinrichs, 1902). Collins sees books 3 and 5 as part of a coherent and developing tradition of political oracles. On similarities and comparison with Revelation, see Collins, *OTP* 1:392; Yarbro Collins, *Crisis and Catharsis*, 46–9, 90–94; Bauckham, *Climax of Prophecy*, 378–83.

[80]See Yarbro Collins, *Crisis and Catharsis*, 49, who notes that sibylline traditions already existed in Phrygia around the time of Augustus.

[81]On matters of introduction, see Collins, *OTP* 1:354–61. The main corpus of book 3 was composed in Egypt between 163 and 145 BCE. Later additions to this main corpus include *Sib. Or.* 3:350–488; and 3:1–96, various parts of which

Romans as sexually immoral, as oppressive and bloodthirsty rulers, and as consumed with the desire for wealth (see *Sib. Or.* 3:175–195). The oracle against Rome in *Sib. Or.* 3:350–380 draws on the personification of Babylon as courtesan-queen and slave from Isaiah 47, as does Revelation 18, in its attack on Roman wealth:

> However much wealth Rome received from tribute-bearing Asia,
> Asia will receive three times that much again
> from Rome and will repay her deadly arrogance to her.
> Whatever number from Asia served the house of Italians,
> twenty times that number of Italians will be serfs
> in Asia, in poverty, and they will be liable to pay ten-thousandfold,
> O luxurious golden offspring of Latium, Rome,
> virgin, often drunken with your weddings with many suitors,
> as a slave you will be wed, without decorum. (*Sib. Or.* 3:350–358)

Scholars have adduced this oracle as a parallel to Revelation 18 and an indication of the resentment felt in Asia over Rome's commercial power.[82] Both *Sib. Or.* 3:350–380 and Revelation 18 criticize Rome's wealth and both allude to Isa 47:1. The parallel, however, has been overstated and requires more serious analysis. The similar characterization of Rome as a woman in Revelation and *Sibylline Oracles* 3 can be explained by their shared dependence on the Hebrew scriptures; there is no need to posit any literary dependence of Revelation on *Sib. Or.* 3:350–380. But there is an even more significant reason to differentiate this oracle from Revelation 18, namely, its political ideology. John does address his prophetic letter to seven churches in Asia, but he in no way adopts a nationalistic ideology on behalf of Asia against Rome. *Sib. Or.* 3:350–380, in contrast, envisions the restoration of Asia's fortunes within the earthly, political sphere. A "mistress" (δέσποινα) will cut Rome's hair, cast the city from heaven to earth, and bring "serene peace" to the Asian land (*Sib. Or.* 3:359–368). Although this oracle trumpets Asia's cause, it was probably composed in Egypt, as were the rest of *Sibylline Oracles* 3. The "mistress" is most likely Cleopatra, whose ambition was

---

were added between the battle of Actium in 31 BCE and the destruction of the Jerusalem Temple in 70 CE. The passages that mention Babylon or Assyria, 3:160 and 3:265–94, were composed well before the destruction of the Jerusalem Temple by the Romans and refer to the destruction and restoration during the sixth century BCE.

[82] So Yarbro Collins and Bauckham.

to rule the entire Roman Empire.[83] *Sibylline Oracles* 3 exhibits general
enthusiasm for the Ptolemaic house,[84] a political ideology that deepens the
distinction between the oracles and Revelation. While the moral and
social portrait of Rome in book 3 is similar to the depiction of Babylon
in Revelation, the ideology of the two texts is qualitatively different.

The political ideology that distinguishes the attack on Rome in
Sibylline Oracles 3 from Revelation can be found in the other sibylline
books. *Sibylline Oracles* 4 consists of a core Hellenistic political oracle
written close to the time of Alexander the Great and Jewish additions
from around 80 CE (*Sib. Or.* 4:102–51), after the destruction of the
Temple in Jerusalem and the eruption of Vesuvius (see *Sib. Or.* 4:116,
130–35). These additions are most important for comparison to Revelation.[85] Roman wealth appears only once in this book:

> Great wealth [πλοῦτος μέγας] will come to Asia,
>   which Rome itself
> once plundered and deposited in her house of many possessions.
> She will then pay back twice as much and more
> to Asia, and then there will be a surfeit of war. (*Sib. Or.* 4:145–48)

Yarbro Collins points out that this oracle demonstrates that Jews in Asia
Minor shared the feelings of resentment against Rome of their Greek
neighbors.[86] Again, we see in this quotation from *Sibylline Oracles* 4 a
nationalistic ideology that does not fit with Revelation. A second example
of this ideology appears when Nero is cast in the unlikely role as hero for
Asia. *Sib. Or.* 4:119–24 and 4:138–9 contain an expression of the myth
of Nero's flight beyond the Euphrates to the Parthians and his future return, as does Revelation 13.[87] In *Sibylline Oracles* 4, the material prosper-

---

[83]This is the majority view described by Collins, *OTP* 1:358, who dates this
oracle to shortly before the battle of Actium, 31 BCE.

[84]So Collins, *OTP* 1:358.

[85]See *Sib. Or.* 4:107–108, on the earthquake in Laodicea, after which the city
was able to rebuild without imperial aid; see also Tac. *Ann.* 14.27.

[86]Yarbro Collins, *Crisis and Catharsis*, 91.

[87]See *Sib. Or.* 5:93–110; 5:215–227; 5:361–385. Rev 13:3 and 17:11, 16 have
been the focus of commentary in terms of the influence of the *Nero redivivus*
myth on Revelation. See Wilhelm Bousset, *Der Antichrist in der Überlieferung
des Judentums, des neuen Testaments und der alten Kirche: Ein Beitrag zur
Auslegung der Apocalypse* (repr.: Hildesheim: Georg Olms, 1983; orig.:
Göttingen: Vandenhoeck & Ruprecht, 1895); idem., "Antichrist" in *Encyclo-*

ity that Asia will enjoy as its revenge on Rome is a result of Nero's return. Whereas *Sibylline Oracles* 4 depicts Nero as Asia's hero, Revelation 13 incorporates the myth of *Nero redivivus* into a narrative of satanic domination of the social, political, and religious spheres of earthly life.

Book 5 of the *Sibylline Oracles* adds two more motifs to the list of parallels between the Sibyllina and Revelation, the use of the code name "Babylon" for Rome and gematria, or symbolic numbers, for the names of Roman emperors.[88] But these parallels can be misleading. While "Babylon" is a consistent cipher or symbol for Rome in Revelation, the name "Rome" appears frequently in *Sibylline Oracles* 5.[89] There is also an oracle against the real Babylon, "of golden throne and golden sandal," in *Sib. Or.* 5:434–446. The gematria in *Sibylline Oracles* 5 expresses the same political ideology that distinguished *Sibylline Oracles* 3 and 4 from Revelation. The emperor Hadrian is called "a most excellent man" who "will consider everything" (πανάριστος ἀνὴρ καὶ πάντα νοήσει, *Sib. Or.* 5:48). Such a favorable view of an emperor hardly fits with Revelation's ideology. *Sibylline Oracles* 5 also contains a fuller expression of the Nero myth than *Sibylline Oracles* 4 or Revelation 13. Nero's function in *Sibylline Oracles* 5 is not to oppose God but to oppose Rome.[90] Nero receives blame for the war on the Jews (5:150–151). There is no mention of wealth or economic activity in the description of Nero's return and war against the Romans, as in book 4.

The theme of Rome's wealth and economic exploitation of the empire is completely absent from the polemic against Rome in *Sibylline Oracles*

---

paedia of Religion and Ethics, ed. James Hastings et al. (Edinburgh: T.&T. Clark; New York: Scribners, 1979–1981) 1:578–81; and Bousset [commentary], 410–19; also Charles 1:350; Yarbro Collins, *Combat Myth*, 174–86; Prigent, 203; and Bauckham, *Climax of Prophecy*, 384–452.

[88]"Babylon" is used for Rome in *Sib. Or.* 5:143 and 5:159. For examples of gematria, see *Sib. Or.* 5:12, 14, 15, 21, 25, 28, 37, 38, 40, 42, 46–48; Rev 13:18. The catalogue of rulers in *Sib. Or.* 5:1–51 runs from Alexander the Great to Marcus Aurelius, referring to most by gematria.

[89]"Babylon" in *Sib. Or.* 5:143 is preceded by "Rome" in 5:138. *Sib. Or.* 5:168, shortly after the "Babylon" of 5:159, reads "city of the Latin land."

[90]Nero appears as a human figure who has been hiding among the Parthians, rather than as a demonic beast who has returned to life (see Collins, *OTP* 1:391; and Yarbro Collins, *Combat Myth*, 177), although God gives him strength "to perform things like no previous one of all the kings" (*Sib. Or.* 5:220–21).

5.[91] We find the most extended attack on Rome in 5:155–178, of which the following is typical:

> With you are found adulteries and illicit intercourse with boys.
> Effeminate and unjust, evil city, ill-fated above all.
> Alas, city of the Latin land, unclean in all things.
> maenad, rejoicing in vipers, as a widow you will sit
> by the banks, and the river Tiber will weep for you, its consort.
> You have a murderous heart and an impious spirit. (*Sib. Or.* 5:166–171)

The oracle does not discuss Rome's wealth or lust for "ill-gotten gain," as does *Sibylline Oracles* 3, but the charges of sexual immorality in *Sib. Or.* 5:166–167 echo the polemic of *Sib. Or.* 3:185–190.[92] *Sib. Or.* 5:386–396 also attacks Rome's sexual immorality, listing prostitution, incest, and bestiality among the "abominations," but does not mention wealth or greed. The oracle in 5:155–78 alludes to the war against the Jews and the destruction of the Jewish Temple as the reason for Rome's (here called "Babylon") destruction (5:158–161).

Both Revelation and the *Sibylline Oracles* contain strong language written in vehement protest to Rome. Revelation never envisions the restoration of Rome in favorable terms; it thus constructs a more radical critique. Babylon must be completely destroyed and the New Jerusalem can then take its place. Comparison of the *Sibylline Oracles* and Revelation, moreover, highlights the extent to which motifs of wealth and trade are part of Revelation's attack on Rome. I will return to this point below, when considering the imagery of wealth in the oracles of restoration in the Sibylline Oracles in comparison to the description of the New Jerusalem in Revelation. The shared interpretive conventions of Revelation and the *Sibylline Oracles* suggest that John wrote his prophecy with some awareness of the Sibylline tradition. But if this is so, he has greatly intensified the wealth motifs and the attack on Rome.

---

[91]Thus, contra Collins, *OTP* 1:391, the polemic against Rome in book 5 is not as bitter or deep as book 3.

[92]The simile of the widow, found in Isaiah 47 and Revelation 18, probably derives from *Sibylline Oracles* 3.

Conclusion: Babylon and Rome

John constructs his portrait of Rome under the name of "Babylon" by weaving together selections from the prophets of the Hebrew Bible that originally applied to Babylon and Tyre. He thereby constructs a city called Babylon that is quite different from the city of his sources. The commercial power of John's Babylon/Rome, a power evoked by the juxtaposition of prophetic oracles against Babylon with oracles against Tyre, will be a focus of the next chapter when I examine the relationship of wealth and status in the Greco-Roman world. Other texts used the code name "Babylon" when addressing Rome, although no other enemy of Rome weaves the prophetic texts together as John does to produce such a powerful and extended polemic against the wealth of the city.

Second Temple period texts portray Rome as a wealthy and blood-thirsty nation, conquering and plundering in order to get more wealth, sexually immoral, and practicing sorcery and magic.[93] All of these texts, however, both the prophetic texts of the Hebrew Bible and Second Temple texts, include one notable feature that the Apocalypse of John lacks completely—a strong concern for the poor. In Revelation, the opposition is between God's wealth in heaven, which endures, and Babylon's wealth, which is destroyed. But nowhere in the Apocalypse is there a strong concern for social justice or the oppression of the poor, the widowed, or the orphaned. Babylon is condemned for her wealth and love of luxury, but not for her oppression of the poor. In the Jewish tradition, the destruction of the evil power, whether that be Babylon or Rome, leads to a new age of justice, agricultural bounty, and fair economic distribution. As we explore ancient literature anticipating the restoration of Jerusalem, the concern for social justice in the Jewish tradition, a concern totally absent in Revelation, comes even more to the forefront.

The New Jerusalem

The focus of eschatological hope in the Apocalypse of John is the new city of Jerusalem, where God will dwell with humankind. This vision of hope, Rev 21:9–27, is also the most opulent vision in the book of Revelation. Again, John's vision of the New Jerusalem draws heavily on prophetic sources. The motif of the restoration of Jerusalem is part of a

---

[93]In addition to the *Sibylline Oracles* see *Pss. Sol.* 1:4–2:5; 2:19–21; 17; 1QpHab 3:2; 6:1–2 [cf. 6:5–6]; 4QpPsª 2:9–11; 3:8–11.

larger theme in Jewish literature: the anticipation of the future age of the spirit, in which God or God's agents, such as the Messiah, will establish a kingdom and restore Israel's fortunes. Isaiah, Jeremiah, and Ezekiel do not use wealth imagery extensively to describe this future age. Rather, their oracles, hymns, and poems describe the restoration in terms of agricultural bounty, social justice and equality, the service of other nations for Israel, the rebuilding of the Temple, and an intimate relationship with the God of Israel.[94] Of the three major classical prophets, only Isaiah makes abundant use of wealth motifs; John finds his inspiration for the New Jerusalem, if not all its adornments, in Isaiah. This Isaianic tradition of wealth in the New Jerusalem can be found in Tobit and the Dead Sea Scrolls as well as Revelation, suggesting that the wealth in the restored city is part of an established tradition in Jewish literature. But John also draws on biblical passages describing the cult and Temple, in which wealth motifs are prominent, with the result that his vision of the New Jerusalem is the most opulent in ancient Jewish or Christian literature.

Wealth in the New Jerusalem

The restoration of Jerusalem is a particular theme of both Second and Third Isaiah, from which John draws the words to describe his vision of a new, heavenly city.[95] The restoration of Jerusalem, in Isaiah as in Revelation, is linked to the destruction of Babylon (Isa 43:14), from whence the captives return to Israel.[96] Cyrus, God's agent in the destruction of Babylon and the release of the captives, will rebuild the city of Jerusalem.

---

[94]See Isa 2:2–4; 11:1–9; 25:6–10a; 27:12–13; 32:14–20; 33:20–22; 35:1–10; Jer 3:17; 31:1–14, 23–40; 33:9–11; Ezek 36:8–15; 37:1–14; 39:25–29, which includes the valley of the dry bones forming new bodies; and the description of the new Temple starting in Ezek 40:1–49.

[95]Fekkes, *Isaiah and Prophetic Traditions*, 92–103, discusses how the Old Testament passages used in Revelation 21 are drawn from prophetic oracles of renewal or restoration, esp. Ezekiel 40–48; Isa 52:1; 54:11–12; Isaiah 60; and Zechariah 14. This supports Fekkes's thesis that the use of the Hebrew Bible in Revelation shows conscious authorial intention. I have shown the same intentionality in the use of wealth passages. Fekkes goes on to make the bold assertion that John's use of a passage "extends also to the setting and *purpose* of the original biblical passage" (102, emphasis mine). It is far-fetched to imagine that John's free recombination and rewriting of scriptural texts has anything at all to do with the purpose of the original passages.

[96]See also Ezek 38:1–39:29, the battle of Gog and Magog, and the plundering of villages in Ezek 38:10–13. The oracle ends in the restoration of Israel.

When he builds it, they will come, bearing their wealth: "The wealth of Egypt and the merchandise of Ethiopia, and the Sabeans, men of stature, shall come over to you and be yours" (Isa 45:14).[97] God promises to rebuild the city in luxury: "O afflicted one, storm-tossed, and not comforted, I am about to set your stones in antimony, and lay your foundations with sapphires. I will make your pinnacles of rubies, your gates of jewels, and all your wall of precious stones" (Isa 54:11–12; see Rev 21:19–20). The poem in Isa 60:1–22 supplies most of the material that appears in Revelation 21–22.[98] The phrase "wealth of the nations" (גוים חיל) is a refrain in the Isaiah poem celebrating the glory of the restored Jerusalem (Isa 60:5, 60:11, 61:6, cf. Isa 45:1). In Isa 60:5 and 60:11, it forms an *inclusio* around a description of that wealth. Huge caravans of camels from Midian, Ephah, and Sheba (Arabia) carry gold and frankincense; flocks of sacrificial animals come to the altar. Whole fleets from Tarshish bring gold and silver. The gates of the city remain open, both because there are no enemies to attack and because of the constant stream of wealth from the nations into the city. The Lord will also bring new wealth to restore the city, replacing plain and common materials with fine and expensive ones (Isa 60:17). The emphasis on social justice in Isaiah 60–62 is quite strong, appearing in close connection to images of wealth (see Isa 60:17; 61:1; cf. Luke 4:18–21). God reminds the people that "I the Lord love justice, I hate robbery and wrongdoing" (Isa 61:8). The concern for social and economic justice in Isaiah 60–62 is completely absent from Revelation 21–22.

The restoration of Jerusalem becomes a prominent symbol of hope in Jewish literature between the return from the Babylonian exile and the time of the book of Revelation. Other groups besides the community of Third Isaiah saw themselves as exiles awaiting restoration—the Qumran community in the wilderness, the Jewish opponents of Pompey and Aristobulus in 63 BCE, apocalyptic writers after the destruction of the Second Temple in 70 CE and after the Bar Kokhba revolt in 132 CE. The theme was a major *topos* in Jewish literature, apocalyptic or otherwise. A number of texts follow the Isaianic tradition, as does Revelation, of

---

[97]The word translated "wealth" here, יגיע, from the verb יגע, "to exert oneself," has the connotation of production rather than of gold or money. The LXX reads Ἐκοπίασεν Αἴγυπτος.

[98]On the three-part structure of Isaiah 60–62, see Westermann, *Isaiah 40–66*, 373. Cf. also the bride adorning herself with jewels in Isa 61:10; and Fekkes, "Revelation 19–21 and Isaian Nuptial Imagery."

envisioning the restored city of Jerusalem in luxurious and wealthy images. Tobit 13:16–17 provides a close parallel to Revelation:[99]

> The gates of Jerusalem will be built with sapphire and emerald, and all your walls with precious stones. The towers of Jerusalem will be built with gold, and their battlements with pure gold. The streets of Jerusalem will be paved[100] with ruby and with stones of Ophir. (Tob 13:16–17)

The "stones of Ophir" are almost certainly gold,[101] making this passage a remarkably close parallel to Rev 21:21. John almost certainly had this passage in mind, along with Isa 54:11–12, when composing Rev 21:19–21.[102] The Qumran vision of the New Jerusalem, also in the Isaianic tradition, highlights the concentration of wealth motifs in John's vision in Revelation.[103] Wealth motifs occur only once in 5QNJ, in the description of the main street passing through the middle of the city: "And [all the streets of the city] are paved with white stone . . . marble and jasper." Given the tradition in Isaiah, Tobit, and Revelation, we can infer that the missing text included a fuller description of gems or precious metals.

All Jewish texts describing the restoration of Jerusalem, however, do not use wealth motifs. The hymn of comfort in Bar 4:5–5:9 uses themes and images from Isaiah 60–65 without any mention of wealth, gold, or jewels adorning the city. There is joy at the return of the exiles, but they bring no wealth with them (Bar 4:36–37). Although Bar 5:1–2 alludes to Isa 61:10, Baruch clothes Jerusalem in "the robe of righteousness" and "the diadem of the glory of the Everlasting" rather than in Isaiah's garlands and jewels. Restoration is also a theme in *Psalms of Solomon* 17.

---

[99] While it has been argued that Tobit 13–14 are late additions, copies of these chapters have been found among manuscripts of Tobit at Qumran. See Nickelsburg, *Jewish Literature*, 33 and 33n.39.

[100] LSJ, s.v. ψηφολογηθήσονται = ψηφοθετέω, "to make tesselated pavements."

[101] See *2 Bar* 10:19; Dan 10:5; Job 28:16; Ps 45:9; Isa 13:12; and Collins, *Daniel*, 373.

[102] See the discussion by Fekkes, *Isaiah and Prophetic Traditions*, 238–53. I shall return to this in more detail in chap. 7.

[103] Aramaic fragments (QJN ar) include 1Q32, 2Q24, 11QJN ar, unpublished fragments from Cave 4; and 5QJN ar [5Q15], pub. "Description de la Jérusalem nouvelle," DJD III, 184–93; trans. of 5QJN ar from Geza Vermes, *The Dead Sea Scrolls in English*, 3rd ed. (Sheffield UK: JSOT Press, 1987).

Rather than using images of wealth to describe the righteousness of the Messiah and the glory of Jerusalem, the psalmist explicitly uses wealth as a foil to show what the Messiah will *not* be. The Messiah "will not rely on horse and rider and bow, nor will he collect gold and silver for war" (*Pss. Sol.* 17:33); "his words will be purer than the finest gold, the best" (17:43). The Messiah makes Jerusalem holy so that the nations return, bearing gifts—but the gifts are "her children who had been driven out" (*Pss. Sol.* 17:30), not, as in Isaiah 60–61, gold and silver. The exiles of the diaspora themselves are the glory of Jerusalem. The Messiah blesses the Lord's people with wisdom and happiness (*Pss. Sol.* 17:35), rather than with gold and frankincense (Isa 60:6). Apocalyptic literature, as we have seen throughout this chapter, does not include the concentration of wealth motifs found in Revelation. The eschaton in the Book of the Watchers (*1 Enoch* 1–36) brings peace and agricultural bounty to Jerusalem, rather than gold or jewels.[104] While *2 Baruch* includes hints of wealth in the earthly Jerusalem that was destroyed (*2 Bar* 6:4–7; 10:19), there are no wealth motifs in the description of the New Jerusalem that was prepared by God before creation (*2 Bar* 4:1–7; cf. 32:4). As with *1 Enoch*, the depictions of the blessings of the eschaton in *2 Baruch* focus on agricultural bounty and peace (*2 Bar* 29:5–8; 73:1–74:4).

We looked above at the portrayal of Rome in the *Sibylline Oracles*.[105] Jerusalem's wealth, both before and after the destruction of the city, also receives attention in books 3 and 5.[106] But the depiction of the wealth of the city is tempered by a strong concern for economic justice as well. In a discrete section describing the Babylonian exile and restoration (3:196–294), the Sibyl praises the Jews as "a race of most righteous men" (γένος δικαιοτάτων ἀνθρώπων, 3:219; cf. 3:580–600). The Jews are righteous in part because their deeds exhibit a strong sense of economic justice (3:234–237).[107] They have just measurements and boundaries; the rich do not take advantage of the less powerful; and the prosperous share with the poor. This passage is a short treatise on economic morality and functions as a stark contrast to some of the

---

[104]See *1 Enoch* 10:18–20; 11:1; 24:4–25:6; 26:1–2.

[105]See above, 65–70.

[106]See the remark by Collins, *OTP* 1:356, that "the third Sibyl displays an interest in the Temple which is unparalleled in any document from Egyptian Judaism."

[107]The oracle also commends the Jews for not practicing sorcery, magic, or astrology (*Sib. Or.* 3:220–33).

polemical charges against the greed and oppressive rule of the Romans in book 3.[108] The eschatological kingdom, according to *Sibylline Oracles* 3, brings agricultural blessings rather than wealth (3:619–623, 744–751) although there is one mention of "just wealth [πλοῦτος δίκαιος] among men, for this is the judgment and dominion of the great God" (3:783–784). Book 5 also uses agricultural imagery to describe the blessings of the eschatological kingdom (5:81–285, 328–332). This later book of oracles anticipates a more glorious restoration of Jerusalem than *Sibylline Oracles* 3, but the descriptions in *Sibylline Oracles* 5 do not approach the opulence and splendor of Revelation. The savior messiah who comes[109] after the destruction of the Temple redistributes wealth to "all the good" that previous men had taken away (*Sib. Or.* 5:417) and destroys evil nations and cities with fire. He also restores Jerusalem:

> And the city which God desired, this [the blessed man] made
> more brilliant than stars and sun and moon,
> and he provided ornament [κόσμον] and made a holy temple,
> exceeding beautiful in its fair shrine, and he fashioned
> a great and immense tower over many stadia
> touching even the clouds and visible to all,
> so that all faithful and all righteous people could see
> the glory of eternal God, a form desired. (*Sib. Or.* 5:420–427)

This description hints at the wealth of the city by noting its ornamentation, beauty, and size, but provides no concrete list of jewels or luxury items. While the Isaianic tradition of wealth in the New Jerusalem runs strong through texts such as Tobit, 5QNJ, and Revelation, we may add the *Sibylline Oracles* to Baruch, *Psalms of Solomon*, *1 Enoch*, and *2 Baruch* as part of a list of texts which do not include wealth imagery in their descriptions or actually oppose wealth and other luxuries.

Wealth and the Jerusalem Temple

The vision of the New Jerusalem in Rev 21:1–27 is a vision of a city; the narrator clearly states that he saw no temple, "for the Lord God, creator of all, and the Lamb are the temple" (Rev 21:22). But this passage draws much of its wealth imagery from descriptions and visions of the Jerusalem Temple and priestly vestments.[110] John has again radically

---

[108]For example, 3:175–95.

[109]See Collins, *OTP* 1:403, n. y3, on the use of the past tense in anticipation.

[110]So also Fekkes, *Isaiah and Prophetic Traditions*, 98–101.

recombined biblical texts to concentrate wealth motifs in his visions by using both "restored Jerusalem" and "Temple" passages. Whereas the tradition of wealth in the New Jerusalem is mixed in Jewish literature, the descriptions of the Temple of Jerusalem, like the tabernacle that preceded it, are usually quite opulent. The earliest traditions call for blue, purple, and crimson fabrics, fine linen, and liberal amounts of gold in the decoration of the garments and the tabernacle (Exod 28:1–39; 35:20–29; 39:8–14). Nine of the twelve jewels that decorate the twelve gates of the New Jerusalem in Rev 21:19–20 appear in the list of twelve jewels that decorate the breast piece of Aaron (Exod 28:17–20).[111] Solomon's Temple, according to the description in 1 Kings 6–7, was decorated with fine luxury items and tremendous amounts of gold. The opulence of the Herodian Second Temple could well have been a fresh memory for John and other Christians in Asia at the end of the first century CE (see *Ep. Aris.* 85; Jos. *J.W.* 5 §§184–226).

The architectural plan of the city described in Revelation 21 follows the plan set out in Ezek 48:30–35. Ezekiel's vision of the new Temple that precedes the layout of the city (Ezek 40:1–46:24), however, is remarkably plain, considering the tradition in Exodus, 1 Kings, and the descriptions of the Second Temple in later texts. A man with a linen cord and measuring reed shows the temple to the prophet (Ezek 40:3–5). John's tour of the New Jerusalem, in contrast, is conducted by an angel with a *golden* measuring rod (Rev 21:15). In Ezekiel, the tables for the preparation of sacrifices and offerings are made of hewn stone (Ezek 40:38–43). The walls, doors, door posts, and porch for all three chambers of this temple are paneled with wood. The only decorations for these walls are carvings of cherubim and palm trees (Ezek 41:15b–26). The vestments for the Zadokite priests who run the sanctuary are to be linen (פֵּשֶׁת, λίνεος), not wool; no other finery is mentioned (Ezek 44:17–18). Zimmerli remarks that a comparison of this temple with Solomon's in 1 Kings 6 makes everything in Ezekiel appear much more modest; the absence of gold is particularly striking in comparison with Solomon's temple.[112]

When John uses Ezekiel's vision in Revelation, he restores the missing elements of wealth and luxury. Other Second Temple Jewish

---

[111]See Himmelfarb, *Ascent to Heaven*, 18, on the general rule for garments and curtains in the Priestly document that "the more important the object, the more expensive and magnificent it has to be."

[112]See Zimmerli, *Ezekiel 2*, 387.

texts do the same. The Temple Scroll conflates and reworks several traditions, including Ezekiel 40–49, to construct a vision of the ideal
temple.[113] The description of the sanctuary and its furnishings is mostly
fragmentary, but we can discern a variety of luxury materials, such as
blue and purple, silver, pure gold (several times), and bronze, in the
decorations of the Temple. Liberal amounts of gold are used in the
Temple vessels and furnishings (11QTemple 3; 7:13; 9:12) and as overlay
for the walls, gates, pillars, and roof (11QTemple 31:8–9; 36:11;
41:16–17). The only reference to any luxury in the eschatological kingdom in *Sibylline Oracles* 3 refers to the restored Temple (*Sib. Or.*
3:657–668), another demonstration of the tradition of wealth in the Jerusalem Temple. By using Temple imagery for his city without a temple
(Rev 21:22), John taps into this tradition and another source of wealth for
the New Jerusalem.

A Final Note

In this chapter, I have treated the Apocalypse as hypertext and double
clicked on wealth passages, opening a cyberworld of parallels and contrasts in Jewish literature from the prophets through the Second Temple
period. But using Revelation as a guide to this world of literature runs the
risk of ignoring themes that are not present in the Apocalypse but are
prominent in ancient Jewish literature. This is significant, because some
of the most important Jewish texts dealing with economic morality have
no parallel in John's Apocalypse. The more one reads Jewish literature
with an eye for passages about wealth and trade, the more striking it is
that nowhere in the Apocalypse is there any strong concern for social
justice, the poor, the widowed, or the orphaned. The opening chapter of
Isaiah raises the issue of social justice in Judah (Isa 1:16-17, 1:21-23) and
this moral concern is strong throughout the book.[114] There are numerous
passages in Jeremiah and Ezekiel that call for social justice, particularly
in terms of care for the poor, the widowed and the orphaned.[115] The
theme runs strong throughout Second Temple literature.[116] The Qumran

---

[113]On the composition of the scroll, see Yigael Yadin, *The Temple Scroll*
(Jerusalem: Israel Exploration Society, 1983) 1:71–88.
[114]See Isa 3:13–15; 5:8, 23; 9:13–17; 10:1–4; 41:17; 42:1–8; 58:6–12.
[115]Jer 5:27–28; 6:13; 7:5; 21:12; 22:3, 13–17; Ezek 18:5–18; 22:12–29;
34:1–6; see also Amos 2:6–8; 5:10–13; Micah 2:1–5; 3:9–12; 6:8–16.
[116]*As. Mos.* (= *T. Mos.*) 5:1–6; 7:1–4, 6–9; *1 Enoch* 10:4–22, 16–21; 11:1–2;

sectarian documents contain rules for the sharing of possessions; the practice was well known to outsiders.[117] The Jewish moral tradition treats wealth in terms of economic justice or oppression, fair distribution or excessive greed. Revelation does not enter into a discussion of wealth in these moral terms but presents wealth as either good or bad, God's or Babylon's.

Summary and Conclusions

Tradition-historical analysis of the wealth passages in the Book of Revelation has shown how the visions in the Apocalypse compare to their Old Testament sources and to Jewish literature of the Second Temple period. In Revelation, John rewrites and conflates biblical passages to create new versions of old characters and scenes. Each vision in Revelation—the Human One, the throne room, Babylon, the New Jerusalem—includes several different Old Testament texts. The author concentrates wealth motifs in his visions with the result that each one is much wealthier than its biblical antecedents. He often uses only a word or phrase from his biblical sources, so that one sentence in Revelation might draw on four different Old Testament passages. John's free use of biblical texts to construct opulent visions of heaven and the New Jerusalem stands out within Second Temple Jewish literature. No other text decorates the Human One in gold, as Revelation does; indeed, the description in Revelation goes against the early Jesus traditions about wealth. Rev 4:2–11 has a higher concentration of wealth motifs than any other Second Temple throne vision. By combining oracles against Tyre with oracles against Babylon,

---

Pss. Sol. 4:9–22; *Sib. Or.* 3:234–248, 783–784; *T. Levi* 14:1–8; CD 6:15–16, 21; 8:3–7 (=19:15–19); 1QS 1:1–15; 2:2.

[117]See 1QS 5:1–4, 14–20; 6:2, 13–25; 7:6–25; 8:23; 9:22; CD 13:11–16; 14:13–17; Pliny *HN* 5.15 [73]; Philo, *Quod omn. prob.* 12.75–87 [457–9]; *De vit. cont.*16 [474]; Jos. *J.W.* 2 §§119–61; *Ant.* 13 §§171–72; 18 §§11, 18–22; 15 §§370–79. Yigael Yadin, *The Scroll of the War of the Sons of Light against the Sons of Darkness* (Oxford: Oxford University Press, 1962) 311, commenting on 1QM 11:9, 13; 13.13-14 refers to 1QpHab 12:10 as evidence that the words for poor (אביון, אני) are metaphorical and equivalent to phrases such as "poor in spirit" and other Old Testament phrases such as found in 1 Sam 22:8; see also Knibb, *Qumran Community*, 245. The clear economic reference in 1QpHab 12:10 and the importance of wealth in the Community Rule make this "metaphorical" or "spiritual" interpretation inadequate for the range of uses of the words in sectarian literature. See also 1QH 2:32–35; 3:25; 4QpPsᵃ 2:9–11; 3:8–11.

John constructed a new "Babylon" that is a wealthy, commercial power. The portrayal of Babylon in Revelation exhibits similarities to the portrayal of Rome in Second Temple Jewish texts, in particular the *Sibylline Oracles*. But the commercial focus of John's description of Babylon/ Rome is unique. Revelation's ideological opposition to Rome goes against early Christian tradition such as found in Paul and 1 Peter while its rejection of earthly political solutions differentiates its ideology from the *Sibylline Oracles*. Revelation stands in a tradition, with Isaiah, Tobit, and 5QNJ, of anticipating an opulent New Jerusalem. Other texts, such as Baruch and the *Psalms of Solomon*, do not use wealth motifs or explicitly oppose wealth in the restored city. The implied author describes a wealthier vision of the heavenly city than does any other text by drawing on descriptions of the Jewish Temple and cult for the New Jerusalem in Revelation, passages in which we find a high concentration of wealth motifs.

I have asked throughout this chapter how the audience of Revelation, particularly hearers knowledgeable in the Hebrew Bible, would have reacted to these visions. Given the intricacy of allusions, echoes, and borrowed phrases in Revelation, it is doubtful whether any listener could have kept up at all. Perhaps some Christians who had studied the Jewish scriptures extensively would have caught some of the references; heard some of the allusions; and pondered their significance. But most of the audience would have missed the allusions and echoes because it is highly unlikely that many of them had such deep scriptural knowledge. This hypothesis is made even more probable by the absence of clues in Revelation itself suggesting that any of its images have been borrowed from biblical texts. Revelation has no citation formulas, no names of the prophets who are its sources, and no direct quotations. These are all typical literary conventions in other New Testament texts. Borrowing from the prophets is not unusual; I have shown how Ezekiel 1 and Daniel 7 influenced other apocalyptic visions. But the extent and manner in which Revelation borrows from and rewrites Daniel, Ezekiel, Isaiah, and Jeremiah is unique. The use of the Hebrew Bible in the Apocalypse undercuts the authority of the Hebrew scriptures because it does not acknowledge that authority. Instead, Revelation claims authority as a text on its own terms (Rev 1:1–3; 22:10–20). Ultimately, then, exegesis of the Hebrew scriptures and the author's sources in Revelation directs us to a different context for interpretation of its wealth motifs that was much more accessible to its original audience than the intertextuality and allusiveness of the Apocalypse; that is, the world of Greco-Roman culture.

Wealth Motifs in Greco-Roman Literature and Culture

Introduction

In this chapter, we turn to the ways in which the imagery and motifs of wealth and trade in Revelation would have been heard in the cities of Asia Minor around 95–100 CE. But, in light of the previous chapter, this task might strike a dissonant note. As we have seen, the language and characters of the Apocalypse originate in the narrative worlds of Jewish prophetic and apocalyptic literature. So what do demonic beasts and angelic guides have to do with philosophical treatises and polished speeches? The anti-Roman stance of the Apocalypse deepens this sense of dissonance between the narrative world of Revelation, with its prophetic and apocalyptic Jewish sources, and the social world of Greco-Roman culture. But Greek culture and Roman authority are major moral issues in the Apocalypse because this text came to life in a Greco-Roman context. John chose to write in Greek, idiosyncratic though his may be, because it was the language of the eastern Empire and of the early Christian communities. Few of the Christians who heard the Apocalypse would have had the knowledge of the Hebrew scriptures that John had, whereas all would be conversant in the public aspects of Greco-Roman culture that organized social life in the cities of Asia Minor. Some, such as "Jezebel" and her students, might have studied Greek philosophy as well.

The Apocalypse of John was written and first read in an era of increasing prosperity and cultural activity in Roman Asia. Vespasian built a road from Pergamum to Smyrna through Ephesus, Thyatira and Sardis, linking the Asian cities to which John wrote his Apocalypse. There was a significant amount of cultural and building activity during the 80s and 90s, despite the negative image given to Domitian's reign after his assassination.[1] Domitian advanced the progress of prominent Asians in the

---

[1]See David Magie, *Roman Rule in Asia Minor: To the End of the Third*

imperial administration. He favored Ephesus to the point where it became the most prosperous and important city in the eastern Roman empire, a distinction usurped by Smyrna during Hadrian's reign. The temple of the Sebastoi that was erected at Ephesus under Domitian included a colossal statue of the emperor.[2] The council of Ephesus, acting with the Senate in condemning Domitian after his death, later removed the statue. The renaissance of Greek culture called the Second Sophistic was gathering momentum at the end of the first century CE; Ephesus and Smyrna were major centers of rhetoric.

Revelation was written and read in the context of these cultural changes. Images and phrases which may have derived from the Hebrew Bible could nevertheless have been understood quite differently by someone with a gentile Greek background. To understand how wealth imagery in Revelation functioned as part of the ideological critique of Rome and John's Christian opposition, it is necessary to understand the variety and ambiguity of ancient ways of thinking about and through wealth. The goal of this chapter is to show how the wealth imagery of the Apocalypse, though carefully crafted from the Jewish scriptures, evoked different associations of status in Greco-Roman culture. Whereas the wealth of heaven shines with aristocratic and philosophical luster, the tawdry wealth of Babylon/Rome is tied to the denigrating activity of trade.

Christ as Moral Philosopher

The two wealth passages not covered in the previous chapter, the moral exhortation about poverty and wealth in the oracles to Smyrna and Laodicea, lead us into our Greco-Roman sources. If we were able to ask someone in ancient Smyrna or Laodicea who they would expect to issue exhortations on the virtue of poverty or the moral perils of wealth, they would surely point to the moral philosophers. Philosophy in the early Roman empire was concerned primarily with ethics. The oracles to Smyrna and Laodicea cover several issues that philosophers pondered in antiquity: the relation of freedom and hardships, or περιστάσεις (*peristaseis*); the nature of true wealth; finding wealth in poverty; avoiding reliance on possessions and wealth; and the moral peril of seeking

---

Century after Christ, 2 vols. (Princeton NJ: Princeton University Press, 1950) 1:570–89; and Thompson, *Revelation*, 95–115.

[2]Friesen, *Twice Neokoros*, 41–49, establishes that the cult was founded in Ephesus during Domitian's reign; see 59–75 on the temple.

excessive gain. Less than fifty years after the Apocalypse was written, Justin Martyr studied the four schools of philosophy in Ephesus before settling eventually on Christianity.[3] The Christians addressed in the Apocalypse were probably not leisured enough to engage in such philosophical education, but we can assume some awareness of and contact with philosophers, particularly Cynic and Stoic street-corner preachers. As I will show, Christ's exhortation to the churches of Smyrna and Laodicea would have suggested to the Asian Christians the exhortation of a moral philosopher.

The Cynics and the Stoics are the best candidates for the type of philosopher evoked by Christ in Revelation 2–3, but some clarification is necessary before evaluating these two options. The eclectic nature of Hellenistic and Roman philosophy blurs the distinctions between different systems, and the Cynics were not particularly systematic.[4] The regular appearance of the term "Cynic-Stoic" in scholarly literature should alert us to some of the difficulties we face in using the categories of Greco-Roman moral philosophy.[5] Stoicism began with a strong dose of Cynic influence, as Zeno was a disciple of Crates.[6] While Stoicism had universal respectability throughout the Hellenistic period, Cynicism faded in the second and first centuries BCE, being absorbed by Stoicism, and then revived in the first century CE. This revival was in part a result of a new interest in earlier Cynicism by Stoics such as Musonius Rufus and

---

[3]See Just. Mart. *Dial.* 2; the search for the true philosophy was a literary convention.

[4]See Abraham J. Malherbe, "Self-definition among Epicureans and Cynics," in *Self-Definition in the Graeco-Roman World*, ed. Ben F. Meyer and E. P. Sanders, vol. 3 of *Jewish and Christian Self-Definition* (Philadelphia: Fortress Press, 1982) 46–59, esp. 48–50.

[5]Note the title of Rudolf Bultmann's 1910 dissertation, *Der Stil der paulinischen Predigt und die kynische-stoische Diatribe*, FRLANT 13 (Göttingen: Vandenhoeck & Ruprecht, 1984). Stanley K. Stowers, in his important revision of Bultmann's work, *The Diatribe and Paul's Letter to the Romans*, SBLDS 57 (Chico CA: Scholars Press, 1981) 77 and 77n.423, notes that examples of the diatribe come from either Stoics or Platonists with Stoic and Cynic traditions. See also H. D. Betz, "Jesus and the Cynics: Survey and Analysis of Hypothesis," *JR* 74 (1994): 472, where he describes Epictetus as an austere Cynic who turned to Stoicism and then created own version of Cynic-Stoic philosophy.

[6]See A. A. Long, *Hellenistic Philosophy*, 2nd ed. (Berkeley and Los Angeles: University of California Press, 1986) 3–4, 109–11; Abraham J. Malherbe *The Cynic Epistles*, SBLSBS 12 (Missoula MT: Scholars Press for SBL, 1977) 1.

his students. Both schools focused on ethics and used much of the same vocabulary to describe the pursuit of virtue. Nonetheless, two discernibly different ethical teachings on wealth can be identified within "Cynic-Stoic" philosophy and labeled, for heuristic purposes, "Stoic" and "Cynic," whether or not these teachings were consistently followed by various philosophers in the first and second centuries CE. The Stoic teaching is that wealth and poverty are not constituents of virtue but are classed as τὰ ἀδιάφορα (the *adiaphora*), things indifferent to virtue. The Cynic teaching is that wealth and possessions are impediments to virtue and happiness and that a poor person is closer to virtue and happiness than a wealthy one. The true Cynic was thus expected to be poor while the Stoic could be, and often was, quite wealthy. Although commentators regularly assume that Christ praises poverty in the messages to Smyrna and Laodicea, closer examination of both the Cynic and Stoic teaching on wealth shows that Christ's moral exhortation in these messages has strong affinities with Stoic philosophy.

The Cynic View of Wealth

Christ's exhortation to the Smyrnan church might sound at first very much like the Cynic view of wealth and poverty. Christ characterizes the Smyrnans by their poverty and their afflictions, which include slander (βλασφημία) at the hands of the Jews and imprisonment (2:9–10). Christ says that, despite their poverty (πτωχεία), the Smyrnans are really rich. The teaching of Cynics focused entirely on ethics and behavior, including wealth, poverty, and appearance.[7] The attitude of the Cynics toward wealth stems from their goals of a life "according to nature," κατὰ φύσιν (*kata phusin*). The Cynics did not define "nature"

---

[7]For a general introduction, see Abraham J. Malherbe, "Self-Definition," and idem, "Cynics," *IDBSup*, 201–203; for more thorough discussion of the ancient Cynics and Cynicism, see Marie-Odile Goulet-Cazé, "Le cynisme à l'époque impériale," *ANRW* 2/36/4, 2721–2833; and the articles collected in Marie-Odile Goulet-Cazé and Richard Goulet, eds., *Le Cynisme ancien et ses prolongements. Actes du colloque international du CNRS*, (Paris: Presses Universitaires de France, 1993). For a general discussion of the philosophical attitude toward poverty, see Herbert Grassl, *Sozialökonomische Vorstellungen in der kaiserzeitlichen griechischen Literatur (1.–3. Jh. N. Chr.)*, Historia 41 (Weisbaden: Franz Steiner, 1982) 65–90. There was a debate in antiquity over whether Cynicism was truly a philosophy or a way of life, since they did not develop a system of logics or physics but focused entirely on behavior; see Diog. Laert. 6.103; Malherbe, "Self-Definition," 48–50.

but seemed to have assumed that a life *kata phusin* was both virtuous and governed by reason. The Cynics equated happiness with virtue; therefore, their goal was the virtuous life. For the Cynics, this virtuous, reasonable life was an attainable goal; they were less tolerant of partial efforts than the Stoics.[8] Cynics strove to achieve self-sufficiency, or αὐτάρκεια (*autarkeia*), in all things. They emphasized the independence of the wise person from social custom and life *kata phusin*. They shunned externals such as wealth and possessions and ignored hardships (*peristaseis*) in order to live a virtuous, independent, and self-sufficient life *kata phusin*.

The virtues of poverty and simple living and the moral evils of wealth and possessions were central parts of Cynic philosophy. These ethical leitmotifs go back to the founder of the school, Diogenes of Sinope, whose life and deeds had acquired a legendary character by the first century CE. Diogenes Laertes, in *Lives of the Eminent Philosophers* 6.20–81, records a number of stories concerning Diogenes that had circulated for hundreds of years; some 51 epistles were written by Ps.-Diogenes (really at least four different authors) between the first century BCE and the fourth century CE.[9] According to tradition, Diogenes of Sinope sought out hardships, avoided reliance on possessions, and broke social conventions. Diogenes attacked the love of money and the pursuit of wealth as part of his assault on social convention, finding nothing more silly in the animal world than those "puffed up with conceit of wealth" (Diog. Laert. 6.24).[10] Criticism of wealth and praise of poverty

---

[8]See Ps.-Diogenes 30 (Malherbe, *Cynic Epistles*, 131); and Marie-Oudile Goulet-Cazé, *L'ascèse cynique: Un commentaire de Diogène Laërce VI 70-71* (Paris: J. Vrin, 1986) 23–27.

[9]See Malherbe, *Cynic Epistles*, 14–15.

[10]See also Diog. Laert. 6.28, 44, 50. See the description of Crates in Diog. Laert. 6.85–93, including his comment that his country was ἀδοξία καὶ πενία. The teachings of Demonax, in contrast, as presented by Lucian, do not focus on wealth, but it is not clear whether or not to take the *Demonax* at face value (as is always the case with Lucian). See J. Bompaire, *Lucien écrivain: Imitation et Création*, Bibliothèque des Ecoles Françaises d'Athènes et de Rome 190 (Paris: Boccard, 1958) 472–514. Dudley, *Cynicism* 158–62, and C. P. Jones, *Culture and Society in Lucian* (Cambridge MA: Harvard University Press, 1986) 90–98, take Demonax as a Cynic philosopher; but compare the intertextual approach of Graham Anderson, which leans towards deconstruction, in *Lucian: Theme and Variation in the Second Sophistic*, Mnemosyne Supp. 41 (Leiden: E. J. Brill, 1976).

and hardships are regular features of the Cynic Epistles.[11] For the true strict Cynic, what is "really honorable" is "to learn to be steadfast under blows, not of puny men, but of the spirit, not through leather straps or fists, but through poverty, disrepute, lowly birth, and exile" (Ps.-Diogenes 31).[12] An epistle attributed to Crates tells the wealthy who "engage in trade and cultivate much land" to "go hang yourselves." The same epistle claims that true wealth is to be found only in poverty: "although we possess nothing, we have everything" (Ps.-Crates 7).[13]

The notion that poverty is superior to wealth is widespread in Cynic literature.[14] Dio Chrysostom, a student of Musonius Rufus, was influenced by both Stoicism and Cynicism. Diogenes of Sinope is a central figure in Dio's *Orations* 6, 8, 9, and 10. Dio sounds the standard Cynic cries against wealth, luxury and convention in the sixth oration, but his remarks against the tyranny of the "Persian King" show the degree to which he has coopted Diogenes to describe his own situation in exile under Domitian.[15] Dio's "conversion" to philosophy during exile, as presented in *Oration* 13, has been taken recently more as rhetorical posturing than an actual account.[16] Whatever the actual commitment to Cynicism might have been, his writings show the influence of Cynic ideas. In the seventh or "Euboean" oration, Dio argues for the moral superiority of the rural poor. He begins by telling a tale of shipwreck among Euboean hunters to illustrate that the rich are at a disadvantage to the poor in living a decent life "in accordance with nature" (*kata phusin*,

---

[11]A major methodological argument of Malherbe, "Self-Definition," is for the use of the Cynic Epistles as sources for understanding Cynicism during our period, rather than the more idealized versions of Cynicism one finds in the writings of Lucian, Epictetus, or Julian.

[12]Malherbe, *Cynic Epistles*, 136–37.

[13]Malherbe, *Cynic Epistles*, 58–59. See also Ps.-Xenophon 18; 20; Ps.-Anacharsis 9; 10; Ps.-Crates 8; 26; Ps.-Diogenes 36; 37; Ps.-Socrates 1; 6.

[14]See also Musonius Rufus *Frags.* 7; 18A–20; Maximus of Tyre *Disc.* 36; Julian *Or.* 7.214BCD; and Ronald F. Hock, "Simon the Shoemaker as an Ideal Cynic," *GRBS* 17 (1976) 41–53.

[15]See *Or.* 6.5, 35–37, 49–50, 58–60.

[16]Compare the interpretations of Dudley, *Cynicism* 148–58, who relies on H. von Arnim, *Leben und Werke des Dio von Prusa* (Berlin, 1898); C. P. Jones, *The Roman World of Dio Chrysostom* (Cambridge MA: Harvard University Press, 1978) 45–55; and D. A. Russell, ed., *Dio Chrysostom Orations VII, XII and XXXVI* (Cambridge: Cambridge University Press, 1992) 6: "the signs of a studied performance and the adoption of a recognized pose are evident."

Or. 7.81; cf. 7.103). Dio's description of the life of the hunter's family shows the "true wealth" they have found in their rural poverty.[17] In *Or.* 7.65–66, a pastoral banquet scene, the speaker draws a direct comparison between the happiness of this family in their poverty and the misery among the rich and powerful.

> I could not help deeming these people fortunate and thinking that of all the men that I knew, they lived the happiest lives. And yet I knew the homes and tables of rich men, of satraps and kings as well as of private individuals; but then they seem to me the most wretched of all; and though they had so appeared before, yet I felt this the more strongly as I beheld the poverty and free spirit of the humble cottagers and noted that they lacked naught of the joy of eating and drinking, nay, that even in these things they had, one might say, the better of it (*Or* 7.65–66).

Dio inscribes in "nature" the life *kata phusin*, illustrating, with considerable literary artifice, Cynic ideals such as freedom, self-sufficiency, and the happiness attained through virtue.[18] In this philosophical view, wealth is clearly an impediment to virtue while poverty is in and of itself virtuous.

Thus far, Christ in Rev 2:9–11 sounds very much like a Cynic philosopher. But closer examination of the message to the Smyrnans places some distance between Christ in Revelation and the Cynics in Roman antiquity. Christ does not dwell on the Smyrnans' poverty or wealth, nor does he draw any explicit connections between their poverty and the slander from the Jews. Poverty on its own does not bring virtue to the Smyrnans. It is because of their suffering, not their poverty, that the Smyrnans rank high in Christ's characterization of the seven churches. Furthermore, the character dictating these messages, Christ, was seen by John dressed in gold and surrounded by golden lampstands. Surely gold cannot be evil if Christ wears a golden belt. And, as we saw in the previous chapter, Christ summons John to view "what must soon take place" from the vantage point of the wealthiest heavenly throne room in Jewish literature. Appearance was very important for the Cynic philosopher. A cloak, staff, and wallet were all the possessions Diogenes carried; in one episode, he threw away his cup when he saw a child drinking from

---

[17]See esp. Dio *Or.* 7.2, 9–12, 22–63, 80.
[18]See also Dio Chrys. *Ors.* 4.83–96; 6.5, 13–17, 31, 35–37, 49–50, 60; 13.13; 77/78.15–17, 26–28, 30–31, 33, 34–45; and 62.1.

his hands.[19] The plain dress of Diogenes was important to later Cynics and served as their uniform; "consider the ragged cloak to be a lion's skin, the staff a club, and the wallet land and sea, from which you are fed."[20] Lucian, in *The Runaways*, derides manual laborers and slaves who leave their jobs to become "philosophers" merely by donning a short cloak and carrying a staff and wallet (*Fug.* 14, 27).[21] The "Heracles of Herodes," called "Sostratus" by Lucian, wore wolf skins and lived on milk and barley meal (Philostr. *VS* 2.1 [552–553]; Luc. *Dem.* 1).[22] Christ does not adopt the pose or dress of the Cynic philosopher; he does not praise poverty for its own sake or as the necessary for virtue. Rather, Christ adopts a more aristocratic tone befitting the school of philosophy that preached the perils of reliance on wealth while allowing the possession of vast quantities, Stoicism.

"Adiaphora": Stoic Indifference to Wealth

Attacking reliance on wealth rather than wealth itself as a moral peril is a key difference between Cynic and Stoic attitudes toward wealth. In the oracle to Laodicea, Christ sees poverty, wretchedness and misery where the Laodiceans see security in their wealth (Rev 3:17). The Laodiceans are not condemned for being wealthy per se; rather, their "lukewarm"

---

[19]Diog. Laert. 6.37; see also 6.23 (the famous tub) and 6.87 on Crates.

[20]Ps.-Crates 26 [Malherbe, *Cynic Epistles*, 118–19]; see Malherbe, "Self-Definition," 49–50. Practices such as Cynic dress have been adduced as similarities between the early Jesus movement and Cynics (cf. Luke 9:3); see F. Gerald Downing, "Cynics and Early Christianity," in *Le Cynisme ancien*, 281–304.

[21]The companion treatise deriding hypocritical and greedy Cynic philosophers is *The Passing of Peregrinus*; see also Luc. *Bion* 7–11; and Arr. *Epict. Diss.* 3.22.9–12; 3.22.50. The suspicions reserved for false philosophers and wandering Cynics met early Christian teachers such as Paul; see Abraham J. Malherbe, "Gentle as a Nurse: The Cynic Background to I Thess ii," *NovT* 12 (1970): 203–17.

[22]Demonax, who followed Diogenes in appearance, mocked the Cynic Honoratus, who dressed himself in bearskins (Luc. *Dem.* 5, 19). On the milder strain of Cynicism, introduced by Crates in contrast to Diogenes' harsh demeanor, see Malherbe, "Self-Definition" and "Cynics." Appearance was an important aspect of the self-presentation and characterization of ancient philosophers. See for instance Luc. *Icar.* 29–31 and *Per.* 15 on the appearance of philosophers; see also the study of Epicurean recruitment by Bernard Frischer, *The Sculpted Word: Epicureanism and Philosophical Recruitment in Ancient Greece* (Berkeley: University of California Press, 1982), which explores the appearance of the philosopher in statues in terms of social expectations and Epicurean physics.

attitude is the real problem. The assertion that Stoicism focuses on reliance on wealth rather than wealth itself requires some explanation and context. Stoic ethics differ from Cynic not only in the attitude toward wealth but in the complexity of the philosophical system that underlies the ethics. It is impossible to describe the Stoic attitude toward wealth without a fuller explanation of Stoic ethics; and indeed it is difficult to describe Stoic ethics without delving into a full discussion of the entire philosophy.[23] Stoicism took from the Cynics the notion that virtue is the only good. They developed, however, ontological and epistemological theories, which they called physics and logics, to account for the reliability of the self's perceptions of the universe and the ability to know what is good or virtuous. The Stoics, like the Cynics, attempted to live virtuously by living in harmony with nature, *kata phusin*. But the Stoics defined "nature" as reason (λόγος, *logos*), which they equated with the will or mind of God. Reason or *logos*, the divine spirit, pervades the universe and the soul. For a rational being, reason is the highest power and governs the life according to nature. Governed by reason, the orientation (οἰκείωσις, *oikeiōsis*) of a rational being is toward virtue since reason crafts the rational being's primary impulse (ὁρμή, *hormē*).[24] The effort of the wise person to choose appropriate actions (τὰ καθήκοντα, *ta kathēkonta*; Latin *officia*) is hampered by human limitations in knowing the will of Zeus in every circumstance. Virtue remains within the power of the rational being, however, since any action can be done in a virtuous way.

The orientation or *oikeiōsis* of the rational being in ethical decisions is to choose virtue, the only good, and to live *kata phusin*, governed by reason. But everything is not readily classed as virtuous or not virtuous, in accord with nature or contrary to nature. There existed in Stoic thought a third category, the *adiaphora*, that which is morally indifferent. In its broadest sense, the *adiaphora* are those things which are neither good nor bad; therefore, all externals. But the Stoics used narrower definitions as

---

[23]For a discussion of Stoic ethical theory as it derives from their philosophical system, see Long, *Hellenistic Philosophy*, 172–99; F. H. Sandbach, *The Stoics*, 2nd. ed. (Bristol UK: Bristol, 1989) 28–38; and esp. Brad Inwood, *Ethics and Human Action in Early Stoicism* (Oxford: Clarendon, 1985) 182–215.

[24]The centrality of *oikeiōsis* to Stoic ethical theory, as the "the most economical theory of animal behaviour," is the crux of Inwood's project. The Stoic theory of impulse is much more complicated than presented here, but is not germane to the present discussion; see *Ethics and Human Action*, 47–53, 224–57.

well. Within the *adiaphora*, there can be discerned the "absolute indifferents," which have no ethical significance; and the indifferents which are not constitutive of virtue but which can be used well or badly. Such *adiaphora* or indifferents are preferred things, such as health and property. The similarity to Cynic ethics can be seen here in that wealth is external to virtue. The Stoics, however, did not necessarily avoid wealth as an impediment to virtue. While the wise person always chooses the good or virtuous, that person also selects among preferred things. Wealth and poverty are both indifferent, but wealth is preferred to poverty. To quote Long,

> Wealth accords with Nature in the sense that a rational being is naturally predisposed to prefer wealth to poverty if it is open to him to select either of these. Wealth is a state which is objectively preferable to poverty, but wealth is not something which it is the special function of a rational being to possess [in contrast to virtue]. The value of wealth is relative to poverty, but wealth has no value relative to virtue. Morally speaking, wealth and poverty are indifferent; for it makes no difference to a man's moral worth (or welfare) whether he is rich or poor.[25]

A wise person might use poverty wisely and a foolish person might use wealth foolishly, but given the choice, the wise person will select wealth over poverty as long as it does not conflict with reason, or life *kata phusin*, and hence impinge on virtue. Seneca, who gives a classical expression of the Stoic notion of wealth as a preferred *adiaphora* in his *De vita beata*, claims that he does not care if he is in a sumptuous palace or under a bridge with beggars—but he prefers the palace, a nice toga, and a comfortable mattress (*De vita beata* 25.1–3). This is a considerably different teaching on wealth than the Cynic views examined above.[26]

As we noted above, Cynic and Stoic ideas about wealth were not always clearly distinguished in the writings of the moral philosophers.[27] Epictetus, who shows the strong influence of Cynicism on Stoic moral

---

[25]Long, *Hellenistic Philosophy*, 192–93. For a recent philosophical analysis of the Stoic concept of *adiaphora*, see Nicholas P. White, "Stoic Values," *The Monist* 73 (1990) 42–58.

[26]See Ps.-Crates 29 (Malherbe, *Cynic Epistles*, 78–79), which makes the distinction between being a Cynic and being "indifferent to everything."

[27]See Betz, "Jesus and the Cynics," 472–5, on Epictetus as a Cynic-Stoic; and Philo, who used Cynic ideas but was certainly never considered a Cynic.

teaching during our period of study, is a case in point.[28] The philosophical basis of Epictetus's attitude toward wealth is essentially the same as Seneca's.[29] Wealth is an *adiaphora*, external to virtue.[30] But the use (χρῆσις, *chrēsis*) that one makes of material things such as wealth is not a matter of indifference.[31] Furthermore, Epictetus frequently chides those who can recite the philosophical creed of what is good, bad, and indifferent, but lack the training (ἄσκησις, *askēsis*) to put this idea into practice.[32] Unlike Seneca, he tried to live with as few attachments and possessions as possible and preached against the burdens of wealth as impediments to a life according to nature.[33] In his diatribes, which were directed toward aristocratic students and visitors, Epictetus regularly attacks the triad of health, wealth, and fame—"we are anxious about our wretched body, about our trifling estate, about what Caesar will think" (Arr. *Epict. Diss.* 2.13.11).[34]

The example of Seneca points us to the two sides of the Stoic attitude toward wealth. One the one hand, the concept of the *adiaphora* fits elegantly into the complete Stoic system describing human nature and psychology, the structure of the universe, and the path to happiness. On

---

[28]On the true Cynic, see Arr. *Epict. Diss.* 3.22; and Margarethe Billerbeck, *Epiktet vom Kynismus*, Philosophia Antiqua 34 (Leiden: E. J. Brill, 1978) 1–4; on the true Stoic, see 2.9.19–22; 2.19.19–26. Epictetus's teachings have been recorded in the lecture notes (ὑπομνήματα) of his student Arrian. See P. A. Brunt, "From Epictetus to Arrian," *Athenaeum* 55 (1977): 19–48, on the social setting of Epictetus's school and the influence Epictetus had on Arrian's later political and literary career.

[29]Epictetus argures that happiness comes from regarding one's own good and advantage (τὸ ἀγαθὸν τὸ αὑτοῦ καὶ συμφέρον) in those things that are under one's control. Placing happiness in externals results in slavery to things and others (Arr. *Epict. Diss.* 4.7.9–11). The goal of detachment or freedom from externals allows one to be wealthy: "Now if you regard yourself as a thing detached [ἀπόλυτον], it is natural [κατὰ φύσιν] for you to live to old age, to be rich [πλουτεῖν], to enjoy health" (2.5.25).

[30]See Arr. *Epict. Diss.* 1.30; 2.6; 2.13.10–11; 2.19.13.

[31]See Arr. *Epict. Diss.* 2.5.1, 6–7.

[32]See esp. Arr. *Epict. Diss.* 2.19.13, 15–16, 19–22. An interesting note to this diatribe is Epictetus's characterization of "Jews," by whom he probably means Christians (note "baptists," 2.19.21), as people who practice what they believe. See also 4.7.6 on the attitude of "Galileans" toward possessions.

[33]Arr. *Epict. Ench.* 33.7.

[34]See Arr. *Epict. Diss.* 2.6.25; 2.19.32; 2.24.21–29; 3.14.11–14; 3.22.26–32; 4.1.60; 4.6.4, 22–24; 4.7.22–24; 4.7.37; *Ench.* 44.

the other hand, the Stoic attitude toward wealth fit the lifestyle of the fabulously wealthy Seneca quite well.[35] Some time after our period, Clement of Alexandria, in his *Quis dives salvetur?*, used the concept of *adiaphora* to allegorize Mark 10:17–31 and remove the threat to wealthy Christians of actually having to sell all their possessions. A modern conception of human nature, which is a considerably different view from the Stoic conception of nature as reason, makes it difficult for us to view the Stoic attitude toward wealth without a strong hermeneutic of suspicion.

Modern suspicion that Stoic philosophy was a convenient ideology for the wealthy finds support in ancient descriptions of the Stoics. Perceptions of Stoic ideas of *adiaphora* and wealth are as important as the theory of *oikeiōsis* for understanding attitudes toward wealth in the Greco-Roman world. Plutarch, a Platonist who wielded a sharp pen against other philosophical schools, attacked the Stoic notion of *adiaphora* as providing a double standard for Stoics to continue to enjoy those things which they deemed indifferent to virtue (*Mor.* 1063C–1064F).[36] The Stoics, of course, were not the only ones who were attacked. Hypocritical Cynics were a favorite target of Lucian's (*Per.* 11–13). In *The Runaways*, when Kantharos, the slave-turned-Cynic-philosopher, is discovered to have a purse of gold, Heracles remarks that while he claimed to be a Cynic, his gold shows him to be in fact a Chrysippean, or Stoic (*Fug.* 31). Lucian draws the caricature of the Cynic as abusive and poor and the Stoic as rapacious and wealthy in greater detail in *Lives for Sale* (*Bion* 7–11, 20–25).[37] Such polemical accounts of Stoics and Cynics show us that the teachings of the two philosophies on wealth, divorced from their systematic rationale, had become the basis of

---

[35]See Miriam T. Griffin, *Seneca: A Philosopher in Politics* (Oxford: Clarendon, 1976) 286–314 ("Seneca *Praedives*"); John Ferguson, "Seneca the Man," in *Neronians and Flavians: Silver Latin I*, ed. D. R. Dudley (London and Boston: Routledge & Kegan Paul, 1972) 12–14; and John M. Rist, "Seneca and Stoic Orthodoxy," *ANRW* 2/36/3 (1989): 1994–95.

[36]Plutarch's sharpest critique of Stoicism may be found in *De communibus notitiis adversus Stoicos* (*Mor.* 1058E–1086B) and *De Stoicorum repugnantiis* (*Mor.* 1033A–1057B). Jackson P. Hershbell, "Plutarch and Stoicism," *ANRW* 2/36/5 (1992): 3336–52, discusses the ambiguous attitude of Plutarch towards the Stoics.

[37]See Bompaire, *Lucien écrivain*, 182–91, 350–61, 485–91; Dudley, *Cynicism*, 144–45; and Malherbe, *Cynic Epistles* 1, on Lucian and the Cynics.

caricature. The Cynics were described as sullen, dirty, and abusive beggars while the Stoics were wealthy hypocrites whose hairsplitting rationalizations allowed them to enjoy the so-called "indifferents."

True Wealth in Jewish and Christian Literature

A legitimate concern at this point might be that we have strayed into the arcane world of philosophical discussion, a world beloved by academics but totally separate from the social world of the early Christians. But the broad influence of Stoic and Cynic moral philosophy on Greco-Roman culture can be seen in ancient Jewish and Christian literature closer to John's Apocalypse than are the essays of Seneca and Epictetus. The literary convention of "true wealth" as something moral, spiritual, heavenly—anything but actual gold, silver, and jewels—demonstrates this influence. When Christ says that the Smyrnans, despite their poverty, are actually rich, his words echo this *topos* (Rev 2:9; see Matt 6:19–21; Luke 12:33–34). The story of the Euboean hunters in Dio's seventh *Oration* and the story of Micyllus in Lucian's *The Cock* are illustrations of this philosophical convention with particularly strong Cynic themes, for in both these instances "true wealth" is found in actual poverty.[38] But, like the Stoic concept of the *adiaphora*, the idea of "true wealth" as moral or spiritual also functioned as an ideology for the wealthy.[39]

Philo's discussion of a Stoic paradox in "Every Good Person is Free" (*Quod omnis probus liber sit*) contains several parallels to the message to the Smyrnans in Revelation. Philo, like Christ in Revelation, calls the poor "wealthy" and the rich "poor" and extols the virtue of endurance (ὑπομονή, *hypomonē*) in the face of the trials of fortune. Philo takes the Stoic position that slavery and freedom are matters of the soul as well as the body. Thus freedom is freedom from vice and wealth is wealth in virtue (3.17–18 [448]). Wealth brings status but carries encumbrances for the soul such as "love of money or reputation and pleasure" (3.21 [448]).

---

[38]See Luc. *Gall.* 9, 13–14, 21–27, 29–33; cf. Sir 31:1–11. For a comparison of this story to the parable of Lazarus and Dives, see Hock, "Lazarus and Micyllus," who argues that the moral point is not wealth and poverty per se but the virtue and vice associated with each social condition.

[39]See Horace *Eps.* 1.1.106–107; 1.10.39–41; Plut. *De cup. div., Mor.* 523C–528B; *De vit. aer. ali., Mor.* 827E–832A; Edward O'Neil, "De cupidatate divitiarum (Moralia 523C–528B)" in *Plutarch's Ethical Writings and Early Christian Literature*, SCHNT 4, ed. H. D. Betz (Leiden: E. J. Brill, 1978) 289–362; and Grassl, *Sozialökonomische Vorstellungen*, 161–66.

The good person has no such encumbrances; he or she is truly free because his or her soul is truly free. Philo discusses the Essenes as an example of virtuous people who have found true wealth and freedom by giving up their possessions (12.75–91 [457]); they are considered "exceedingly rich [πλουσώτατοι], because they judge frugality with contentment to be, as indeed it is, an abundance of wealth" (12.77[457]). Philo strikes a Cynic pose when he claims that "exemption from slavery belongs to him who takes no thought not only of death but also of poverty, disrepute and pain" (4.23 [449]). Philo's real concern, however, is the slavery of the soul; his depiction of the trials of poverty and manual labor for the freeborn poor belies his Cynic pose and call to endurance (6.34 [450]). The virtuous person, according to Philo in "Every Good Person is Free," can be wealthy as long as their soul is free and unencumbered by his or her possessions. This is the classic Stoic position.

Both endurance and true wealth are prominent in the *Testament of Job*, a first century CE revision of the biblical story of Job (see *hypomonē*, *T. Job* 1:3).[40] In the *Testament of Job*, Job (at that time "Jobab") receives instructions from the Lord to destroy a temple, thereby risking the wrath of Satan. Job is told that Satan will afflict him and take all of his possessions, which were extensive. If he endures these afflictions, the Lord will restore his fortunes and he will receive a "double payment" (διπλάσιον) in this life and resurrection after death (*T. Job* 4:4–9).[41] The promise of this "double payment" helps Job to endure patiently the tremendous afflictions and sufferings brought upon him and his family by Satan. It becomes clear that the reward for his endurance is not just twice

---

[40]On matters of introduction see John J. Collins, "Testaments," *JWSTP*, 349–54; and Russell P. Spittler, "The Testament of Job: Research and Interpretation," in *Studies on the Testament of Job*, SNTSMS 66, ed. Michael A. Knibb and Pieter W. van der Horst, (Cambridge: Cambridge University Press, 1989) 7–32. Cees Haas, "Job's Perseverance in the Testament of Job," in *Studies on the Testament of Job*, 117–54, shows the Hellenistic Jewish provenance of the different terms for perseverance in the *Testament of Job*. All Greek and English quotations of *T. Job* are from *The Testament of Job according to the SV Text*, SBLTT 5, SBL Pseudepigrapha Series 4, ed. Robert A. Kraft et al. (Missoula MT: Scholars Press, 1974).

[41]Susan R. Garrett, "The God of This World and the Affliction of Paul: 2 Cor 4:1–12" in *Greeks, Romans, and Christians: Essays in Honor of Abraham J. Malherbe*, ed. D. L. Balch, E. Ferguson and W. A. Meeks (Minneapolis: Fortress, 1990) 112, points out that this promise diminishes the pathos of the canonical story.

as much wealth but a different sort of wealth, a "great treasure" (μεγάλος πλοῦτος, 26:3) from heaven. The "heavenly" wealth that Job looks forward to receiving will endure when all earthly things have faded or passed away (33:4–5).[42] In the *Testament of Job*, almost all luxury items are used in the description of Job's wife, Sitidos, rather than in connection with Job.[43] Job does receive extensive earthly reward after his afflictions. The description of Job's wealth at the end of the *Testament* (44:1–45:3; 53:1–5) as well as the list of his previous possessions (8:1–2; chs. 9–13; 15:7–9) focus on social justice and charity for the poor. This strong emphasis on almsgiving and acts of charity in the *Testament of Job* is absent from Revelation, as I noted in the previous chapter.

The Apocalypse was likely written in conscious dialogue with the Pauline epistolary tradition and to an audience with some knowledge of Paul or his letters. Paul's argument in Rom 1:18–2:26 shows the influence of Stoic concepts such as the ability to know God through the natural order and the necessity therefore to live according to nature.[44] In Gal 2:6, Paul writes that the status of the Jerusalem leaders "makes no difference" (οὐδέν μοι διαφέρει) to him because God shows no partiality. This has been taken as a reference to the Stoic notion of *adiaphora*.[45] But in discussions of wealth and poverty, Paul shows affinity with Cynic rather than Stoic philosophy. In 2 Cor 6:8–10, Paul uses antithesis to describe the difference between his outward appearance and

---

[42]See also *T. Job* 36:4–5; Job's vision of his seven children enthroned in heaven (40:5) and the "inheritance" he gives to his three daughters, golden cords which turn their minds to heavenly things (46:1–50:3).

[43]On the fundamentally negative view of females here, see Susan R. Garrett, "The 'Weaker Sex' in the *Testament of Job*," *JBL* 112 (1993): 55–70.

[44]In addition to the standard commentaries on Romans, see John W. Martens, "Romans 2.14–16: A Stoic Reading," *NTS* 40 (1994): 55–67; and esp. Stanley K. Stowers, *A Rereading of Romans* (New Haven CT: Yale University Press, 1994), who argues that Romans must be read entirely from the perspective of the Greco-Roman context of its original audience.

[45]The proposal originally made by H. D. Betz (*Galatians: A Commentary on Paul's Letter to the Churches in Galatia*, Hermeneia [Philadelphia: Fortress Press, 1979] 94) has been revised, with additional evidence, by James L. Jaquette, "Paul, Epictetus, and Others on Indifference to Status," *CBQ* 56 (1994): 68–80. See also "Life and Death, *adiaphora*, and Paul's Rhetorical Strategy," *NovT* 38 (1996): 30–54, in which Jaquette discusses Paul's use of the *topos* of life and death as *adiaphora* in Phil 1:21–26; 1 Thess 5:10; Rom 8:31–39; and Rom 14:7–9.

inner disposition. He describes himself as dying yet alive, sorrowful yet rejoicing, "poor, yet making many rich; as having nothing, and yet possessing everything." Paul's self-characterization parallels his description of Christ: "though he was rich, yet for your sakes he became poor, so that by his poverty you might become rich" (2 Cor 8:9). In these two passages from 2 Corinthians, Paul trades heavily on the idea of true, "heavenly" wealth, a theme we identified in the *Testament of Job* and can see developed in early Christian texts such as 1 Pet 1:3–21.[46] He also expresses the Cynic attitude toward wealth and poverty.[47] The Stoic notion of *adiaphora* sees wealth as indifferent to virtue; Gal 2:6 expresses this well with regard to status. But in 2 Corinthians, poverty, for both Christ and Paul, is a means to the end of sharing with the churches the "treasure in clay jars" (2 Cor 4:7) so that they might have access to the true, spiritual "wealth" of salvation.

These three examples, Philo, the *Testament of Job*, and Paul, help place the moral exhortation on wealth in Revelation 2–3 in context. They show that moral philosophy influenced ancient Jewish and Christian discussion of wealth and poverty and they sharpen the distinction between the Cynic and Stoic attitudes toward wealth. Cynic philosophy propounded freedom from wealth, possessions, and social convention. Stoic philosophy emphasized freedom from reliance on *adiaphora*, such as wealth, as a way to happiness rather than seeking out poverty as a means to virtue and happiness. The praise of the Smyrnans's poverty by the gold-clad Christ and the denigration of the Laodicean's reliance on wealth evokes the image of the Stoic philosopher.[48] Christ's golden attire, as he

---

[46]I will treat 1 Peter in more detail in chap. 7. The unlikely idea that Jesus was in fact wealthy and raised in an upper-class setting, set forth by G. W. Buchanan, "Jesus and the Upper Class," *NovT* 7 (1964–1965): 195–209, which is revived and labeled "attractive" by Schmidt, *Hostility to Wealth*, 119–20, is not entertained here.

[47]See Ps.-Crates 7 (Malherbe *Cynic Epistles* 58–59); Victor P. Furnish, *II Corinthians*, AB 32A (New York: Doubleday, 1984) 347–48; John J. Fitzgerald, *Cracks in an Earthen Vessel: An Examination of the Catalogues of Hardships in the Corinthian Correspondence*, SBLDS 99 (Atlanta: Scholars Press, 1988) 199–201.

[48]In addition to philosophical discourse on wealth and poverty, the messages to Smyrna and Laodicea in Revelation call to mind the motif of the reversal of fortunes. Aristotle, in the *Poetics*, considers change (μεταβολή) of fortune essential to the plot (μῦθος) of tragedy. A complex (πεπλεγμένος) plot involves reversal (περιπέτεια) or transformation (μετάβασις) of fortune; see *Poet.*

appears to John on Patmos and delivers the messages to the seven churches in Asia, places him at odds with Cynic teaching on wealth and possessions. The associations evoked by Christ's Stoic philosophical demeanor add considerable luster to heaven's wealth in Revelation. This is not just any gold that Christ flashes to John on Patmos but true wealth in the best philosophical tradition. Heaven's wealth acquires status along with its luster. The association of status with heaven's wealth is developed further in the subsequent visions in the Apocalypse so that it becomes the dominant ideology in the polemic against Babylon/Rome.

Courts, Thrones, and Golden Crowns

The messages to Smyrna and Laodicea are bracketed by two displays of God's wealth, the vision of Christ on Patmos (Rev 1:12–16) and the tremendous display of gold and jewels in John's first vision of the heavenly throne room (Rev 4:2–11). As we saw in chapter 2, these two visions, crafted from the Hebrew scriptures, have a much higher concentration of wealth motifs than John's biblical sources. An ancient Christian with no knowledge of the Hebrew Bible might still have found the results of John's intertextual raiding recognizable, however, since these two visions of heavenly wealth have a number of parallels in the Greco-Roman epiphany tradition and in descriptions of Hellenistic and Roman court ceremony. Unlike the visions of the "Human One" in the Jewish tradition, the physical characteristics of the gods were usually

---

7.12; 10.1–11.3. Luke 16:19–31 could have been known to the audiences of Revelation; see Ronald F. Hock, "Lazarus and Micyllus: Greco-Roman Backgrounds to Luke 16:19–31," *JBL* 106 (1987): 447–63; and Richard Bauckham, "The Rich Man and Lazarus: The Parable and the Parallels," *NTS* 37 (1991): 225–46. Other reversal stories include Lucian's *Cataplus;* the Egyptian story of Setme and Si-Osiris; and the story of the rich tax collector Bar Ma'yan and the poor Torah scholar of Ashkelon in *y. Sanh.* 23c; *y. Sanh.* 6.6; *y. Hag.* 2.2; *y. Hag.* 77d. The moral of each of these stories is that the wealthy will be punished after death for the sins committed in this life. The stories do not condemn wealth per se but the sins committed by the wealthy, especially their lack of charity on behalf of the poor. The messages to Smyrna and Laodicea do not include any of the formal narrative features of these stories, such as the revelation of the different fates of the rich and poor after their death. The motif of the reversal of fortunes offers more of a contrast than comparison for the messages to Smyrna and Laodicea, which focus on the true wealth or poverty of these churches in the present.

described in Greco-Roman epiphanies.[49] The Greek and Roman gods did not, of course, always look like Christ in Revelation. Often, the god was disguised as a mortal. This is the case, for instance, with Athena throughout the *Odyssey* or in the well-known story of Zeus and Hermes' visit to Baucis and Philemon (Ov. *Met.* 8.611–725; cf. Acts 14:10–12). Gods might appear as superhuman figures, monsters, or animals.[50] The appearance of Aphrodite, Demeter and Dionysus moved mortals to describe the beauty of the god.[51]

Wealth motifs appeared in Greco-Roman epiphany accounts, but they were not a regular feature. The epiphanies of Asclepius in Aelius Aristides' *Sacred Tales*, for instance, do not include any wealth motifs.[52] The gold in the epiphany of Christ on Patmos is not without precedent in the Greco-Roman tradition but it is unusual. The brightness of Christ as described in Rev 1:12–16 connects this vision most strongly with Greco-Roman epiphanies, in particular descriptions of Apollo, the god of prophecy.[53] In typical literary epiphanies, Apollo gleamed with golden hair and a silver bow; his appearance brought about storms and earthquakes and provoked fear and helpless amazement among mortals.[54] In the Homeric *Hymn to Apollo*, Delos is laden with gold because Zeus and Leto chose the island for the birth of Apollo (3.135–40). These parallels between Christ and Apollo are all the more intriguing because of other parallels with Apollo traditions in Revelation.[55] John's reaction to Christ's appearance, falling as though dead, is also typical of Greco-Roman

---

[49]See the discussion in F. Pfister, "Epiphanie," *PWSup* 277–323.

[50]See Hdt. 8.38; Dion. Hal. 6.13; Plut *Aem. Paul.* 25; Plut *Arat.* 32; *POxy.* 1331; Ap. Rhod. *Argon.* 3.1194–1224; 4.1551, 1591, 1602–18.

[51]See *Hymn. Hom. Dem.* 2.188–90, 275; *Hymn. Hom. Ven.* 5.64–65, 81–90; Hdt. 1.60; Eur. *Bacch.* 453; Virg. *Aen.* 2.589–93; 8.608; Ael. Aris. *ST* 2.4.

[52]See Ael. Aris. *ST* 1.71; 2.18, 32; 3.21; 4.50.

[53]See *Hymn. Hom. Ap.* 3.440–5; *Hymn. Hom. Ven.* 5.64–65, 81-90; Virg. *Aen.* 2.589–93; 8.608. The word ὄψις (Rev 1:16) was also used for epiphany visions; see Pfister, "Epiphanie," col. 280.

[54]See *Hymn. Hom. Ap.* 3.133–40; 4.440–45; Ap. Rhod. *Argon.* 2.669–85; 4.1701–10 (here the bow is gold rather than silver); *Hymn. Hom.* (to Helios) 31.7–14; Pausanius 1.17.1.

[55]See Allen Kerkeslager, "Apollo, Greco-Roman Prophecy, and the Rider on the White Horse in Rev 6:2," *JBL* 112 (1993): 116–21; and Yarbro Collins, *Combat Myth.*

epiphanies, which were generally marked by amazement, fear, and dread, and sometimes joy.[56]

Gods in antiquity looked like kings, since royal ideology was projected onto the cult, and rulers tried to look like the gods as much as possible. John's visions of Christ and of the heavenly throne room (Rev 1:12–16; 4:2–11) would likely have suggested the ceremony of Hellenistic monarchs and the Roman imperial court to the audience of the Apocalypse, especially when heard in conjunction with the prominent kingship motifs in Revelation (1:5–6, 9; 5:10; 11:15–17, 12:10, 15:3).[57] The display of gold was an important part of Hellenistic and Roman ceremony as a symbol of royal ideology, as it was in Jewish and Persian ritual.[58] God sits on a jeweled and golden throne in Revelation just as Hellenistic and Roman rulers sat under golden canopies and covered their palaces with gold; Christ wears a golden sash and Nero paraded through the streets of Rome in a golden cape.[59] The entourage or court around the

---

[56]Astonishment: Od. 1.323; Od. 19.36; Il. 3.398; *Hymn. Hom. Ven.* 5.64-65; *Hymn. Hom. Bacch.* 7.34-42; Plut. *Arat.* 32; *Them.* 30; Hdt. 8.37; Vir. *Aen.* 3.173; Luke 24:41; Luc. *Luc.* 54; Apul. *Met.* 11.13–14; Mark 1:27; Luke 4:36. Fear or dread: Hom. *Il.* 20.130ff; 24.170; *Od.* 16.178f; 24.533; Ap. Rhod. *Argon.* 4.1602–18; Vir. *Aen.* 4.279–82; Hdt. 8.37–8; Matt 16:5; 28:4; Luke 1:2, 29. Joy: *Hymn. Hom.* 33.16-17 (Dioscuri); Ap. Rhod. *Argon.* 1.1329; 4.1591. Silence: *Od.* 19.42; Eur. *Bacch.* 1084; *Aen* 4.279; Apul. Met. 11.14; Luke 1:20; Ael. Aris. *ST* 2.33.

[57]See Aune, "Roman Imperial Court," 5–26. Aune's thesis is that the resemblance of the ceremonies in Revelation and the Roman court must be explained by the imperial court being understood as a parody of the heavenly court. While Aune's research and parallels are illuminating, his exegesis summarizes Rev 4–5 from the author's perspective rather than providing critical insights into how the text would have been heard by the audience. John might have hoped to cast the Roman imperial court as a parody of God's court, but Rev 4–5 borrows imperial ideology and motifs so that in effect God's court parodies Caesar's.

[58]See chap. 2; Newsom, "The Development of *1 Enoch* 6-19"; Exodus 25–31; and 1 Kings 6–10.

[59]For the use of gold in Hellenistic or Roman ceremony, see Plut. *Alex.* 37; Diod. Sic. 17.66; Arr. *Herod.* 8.7.2; Plut. *Dem.* 41.4-5; *De frat. amor.* (Mor. 488D); Jos. *Ant.* 3 §§179–87; 6 §372; 7 §4; 9 §149, 151; 19 §§343–46; Suet. *Dom.* 4.4; Dio Cass. 44.11.2; Gregory M. Stevenson, "Conceptual Background to Golden Crown Imagery in the Apocalypse of John (4:4, 10; 14:14)" *JBL* 114 (1995): 259–60. See Suet. *Ner.* 31.1–2 on Nero's "Golden House" and *Ner.* 25, which describes Nero riding through Rome in a golden cape. Aune, "Roman Imperial Court," cites Tac. *Ann.* 12.51 that Claudius is reported to have appeared in a golden robe as well. The citation should be *Ann.* 12.56; Agrippina, not

ruler functioned as part of this royal ideology. In Revelation, the entourage includes the 24 elders, who sit on their own 24 thrones around the throne of God (Rev 4:4).[60] The golden crowns (στέφανοι χρύσοι) of the 24 elders, which have no parallel in apocalyptic literature, have been interpreted as symbols of royalty or victory.[61] It was a widespread practice in the Roman empire for emperors to receive golden crowns from cities or as part of a triumph.[62] The act of throwing down the crowns by the elders (Rev 4:10) ties this vision of the heavenly throne room in Revelation to Hellenistic and Roman court ceremony.[63]

The audience of Revelation, however, would probably have not had any contact with the imperial court itself and might not have been aware of this common practice of doffing crowns to rulers and benefactors.[64] The honorific function of golden crowns, well attested in the inscriptions, is a more likely point of comparison for the elders' crowns in Rev 4:4 and 4:10. A review of inscriptions from Asia reveals a number of refer-

---

Claudius, wears "a Greek mantle of cloth of gold" (*chlamyde aurata*).

[60]See the discussion in chap. 2.

[61]For royalty see Ramsay, *Letters*, 58; Caird, 194; for victory, Swete, 74, on Rev 4:10; Charles 2:20 on Rev 14:14. The breadth of the significance of crowns, wreaths, and diadems in antiquity has been recently explored by Stevenson, "Golden Crown Imagery," 257–72 (see also Aune, 172–75). Stevenson shows how crowns and wreaths could have symbolized victory, royalty, divine glory, and honor. According to Stevenson, 259, the diadem (διάδημα), not the crown or wreath (στέφανος), was a symbol of royalty.

[62]Aune, "Roman Imperial Court" 12; Fergus Millar, *The Emperor in the Roman World, 31 BC–AD 337* (Ithaca NY: Cornell University Press, 1977) 140–43; Theodor Klauser, "Aurum Coronarium," *Gesammelte Arbeiten zur Liturgiegeschichte, Kirchengeschichte, und christlichen Archäologie*, ed. E. Dassman, JAC Ergänsungsband 3 (Münster: Aschendorffsche, 1974) 292–309; Arr. *Anab.* 7.23; *Herod.* 8.7.2; Jos. *Ant.* 14 §§304–23; Livy 37.46.4; 38.37.4; 39.7.1; Plut. *Aem.* 34.5; Pliny *HN* 33.16; Dio Cass. 44.11.22; 45.6.5; cf. Ael. Aris. *ST* 1.41 on "the sort [of crown] men particularly bring to Asclepius."

[63]See Aune, "Rome Imperial Court," 12–13; and Stevenson, "Golden Crown Imagery," 268–71.

[64]Aune's five points explaining "how a provincial resident of the eastern Mediterranean world could possibly know enough about the ceremonial of the imperial court to use it as a model for the ceremonial of the heavenly throne room" ("Roman Imperial Court," 6) do not adequately address this point. Most significantly, no Roman emperor visited Asia in the first century CE; see S. R. F. Price, *Rituals and Power: The Roman imperial cult in Asia Minor* (Cambridge: Cambridge University Press, 1984) 2.

ences to golden crowns.[65] Crowns were often awarded to honor a wealthy patron who had given a building or performed some other service for the city.[66] A civic group, such as the *dēmos* (δῆμος), the *boulē* (βουλή), or the association of Roman businessmen (οἱ πραγματευόμενοι παρ' ἡμῖν Ῥομαῖοι) would grant a golden crown to this person in recognition of the gift. The honoree need not be a senator or equestrian, however.[67] The awarding of a golden crown was also a common decoration, or *donum*, in the Roman army. Centurions and lower ranks, as well as consuls and equestrians, could receive the golden crown (*corona aurea*).[68]

These golden crown inscriptions offer more than a context for reading Rev 4:2–11. They also point to the complicated relation of wealth and status in antiquity. Gold was the most precious metal and the basic standard of wealth and currency, and yet the golden crown was the lowest of the crowns granted as a *donum* in the Roman army. The *corona aurea* served as a catchall decoration for valor. A *corona civica*, generally made of oak and sometimes referred to as the "oaken crown," was awarded for saving the life of a Roman citizen and holding the ground in battle for a day. This crown carried such status that a simple private wearing one was entitled to sit with the senators at the games.[69] The wreath made of the most precious material, gold, was not the wreath that conferred the highest status. Wealth was a precious commodity in ancient society, but status was even more precious, as we will see in the next section.

---

[65]See *IG Rom* 4, nos. 247, 254, 258, 292, 293, 295, 905, 913, 916, 917, 918, 1087, 1108, 1110; *CIG* 3067; 3068; 3595; add. 3641b; add 3831 a[14]; add 3847 p; 3971; 4040 II; E. L. Hicks, ed., *The Collection of Ancient Greek Inscriptions in the British Museum*, Part 3: *Priene, Iasous, and Ephesos* (Oxford: Clarendon, 1890) 545; Pliny *HN* 33.38 [11]; Arr. *Epict. Diss.* 1.19.29.

[66]So also Stevenson, "Crown Imagery," 265, who finds the wreath has its "clearest expression as a symbol of honor within the contexts of military awards and benefactor relationships."

[67]A doctor was honored at Cos for his excellence (ἀρετή), skill (τέχνη), and kindness (εὔνοια, *IG Rom* 4.1108); Stratonicea honored a war hero (*IG Rom* 4.254).

[68]See Valerie A. Maxfield, *The Military Decorations of the Roman Army* (Berkeley and Los Angeles: University of California Press, 1981) 81.

[69]Ibid., 70.

Merchants and Commerce

The epiphany of Christ on Patmos and the visions of the heavenly throne room present God's wealth to the audience of the Apocalypse in a strongly positive light. These visions of heaven's wealth provide the narrative context for the polemic against Babylon in Revelation 17–18. We have already seen that the description of Babylon in Revelation does not agree with the portrayal of that city by the prophets Isaiah, Jeremiah, and Ezekiel, from whom John drew much of his imagery. I discussed in chapter 2 how John drew on oracles from the Hebrew Bible directed against both Babylon and Tyre to construct the Babylon/Rome of Revelation. This separates the wealth of heaven from the wealth of Babylon/Rome, casting the latter as lower-status wealth. By using the lament and woes over Tyre, John cast his Babylon as a commercial power, trading with merchants and sailors, lavishing luxuries on client kings. This characterization would have been heard as negative in the ancient Roman empire, particularly in the Greek East. Merchants of all sorts were held in low esteem and wealthy merchants did not receive the high status their riches might suggest.[70] Agriculture and investment in land, not trade and shipping, were the means to both wealth and status, whereas commerce was not. This attitude was widespread in the Roman world and informs our understanding of how the polemic against Babylon/Rome in Revelation 17–18 would have been heard. I will focus here on three examples of this attitude: the classic philosophical statement of "proper" occupations by Cicero; the famous satire of wealthy freedmen by Petronius; and a lengthy inscription from Ephesus, written very close to the time of the Apocalypse.

Cicero's De officiis

A classic expression of ancient aristocratic disdain for commerce is Cicero's *De officiis* 1.150–151, which discusses the status of a variety of occupations according to the "accepted view."[71] Cicero describes a social

---

[70]See Finley, *Ancient Economy*, 78–89, 95–122; MacMullen, *Romans Social Relations*, 5–22, 98–126; Ste. Croix, *Class Struggle in the Ancient Greek World*, 120–33, 270–74; H. Pleket, "Urban elites and business in the Greek part of the Roman Empire" in *Trade in the Ancient Economy*, ed. P. Garnsey, K. Hopkins, and C. R. Whittaker (Berkeley: University of California Press, 1983) 131–44.

[71]Cicero works within the Stoic tradition of appropriate actions (*officia*, τὸ

and moral ideal that did not necessarily fit with his own and his colleagues' financial practices.[72] But it is the ideal, not the practice, that I am concerned with, and how such philosophical ideals would have affected the perceptions of status among the early Christians in Asia Minor. Cicero writes that those who buy from merchants (*mercatores*) in order to retail immediately are vulgar (*sordidi*), because their profits depend on lying about their merchandise (*De off.* 1.150).[73] Cicero does not name this group; these merchants suggest modern arbitragers or entrepreneurs. Where the modern capitalist sees initiative, the ancient Roman sees *vanitas*. Retail entrepreneurship is grouped with other "sordid" occupations: tax collecting; manual labor; and service industries catering to pleasures.[74] Trade (*mercatura*) on a small scale is also vulgar (*sordida*); Cicero is quite clear about the status of petty merchants and small shopkeepers (*De off.* 1.151). He offers qualified praise for large scale trade of global proportions, if it is performed without misrepresentation (*sine vanitate*). But large-scale trade is not proper for a "gentleman" for any length of time. The trader should retire from business as soon as a fortune (*quaestus*) has been made and invest all his money into a country estate.[75] Cicero praises agriculture as the most liberal occupation of all for a "gentleman."[76] Cicero's strong condemnation of entrepeneur-

---

καθήκοντα), most likely from an earlier treatise by Panaetius, but the point of this source is debated; see P. A. Brunt, "Aspects of the Social Thought of Dio Chrysostom and of the Stoics," *Proceedings of the Cambridge Philological Society* n.s. 19 (1973): 9–34.

[72]The issue was moneylenders or *faeneratores*, condemned in *De off.* 1.150 as "undesirable" but used by Cicero on occasion; several of Cicero's peers participated in moneylending. See the discussion in chap. 1; Susan Treggiari, *Roman Freedmen During the Late Republic* (Oxford: Clarendon Press, 1969) 88–89; and Brunt, "Aspects of the Social Thought of Dio Chrysostom," 30–34.

[73]See also MacMullen, *Roman Social Relations*, 115. The attitude is paralleled by Ben Sira when discussing merchants (ἔμπορος) and traders (κάπηλος); see Sir 26:29; 27:2; 37:11; 42:5.

[74]On ancient attitudes towards manual labor, see Ronald F. Hock, *The Social Context of Paul's Ministry: Tentmaking and Apostleship* (Philadelphia: Fortress Press, 1980) 35–37.

[75]*Si satiata quaestu vel contenta potius, ut saepe ex alto in portum, ex ipso portu se in agros possessionesque contulit, videtur iure optimo posse laudari.* The subject of this clause is not defined precisely but probably refers to *negotiatores* rather than *mercatores*, since he mentions seaborne commerce.

[76]*Omnium autem rerum, ex quibus aliquid acquiritur, nihil est agri cultura*

ism and petty trade, coupled with his ringing endorsement of agriculture, seriously undercuts the praise he offers for large-scale trade. While equestrians and perhaps even senators in Rome might have sought to make profits through commercial ventures, using clients and freedmen as their agents, the taint of *sordidus*— disreputable, degrading, mean—was firmly attached to commerce and merchants in the Roman empire.

Trimalchio: "Concupivi negotiari"

The *Cena Trimalchionis*, or dinner party of Trimalchio, in Petronius's *Satyricon* brings the attitudes toward trade expressed in Cicero's *De officiis* 100 years forward to the court of Nero. The literary complexities of the *Satyricon* are notorious.[77] This has not prevented social historians from plumbing the text with questions about social mobility, the careers of freedmen, and attitudes toward wealth. Trimalchio has been taken as "typical" of any number of positions.[78] The satirical nature of the *Satyricon* has been called into question in that Petronius does not really

---

melius, nihil uberius, nihil dulcius, nihil homine libero dignius. The sentiment was universal among the ancient aristocracy. For the praise of agriculture and the leisure (σχολή, *otium*) of owning land, see also *De off.* 1.92 and Xen. *Oec.* 6.8–9; Columella, *Rust.* 1.*praef.*20; Hor. *Sat.* 2.6.1–15.

[77]Kenneth Rose, "Time and Place in the Satyricon," TAPA 93 (1962) 402–409 discusses these basic narrative issues. On problems of language, grammar and latinity, see Peter George, "Style and Character in the Satyricon," *Arion* 5 (1966): 336–58; J. P. Sullivan, "On Translating Petronius," in *Neronians and Flavians*, 155–83; and W. Martin Bloomer, *Latinity and Literary Society at Rome* (Philadelphia: University of Pennsylvania Press, 1997) 196–231. On problems in narration and the reliability and character of Encolpius, see P. Veyne, "Le 'je' dans le Satiricon," *REL* 42 (1964): 301–24; and Roger Beck, "Encolpius at the Cena," *Phoenix* 29 (1975): 271–83; and idem., "The Satyricon: Satire, Narrator, and Antecedents," *Museum Helvetica* 39 (1982): 206–14. On sexual language and imagery, see Christopher Gill, "The Sexual Episodes in the Satyricon," *CP* 68 (1973): 172–85; and Amy Richlin, *The Garden of Priapus: Sexuality and Aggression in Roman Humor*, rev. ed (New Haven CT: Yale University Press, 1992) 190–95.

[78]See Finley, *The Ancient Economy*, 50-51, 61; Rostovtzeff, *SEHRE*[2], 57–58 ("A typical representative" of city *bourgeoisie*), and 151 ("Trimalchio exists no more, or he lives now not in Campania but somewhere in the provinces"). D'Arms raises an important interpretational issue in the chapter "The Typicality of Trimalchio" in *Commerce and Social Standing*, 97–120, by noting that several scholars have cited Trimalchio as typical of their conception of ancient society. D'Arms proceeds, then, to show how Trimalchio is typical of *his* understanding. See MacMullen, *Roman Social Relations*, 102, "Trimalchio is typical."

stand for anything and therefore nothing in the text is authorially privileged.[79] But even if Petronius does wield his pen against Roman literary society and the aristocracy, he certainly also takes aim at the boorish freedmen or *libertini* such as Trimalchio, who measure worth (*aestimatio*) in *sesterces* and who thrust themselves above their station. As parody of Cicero's advice to move from trade to agriculture in order to be a "gentleman," the story of Trimalchio shows how great amounts of new, commercial wealth did not confer high status in the aristocratic circles of the early Roman empire.

Appearance and reality are prominent themes in the *Cena*; the dishes and entertainments at the party regularly turn into something other than what they appear to be.[80] Perhaps the most damning of qualities about Trimalchio is that he *is* what he appears to be—and advertises it rather than hides it. A mural in the entry hall of his house depicting Trimalchio's life story (the porter identifies these paintings as the *Iliad* and *Odyssey*, *Sat.* 29) and a speech about his career (*Sat.* 76–78) frame the *Cena* and define Trimalchio as a touchstone where appearance and reality intersect. Proper Romans could brag of their wealth, but only as inherited wealth, agrarian wealth, or the gifts of friends. In both mural and speech, Trimalchio boasts of his slave origins and the enormous wealth that he gained through commerce. Trimalchio came to Italy from Asia as a slave, purchased by "C. Pompeius," one of the old nobility, most likely having been sold by his parents for money.[81] He was a domestic rather than field slave and thus able to win the favor of both master and mistress, partly by performing sexual favors for both of them and partly by his business acumen.[82] Trimalchio becomes the *dispensator* (*Sat.* 29.4), the treasurer or steward, of his master's household. Trimalchio's services to his noble master bring him freedom after his master's death along with an estate "fit for a senator" (*patrimonium laticlavium*), a fortune of 30 million *sesterces*.[83] The irony in this phrase is palpable. He has enormous wealth "fit

---

[79]So Beck, "The Satyricon," 206.

[80]See Shadi Bartsch, *Actors in the Audience: Theatricality and Doublespeak from Nero to Hadrian* (Cambridge MA and London: Harvard University Press, 1994) 197–99, on representation and reality in the dinner party.

[81]See Paul Veyne, "Vie de Trimalcion," *Annales (ESC)* 16 (1961): 214–15.

[82]See Veyne, "Vie de Trimalcion," 216 and MacMullen *Roman Social Relations*, 98–99, on slaves in *familia urbana* and the opportunities there for advancement.

[83]See Veyne, "Vie de Trimalcion," 217. Slavery was a juridical rather than

for a senator," but all of this wealth can never bring him or his family the corresponding status. Trimalchio is not satisfied with his inheritance and "conceives a passion for business" (*concupivi negotiari*, 76.1). Already a marginal character in society as a freedman, he chooses the marginal career of commerce. Trimalchio sells the respectable fortune he had inherited in order to finance a career as merchant and shipper.[84] He eventually makes a new fortune, buys back his patron's estates, and retires from commerce. Trimalchio settles down on his estates, finances other freedmen (*libertos faenerare*), and tries to live like the landed aristocracy.[85]

Trimalchio attempts to take on the aristocratic values of the patrician culture of his old master once he is a wealthy master himself, but his efforts fail. He stages an aristocratic dinner party and repeatedly violates the rules for a symposium.[86] His associates are all *conliberti*, fellow freedmen, whose wealth derives similarly from inheritance, commerce, or a combination of the two.[87] These freedmen also try to better themselves on the aristocratic model.[88] While Trimalchio plays at aristocratic culture,

---

social condition. Those who were freed with a substantial legacy, like Trimalchio, could advance in society while a freed sharecropper would not be able to.

[84]The *plebiscitum Claudianum* (218 BCE) prohibited a senator or senator's son from owning an ocean-going ship. These laws were still in effect in the early third century CE, but by the first century senators were involved in trade through freedmen; see D'Arms, *Commerce and Social Standing*, 48–71, 152–59. Pleket, "Urban Elites and Business," 134, finds only one example from Asia Minor of a person who calls himself both a shipper (ναύκληρος) and a member of the council (βουλευτής). On dreams of making a fortune through shipping, and the risks of associated with fortune, see Luc. *Navig.*

[85]D'Arms, *Commerce and Social Standing*, 97–120, who champions Rostovtzeff's thesis that commerce played an important role in creating wealth in the first and second centuries, argues against Veyne that the social attitude against commerce and trade motivated Trimalchio to remain in mock-aristocratic retirement. His argument, however, goes against the grain of the satirical point of the *Cena*.

[86]See Bloomer, *Latinity*, 205–24. He has a silver skeleton brought in at the start of his symposium (*Sat.* 34); treats his guest to a discussion of his problems with constipation and suppositories (*Sat.* 47); and has his will read during the dinner party "so that my slaves may love me now as if I were dead" (*Sat.* 71). Trimalchio starts absurd topics of conversation and reads his own, horrible verse. He butchers Homer, reading Latin while his players act in Greek and telling a fantastic story about the war between Troy and Parentium (*Sat.* 59).

[87]See *Sat.* 38.7–12; 45; 57; 62; 43.1–6; 57.5; 44.15; 57.11; 58.12; 70.1; Veyne, "Vie de Trimalcion," 230.

[88]See *Sat.* 46; 58.7; Bloomer, *Latinity*, 216–21

his mind and the minds of his *conliberti* focus on cash (*Sat.* 43). The language of the *libertini* shows the value they place on money.[89] Trimalchio's "retirement" from commerce to estate life is meant to mimic the aristocratic ideal of wealth befitting a "gentleman" spelled out by Cicero. Trimalchio cannot, however, buy status. Like the ring he wears, Trimalchio tries to look like gold but is really iron (*Sat.* 32).[90] Trimalchio's ostentatious display of wealth becomes the proverbial type for a *parvenu*. But as Veyne writes, a parvenu must have arrived, and Trimalchio never arrives.[91]

The Foundation of C. Vibius Salutaris

The third illustration of the low status of even the wealthiest merchants and traders is a lengthy inscription in Ephesus from 104 CE.[92] C. Vibius Salutaris, born a Roman citizen and a member of the equestrian order, belonged to a prominent family which owned estates near Ephesus. His friends included legates and proconsuls of Asia, at least one *consul ordinarius*, and other equestrian and senatorial families.[93] The inscription records the details of a foundation or endowment of a yearly, public distribution of funds and a biweekly procession of statues through the streets of Ephesus. The foundation can be read as a public expression of patriotism for Rome and Ephesus and self-promotion by an aristocratic citizen and member of the *boulē*, or council, in Ephesus. It thus gives us

---

[89]See Bloomer, *Latinity*, 208, 218–21; *Omne me lucrum transeat, nisi iam dudum gaudimonio dissilio, quod te talem video* (*Sat.* 61): "May I never turn another penny if I am not ready to burst with joy at seeing you in such a good humour"; *ita crescam patrimonio, non corpore*: "As I hope to grow in gains not in girth" (*Sat.* 70).

[90]See the comment by Beck, "Encolpius at the Cena," 272n.4, that no unambiguously favorable comment is passed on Trimalchio except that of the undertaker in *Sat.* 78.6, whose trumpet-blast ends the party.

[91]Veyne, "Vie de Trimalcion," 213: "Le mot est bien impropre; un parvenu est effectivement arrivé, tandis que Trimalcion ne peut échapper à sa caste; il ne parviendra qu'à s'évader dans l'irréalité." See *Sat.* 74; cf. the dinner party in Luc. *Merc. Cond.* 14–18; the theme of wealth and status in the discussion of salary (19–22); and the contrast in status between Greek culture and Roman wealth (23, 25, 35–36, 40).

[92]See Guy M. Rogers, *The Sacred Identity of Ephesos: Foundation Myths of a Roman City* (London and New York: Routledge, 1991). I follow N.T. convention and use the spelling "Ephesus" instead of Roger's "Ephesos."

[93]See Rogers, *Sacred Identity*, 16–19.

an insight into the social world and power relationships of Ephesian society around 100 CE.

The inscription itself is tremendous, consisting of 568 lines engraved in six columns on stones almost 500 cm in breadth and ranging from 200 to 430 cm in height, standing well above eye level on a wall in the theater of the Artemision in Ephesus.[94] Citizens and residents probably could not have read the inscription, since it was so high and so large, but it was nevertheless an extremely public text. Salutaris's foundation carefully and legally endowed two public performances. First, he established an endowment of 21,500 *denarii*, the interest from which funded a complex scheme of lotteries and distributions. The lotteries and distributions took place on the day before and the day of the celebration of the birthday and mysteries of Ephesus's patron goddess, Artemis. The disbursement of the money took place in the Temple of Artemis itself. The foundation specified some 2,702 allotments. Some of the money was distributed to cultic officials and Temple servants, but most went to members of the Ephesian aristocracy.[95] The second public performance was a regular procession. Salutaris dedicated thirty-one type statues of gold, gold overlay, and silver to be carried in a procession through the city of Ephesus, approximately every two weeks, in a large circle that began and ended at the Temple of Artemis. Members of the procession included 10 temple functionaries and 250 *ephebes* (ἔφεβοι), the most important youth association. The gold and gold-overlay statues were *eikons* (εἰκόνες) of Artemis and two deer, dedicated to Artemis and the *boulē*. Silver statues included representations of Artemis; Trajan and his wife Plotina; the Roman people; the Senate; the equestrian order; Athena; and the tribes of Ephesus.[96]

Rogers carefully interprets this inscription within the context of Ephesian social life as a public text that symbolized and legitimized power relationships within the city.[97] Roman rule raised questions of social, historical, and religious identity for the *boulē*, *dēmos*, *gerousia* (γερουσία), and tribes of Ephesus, which were the social institutions

---

[94]Ibid., 20–21; diagram and photographs, 198–99.

[95]Ibid., 41–50. Salutaris's endowment actually consisted of a 20,000 initial endowment and a 1,500 addendum.

[96]Ibid., 83–85. Roger notes, 28, that the amount of expenditure by Salutaris for this foundation falls within the middle of the range of expenditures for foundations in Asia Minor during the Roman Empire.

[97]Ibid., 19–23.

historically holding power in the city before Roman rule. The establishment of the foundation by Salutaris was carefully worked out with the
dēmos and *boulē* and symbolizes their power to transfer and distribute
property in Ephesus. Letters from the *proconsul* and *legatus* of Asia,
signifying Roman sanction for historical Ephesian power, are included in
the text of the inscription. Most important in the performance of the
distribution and procession was the presence of the *ephebes*, the elite
youths of the city. The lottery and distribution reenacted the power
relationships of Ephesus for the future members of the elite, symbolically
portraying the power structures into which the *ephebes* would take their
place. The procession, moreover, recreated the history of Ephesus, placing
the power of Rome within the context of the Hellenistic, Ionian, and
ultimately, mythological foundations of the city.

The Salutaris inscription narrates for us the power relationships of the
society in which Revelation was written and read. It is important to note
who was included in the performance of the lottery and procession and
how their inclusion reflects the reigning social hierarchy in Ephesus.[98] At
the top of the hierarchy are the members of the tribes, symbolizing the
Greek character of the city, followed by the *boulē* and *gerousia*, and then
the *paidonomoi* (παιδονόμοι) and *ephebearchos* (ἐφήβαρχος), officials who trained the youth associations. The next level consisted of the
youth associations, the *ephebes* and the *paides* (παῖδες). The bottom
level consisted of functionaries of the Artemision and the imperial cult.
The relatively low position of the priestess of Artemis might be explained
by the essentially patriarchal nature of power in Ephesus. While Roman
power was represented in the procession by both type statues and the
order of the procession, in the lottery and distribution it was the Greek
institutions that received pride of place, thereby pointing the *ephebes* to
their Ionian and Hellenistic past rather than Roman present. The elite
youths assembled for the lottery and distribution of Salutaris's endowment would witness the entire social hierarchy of Ephesus and become
acculturated to the roles they would take in the civic order.

Officials and groups associated with trade or commerce were not
included in Salutaris's scheme. Rogers finds conspicuous the absence of
some of the most important financial officials of the city, such as the
oikonomoi (οἰκονόμοι), treasurers of sacred monies, and the *agora-
nomos* (ἀγορανόμος), who supervised the sale of commodities and set

---

[98]Ibid., 66–70.

the price for bread. The association of these offices with commerce and trade would have made them unworthy examples for the *ephebes* and *paides* who witnessed this public performance of social power in Ephesus.[99] The omission of the *collegia* of Ephesus shows the disdain of the aristocracy for labor and trade. The story of Paul and the silversmiths in Acts 19:23–41 demonstrates the social power of these organizations. Epigraphical evidence attests to the existence of organizations of wool workers, wool dealers, cloak dealers, flax workers, cobblers, and perfume makers in Ephesus.[100] These organizations had some social privileges in Ephesus; many members would have acquired significant wealth; and their work was essential to the economic life of the city. But they are completely excluded from Salutaris's foundation:

> The wealth of the members of the guilds came from the wrong sources, and their commercial occupations, however critical to the city even feeding itself, were not appropriate ones to hold up to the paides and ephebes as worthy of their social and political aspirations. . . . The guilds could not belong to the ideal civic hierarchy; if they were admitted, the club of the aristocracy would no longer be worth joining for the ephebes and paides.[101]

Salutaris's foundation casts in stone and in public ritual the social bias against labor, trade, and commerce expressed in Cicero's treatise. There is ample evidence in other inscriptions that the exclusion of collegia was not limited to Salutaris's foundation or to Ephesus.[102] Although 150 years

---

[99]Ibid., 70–71.

[100]Ibid., 71; and *ESAR* 4.817–47.

[101]Rogers, *Sacred Identity*, 72.

[102]See *ESAR* 4.734–770 and the following inscriptions for the seven cities of Revelation. Smyrna: a distribution to an association in the gymnasium by Ti. Cl. Carteromachus (*IG Rom* 4.1429, *CIG* 3203); Thyatira: foundation for council from income of gardens about tombs, *BCH* 11 (1887) 457; annual gift to council of one *denarius* (*IG Rom* 4.1222); Sardis: gifts of grain and cash to all citizens in time of need (*ESAR* 764–65); Philadelphia: gifts to council and *gerousia* (*IG Rom* 4.1629 *CIG* 3417); grain, cash to council and *gerousia*, *IG Rom* 4.1632; Laodicea: gifts for council as garland money by Pythodorus, Menander and Domitia, *MDAI(A)* 16 (1891) 146. The *collegia*, of course, tried to establish their own power through public displays of gifts promoted by inscriptions; see, for instance, the triple gateway, *stoas*, and shops dedicated to the Sebastoi by the garment makers (ἱματευόμενοι) in Thyatira (*IG Rom* 4.1209). But the evidence of other inscriptions supports Rogers's hypothesis that the local aristocracy excluded the merchants and *collegia* from their rituals of power.

separate Cicero's *De officiis* and the Salutaris inscription, the attitudes toward merchants and commerce are quite similar.

Summary: Merchants and Commerce

There is considerable evidence of the low opinion of banausic pursuits across the ancient Mediterranean world, from the last days of the Roman Republic to the early Empire.[103] These three illustrations, Cicero's *De officiis*, Petronius's *Satyricon*, and the foundation of C. Vibius Salutaris, demonstrate the low status accorded to commercial wealth. The status-ambiguous and status-conscious members of the early Christian churches in Ephesus and the other cities of Asia Minor would be well aware of these social biases against wealth derived from commerce. When John, through ingenious manipulation of the Hebrew scriptures, portrays Rome as a commercial power, the message would have been clear: Roman wealth was new, low status, *sordidae et vulgares*. Revelation couples this condemnation of Babylon with praise of another wealthy city. The rhetorical acts of praising and condemning cities would also have been familiar to Asian Christians, who lived in the time and place of the greatest rebirth of the rhetorical arts in antiquity since fourth-century Athens.

Praise and Vilification of Cities

The Second Sophistic

John took his material for the description of the New Jerusalem from the Hebrew prophets, but his audience would have likely heard speeches praising their own cities by the sophists. During the second century of the common era, the cultural movement called the Second Sophistic reached

---

[103]See also Dio *Or.* 7.81, 104, 117–23, 13–137; the discussion of traders in search of "base gain," *Or.* 31.37; the critique of Alexandria's sea-borne wealth, *Or.* 32.37; *Or.* 46.8–9, in which he defends himself from money-lending and extols his agricultural activities before the mob in Prusa; and the discussion of trades and professions in *Or.* 77/78.3-4, 8, 12-14, 18-23, 33; Plut. *Solon* 2.6–8; Ps.-Plut. *Quomodo adul.* 7; Philostr. *VS* 1.17 [506]; Libanius *Orat.* 42.21, cited by Ste. Croix, *Class Struggle*, 122, and the examples he cites from legal codes, 126–28; the Erastus inscription (Dittenberg, *SIG* 838), discussed by Pleket, "Urban Elites and Business," 134, also 136–41; D'Arms, *Commerce and Social Standing*, 159–62; Grassl, *Sozialökonomische Vorstellungen*, 101–10; P. Garnsey, "Aspects of the Decline of the Urban Aristocracy in the Empire," *ANRW* 2/1:229–52, esp. 233; and Fik Meijer and Onno van Nijf, *Trade, Transport and Society in the Ancient World* (London: Routledge, 1992) 69–89.

full flower in the cities of Asia.[104] The Second Sophistic as a rhetorical
and cultural movement attempted to emulate the language and glory of
classical Athens.[105] After Athens, Ephesus and Smyrna were the leading
centers of rhetorical training in the Roman Empire and other parts of Asia
were also famous for teachers of rhetoric.[106] While the Second Sophistic
reached its zenith in the second half of the second century, the careers of
many important sophists span the period when Revelation was written
and read. Dio Chrysostom and Lucian, whose early career included
rhetorical performances, can be read within the context of the Second
Sophistic and its literary conventions.[107] The lives of these very public
figures were interconnected; Polemo, for instance, who was born in
Laodicea and settled in Smyrna, traveled to Bithynia to study with Dio.[108]
While the rhetorical performances of the sophists were often for their
aristocratic students or elite gatherings such as the salon of Hadrian or
Marcus Aurelius, declamations were also public performances in the

---

[104]See G. W. Bowersock, *Greek Sophists in the Roman Empire* (Oxford:
Clarendon, 1969); idem., ed., *Approaches to the Second Sophistic: Papers Pre-
sented at the 105th Annual Meeting of The American Philological Association*
(University Park PA: American Philological Association, 1974); and Graham
Anderson, *The Second Sophistic: A Cultural Phenomenon in the Roman Empire*
(London and New York: Routledge, 1993). Philostratus, the third-century chroni-
cler of the sophists, coins the phrase "second sophistic" in the prologue of his
Lives of the Sophists (*VS* 1 [481]), a text which seeks to incorporate the
principles of declamation which it discusses.

[105]See E. L. Bowie, "Greeks and their Past in the Second Sophistic," in
Finley, ed., *Studies in Ancient Society*, 166–209.

[106]"All Ionia is, as it were, an established seat of the Muses; Smyrna holds
the most important position, like the bridge in musical instruments" (Philostr. *VS*
1.21 [516]). A number of sophists came from or settled in the cities of Asia
addressed in Revelation. In addition to Polemo, Nicetes, Scopelian, Lollianus,
and Aelius Aristides, whom I discuss below, Philostratus lists Aristocles of
Pergamum (*VS* 2.3 [567–568]); Heracleides of Lycia (*VS* 2.26 [613–615]); and
Varus of Laodicea (*VS* 2.28 [620]).

[107]On Dio, see Philostr. *VS* 1.7 [487–488]. Lucian, according to the *Dream*,
began his career as a sophist. Specific works that treat rhetoric include
Lexiphanes, A Professor of Public Speaking (*Rhet. Did.*), *Double Indictment,* and
A Slip of the Tongue in Greeting (*Pro Lapsu*). See Jones, *Culture and Society in
Lucian*, 10–16.

[108]See Philostr. *VS* 1.25 [539].

theaters of the cities.[109] The Second Sophistic, as a cultural movement, would have reached a wide audience.

The sophists were important men of affairs in the lives of the cities of Asia and the Roman Empire and could have been known by reputation to the Christian audience of Revelation.[110] A number of sophists, such as Nicetes of Smyrna, Scopelian of Smyrna, and Polemo of Laodicea were active between the reigns of Nero and Hadrian.[111] Second century sophists such as Lollianus of Ephesus, Herodes Atticus, and Aelius Aristides were even more prominent.[112] Sophists staged their careers for the public just as they staged their declamations. Philostratus writes that the Second Sophistic "sketched the types of the poor man and the rich" (*VS* 481). The public display of wealth was part of the performance of the sophist. The most famous and notorious displays were by Herodes Atticus, whose wealth was legendary and whose civic projects extraordinary.[113] But

---

[109]See Philostr. *VS* 1.19 (511) on Nicetes' fear of speaking in the public assembly and the accusations of the crowd; 1.21 (518) on how Scopelian appeared to the crowd; and 1.25 (537–38) on how Polemo would prepare for the crowd.

[110]See Bowersock, *Approaches*, appendix 2, 35–40, for epigraphical evidence of the sophists; Bowersock, *Greek Sophists in the Roman Empire*; and E. L. Bowie, "The Importance of Sophists," *YCS* 27 (1982) 29–59.

[111]Nicetes of Smyrna was summoned to Rome by Nero over a disagreement with a consul concerning the finances of Smyrna; he won his case (*VS* 1.19 [512]). Scopelian of Smyrna served as high priest of Asia (*archiereus*), as had his family before him (*VS* 1.21 [515]); "during the period before a declamation he was generally in the society of the magistrates of Smyrna transacting public business" (τοῖς τῶν Σμυρναίων τέλεσιν ὑπὲρ τῶν πολιτικῶν [*VS* 518]). He was chosen to represent Smyrna on many embassies to Domitian, including arguing against the prohibition of viticulture in Asia; he, too, won his case, and returned with imperial gifts and sanctions against anyone who did not plant vines (520). See also *VS* 518, on Scopelian's draw of students from all over the Empire, including "all the youths of Asia." Polemo's family in Laodicea included many of consular rank (*VS* 1.25 [530]). He brought his extensive political skills to bear on ending factions in Smyrna's government and swaying the Emperor Hadrian to favor Smyrna over Ephesus in imperial building projects (531). See Maud W. Gleason, *Making Men: Sophists and Self-Presentation in Ancient Rome* (Princeton NJ: Princeton University Press, 1994) 21–54, "Portrait of Polemo: The Deportment of the Public Self."

[112]On Lollianus of Ephesus see *VS* 1.23 (526) and Bowersock, *Approaches*, 39. On Herodes Atticus, see *VS* 2.1 (546–66) and Bowersock, *Approaches*, 33, 38. On Aristides, see *VS* 2.9 (582–85); and C. A. Behr, *Aelius Aristides and the Sacred Tales* (Amsterdam: Adolf M. Hakkert, 1968) 61–90.

[113]See *VS* 2.1 (546–66). Herodes built a marble stadium and a theater, in

sophists closer to the time and place of Revelation had their own public displays of wealth. Nicetes built the gate in Smyrna which looks toward Ephesus. Philostratus describes the high priesthood of Asia, held by Scopelian and his ancestors, as "a great crown of glory and more than great wealth" (*VS* 1.21 [515]). Polemo received gifts from Emperors such as free travel by Trajan, a benefit extended to his descendants by Hadrian, along with a seat at the high table of the Alexandrian museum. He demanded 250,000 drachmae for Smyrna from Hadrian and got it.

The public displays of wealth and rhetoric by the sophists were part of the social world of the audience of Revelation. The sophists and their cities functioned in a symbiotic relationship of mutual admiration, each vying for honor, glory, and status. The rivalries were proverbial among cities in Asia Minor, particularly Ephesus and Smyrna, for titles such as "the greatest," "the largest," "chief city of Asia," or for imperial recognition, titles that were advertised in inscriptions in the cities where Revelation was read.[114] The sophists gave voice to these intense civic aspirations for honor and status. Philostratus makes special mention of Dio Chrysostom's speeches blaming or praising different cities. Dio gave addresses in Rhodes, Alexandria, Apamea, and Tarsus as well as in his native Prusa. These encomiums discussed civic pride, aspirations, and rivalries, with frequent comparisons to other cities; the natural and

---

memory of his wife Regila, in Athens; a theater in Corinth; a stadium at Pytho; an aqueduct at Olympia; bathing pools at Thermopylae; established a colony in Epirus, including an water supply; and made other bequests to various cities and temples.

[114]See "Flavians, Antonines, Severi: The Age of Display," *ESAR* 4:734–94. Cities vied for privileges such as freedoms and immunities granted by the emperor; holding of Assizes (Dio *Or.* 35.15 at Apamea, Luc. *Alex.* 57); and the titles "metropolis, first or leading city, and possessor of a imperial temple (neocorus)." On the term *neokoros*, see Friesen, *Twice Neokoros*, esp. 142–68. On the proverbial rivalry between Ephesus and Smyrna, see Dio *Or.* 34.48, Aristides *Or.* 23.65, Philostr. *VS* 1.25. See *ESAR* 4:742–43 for a list of "splendid metropolis" inscriptions: Pergamum, IG Rom 4.331; Smyrna, IG Rom 3.1431; *CIL* 3.741; Ephesus, Barclay V. Head, *Historia numorum: A Manual of Greek Numismatics* (Oxford: Clarendon, 1911; repr.: Chicago: Argonaut, 1967) 577; P. Le Bas and W. H. Waddington, *Voyage archélogique en Grece et en Asie Mineure*, 3 vols (Paris, 1870) 3:146, 147; Philadelphia, IG Rom 4.1619; Laodicea, Head, *Historia numorum*, 678. See also Magie, *Roman Rule*, 599–600; Ramsay MacMullen, *Enemies of the Roman Order: Treason, Unrest, and Alienation in the Empire* (Cambridge MA: Harvard University Press, 1966) 169, 185–87; and MacMullen, *Roman Social Relations*, 58–77.

commercial wealth of cities; and vices characteristic of certain cities, such as overattention to chariot racing and the citharode in Alexandria or the behavior of rich citizens at Rhodes.[115] The Christians in Asia Minor probably did not consciously compare Revelation to the public declamations of the sophists. But sophistic rhetoric sets the context for civic discourse and for discourse about cities in Asia Minor in the first and second century. John vilifies one city and praises another using the imagery of wealth. The sophists used similar motifs to vilify and adorn their cities of choice. In order to explore the cultural and rhetorical context of the Second Sophistic more fully, I will look at two speeches about Rome in detail, Aelius Aristides' "Regarding Rome" and Lucian's *Nigrinus*, that provide pertinent comparisons with the portrait of Babylon/Rome in Revelation 18.

Aelius Aristides, "Regarding Rome"

P. Aelius Aristides is best known to students of early Christianity for his *Sacred Tales* and the insights they offer on the religious culture of the second century. But his fame in antiquity came from his career as a sophist. Aristides studied with the most prominent sophists of his day, including Polemo in Smyrna. Like Dio, he addressed a number of cities, including Cos, Cnidus, Rhodes, and Alexandria in the early part of his career. Aristides was plagued by extended illness (or hypochondria) and turned to the healing god Asclepius for a cure, as he describes in his *Sacred Tales*. He was also notorious for his fanatical avoidance of civic duties.[116] In 155–6 CE, free after years of struggling with these two afflictions, he undertook a grand rhetorical tour, delivering orations in

---

[115]See Philostr. *VS* 1.7 [487]; Dio *Or.* 31, a tirade against Rhodes, and Jones, *The Roman World of Dio Chrysostom*, 26–35 (see also Aristides *Or.* 24); *Or.* 32 and Jones, *Roman World*, 36–44, on Alexandria; *Or.* 33 and 34 and Jones, *Roman World*, 70–82, on Tarsus, including order and luxury (34.11, 27, 45, 48); on the proverbial rivalry between Ephesus and Smyrna, *Or.* 34.48 (see also Aristides *Or.* 23); *Or.* 35, delivered at Apamea in Phrygia, and Jones, *Roman World*, 65–70; Dio on Ephesus and the Ephesian Temple, *Or.* 31.54, 40.11; Prusa and Dio's struggles to beautify city in opposition to the poor, who really wanted grain (40.3–7, 45.15–16, 47.19.); on the complaint that cities spent too much, *Or.* 47.13, 45; also *Ors.* 44, 47, 48 on Prusa.

[116]Behr, *Aelius Aristides and the Sacred Tales*, 61–90, discusses Aristides' efforts to avoid liturgies; and 162–170, Galen and Aristides' illness. Galen, interestingly enough, opposed charlatans and quacks but not "Temple medicine." It was a dream from Asclepius to his father that launched his medical career.

Delos, Athens, Rome, and Corinth. His 26th Oration, "Regarding Rome" (Εἰς Ῥώμην), offers one of the most important pagan comparisons to Revelation 18.[117] He delivered his encomium to Rome before the imperial court. The speech is an extended praise of the *pax Romana*, describing Rome's economic, legal, administrative, and military power.[118] I will explore this speech in some detail, quoting at length because it is generally not well known and because the wealth of Rome is a major topic of the speech. While "Regarding Rome" is usually cited as an example of praise of Rome and its wealth, deeper analysis and comparison of the speech with Aristides' "Panathenaic Oration" (*Or.* 1) shows a disdain for Rome's commercial wealth and cultural inferiority to Athens, themes that would have resonated in the cities where Revelation was read. It is important to explore this disdain because John draws on the same cultural iconography in his polemic against Rome in Revelation 18.

A panegyric or encomium typically began with a description (*ekphrasis*) of the geography of the city being praised.[119] Aristides uses this section to describe Rome as the center of a vast commercial empire. He begins with the size of the city of Rome itself, which covers hills, fields, interior plains, and "even descends down to the sea, where lies the common trading center of mankind and the common market of the produce of the earth" (τὸ κοινὸν ἀνθρώπων ἐμπόριον καὶ ἡ κοινὴ τῶν ἐν γῇ φυομένων, 26.7). Aristides characterizes the city of Rome and its port at Ostia first and foremost as the commercial center of

---

[117]See Meeks, *Moral World*, 144, and Bauckham, "Economic Critique of Rome," *Climax of Prophecy*, 375–76; Behr, *Aelius Aristides and the Sacred Tales*, 88–89, suggests that this was his greatest speech. *P. Aelius Aristides: The Complete Works*, 2 vols, trans. Charles A. Behr (Leiden: Brill,, 1986) 2:73–97; text Bruno Keil, *Aelii Aristidis Smyrnaei quae supersunt omnia*, vol. 2, *Orationes XVII–LIII* (Berlin: Weidmann, 1958).

[118]The outline of the speech is as follows: 26.1–5, proem introducing the difficulty of the speech; 26.6-13, *ekphrasis* of the geography of Rome; 26.14–57, comparison with the Persian and Greek empires; 26.58–71, discussion of civil policy and administration; 26.72–89, Roman military policy; 26.90–91, the Roman constitution; 26.92–106, the *pax Romana*; 26.107, the Emperor; and 26.108–109, peroration (adapted from *P. Aelius Aristides*, trans. Behr, 2.374, with my comments).

[119]See the discussion of the praise of cities in Menander Rhetor's first treatise on epideictic (346.26–367.8); and George A. Kennedy, *Greek Rhetoric under Christian Emperors* (Princeton NJ: Princeton University Press, 1983) 25–26, on the interchangeable use of the terms *encomium* and *panegyric* in later antiquity.

the world. But "Rome" is more than the city; it is also the empire, which is so immense that "the sun's course is always in your land" (26.10). There are no boundaries for the Roman empire, he continues, rather the sea is the internal "belt" around which the continents of the Empire lie, sending their products to Rome. His description of Rome as commercial power, consumer, and importer then follows; I have italicized parts of Behr's translation to bring out the rhetorical *amplificatio* in this section:

> Here is brought from *every* land and sea *all* the crops of the seasons and the produce of *each* land, river, lake, as well as the arts (τέχναι) of the Greeks and barbarians, so that if someone should wish to view *all* these things, he must either see them by traveling over the *whole world* or be in this city. It cannot be otherwise than that there *always* be here an *abundance* of *all* that grows and is manufactured among *each people*. *So many* merchant ships arrive here, conveying *every kind* of goods from *every people every hour* and *every day*, so that the city is like a factory *common to the whole earth*. It is possible to see *so many* cargoes from *India* and even *Arabia Felix*, if you wish, that one imagines that for the future the trees are left bare for the people there and that they must come here to beg for their own produce if they need anything. Again there can be seen clothing from *Babylon* and ornaments from *the barbarian world beyond*, which arrive in much larger quantity and more easily than if merchantmen bringing goods from *Naxus* or *Cythnus* had only to put into *Athens*. Your farmlands are *Egypt, Sicily*, and all of *Africa* which is cultivated. The arrivals and departures of the ships *never* stop, so that one would express admiration not only for the harbor, but even for the sea . . . . So *everything* comes together here, trade, seafaring, farming, the scourings of the mines, *all* the crafts that exist or have existed, *all* that is produced or grown (26.11–13).

Aristides does not talk of Rome's gold or jewels—words which do not appear in the speech at all—but characterizes Rome's wealth strictly in terms of the city's commercial power. With proper rhetorical *amplificatio*, Aristides develops his central point that Rome is the commercial center of the world. Italics in the English translation only emphasize the hyperbolic and, to modern ears, bombastic style of the speech. The idea of production, using transitive forms of the verb φύω, is repeated three times. Four times he mentions merchant ships bringing cargoes from around the empire;[120] he includes nine different place names as well as

---

[120]Behr's translation supplies "merchant" where it does not actually occur in the Greek. The first occurrence is elegantly understated with an understood τοσαῦται (26.11 [p. 95 l. 2 in Behr's translation]); the second mention of cargo is the Attic φορτίον (26.12, [95.5]); the third mention is, again, the understood

mentioning the Greeks and the barbarian world to magnify the portrait of Rome's commercial network. Twice Aristides says that ships are coming in constantly, but he says this in two different ways. His elegant *variatio* expresses the central theme of Rome's commercial power; the city, he says is an ἐργαστήριον for the whole world, using the proper Attic term for a workshop.[121]

The alert reader of the previous section on the status of merchants and traders might wonder how complimentary this description of Rome's commercial power in Aristides' oration was meant to be. This is a serious point to consider. The Second Sophistic looked to Athens, not Rome, as its home; "Regarding Rome" was delivered in Greek to the court of the Roman Emperor. Perhaps the speech does not praise Rome so much as place Rome's achievements within the context of Greek culture. Aristides begins and ends the panegyric with a discussion of rhetoric, presenting the problem of language to his Roman audience. In 26.6, Aristides exclaims that "this city is the first to have exposed the power of oratory [λόγου δύναμιν] as not entirely sufficient" (cf. 26.108). Aristides' praise of Rome is mediated by the Greek language and references to Greek culture within the speech. To understand these references to Greek rhetoric and culture and how they deconstruct Aristides' praise of Rome, we need to situate "Regarding Rome" in the context of another speech, the First or "Panathenaic Oration," delivered in Athens on the same speaking tour.

In the Panathenaic Oration, Aristides recounts the military glories of Greece in great detail (1.75–321), just as he describes the military power of Rome in his 26th Oration. But the military glories of Athens are long past and overshadowed by the conquests of Alexander and Rome. Aristides does not discuss these conquests (1.317), although they overshadow his discussion of Athenian military might. He turns in section 322 to a new subject, "the topic of speech itself." Aristides has already

---

τι (26.12, [95.11]); fourth, for "the arrival and departure of the ships" in 26.13, he uses κατάπλοι δὲ καὶ ἀπόπλοι. The word for market, ἐμπόριον, cognate of the words for merchant, ἔμπορος, and trade, ἐμπορία, appears in 26.7.

[121]See also the wealth imagery in 26.92–106, in which Aristides lists the benefits of the *pax Romana*; note especially the comparison of Alexandria to the "bracelet of a rich woman," 26.95, casting Rome as the γυνή πλουσία, the wealthy woman. The proper mark of Attic style, of course, was not only diction but the avoidance of hiatus.

introduced this topic in the opening of the Panathenaic Oration, where he takes the conceit of praising oratory by means of oratory as the theme of the proem (1.3; see 1.2–7). In this discussion of speech or rhetoric (λόγος, 1.322–330), he contrasts the power of Greek language and culture with her limited and now distant triumphs in battle. Greek language is a "bloodless trophy"; the Athenians "have won an honoured and great victory for all time . . . . for all the cities and all the races of mankind have turned to you and your form of life and dialect" (1.322). The entire civilized world shows emulation (ζῆλος) for Greek culture, wisdom, and language so that Greek has become the universal language of humanity (1.324). Greek is the "mark of education," (ὅρος παιδείας); language, not lands such as Ionia or Thrace, comprises the empire of Greece (1.326–7). The reference to the conquering Romans who had taken these lands would have been clear to his audience.

Read through his discussion of Greek language in the Panathenaic Oration, Aristides' "Regarding Rome" is not so much praise of Rome as evidence of the triumph of Greek culture over the current military power. The subtext of the timeless and conquering power of Greek language and rhetoric and Aristides' fundamental self-identification as a Greek subverts his praise of Rome. In "Regarding Rome," Aristides notes that the Greeks and their arts flourish under Roman rule (26.94). Given Aristides' praise of oratory in both speeches, his comment that (only) the science of administration was left for the Romans to discover (26.58) highlights the extent of Greek advances in culture. Rome turns culture into a commodity: they import Greek arts (τέχναι) just as they import Egyptian wheat and Indian spices (26.11); . In "Regarding Rome," he writes that the Romans surpass the barbarians in wealth and power while surpassing the Greeks in knowledge and moderation (26.41). Aristides' praise is hollow, for the Athenians, according to the Panathenaic Oration, were the first not to be awed by wealth (1.390).

My rhetorical comparison or *synkrisis* of Athens and Rome in Aristides' two speeches show the aristocratic disdain for Rome's commercial wealth that can be discerned beneath the surface of the most famous ancient speech praising Rome. As an intertextual reading, this comparison was not available to Aristides' historical audience—nor would he have wished that the Imperial Court draw these conclusions from his "praise" of Rome or his reception would not have been favorable. Nor would the ordinary auditor of Revelation have been used to such subtle nuances in the hermeneutics of panegyric, although it has figured so prominently in other treatments of wealth in Revelation that an exegesis is required in this study. But the Christians who heard Revelation and the non-Roman Easterners who heard or read Aristides' speech on Rome would have had the same cultural ideas about the vocabulary and figures of the praise of cities. The faint praise of Rome's commercial wealth in "Regarding Rome" highlights the harshness of the polemic against Babylon/Rome commercial wealth in Revelation. In drawing his portrait, John of Patmos was tapping into a wider sentiment in the Greek East, expressed by Aristides as well, that his audience would have recognized.

Lucian's Nigrinus

There is further confirmation of this widely held view of Rome in the ancient Greek East in the work of another second century author, Lucian of Samosata. With its satire of the city of Rome and the foibles of wealthy patrons and sycophantic clients, Lucian's *Nigrinus* has been called the antithesis to Aelius Aristides "To Rome."[122] It is important to ask if *Nigrinus*, as with all of Lucian's writings, should be read as social commentary or literary showmanship.[123] Although not strictly speaking an oration like Aristides' "To Rome," *Nigrinus* is nevertheless an epideictic showpiece.[124] The disequilibrium between the opening dialogue between "Lycianos" and a friend, and the central monologue, which purports to describe the views and philosophy of Nigrinus, signals that the *Nigrinus* may be more sophistic show than Cynic philosophy.[125] There are a number of clues in the opening sections (*Nigr.* 1–12) that Lycianos will deliver a declamation on Athens and Rome, playing the part of the philosopher Nigrinus. For instance, in the letter which precedes the dialogue, Lycianos calls attention to the epideictic genre of the text and

---

[122]R. Helm "Lukianos," *PW* 13.2 (1927) 1752; Bompaire, *Lucien écrivain*, 502. See also Lucian's "Hirelings in Great Houses" (*Merc. cond.*).

[123]See Bompaire, *Lucien écrivain*, 499–512. Major interpretational issues for *Nigrinus* include its relation to anti-Roman sentiment in Hellenistic and Roman writers whose satire of Rome parallels Lucian such as Juvenal's *Third Satire*; the attitude towards Rome in the *Nigrinus* within the context of Lucian's other writings, particularly *Merc. cond.*, *Laps.* and *Apol.*; and the "platonic" Nigrinus whose philosophy sounds quite Cynic. See also Jones, *Culture and Society in Lucian*, 8–10, 25, 78–89 for more recent investigation of the historical issues and Anderson, *Lucian: Theme and Variation*, 81–89, on the literary problems.

[124]See Kennedy, *New Testament Interpretation*, 3, on *letteraturizzazione*, rhetoric as a literary style.

[125]Bompaire, *Lucien écrivain*, 509: "un déséquilibre entre le dialogue et le monologue central."

Nigrinus's skill with words. He writes that for him to display his own rhetorical skill (δύναμιν λόγων ἐπιδείξασθαι) in a book sent to Nigrinus would be as absurd as sending owls to Athens. The inference is that the "philosopher" Nigrinus himself has demonstrated impressive rhetorical skill to Lycianos. There then follows an *amplificatio* of rhetorical terms in the proem of *Nigrinus* (*Nigr.* 1–10).[126] The proem thus characterizes Lycianos's rendition of Nigrinus's speech as a sophistic declamation; Lycianos has practiced Nigrinus's words so much (τὸ μεμνῆσθαι) that he has made them a μελέτη, or declamation (*Nigr.* 6). Nigrinus the philosopher is also a teacher of rhetoric whose rhetorical skill overshadows Lycianos's performance in this dialogue. The comparison or *synkrisis* of Athens and Rome that follows the proem, then, can be read as a sophistic declamation which, like Aristides' "To Rome," illumines our understanding of the negative view of the Greek East toward their Latin rulers.

Nigrinus's encomium of Athens runs from *Nigr.* 13 to *Nigr.* 15 and his attack (*psongos*) against Rome extends through *Nigr.* 34. This central portion of the dialogue includes scathing descriptions of wealthy Roman society dinners, *salutatio*, horse racing, baths, and client-philosophers. Within this extensive condemnation of Rome are two sections praising Nigrinus and his philosophy as an antithesis to the city (*Nigr.* 17–20 and 26–28). These glimpses of Nigrinus's philosophy present the problem of the Platonist who talks very much like a Cynic. The epilogue begins in *Nigr.* 35 and continues to the end of the dialogue.

Poverty and wealth are major themes in Nigrinus's descriptions of Athens and Rome. The talk between Lycianos and Nigrinus begins with praise of Athens, "because Philosophy and Poverty have ever been their foster brothers" (*Nigr.* 12). The Athenians live simple lives in accord with Cynic morality, according to the Platonic philosopher Nigrinus. Their atti-

---

[126]In *Nigr.* 1, the interlocutor begs to hear more than just a *kephalaion*, a technical rhetorical term for the topic of an argument. The interlocutor describes the time spent with Nigrinus by Lycianos as a συνουσία, a technical term used for the attendance of student upon a teacher of rhetoric (*Nigr.* 10). The interlocutor, swearing by Hermes, the god of orators, then exclaims that Lycianos has been "proemizing" (πεπροοιμιάζομαι) according to rules of rhetoricians (κατὰ τὸν τῶν ῥητόρων νόμον). He anticipates the excuse by Lycianos that he was not prepared for this speech, a reference to the sophistic practice of extemporaneous speech (αὐτοσχεδιασμός). The interlocutor then takes the role of the audience for this rhetorical contest and will shout and cheer or hiss according to the merits of the declamation.

tude toward wealth and luxury is the primary example of the simple life
given by Nigrinus; he also mentions freedom and free speech. Nigrinus
tells of a conspicuously wealthy and vulgar person (ἐπίσημος καὶ
φορτικός) who came to Athens and scandalized the citizens by his
clothes, jewelry, and number of attendants. The Athenians educated him
(παιδεύω) in a gentle way, much in the manner of the Cynics, by mock-
ing his appearance and manners.[127] Although Nigrinus never tells where
the millionaire comes from, the implication is that he is from Rome.
Athens, the philosopher concludes, is suited for the serious person "who
has been taught to despise wealth and elects to live for what is intrinsically good" (*Nigr.* 14).

But anyone who loves wealth, gold, purple, and power will find
Rome better suited to them (*Nigr.* 15). Just as simple lives of poverty and
the avoidance of wealth and luxury were themes in Nigrinus's description
of Athens, the adulation of the wealthy and the trappings of wealth are
part of his description of Rome. Nigrinus expresses the disdain we have
already seen for the ostentatious display of wealth by Romans (*Nigr.* 21).
It is the voice of philosophical Athens criticizing Rome's vulgarity, the
same subtext we identified in Aristides' speeches to Athens and Rome.[128]
Nigrinus excoriates the rich's use of the *nomenclator* to greet their guests
and their demands for "Persian" obeisance. He also notes the excessive
attention to wills and the hypocrisy of legacy hunting; gluttony and
fixation on luxurious dainties; and rude behavior in the baths (*Nigr.*
30–34). Nigrinus criticizes the vice that wealth promotes and the
flattering servitude that wealth provokes as much as the wealth itself
(*Nigr.* 22). Excessive wealth leads to excessive desire for pleasure and,
subsequently, vice: the "ever-flowing, turbid stream" of pleasure brings
in "adultery, avarice, perjury, and the whole family of the vices [τῶν
ἡδονῶν], and sweeps the flooded soul bare of self-respect, virtue, and
righteousness" (*Nigr.* 16).[129]

---

[127]See Malherbe, "Self-Definition" and "Cynics," on harsh and gentle
methods used by different schools.

[128]See Bompaire, *Lucien écrivain*, 499–504, on the Cynic themes here and
Fuchs, *Geistige Widerstand*, 17–19, 47–57, on anti-Roman sentiment among
Greek philosophical writers. See also Philo *De vit. cont.* 6.48 [478]; Jos. *Ant.* 15
§§271–76; Dio *Or.* 13.34; 31.121, 157; 32.69–95; 34.38; 38.66; Luc. *Dem.* 40,
57; *Anach.* 37; Philostr. *VA* 1.16; 4.22; 4.42.

[129]Harmon's Loeb translation supplies "the whole family of the vices" for τὸ
τοιοῦτο φῦλον τῶν ἡδονῶν, presumably as a better parallel for virtue,

Lucian's *Nigrinus* tells us much about "true wealth"; Lycianos reports to his friend that, after his trip to Rome, he is "once poor, now truly rich indeed" (*Nigr.* 1). Lycianos then describes to his friend how Nigrinus praised philosophy, ridiculing "the things that are popularly considered blessings—wealth and reputation, dominion and honour, yes and purple and gold—things accounted very desirable by most men, and till then by me also" (*Nigr.* 4). The philosopher criticized "what was dearest to me—wealth and money and reputation." The narrator "Lycianos" makes the philosopher Nigrinus sound very much like Diogenes of Sinope. Rome, in *Nigrinus*, is a symbol of not only excessive wealth and vice but the excessive, even ostentatious, display of wealth, power, purple and gold. This rhetoric of blame would have been familiar to Asian audiences when they heard John's attack on Rome in Revelation.

Summary and Conclusion

The complexity of wealth imagery in the Apocalypse of John reflects the complex and different attitudes toward wealth in Greco-Roman society. The philosophical tradition regularly criticized the trappings of wealth and power. At the same time, citizens and sophists celebrated these trappings in speeches and inscriptions that glorified their wealth and power. Wealth could function as part of philosophical critique or civic praise, just as it does in the Apocalypse. Each section of this chapter demonstrated this correspondence between the narrative world of the Apocalypse and the social world of its audience. First, I showed that the exhortation of the gold-clad Christ in Revelation evoked Stoic attitudes toward wealth, particularly as it was translated into wider moral discourse under the *topos* of "true wealth." While the Cynic attack on wealth and praise of poverty was too narrow in comparison to the messages to Smyrna and Laodicea, the Stoic notion of the *adiaphora*, which functioned as an ideology for the wealthy but still allowed for a surface critique of wealth, made for an informative parallel. Second, I noted the parallel between the descriptions of Christ and Greco-Roman epiphanies and between the heavenly throne room and Hellenistic and Roman monarchs and courts. Third, I showed how the wealth of heaven is distinguished in Revelation from the wealth of Babylon/Rome. A number of examples demonstrated that commerce was held in low esteem, particularly when compared to

---

ἀρετή. But the paragraph is about the flow of pleasures into every gate of the body and through the gates and streets of Rome.

inherited and established landed, wealth. Fourth and finally, I demonstrated how wealth was part of the praise and blame of cities in epideictic rhetoric. Here again, wealth could function in praise and blame, just as it does in the Apocalypse. While the sophists praised the Asian cities for their wealth, the Greeks retained a disdain for Roman commerce and culture well into the second century CE.

Each of the points of this chapter will inform the exegesis in the following chapters; I will draw on this evidence as I examine the passages in Revelation in more detail. The evidence of this chapter also suggests a broader conclusion for the study of the Apocalypse. Taken as a whole, the exploration of attitudes toward wealth here sets the interpretive context for a rhetorical analysis of the Apocalypse. We saw in chapter 2 how the imagery of Revelation comes from the Hebrew Prophets, but we have seen here how the themes of the Apocalypse reflect the discourse of Greco-Roman culture. This chapter has shown the ways in which the audience could have heard the wealth imagery of the Apocalypse. While John drew on biblical sources for the imagery of the Apocalypse, his audience would have seen his visions in the light of their own social world.

Wealth and Rhetoric
in Revelation

The Rhetoric of Revelation

The literary results of the previous two chapters are impressive. In chapter 2, we discussed in detail the biblical sources for Revelation and compared the wealth motifs to Second Temple Jewish and early Christian literature. This research showed how John selected and concentrated source materials so that the visions of his Apocalypse are wealthier than other apocalyptic texts. The intricate layers of intertextuality in Revelation, moreover, cast a strong doubt on how well the audience could have understood or even heard the biblical allusions. Revelation does not have any citation formulas or other clues to help its audience to recognize biblical quotations or allusions.[1] Modern scholars, with printed texts and concordances at hand, disagree over the number and extent of many of the allusions and echoes in Revelation. This doubt about the effectiveness of purely literary exegesis was strengthened by the extensive correspondences uncovered in chapter 3 between the wealth passages in Revelation and discourse about wealth in Greco-Roman culture.

The correspondences between Revelation and Greco-Roman sources offer more than parallels; they point to an interpretive context as well. The literary results of chapters 2–3, then, have broader interpretive implications. The search for literary sources and parallels has also been a search for the context in which to read Revelation. As I discussed in the Introduction, the relation of text and context is particularly difficult for Revelation. Interpretations of the Apocalypse have struggled to bridge the

---

[1]As noted in chap. 2, n. 1; see Paulien, *Decoding Revelation's Trumpets*, 100–54; Fekkes, *Isaiah and Prophetic Traditions*, 59–63; Boring, 27; and Moyise, *Old Testament in Revelation*, 14–19. Moyise's criticism of Fekkes's attempt to divide allusions to Isaiah into categories of probability or doubt as a way of better appreciating the "authentic" allusions is apt: "it is often the subtle nuances that separate it from other members of the genre. After all, we would not expect a music critic to limit his or her comments to the loudest instruments in the orchestra!" (p. 18).

abyss between its phantasmagorical narrative world and the social world of the implied audience. Part of the difficulty may be that the study of Revelation has been preoccupied with the author's sources and background. This preoccupation leads the reader deeper and deeper into the narrative world of Revelation—deeper into the abyss, as it were—and deeper into constructions of the author's mind and intent, all the while moving further and further away from the Asian Christians who read the text aloud in their assemblies. Rhetorical criticism keeps the audience ever in mind, and the book of Revelation is a highly rhetorical work.[2] We can try to hear Revelation as the audience in ancient Asia Minor would have heard it by focusing on the rhetoric of the text. Keeping attention on the rhetorical nature of the Apocalypse avoids separating the text from its context, or its "rhetorical situation."[3]

George Kennedy has defined rhetoric simply as "that quality in discourse by which a speaker or writer seeks to accomplish his purposes."[4] We should be cautious in assuming too much formal rhetorical knowledge in the Christian communities at this time, nor should we sell them too short as uncultured and uneducated. A certain amount of rhetoric was "in the air," particularly in the cities of Asia Minor where sophists performed for the public.[5] The author of Revelation digested vast amounts of the Hebrew and Greek scriptures, which provided him with a form of rhetorical training. There were also rhetorical handbooks in circulation. Classical rhetorical theory furnishes a more emic analytical tool for studying the argument of Revelation than modern linguistic theories.[6] If nothing else, it provides a vocabulary for discussing the

---

[2]By "rhetoric" I mean the practice and study of persuasive speech in Greco-Roman antiquity, and by "rhetorical criticism," the method introduced to N.T. studies by George A. Kennedy, *New Testament Interpretation through Rhetorical Criticism* (Chapel Hill and London: University of North Carolina Press, 1984). The standard reference work on ancient rhetorical forms and figures is Heinrich Lausberg, *Handbuch zum literarischen Rhetorik: Ein Grundlegung der Literaturwissenschaft*, 2 vols. (Munich: Max Hueber, 1960).

[3]See Lloyd F. Bitzer, "The Rhetorical Situation," *Philosophy and Rhetoric* 1 (1968): 1–14.

[4]Kennedy, *Rhetorical Criticism*, 3.

[5]See the discussion of sophists in chap. 3, pp. 111–15; Kennedy, *Rhetorical Criticism*, 8–10, for a reasoned historical justification for using classical rhetoric to study the N.T.; and Aune, "Roman Imperial Court," 6–7.

[6]Compare the shockingly etic approaches of Schüssler Fiorenza, *Justice and*

rhetoric of Revelation that corresponds to the vocabulary of Greco-Roman antiquity for discussing public discourse. The Greek of Revelation may not be up to Attic standards, but the text lends itself to analysis in terms of epideictic invention, arrangement, and style.

The rhetorical nature of the Apocalypse, like other New Testament writings, begins with its performative character. This was a text to be read aloud and to be heard by an audience.[7] Of the three types or "species" of classical rhetoric, Revelation may be compared to either deliberative rhetoric, (λόγος συμβουλευτικός), which seeks to persuade an audience to follow or not to follow a specific course of action, or epideictic (λόγος ἐπιδεικτικός), which seeks to affect an audience's values or their views toward a person or city. The third species, judicial or forensic rhetoric (λόγος δικανικός), applies to the setting of the law court. Judicial rhetoric takes the forms of prosecution and defense (ἀπολογία). Deliberative rhetoric takes the forms of exhortation and dissuasion. Epideictic takes the forms of praise or encomium or panegyric (Lat. *laudatio*), and blame (ψόγος [*psongos*], Lat. *vituperatio*). Of these three species and their constituent positive and negative forms, Revelation has clear affinities with epideictic rhetoric.[8] First, epideictic tries to affect an audience's view, opinions, or values. The Apocalypse tries to convince its audience to hold a favorable point of view toward John and his allied prophets and their version of Christianity and to take a negative point of view toward the Roman authorities, the Jews, and Christian teachers, prophets, or functionaries who hold different views from John.[9] Second, epideictic includes speeches of praise and blame of persons and cities. Revelation begins with the praise or blame of the seven cities in Asia and builds to extended invective against Babylon and encomium on the New Jerusalem. Third, epideictic rhetoric is distinguished by its amplification of topics and imagery (ἐργασία [*ergasia*], Lat. *amplificatio*); vivid description (ἔκφρασις [*ekphrasis*]); and comparison (σύγκρισις [*synkrisis*]). All

---

Judgment, 159–80; and David Hellholm, "The Problem of Apocalyptic Genre and the Apocalypse of John," *Semeia* 36 (1986) 13–64.

[7] Note ἀναγιγνώσκω, Rev 1:3, and the forms of ἀκούω in Rev 1:3; 22:17, 18; 2:7, 29; 3:6, 13, 22.

[8] Schüssler Fiorenza, 15–37, discusses all three species as aspects of the rhetoric of Revelation.

[9] See Kennedy, *Rhetorical Criticism*, 19–23, 73–77, on the goals of epideictic rhetoric.

three of these characteristics are prominent features in Revelation, as I will note in this and the following chapters. There are elements of deliberative rhetoric in the exhortations to "stand firm" and dissuasion from eating idol meat in the messages in Revelation 2–3; there are elements of accusation against Rome/Babylon in Revelation 18 that might suggest the law court.[10] But the few calls for action in the text are vague; what does it mean to "hold fast" (3:11), "rest a little longer," (6:11), or "calculate the number of the beast" (13:18)? Rev 13:18 also calls for wisdom; understanding is more important than action. The visions describe "what is, and what is to take place" (1:19) rather than what the audience should do. While the implied author asserts that events are going to happen in the future, the rhetorical function of these assertions is to change the audience's mind in the present. Revelation should be read as epideictic rhetoric.[11]

Again, the use of classical terminology should not be taken as a claim that John and his audience were trained rhetoricians who analyzed discourse in light of these classical categories. The terms are helpful for describing what is going on in the text and were also being used by theorists around the time Revelation was written and first read. A comparison with a modern method of interpretation, the sociology-of-knowledge approach, shows the value and flexibility of classifying Revelation as epideictic rhetoric. Analysis of Revelation in terms of the sociology-of-knowledge discusses how Revelation tries to change the symbolic universe of the audience by imparting new knowledge that differs from the publicly accessible knowledge of Greco-Roman society.[12] Revelation tries to change the way the audience sees their social world. This is the function of epideictic rhetoric, which tries to change an audience's values or opinions.

---

[10]Kennedy, *Rhetorical Criticism*, 74, notes there is always a "subtle deliberative purpose" in epideictic rhetoric but the primary goal is the strengthening of values.

[11]Kirby, "Rhetorical Situations," 200, mistakenly contends that Revelation is deliberative rhetoric because it "is concerned with events in the future (Rev 1. 1, 3) and with a course of action expedient to the audience (22. 11–12)." In effect, he takes these statements at face value, abrogating his critical position, rather than examining their rhetorical purposes.

[12]See Susan R. Garrett, "Chaos or Community?" 73–87; Meeks, *Moral World*, 143–44; on public and deviant knowledge, Thompson, *Revelation*, 186–97; and the discussion in the introduction.

The outline or arrangement of a speech in antiquity varied according to the species of rhetoric, but all three types moved in good Aristotelian fashion from beginning (*proem* or *exordium*) through the middle (including the *narratio, propositio, argumentatio, exempla,* etc.) to end (*epilogue* or *peroratio*).[13] The general structure of the Apocalypse can be compared to the arrangement of epideictic rhetoric, "an orderly sequence of amplified topics dealing with the life of the person being celebrated or with the qualities of the concept under consideration, often adorned with vivid description (ecphrasis) or with a comparison of the subject to something else (synkrisis)."[14] The amplified topics of the Apocalypse are John's visions, which are hardly in orderly sequence according to classical standards. Indeed, almost two thousand years of interpretation has yet to produce a satisfactory outline. But John's visions do suggest epideictic arrangement in the way his carefully constructed, literary pieces incorporate vivid description (*ekphrasis*) and are contrasted with each other (*synkrisis*). *Synkrisis*, often called polemical parallelism or the mirroring motif by commentators, is a major structuring device of the Apocalypse.[15] Satan and Satan's allies mimic God and God's creatures throughout the book of Revelation. The Beast from the Sea, with ten horns and seven heads and a deadly wound that had been healed (Rev 13:1–3), mimics the Lamb of God who was slain and has seven horns and seven eyes (Rev 5:6–7). An angel seals the slaves of God upon their forehead, protecting them from the disasters that beset the earth (7:3); the Beast from the Land causes everyone to be marked on their forehead or right hand (13:16), designating them for eventual death and destruction. Both God and Satan have armies fighting for them. The cities of Babylon and the New Jerusalem are set in clear contrast. Not all of the comparisons in the Apocalypse can be set in neat, binary oppositions.[16] But the

---

[13]See the table of authorities in Lausberg, *Handbuch,* 148–49 (§262).

[14]Kennedy, *Rhetorical Criticism,* 24; see 23 on the *ekphrasis* of the visions in Revelation.

[15]Adolf Deissmann might not have been the first to notice this pattern but deserves credit for coining the phrase "polemical parallelism" to describe the cult of Christ in opposition to the cult of Caesar; see Paul Barnett, "Polemical Parallelism: Some Further Reflections on the Apocalypse," *JSNT* 35 (1989): 111–20. See esp. Meeks, *Moral World,* 144–45. The pattern of binary oppositions has been used by structuralist commentators on Revelation such as Gager, *Kingdom and Community,* and Yarbro Collins, *Combat Myth* and *Crisis and Catharsis.*

[16]This is a main point of Leonard L. Thompson, "The Literary Unity of the

mirroring motif as a literary device expresses the cosmic conflict in the narrative world of the Apocalypse between the forces of heaven and the demonic powers.

Outlines of Revelation have been notoriously unsuccessful in proving very much.[17] Most commentators discern units in Rev 1:1–20, which I will discuss as proem and *narratio* in detail below; Rev 2:1–3:22, the messages to the seven churches; and an epilogue (*peroratio*) in 22:6–21. The main point of contention is how to divide up Rev 4:1–22:7, with its complicated patterns of interlocking, interwoven, and intercalated visions.[18] The "septenaries" or series of sevens (seven messages, seven

---

Book of Revelation," *Mappings of the Biblical Terrain: The Bible as Text*, ed. V. L. Tollers and J. Maier (Lewisburg PA: Bucknell University Press; London and Toronto: Associated University Presses, 1990) = *Bucknell Review* 33/2:347-63.

[17]The study and comparison of literary outlines of Revelation would be a major work in its own right, although the value of such a work would be questionable. I have chosen three of the most important recent scholars for illustrative purposes; further examples abound (for analysis see esp. Christopher R. Smith, "The Structure of the Book of Revelation in Light of Apocalyptic Literary Conventions," *NovT* 36 [1994]: 373–93; and Humphrey, *Ladies and the Cities*, 84–95). Schüssler Fiorenza, *Justice and Judgment*, 174, proposes a series of four, sometimes overlapping, major parts: (1) the inaugural vision and letter septet, 1:9–3:22; (2) the seven sealed scroll, 4:1–9:21; 11:15–19; 15:1, 5–16:21; 17:1–19:10; (3) the small prophetic scroll, 10:1–15:4; and (4) visions of judgment and salvation, 19:11–22:9. Yarbro Collins, *Combat Myth*, 19–32, divides Revelation into two "great cycles" of visions, 1:1–11:19 and 12:1–22:21, including two series of seven unnumbered visions, 12:1–15:4 and 19:11–21:8 (following here Farrer, *Rebirth of Images*, 47–49). Collins also introduces the unfortunate terms "Babylon Appendix" (17:1–19:10) and "Jerusalem Appendix" (21:9–22:5). Bauckham, *Climax of Prophecy*, 5–6, 17, questions the actual count of the markers for these "unnumbered series," καὶ εἶδον and ὤφθη. He proposes an inaugural vision in 4:1–5:14, leading into three numbered series of sevens, with two intercalations (6:1–8:1; 8:3–5 / 8:2; 8:6–11:19 / 15:1; 15:5–16:21). "The story of God's people in conflict with evil," 12:1–14:20 and 15:24, falls between the seven trumpets and seven bowls. Bauckham's Babylon section is 17:1–19:10; 19:11–21:8 is transitional; and 21:9–22:9 the New Jerusalem, followed by the epilogue (see *Climax of Prophecy*, 2–22).

[18]Problems in terminology are symptomatic of the difficulties in describing the structure of Revelation. A passage such as Rev 6:1–8:5 demonstrates this well. The seven seals are opened in 6:1–16 and 8:1–2. The visions in Rev 7:1–17

trumpets, etc.) would have been evident as a structuring device to an audience hearing the Apocalypse even for the first time. There are also a number of recurring phrases, in particular "after this I saw" (or "heard"), which would guide the audience (see Rev 4:1; 7:1; 15:5; 18:1; 19:1). Problems arise when commentators attempt to be more precise than this—for there are a number of confusing twists and turns—or, in a variation of the same error, when commentators see more structure in the Apocalypse than there really is. Hinge texts, such as Rev 10:1–11:14 and 19:1–10, which interrupt septenaries or start new sections before another has finished, complicate analysis of the units even more. Attempts to group visions in "unnumbered series of sevens," interludes, appendices, and intercalations, however justified by detailed analysis of the text, offer little insight into how the audience would have heard the Apocalypse since these complicated structures would not have been accessible to auditors. The distinction between rhetorical *style* and *arrangement* or structure is helpful to keep in mind when considering the structure of the Apocalypse. Style, in rhetorical criticism, may be divided into *lexis* (λέξις) or diction, the choice of words, including metaphors and tropes; and *synthesis* (σύνθεσις) or composition, including figures of speech and thought.[19] The recurrence of stylistic features might be mistaken for structural clues and such a mistake could produce a more complicated arrangement than necessary. Furthermore, the cyclical, repetitive, and

---

are thus inserted between the sixth and seventh seal, a process called "intercalation" (Bauckham, *Climax of Prophecy*, 9) or "interlude" (Schüssler Fiorenza, *Justice and Judgment*, 172–73). But Schüssler Fiorenza uses the term "intercalation" to describe the linking process in 8:1–2 in which the seventh seal leads immediately to the seven trumpets; Yarbro Collins, *Combat Myth*, 16–18, calls this second device "interlocking" and Bauckham, *Climax of Prophecy*, 8–9, "overlapping or interweaving." Schüssler Fiorenza thus describes "double intercalations" in Rev 10:1–11:14 and 17:1–19:10.

[19]See Kennedy, *Rhetorical Criticism*, 26–30. A convenient list of figures and tropes is in Herbert W. Smyth, *Greek Grammar*, rev. by Gordon Messing (Cambridge MA: Harvard University Press, 1984; orig. 1916, 1920) 671–83. Bauckham identifies a number of repeated phrases exhibiting "remarkable" variation (*Climax of Prophecy*, 22, 27). While John's use of *variatio* is skillful, it is hardly remarkable within the context of ancient rhetorical conventions. A number of these features Bauckham identifies, as he himself notes, would not have been evident to the audience nor to most careful readers today (29).

confusing structure of the visions is in itself a rhetorical technique designed to destabilize the audience's view of their social world.

Rhetoric tries to convince an audience about something and requires proof to do this. In Revelation, despite the enormous complexity of the visions, the rhetorical task boils down to the relatively simple one of convincing the audience that John's worldview is correct while his opponents' (Roman, Jewish, and Christian) is fundamentally, even diabolically, wrong. Rhetorical theory describes the proofs in the argument (πίστις, Lat. *probatio*) of a speech as "inartistic" or external (ἄτεχνος, Lat. *inartificialis*) and "artistic" or internal (ἔντεχνος, Lat. *artificialis*) proofs.[20] External proofs, such as the testimony of witnesses or court documents, would be of particular importance in judicial or forensic rhetoric but are helpful for describing the argument in Revelation as well. The visions of the Apocalypse function as external proofs. While a critical reader might argue that these are literary creations of John and therefore internal proofs, in the narrative-rhetorical situation they are presented to the audience as something John sees, records, and reports to the seven churches. The function of the visions in Revelation as external proofs is analogous to the function of the miracles of Jesus in the Gospels.[21] John's visions acquire additional authority from their correspondence to earlier prophetic and apocalyptic visions and their use of biblical language, since the Hebrew scriptures frequently functioned as external proofs in early Christian writings. The visions could seem authoritative to members of the audience familiar with Jewish and Christian apocalyptic traditions, but they might seem quite bizarre to others. The visions cannot stand alone, therefore, but require additional argument or proof.

The second type of proof centers on the author himself, his own authority, and his relation to authority figures in the Christian community, in particular Jesus Christ. If the Apocalypse is to have validity among its intended recipients, the text must successfully convince the audience that John of Patmos has recorded visions received from God through Christ. The validity of John's visions, or external proofs, depends a great deal upon the authority of the narrator and the goodwill of the audience. Throughout the Apocalypse, then, but particularly in the introductory

---

[20]See Lausberg, *Handbuch*, 1:190–93 (§§348–54); Kennedy, *Rhetorical Criticism*, 13–19; Arist. *Rh.* 1.2.2 (1355B); 3.13.4 (1414B); Quint. *Inst.* 5. preface, 1.1.

[21]See Kennedy, *Rhetorical Criticism*, 14–15, on the function of the miracles in the Gospels as external proofs.

proem and narration in Rev 1:1–20, the author presents internal or "artistic" proofs designed to seek their sympathy and goodwill of the audience toward the narrator.[22] Two different types of artistic proofs featured in John's proem are "ethical" and "pathetical" proofs. An "ethical" proof attempts to establish the narrator's character (ἦθος [*ēthos*]) and credibility; a "pathetical" proof works upon the feelings (πάθος [*pathos*]) of the audience with promises and threats.[23] Again, use of these terms should not be taken as a claim that John had a copy of Quintilian's *Institutio Oratoria* or that the audience judged the Apocalypse by its faithfulness to Aristotle's *"Art" of Rhetoric*. The modes of *ēthos* and *pathos* are convenient terms to describe a feature common to discourse in all cultures: a speaker attempts to establish credibility and to play upon the feelings and emotions of his or her audience.

The Rhetoric of Revelation 1:1–20

I will now show how rhetorical theory works in the text of Revelation and how the ideology of wealth functions as part of this rhetoric. Rhetorical theory and practice place a great burden on the beginning of a text. In the opening proem (Rev 1:1–8) and narration (Rev 1:9–20) of the Apocalypse, the implied author attempts to seek the attention and the goodwill of the audience; establish the trustworthy character of his narrator; and introduce the main themes of the Apocalypse. Rev 1:1–20 also introduces the wealth of heaven to the audience in the vision of Christ as the Human One (1:12–16). The proem and narration set the rhetorical and ideological context for the wealth imagery in Rev 1:12–16 by developing the social and political associations of heavenly wealth and power. I will discuss these associations at length as I develop a rhetorical exegesis of Rev 1:1–20. By emphasizing the rhetoric of the text and the ideology of wealth, the exegesis that follows cannot perforce account for every literary detail in this rich text. Rather than following every hint, allusion, and history-of-religion image, I will focus on rhetoric, wealth, and ideology.

---

[22]See on artistic proofs, Lausberg, *Handbuch*, 193–95 (§§355–57); Kennedy, *Rhetorical Criticism*, 14–19; Arist. *Rh.* 1.2.2–5 (1356a); Quint. *Inst.* 5.12.9–12.

[23]Aristotle's third mode, *logos* or logical proof, is not a prominent feature in Revelation, although see on Rev 1:3 below. Kirby, "Rhetorical Situation," uses the categories of *ēthos* and *pathos* in his rhetorical analysis of Revelation 1–3.

The function of the proem is "to obtain the attention of the audience and goodwill or sympathy toward the speaker."[24] The proem of the Apocalypse, Rev 1:1–8, can be divided into the superscript or preface, 1:1–3, and the epistolary prescript, 1:4–8. This division is marked by shift from third-person in the preface to first-person in the epistolary prescript. Revelation in effect begins twice, but there are rhetorical implications in postponing the opening of the letter in 1:4–8 until after the third-person preface in 1:1–3.[25] If Revelation opened with Rev 1:4, it would most likely be called "The Letter of John to the Asians," perhaps referred to as "Fourth John" or "Asians," on the analogy of Ephesians and Hebrews. The epistolary character of the text and John's role as author rather than prophetic witness would be foregrounded rather than mediated through the preface. But rather than presenting itself as a letter from John, the Apocalypse presents itself as the revelation or ἀποκάλυψις of Jesus Christ. This shift is a subtle rhetorical move designed to increase the authority of the visions in the text (the external proofs) by ascribing them to God and Christ while establishing the *ēthos* or character of the narrator as trustworthy to deliver these visions to the audience (an internal, artistic proof).

A number of rhetorical features of the preface in Rev 1:1–3 focus on the *ēthos* or character of the narrator. The Apocalypse is identified as Ἀποκάλυψις Ἰησοῦ Χριστοῦ (1:1), the "revelation" (or "uncovering") of Jesus Christ, only once. The lack of further description, coupled with the expectation that this *apokalypsis* would be read aloud in assembly, shows that the word was familiar to its audience. The audience would likely have understood it as a reference to Christian worship and prophetic activity rather than a description of the genre of the text (see 1 Cor 14:26).[26] The preface claims that this is the revelation "of Jesus

---

[24]Kennedy, *Rhetorical Criticism*, 23–24; see also Lausberg, *Handbuch*, 1:150 (§263); Arist. *Rh.* 3.14 [1414b]; Quint. *Inst.* 4.1.1–79.

[25]This rhetorical move could be attributed either to the historical John of Patmos or to a later editor; the heuristic assumption of the "implied author" includes both possibilities. Aune, "Prophetic Circle," suggests that the Apocalypse was carried to the churches by different prophetic envoys and the prologue legitimates their role.

[26]Revelation is the first "apocalypse" to take this title. Schüssler Fiorenza, *Justice and Judgment*, 150–51 and n. 56, makes a strong case that the title was meant to characterize John's experience as a Christian prophetic experience within the Pauline tradition. See also 1 Cor 1:7; 14:6; 2 Cor 12:1, 7; Gal 1:12;

Christ," given to Jesus by God and then delivered to John by an angel.[27] Although the "historical" John of Patmos may have been a leader of a group of Christian prophets and known to many of the Asian churches, the text itself has to construct the character of the narrator, by means of artistic proofs, so that the audience will find the report of heavenly visions more convincing. Before John speaks directly to the audience as "I," he is introduced as a slave of God, to whom God sent an *apokalypsis* of Christ by means of God's angel. The author introduces himself in the third-person in 1:1–2, at the center of a chiastic structure:[28]

> A   The revelation of *Jesus Christ*,
>   B   which *God* gave him to show his slaves what must soon take place;
>   C   he made it known by sending his angel to his *slave John*,
>   B'   who testified to the word of *God*
> A'   and to the testimony of *Jesus Christ*, even to all that he saw.

The chiasm surrounds the slave John with the highest Christian authority figures, Jesus Christ and God, and introduces the mediating angel. The rhetorical strategy of ascribing this *apokalypsis* to God is part of the overall strategy of cloaking the author's own moral, ideological, and theological convictions in divine garb. Here, in contrast to every other New Testament text, God and Jesus Christ are ascribed authorship. John, a slave of God, merely receives the revelation.

The preface begins to establish the narrator's *ēthos*, by claiming that God has entrusted the "revelation" of Jesus Christ to his slave John, by means of an angel. It also heightens the emotional impact (*pathos*) of the

---

2:2; Eph 1:17; 3:3; 2 Thess 1:7; 1 Pet 1:7, 13; 4:13. The verb ἀποκαλύπτω does not occur in Revelation but is frequent in Paul and Deutero-Pauline texts (Rom 1:17, 18; 8:18; 1 Cor 2:10; 3:13; 14:30; Gal 1:16; 3:23; Eph 3:5; Phil 3:15; 2 Thess 2:3, 6, 8; 1 Pet 1:5, 12; 5:1).

[27]Reading the genitive here as subjective, with Bousset, 210; Swete, 1–2; Charles 1:6; and subsequent commentators.

[28]In Greek, the chiasm is as follows:

A   Ἀποκάλυψις Ἰησοῦ Χριστοῦ
   B   ἣν ἔδωκεν αὐτῷ ὁ θεός,
      C   δεῖξαι τοῖς δούλοις αὐτοῦ ἃ δεῖ γενέσθαι ἐν τάχει, καὶ ἐσήμανεν ἀποστείλας διὰ τοῦ ἀγγέλου αὐτοῦ τῷ δούλῳ αὐτοῦ Ἰωάννῃ,
   B'   ὃς ἐμαρτύρησεν τὸν λόγον τοῦ θεοῦ
A'   καὶ τὴν μαρτυρίαν Ἰησοῦ Χριστοῦ, ὅσα εἶδεν.

text on the audience. This is done in two ways. First, John creates an eschatological time frame with the phrases "what must soon take place" in the first sentence (ἃ δεῖ γενέσθαι ἐν τάχει, 1:1) and "the time is near" in the second (ὁ γὰρ καιρὸς ἐγγύς, 1:3). The preface expresses a clear sense of eschatological urgency; God has revealed the future to John. Second, the preface includes the first of the seven beatitudes in the Apocalypse, with a blessing upon "the one who reads aloud the words of the prophecy" and "those who hear and who keep what is written in it" (1:3). This blessing implies a palpable threat for those who do not keep these words or act within the eschatological time-frame created by the text (see Rev 22:18–19). The blessing is linked to the warning "the time is near" by a causal γάρ (ὁ γὰρ καιρὸς ἐγγύς), so that the final phrase is an *enthymeme* or deductive proof. Those who pay attention to John's Apocalypse are blessed *because* the time is near. The rhetoric of the preface attempts to instill in the audience a sense of urgency and of the importance of this revelation.

Slaves of God

When the preface characterizes both narrator and implied audience as slaves of God, it introduces an important theme for the rhetoric and the ideology of wealth in Revelation.[29] The words "slave" (δοῦλος) or "fellow slave" (σύνδουλος) appear in Revelation as designations of a social order (6:15, 13:16, 19:18) but appear more frequently as terms with positive connotations designating the people of God.[30] There are special references to prophets as slaves of God (10:7; 11:18; 19:10; 22:9) and martyrs, fellow-slaves and brothers of the prophets (6:11). The implied author of Revelation uses a phrase well-established in early Christian theological discourse. The established usage suggests that "slave of God/Christ" had positive connotations; the use of the phrase at the opening of a number of letters (Rom 1:1; Gal 1:10; Phil 1:1; Tit 1:1; Jas 1:1; 2 Pet 1:1; Jude 1) suggests that its appearance in Rev 1:1 might even be expected by a Christian audience.[31] The slave language in Rev 1:1 has

---

[29]Roloff, 20, claims that John rejects any claim to authority or position by describing himself and the members of the churches as slaves. But this overlooks the power and subtlety of the slave metaphor, as I discuss here.

[30]See Rev 1:1 (twice; note προφητεία, 1:3); 2:20; 6:11; 7:3; 10:7; 11:18; 15:3 (Moses); 19:2, 19:5; 22:3, 6, 9.

[31]The positive use of the title slave and its association with prophets in the Apocalypse is well recognized by commentators; see Aune, "Social Matrix," 17;

both ethical and pathetical functions. Martin has shown how the phrase "slave of God/Christ" functioned both as a title of leadership and a symbol of salvation in the New Testament.[32] Both senses are present in Rev 1:1, where John takes the title of "slave of God" as a prophetic leader while the implied audience joins him soteriologically as "slaves of God" in the kingdom established by Christ (see Rev 1:6, 9).

The positive connotations carried by slave metaphors in Revelation, as with its use in other early Christian literature, reflect the positive aspects associated with slavery in the social world of the Greco-Roman audiences of these texts. We should not be misled by the negative connotations the word "slave" has in modern English usage; such negative connotations are surely behind the NRSV's translation of δοῦλος as "servant" while noting that the Greek word is in fact "slave."[33] Our recent contact with one former slave, Trimalchio, who frees several of his own slaves in the course of his dinner party, should alert us to the social ambiguities that surrounded slavery in Roman antiquity. There was a slave hierarchy, ranging from rural farm workers and urban menial laborers to slaves with administrative and financial management responsibilities, such as Trimalchio, who was *dispensator* or steward for

---

and "Prophetic Circle," 108–10, where Aune argues that the slaves in 1:1 and 22:16 are the Christian prophets exclusively. This is challenged by Bauckham, *Climax of Prophecy*, 85–86. The influence of the O.T. on Rev 1:1 is generally recognized; see Amos 3:7; and Charles, 1:6, who holds that the "servants" are prophets.

[32]See Dale B. Martin, *Slavery as Salvation: The Metaphor of Slavery in Pauline Christianity* (New Haven CT and London: Yale University Press, 1990) 50–68; a third function of the slave metaphor in Paul's letters described by Martin is the ideology of the demagogue as slave of the masses. Occurrences of "slave of God/Christ" showing designation of leadership include Matt 21:33–41; 22:1–14; 24:45–51; Luke 2:29; 12:41–46; 17:7–10; Acts 2:18; 4:29; 16:17; 20:19; 34–35; Rom 1:1; Gal 1:10; Phil 1:1; Col 4:12; 2 Tim 2:24; Tit 1:1; Jas 1:1; 2 Pet 1:1; Jude 1. The soteriological sense of "slave of God/Christ" can be seen in Matt 6:24; Luke 12:41–46; Revelation itself; and in Martin's exegesis of Romans 6 and 1 Corinthians 9. Martin's brief summary of the use of the slave metaphor in Revelation (p. 54) incorrectly characterizes the Apocalypse as independent of Pauline Christianity.

[33]The research on the status of slaves in antiquity of Martin, *Slavery as Salvation*, 2–49, confirms the briefer studies in Veyne, "Vie de Trimalcion," 216–23; MacMullen, *Roman Social Relations*, 98–104; and Meeks, *First Urban Christians*, 20–22.

C. Pompeius (*Sat.* 29.4).[34] Slavery and manumission functioned within the patron-client structure of Roman society, in which both parties gave and received honors and influence. Being the slave of a powerful or wealthy person would raise the status of a person of humble origins or limited economic means. Trimalchio and his fellow freedmen attempted to "better" their favorite slaves.[35] Manumission provided one of the only means of social mobility in the Roman Empire.[36] The philosopher Epictetus, for instance, was a freed slave. While slavery was not a necessarily preferable state in antiquity, to be a slave of a wealthy or powerful patron, such as an imperial slave of Caesar, raised one's status over the free, urban poor. This social dynamic applied only within urban cultures such as Rome, Corinth, and the cities of Asia; rural slaves could be much worse off than their free counterparts.

The social context of slave language underscores the importance of the characterization of the audience and narrator of Revelation as slaves. The use of the slave metaphor to describe John and the audience would suggest, by analogy with Martin's work on Paul, a positive function for this language in Revelation. Designation of John and his fellow prophets as slaves of God (1:1; 10:7; 11:18) would imply a position of leadership within the Christian community. The characterization John as *the* slave worthy to receive the revelation of Christ and communicate it to the other slaves is part of the ethical argument of the proem since it helps to establish the narrator's character (*ēthos*) as authoritative. The interpreting angel who leads the narrator in the Babylon and New Jerusalem sections attributes additional authority by stating that he, though an angel, is a "fellow slave" with John and his brother prophets (19:10; 22:9). As slaves of God, prophets had special authority, like the steward of a powerful senator or a slave of Caesar. Those in the implied Christian audience are also "slaves of God," a usage Martin labels soteriological. We can read this as a rhetorical argument appealing to the audience's feelings (*pathos*). They all have the same owner and patron in God.

---

[34]See Veyne, "Vie de Trimalcion," 216–18; Martin, *Slavery as Salvation,* 15–22; and Peter Garnsey, "Slaves in Business," *Roma* 1 (1982) 105–108.

[35]Pet. *Sat.* 46; see Veyne, "Vie de Trimalcion," 216. The rich looked for talent among their slaves because they needed managers for their estates and affairs. The *Satyricon* also suggests a "trophy wife" syndrome as well, in which development of slaves' talents reflected well on the owners.

[36]See Veyne, "Vie de Trimalcion," 216–23; MacMullen, *Roman Social Relations,* 98–104; and Martin, *Slavery as Salvation,* 30–42.

To this point, the slave language in Revelation appears to function in the same way as the slave metaphor in other New Testament texts, such as Paul and the Gospels. The established usage of the slave metaphor in the New Testament drew on the patronal ideology of Greco-Roman society, as does Revelation, but the Apocalypse has a significant difference. Other New Testament texts lack the extensive description of the patron God that we find in Revelation. John characterizes the owner and patron of these slaves, God, and the owner's son, Christ, by means of extravagantly wealthy visions (Rev 1:12–16; 4:2–11), visions which have no counterpart in Paul. The characterization of God as a wealthy monarch in the Apocalypse far exceeds the characterization of God as king, master, or landowner in the Gospels. The implied author adds the imagery of wealth to the patronal ideology inherent in the slave metaphor, amplifying its ideological power. In doing so, he challenges the dominant Greco-Roman power structure on its own terms. John does not subvert the patronal ideology inherent in the "slave of God/Christ" metaphor, as Paul arguably does, but uses it for his own ideological purposes. Revelation portrays God as more powerful, and *wealthier*, than any contender the Romans might put forward: proconsul, high priest, Caesar himself.[37] And, the more powerful the master or patron, the more powerful the head slave. The rhetoric of slavery in Revelation raises the status of John within the Christian communities of Asia, since he is the slave deemed worthy to receive the *apokalypsis* from this wealthy and powerful God.

Ruler of the Kings of the Earth

The preface defines the authority and *ēthos* of John as the head slave deemed worthy by God to receive the revelation of Jesus Christ through an angel. The patronal ideology of the slave metaphor implies wealth and power, both of which will be made more explicit for the audience in Revelation. The epistolary prescript in 1:4–6 also develops the royal-political aspects of heavenly power. Rev 1:4 begins as though it will follow the standard opening of a Pauline letter: "John to the seven churches that are in Asia: Grace to you and peace." While John did not need Paul's example in order to write a letter to the Christian churches, familiarity with the Pauline tradition in Asia is likely and this can be read

---

[37]Martin describes Paul's challenge to the benevolent patriarchal leadership in terms of his assumption of the title "slave of all"; see *Slavery as Salvation*, 86–135.

as another reach for the audience's goodwill.[38] John makes significant changes in the formal elements of Paul's greeting for his own rhetorical and ideological purposes. Paul typically writes "grace from God our father" (Rom 1:1, 1 Cor 1:1), but God is the father only of Jesus in Revelation (Rev 1:6).[39] John sends grace and peace first from "the One who is and who was and who is to come" (Rev 1:4). This phrase, unique in the New Testament, would have evoked comparisons to both Jewish interpretations of Exod 3:14 and popular Greek descriptions of the gods.[40] John adds to the characterization of God as patron of Christian slaves with this evocative phrase, which challenges rival Jewish and Greek conceptions of the deity. The God who has chosen John as the slave worthy of a special prophetic revelation is more powerful than Zeus, Isis, or the God of the Jewish people. Second, greetings are sent from "the seven spirits who are before [God's] throne." The identity of these seven spirits has eluded commentators, but the term seems to refer to some spirit separate from angels (cf. Rev 1:20; 3:1; 4:5; 5:6).[41] Whatever their history-of-religions background, the greeting functions rhetorically by introducing God's throne, the focal point of Revelation 4–22, early on in the proem.

Finally, in the third element of the greeting, John sends grace and peace from "the faithful witness, the firstborn of the dead and the ruler of the kings of the earth" (Rev 1:5).[42] Christ, like God, has a threefold

---

[38]See Roloff, 7–8; Karrer, *Die Johannesoffenbarung als Brief*; on points of contact between Revelation and Pauline Christianity, see Schüssler Fiorenza, *Justice and Judgment*, 85–156.

[39]So also Roloff, 24; see Rev 2:28; 3:5, 21; 14:1.

[40]Noted by Bousset, 214; Charles 1:10; and subsequent commentators. See *Tg. Ps.-J.* Exod 3:14; *Tg. Ps.-J.* Deut 32:39; Paus. 10.12.5; Plut. *De Is. et Os.* 9 (*Mor.* 354C).

[41]Bousset, 214–18, who sees here a primitive Trinitarian formula (cf. Just. Mart. *Apol.* 1.6; *Dial.* 87.1), identifies them as the seven archangels of the presence; so also Charles 1:11–13 (who brackets the phrase nonetheless); Harrington, 46; and Aune, *HarperCollins Study Bible,* 2310. This reading is disputed by Swete, 5–6; Caird, 15; and Roloff, 24, who prefer the sevenfold Spirit of God. Beasley-Murray, 55, maintains that they must be a representation of the holy spirit. Mounce, 69–70, does not take a position.

[42]See Charles 1:13, on the anomalous Greek. Schüssler Fiorenza, *Justice and Judgment*, 70–73, argues that the three predicative statements about Christ in 1:5–6 came from early Christian baptismal language.

description, with each part corresponding to a different aspect of Christ's activity.[43] The idea of Christ as witness (μάρτυς) is unique in the New Testament.[44] The implied author has already described how John "testified [ἐμαρτύρησεν] to the word of God and to the testimony [μαρτυρίαν] of Christ" (1:2). The word μάρτυς carries the idea of "bearing witness" by giving one's life, anticipating the later sense of "martyr."[45] Within the Apocalypse, Christ (1:5, 3:14) shares this appellation with Antipas of Pergamum, who was also put to death (2:13), and the two prophetic olive trees in 11:3–13, who are killed by the beast. John, of course, is not dead but nonetheless can witness to the word of God (Rev 1:2, 9), a usage perhaps designed to communicate the suffering by the author to his audience. Whether verb or adjective, death or not, it is an important concept and lends further authority to the narrator. The second attribution of Christ in the epistolary prescript follows logically from the first: as faithful witness, Christ is also firstborn of the dead. In the early church, this word (πρωτότοκος) had developed from a reference solely to Christ's resurrection to include a titular sense of Christ as sovereign or ruler of the dead and the church itself (Col 1:15, 18; Heb 12:23).[46]

The third aspect of Christ's description in Rev 1:5 introduces a political motif.[47] Whereas the characterization of God, "who is and was and is to come," challenges the ideology of Jewish and pagan Greek theology, the description of Christ as "ruler of the kings of the earth" challenges Roman authority. As part of this challenge, John apparently draws on two lines from Psalm 89 (= LXX Psalm 88), a royal-messianic psalm which may have evoked political associations, with several key

---

[43]See Roloff, 24–25; Aune, 43–49.

[44]So Charles 1:14, noting μαρτυρέω in John 18:37.

[45]See Allison A. Trites, "Μάρτυς and Martyrdom in the Apocalypse: A Semantic Study," *NovT* 15 (1973): 72–80, on the diachronistic development of this word.

[46]See Charles 1:14; Roloff, 25.

[47]Schüssler Fiorenza, *Justice and Judgment*, 68–81, makes the important observation based on exegesis of Rev 1:5–6 and 5:9–10 that John conceives of the theological notions of redemption and salvation in political and socio-economic categories. Her article does not, however, take account of the positive aspects of slavery in the social world of the original audience, which would have an impact on these categories; for instance the notion of being purchased (Rev 5:9) by the Lamb; nor does she retain a keen sense in this article of the ideological argument in Revelation against John's Christian opponents.

substitutions.[48] One change in particular shows how the author has emphasized the political motif. Where Ps 89:28 reads "highest of the kings of the earth," John changes "highest" to "ruler," (ἄρχων [*archōn*]). The Greek word *archōn* is a political title for a chief magistrate in a Greek city. Jesus is ruler, *archōn*, of the kings of the earth. These kings of the earth become major characters in the visions of Revelation 4–22, in particular the Babylon passage in chapters 17–22.[49] The challenge to earthly authority expressed here in the epistolary prescript will be developed at length in the Apocalypse to the point where the social and political consequences of John's theology, both within the context of the Christian churches and between the churches and Greco-Roman society, are paramount in the rhetoric of Revelation.

The epistolary prescript in Rev 1:4–5a segues into a doxology in Rev 1:5b–8. In the epistolary structure of Revelation, this doxology functions like the Pauline thanksgiving, continuing the introduction of major themes and ending with an eschatological climax.[50] The doxology in Revelation focuses on Christ's actions on behalf of the community. There is a clear reach for the audience's goodwill in the use of first-person plural pronouns in 1:5–6 as the narrator forges a bridge to his audience through the words "us" and "our." Christ's actions are cast in political terms; he has established Christians as a kingdom and priesthood.[51] The community which has received the benefits of Christ's death consists of those who have been loved by Christ and washed of their sins and made a "kingdom" (βασιλεία) under this *archōn*. This doxology ends with two prophetic oracles, one announcing the *parousia* of Jesus on the clouds of heaven (v. 7) and the other taking the voice of God (v. 8). The prophetic oracle in Rev 1:7 continues the political motif. According to this oracle, every eye will see Christ upon his return, even those who killed or "pierced" him, while every nation or tribe (πᾶσαι αἱ φυλαὶ τῆς

---

[48]See Ps 89:38 and Ps 89:28.

[49]See Rev 6:15; 17:2, 18; 18:3, 9; 19:19; 21:24.

[50]See Schubert, *Form and Function of the Pauline Thanksgiving*, 4–9; and J. T. Sanders, "The Transition from the Opening Epistolary Thanksgiving to the Body in the Letters of the Pauline Corpus," *JBL* 81 (1962): 348–62.

[51]See Elisabeth Schüssler Fiorenza, *Priester für Gott: Studien zum Herrschafts- und Priestermotiv in der Apokalypse*, NTAbh n.s. 7 (Münster: Aschendorff, 1972) 253–62; *Justice and Judgment*, 68–81; and Andrew J. Bandstra, "'A Kingship and Priests': Inaugurated Eschatology in the Apocalypse," *Calvin Theological Journal* 27 (1992): 10–25.

γῆς) will mourn. The particular prophetic oracle used in Rev 1:7 has rhetorical significance as well. The conflation of Dan 7:13 and Zech 12:10 in Rev 1:7 was probably already in the repertoire of early Christian prophetic tradition.[52] It was thus meant to be recognized by the audience and to provide legitimation for John as a trustworthy prophet. In rhetorical terms, a legitimate prophetic oracle at this point in the proem is part of the establishment of the speaker's *ēthos* or character.

Since the prophetic pronouncement in Rev 1:8 concludes the proem of the Apocalypse (cf. 1:4), a short summary of the rhetorical structure and themes of Rev 1:1–8 is in order before proceeding. The authority of the text and the authority and *ēthos* of the implied author and narrator, John, are the primary rhetorical concerns in this passage, but as we have seen these goals are reached a number of ways. The preface attributes authorship of this Apocalypse to God and selects John as the one slave worthy to transmit it to the rest of God's slaves. This is a prophecy of eschatological urgency and implied threats to be read aloud in the Christian assembly. Those who pay attention and keep its words are blessed, implying that any of God's slaves who ignore the revelation of the prophet-slave John do so at their peril, "for the time is near" (Rev 1:3.) The epistolary prescript trades on Paul's authority and style, but makes distinctive changes that highlight major themes of the Apocalypse. Chief among these themes is the royal-political motif, anticipating the glorious introduction of the Human One in 1:12–16. The proem concludes with recognizable prophetic oracles designed to confirm among the Christian audience the authority of this text as prophecy and the narrator as prophet.

While in the Spirit on the Lord's Day

John turns again to the audience in Rev 1:9, focusing on building the bridge between narrator and audience. The audience might not ever be sure who is "speaking" in the proem. Characters are introduced in the third-person in the preface (1:1–3); John addresses the audience directly in the epistolary prescript (1:4–6); a prophetic oracle describes the

---

[52]On the development of this oracle in Christian tradition, see Norman Perrin, "Mark 14:62: The End Product of a Christian Pesher Tradition?" in *A Modern Pilgrimage in New Testament Christology* (Philadelphia: Fortress Press, 1974) 10–22. On the form of this oracle, see Aune, *Prophecy in Early Christianity*, 255, 280, and 433n.184. The oracle also foreshadows the identification of the voice in Rev 1:13 as that of Daniel's Human One.

parousia of Jesus (1:7); and, finally, God speaks (1:8). After this multiplication of narrative voices, John identifies himself again in 1:9 to keep his audience from becoming lost.[53] This verse is the strongest appeal for the goodwill of the audience by the narrator in the Apocalypse. The narrator is the audience's brother (ἀδελφός), a familial term that was common in Christian theological discourse for members of the community. Here it functions as one of the author's ethical proofs to establish his narrator's credibility with the audience. Paul always uses ἀδελφός at the beginning of his letters (Rom 1:13; 1 Cor 1:10; 2 Cor 1:8; Gal 1:2, 11; Phil 1:12; 1 Thess 1:4) as well as throughout the body. It is used infrequently in Revelation relative to the New Testament, with only five occurrences, and may been a term reserved especially for prophets within John's circle (see Rev 6:11; 12:10; 19:10; 22:9). John uses another Pauline word, "partner" or "associate," συγκοινωνός, (Rom 11:17; 1 Cor 9:23; Phil 1:7; 4:14; Eph 5:11), to describe how he and the audience share in the persecution (θλῖψις), the kingdom (βασιλεία, continuing the political theme introduced in Rev 1:5–6), and the patient endurance (ὑπομονή) that is "in Christ."[54] Where self-description as ἀδελφός was an ethical appeal, the author shifts to *pathos* in this appeal to the ideals of persecution and endurance. Patient endurance in the face of affliction was a Stoic concept, expressed also in Paul's letter and in other Jewish and Christian texts.[55] Whatever persecution John did in fact share

---

[53]This is called "renominalization" by L. Hartman, "Form and Message. A Preliminary Discussion of 'Partial Texts' in Rev 1–3 and 22,6ff." in *L'Apocalypse johannique et l'Apocalyptique dans le Noveau Testament*, 129–49, who notes the border or episode marker of time and place in 1:9–20 but does not connect this transition to rhetorical theory or practice.

[54]The NRSV translation, "I, John, your brother who share with you in Jesus the persecution . . . " fails to take account of the close relationship of ἀδελφός and συγκοινωνός implied by the lack of the article with συγκοινωνός. Problems with this phrase include how to construe ἐν Ἰησοῦ; and whether ἐν Ἰησοῦ goes with all three nouns or only with ὑπομονή; see Charles 1:21.

[55]Susan R. Garrett, "The God of This World and the Affliction of Paul: 2 Cor 4:1–12," in *Greeks, Romans, and Christians: Essays in Honor of Abraham J. Malherbe*, ed. David L. Balch, Everett Ferguson, and Wayne A. Meeks (Minneapolis: Fortress Press, 1990) 99–117, explores the motif of ὑπομονή in Paul as a bridge between Jewish and Stoic traditions. The evidence cited by her (100n.7 and 105n.30) demonstrates the widespread notion of "patient

with the Christians of Asia Minor, it is nothing compared to what the Apocalypse is about to describe. Affliction or persecution, endurance, and the kingdom of Christ are key concepts for access to heavenly wealth in Revelation, as we will see in the next chapter in the discussion of the message to Smyrna (Rev 2:8–11).

The implied author then situates his narrator in time and place. In classical rhetoric, this was called the *narratio*.[56] John is on Patmos "on account of the word of God and the witness of Jesus." John implies that he has been sent to this island as punishment for his prophetic activities.[57] As noted above, the idea of witness, μαρτυρία, carries a sense of suffering to the point of death, underscoring John's self-characterization as the audience's "partner in suffering, kingdom, and endurance." By specifying that John was "in the spirit on the Lord's day," the implied author creates a congruence between the narrator in narrative time and the audience, hearing John's *apokalypsis* read aloud in the Christian assembly.[58] The narrative framework of the Apocalypse is fairly simple, despite the enormous complexity of the intervening visions. John was on Patmos, where he received visions from Christ, which he was commanded to record and send to the seven churches (1:11). The author describes this setting before describing the vision of Christ, a device to simplify the plan for the audience. The formal narration continues in Rev 1:19, when Christ repeats the command to write to the churches, and 4:1, where the voice of Christ summons John to the heavenly throne room. This brackets the seven messages from the central visions, again simplifying the narrative scheme for the audience. The visions of chapter 4–22 are hardly simple, but the structure is intentionally confusing so as to destabilize and thereby challenge the audience's view of their world. Things start to settle down in the epilogue; in 22:8–9, John testifies to the truth of his visions and communicates the command to publish the text rather than seal it up

---

endurance" as a response to hardships or to Satan's testing.

[56]See Kennedy, *Rhetorical Criticism*, 24, 79–80, 145, on the uses of *narratio* in different species of rhetoric.

[57]Most commentators (e.g., Swete, 12; Charles 1:22; Roloff, 32; Boring, 81–82) take this reading but do not recognize that this could be a rhetorical pose.

[58]See David E. Aune, "The Apocalypse of John and the Problem of Genre," *Semeia* 36 (1986): 89, on the strategy of audience participation in order to recreate the revelatory experience; and Thompson, *Revelation*, 72–73, on the worship context for the reading of the Apocalypse.

(22:10; cf. 22:18–19). Asian Christians hearing this Apocalypse would know at least how it came to be read aloud in their church.

Jesus Christ, the Human One

John turns to see the voice and describes the dramatic vision of Christ as Human One amidst the seven golden lamps. This vision (Rev 1:12–16) is the climax of the *narratio*. We have looked at this vision twice already, from the Jewish and Greek perspectives, and can now apply that research into its literary background and social context to understand its rhetorical force, especially as it applies to the characterization of Christ. The implied author has emphasized the *ēthos* of the narrator in the proem and narratio. Another character now takes center stage. The characterization of John as trustworthy slave and prophet, entrusted with a special revelation from God, allows the narrator to fade into the background so that the visions will appear to the audience as accurate prophetic vision reports. Within the narrative framework of the Apocalypse, Christ, the risen Lord of the Christian communities, appears and dictates the messages to John for delivery to the seven churches. The *ēthos* of the narrator masks the literary nature of the visions, allowing them to take on divine authority.

John describes a vision of a deity recognizable to Jewish or Greek Christians. The first thing John describes upon turning around are the seven golden lampstands. Christ himself wears a long robe and a golden sash. This vision of Jesus is the first indication that gold is associated with the divine and with the Christian communities in the narrative world of the Apocalypse. The audience wonders, of course, where Christ's gold comes from, but for that they have to wait for the vision of the heavenly throne room (4:2–11). Christ wears gold and, according to his interpretation (1:20), the Christian churches are represented by seven golden lampstands. Associating gold with Christ and the churches establishes a norm in the text that influences how one perceives every subsequent image of wealth in this narrative world. Heaven sets the gold standard in the Apocalypse. The wealth imagery in this vision also functions as part of the characterization of Christ. The ruler of the kings of the earth and son of the *pantokrator*, "God Almighty," is wealthy as well as powerful.[59] The vision in Rev 1:12–16 adds wealth to Christ's political power.

As we have seen, John uses parts of several different OT passages in Rev 1:12–16: golden lamps from Zechariah (Zech 4:2); golden belt from Daniel (Dan 10:5); and the long "foot-robe" (ποδήρης) from Ezekiel (Ezek 9:2), which evokes the opulence of the Hebrew cult (Exod 25:3–7). The wealth motifs in Rev 1:12–16, drawn from the Hebrew scriptures, foreshadow the glories of heaven soon to be described. The allusions, however, would have been obscure to anyone without a deep knowledge of the scriptures; the implied author offers no interpretive clues for the audience that this vision is in fact a bundle of literary allusions. The only clue for the audience is the action of the narrator. When John sees Christ, he prostrates himself as would be appropriate before a king as well as before a deity (Rev 1:17).[60] This is a standard motif in biblical as well as Greco-Roman epiphany scenes. Daniel falls to the ground in a trance when he sees a vision of Gabriel by the Tigris:

> I looked up and saw a man clothed in linen, with a belt of gold from Uphaz around his waist. His body was like beryl, his face like lightning, his eyes like flaming torches, his arms and legs like the gleam of burnished bronze, and the sound of his words like the roar of a multitude. (Dan 10:5–6)

Those in the audience familiar with the Jewish scriptures might have recognized the decorative motifs in Revelation borrowed from Daniel's vision, although the identification of Christ as the Human One by John in Rev 1:13 begins a tangled web of intertextual confusion difficult for even the hardiest exegete to unravel. The vision of Christ in Rev 1:12–16 would likely have evoked other comparisons for those more familiar with the iconography of Greco-Roman culture rather than the Jewish scriptures:

---

[59]Roloff, 28–29, discusses the Stoic understanding of deity implied in the word παντοκράτωρ (see Rev 1:8; 4:8; 11:17; 15:3; 16:7; 19:6, 15; 21:22; elsewhere in the N.T. only in 2 Cor 6:18, where it is in a quotation of the LXX [regular translation for צבאות]). Roloff relates this to John's focus on Hellenistic Christians but it is also interesting in terms of the Stoic attitude toward wealth expressed in Rev 2–3.

[60]See Aune, "Roman Imperial Court," 13–14.

> And to them the son of Leto, as he passed from Lycia far away to the countless folk of the Hyperboreans, appeared; and about his cheeks on both sides his golden locks fell in clusters as he moved; in his left hand he held a silver bow, and on his back was slung a quiver hanging from his shoulders; and beneath his feet all the island quaked, and the waves surged high on the beach. Helpless amazement seized them as they looked; and no one dared to gaze face to face into the fair eyes of the god. And they stood with heads bowed to the ground. (Ap. Rhodes *Argon.* 2.674–83)

This epiphany of Apollo is illustrative of other Greco-Roman epiphanies.[61] John places seven stars in Christ's right hands and a double-edged sword in his mouth. While both props have extensive intertextual associations in the Hebrew scriptures and intratextual references in Revelation, they also suggest the symbolic weapon or tool regularly carried by Greek and Roman deities—Apollo's bow and lyre; Isis's *sistrum* and *situla*; Hermes' *caduceus*; Athena's *aegis*, helmet, shield, and spear. Golden thrones, capes, and crowns were part of the court ceremony of Hellenistic monarchs and Roman emperors; this cosmic deity, the Human One, is also the ἄρχων of the kings of the earth. John and the audience are the slaves of this ancient, powerful king and his son (1:1).

Conclusion: The Two Messengers

The proem and narration in Rev 1:1–20 lead directly into the messages to the seven churches in Asia. Two messengers present these messages. First is John, slave and prophet of God and narrator of the visions of the Apocalypse. The superscript (Rev 1:1–3) characterizes John the narrator and his audience as slaves of God, a traditional Christian metaphor. This ideology has implications within the Asian Christian community. John, slave and prophet of God, is entrusted with a revelation for the entire church, while other teachers, apostles, or prophets do not have this status. The second messenger is Jesus Christ, whose power is characterized in political language that challenges Roman authority. Christ adds authority to the paraenesis of the messages, authority that John could not command on his own. The appearance of Jesus Christ, ruler of the kings of the earth, to John on Patmos displays the wealth befitting such a regal

---

[61]See chap. 3, pp. 97–99.

figure.[62] The wealth imagery in Christ's appearance on Patmos prepares the audience for the discussion of wealth and poverty in the messages and the wealth imagery in the visions of heaven that follow. The characterization of John and the audience as slaves of God introduces the rhetorical dynamic whereby the imagery of wealth in the Apocalypse becomes an ideology for the community. As slaves of God, the Christians are slaves of the most powerful and wealthiest monarch. Their God is not only wealthier than Caesar, but the wealth of heaven is superior to the wealth of Rome.

---

[62]David E. Aune, "The Apocalypse of John and Graeco-Roman Revelatory Magic," *NTS* 33 (1987): 481–501, argues that John consciously adopts and parodies revelatory magic motifs in the Apocalypse. Two examples he cites are in Rev 1:1–20: Hecate as key-bearer (Rev 1:18); the first and the last or alpha and omega (1:8, 17). The third is the phrase "I am coming quickly" (Rev 2:16; 3:11; 22:7, 12, 20). It is not clear to me that John's audience would see this as parody, nor that they would perceive the political and wealth imagery in 1:12–16 and 4:1–5:14 as "parody" of the imperial court, as Aune contends in "Roman Imperial Court Ceremony," so much as a challenge to Roman power.

The Messages
to Smyrna and Laodicea

Rhetoric and the Social Composition of the Churches

In the previous chapter, I described how John characterizes Christ in Rev
1:1–20 as a regal and wealthy figure powerful enough to challenge
Roman authority. Christ now speaks directly to the churches in Asia. He
dictates seven exhortations, sometimes called letters, to John for the
"angels" of seven churches in Asia.[1] The messages to the seven churches
in Revelation 2–3 are our strongest anchor for a social-historical reading
of the visions in chapters 4–22. These seven messages contain more
discernible references to concrete moral behavior and the social world of
the hearers than do the visions in the rest of the Apocalypse. The
tendency among scholars has been to follow the hermeneutical advice of
Rev 1:19 and read the seven messages as indications of "that which is"
and the visions in Revelation 4–22 as "that which is to take place."[2] But
I strongly question whether we should take John's characterization of
each Christian community at face value.[3] I have maintained throughout

---

[1]See Charles 1:34; the angels have been taken as elders, bishops, messengers,
guardian angels, and the heavenly counterparts of the seven churches. Schüssler
Fiorenza, *Justice and Judgement*, 145–46 and nn. 37–39, identifies the angels as
visionary counterparts of the prophets in each community and thus as evidence
that John is a leader of this group of prophets; so also Aune, "Social Matrix," 23,
and "The Prophetic Circle of John of Patmos." Roloff, 38–40, contends that the
use of angels as recipients of the messages is a criticism of angel worship among
the churches.

[2]"What you have seen" in Rev 1:19 is usually understood to refer to the
vision in 1:12–16. But see the elegant proposal of Caird, 26, who construes καί
. . . καί as "both . . . and," with the following translation: "write what you see,
what now is and what is to happen thereafter."

[3]The search for "local references" in the messages is a positivist-historicist
attempt to prove that messages are descriptions of "that which is." See Ramsay,
Letters to the Seven Churches; Hemer, *Letters to the Seven Churches of Asia*;
and Charles H. H. Scobie, "Local References in the Letters to the Seven

this study that Revelation does not reflect so much as construct a social situation, hence my focus on the rhetoric of the text. Our understanding of "that which is"—the characterization of each community—must take into account the ideological agenda of the Apocalypse. In this chapter, I will focus on how the rhetoric of wealth in the seven messages shapes the ideology of the Apocalypse.

The rhetorical characterization of the seven churches can be understood in ideological terms. As noted in chapter 1, the seven messages focus on two main moral issues: endurance in the face of suffering; and each church's relation to teachers or groups whom the implied author condemns. The messages to Ephesus, Pergamum, and Thyatira deal primarily with the acceptance or rejection of Christian teachers or prophets whom John himself opposes; ideological conflict is a clear issue in these messages.[4] The proclamation to Sardis does not mention any Christian teachers or opponents but divides the congregation into the majority who are "dead" and a minority "who have not soiled their clothes" (Rev 3:1, 4). The call in this message to "remember then what you received and heard; obey it, and repent" (3:3) suggests that the "dead" members of the church have turned away from John's authority (note ἀκούω and τηρέω in both 1:3 and 3:3). The church in Sardis still retains its "name of being alive" (3:1) because they do not acknowledge any of John's Christian opponents as authoritative. They are not active dissenters but are placed on warning. The praise for Philadelphia suggests the rejection or at least absence of John's Christian opponents as well as the author's support for this community's strong opposition to the Jewish community (3:8–10).

But the characterization of Smyrna and Laodicea as the "poor" and the "rich" churches poses a special case, since the praise and blame accorded to these two congregations do not obviously connect to John's ideological agenda. The motifs of poverty, wealth, and trade have obscured the connection. If we accept the characterization of these two churches at face value, the argument would go as follows. The Smyrnans are a poor congregation and thus more susceptible to persecutions and slander. Their poverty has come about because of their strong adherence to the Christian faith, which puts them at odds with Greco-Roman society.[5] The Laodiceans, in direct contrast, boast of their wealth and are

---

Churches," *NTS* 39 (1993): 606–24.

[4]See Rev 2:6, 14–15, 20–24.

[5]So Bousset, 242–43; Swete, 31; Charles 1:56; Caird, 35; Mounce, 92;

chastised by Christ. The assumption here would be that the members of this church are able to avoid suffering because of their wealth, which they have achieved through accommodation to the culture. But these common interpretations accept the characterization in these messages as reliable indicators of "that which is." The powerful rhetorical and ideological agenda of the Apocalypse casts serious doubts on accepting any characterizations without asking how the scripting of these two communities functions as part of that agenda. Disregarding for the moment whether or not the Smyrnan and Laodicean churches were actually poor and rich, I will consider how these two messages advance the rhetorical agenda of the Apocalypse, particularly its Christological rhetoric.

There is second reason for maintaining that a rhetorical strategy is behind the characterization of Smyrna and Laodicea. As discussed in the introduction, the social composition of the seven churches was likely quite diverse, casting some doubt on John's identification of two churches as "poor" and "wealthy." The Pauline churches included imperial slaves, freed slaves, merchants, and soldiers and the seven churches of the Apocalypse are part of Paul's original territory. The emerging consensus reported by Malherbe on the social level of first-century Christians applies to the audience of the Apocalypse as well as the Pauline churches.[6] The audience would have included as wide a variety of economic, educational and social levels as can reasonably be imagined within the constraints of the highly stratified society of the Roman Empire. There is, unfortunately, no prosopographic evidence from Revelation as there is from Paul's letters. John and Antipas (Rev 2:13) are the only two names we have; the names of John's opponents are rhetorical constructions. But there would have been households supporting the seven churches, perhaps more than one in the larger cities of Ephesus and Smyrna, just as there were in other early Christian churches.

More evidence for the social composition of the "poor" church of Smyrna comes from the letters of Ignatius. Whatever their actual situation was when John composed and sent the Apocalypse around 95 CE, this congregation apparently had financial means by 115 CE, when Ignatius wrote the Smyrnans from Troas.[7] In his letter, Ignatius recalls the material

---

Roloff, 48; Harrington, 59.

[6]Malherbe, *Social Aspects*, 29–59; see also Meeks, *First Urban Christians*, 51–73.

[7]On the date and circumstances of this letter, see William R. Schoedel, *Ignatius of Antioch*, Hermeneia (Philadelphia: Fortress Press, 1985) 11.

and spiritual support he received during his stay in this city: "You refreshed me in every way [κατὰ πάντα με ἀνεπαύσατε], and Jesus Christ (will refresh) you" (Ign. *Smyrn.* 9:2).[8] The members of the Smyrnan and Ephesian churches funded a deacon to accompany Ignatius to Troas (Ign. *Smyrn.* 12:1, *Eph.* 1); the Smyrnans accepted and supported two deacons sent by Ignatius (Ign. *Smyrn.* 10:1); and they sent a legate to the church in Antioch (Ign. *Smyrn.* 11:3). These are not the actions of a church struggling for funds. Smyrna was a prominent city in Asia and the Empire. We should not be surprised that the church there exhibited diversity and possessed some wealth. In the closing of his letter, Ignatius mentions several households in Smyrna, including the house of Tavia. It is possible that some wealthier Smyrnans had converted to Christianity and brought their resources to support the church between the time of the Apocalypse and Ignatius. There is no mention in Ignatius's letter of prior poverty or conflict with the Jews; nor indeed do any of Ignatius's letters refer to Revelation, even though Ignatius was in contact with a number of the same churches as John. Ignatius also has Christian opponents; he warns of "beasts in human form" and "those who hold erroneous opinions about the grace of Jesus Christ" (*Smyrn.* 4:1, 6:2), referring to teachers of docetic versions of Christianity. Ignatius rebukes these teachers for their lack of charity: "For love they have no concern, none for the widow, none for the orphan, none for one distressed, none for one imprisoned or released, none for one hungry or thirsty" (*Smyrn.* 6:2). This accusation underscores John's complete disregard for issues of social justice, which we first noted in chapter 2. As in his other letters, Ignatius exhorts the church to support the bishop, elders, deacons, virgins, and widows (*Smyrn.* 8:1–2; see *Magn.* 6:1, *Eph.* 5:1), functionaries and groups absent from Revelation. While John's message to Smyrna scripts this church as "poor but rich," we are justified in assuming more variation in social level than the Apocalypse suggests for Smyrna as well as the other churches.

Form and Function of the Messages to the Seven Churches

Before considering in more detail the rhetoric of wealth in the messages to Smyrna and Laodicea, I would like to analyze the form and function of the messages as a whole. Most commentators now see the seven messages to be an integral part of the Apocalypse rather than separate

---

[8]Ibid., 245; and see p. 11, where Schoedel suggests that the stay was lengthy.

letters.[9] There are numerous intratextual references in Rev 2:1–3:22 to the prologue in 1:1–20 and to the visions in 4:1–22:5. Variations strongly suggest that the messages refer to seven actual churches, although the number seven is clearly stylized to fit the literary structure of the Apocalypse since there were also churches in Colossae, Hierapolis, Magnesia, and Tralles when Revelation was written. Since the Apocalypse is a circular letter, the paraenesis in each message, though focused on one church, applies to the entire audience.[10]

A function of the messages is to draw this audience into the narrative world of the text. John's visions attempt rather dramatically to change the audience's view of their social world by casting the Roman political order as demonic and describing impending death and destruction to most of the earth's inhabitants. The internal evidence of the messages and the external evidence of other NT texts suggest that the audience was not necessarily receptive to this strategy. The Apocalypse itself informs us of rival prophets and teachers in the seven churches.[11] Furthermore, the evidence of other NT writings suggests that second- and third-generation Christians found urban life in Roman Asia much more appealing than did John and his fellow prophets.[12] Therefore, any change in the audience's

---

[9]Charles, 1:37, maintains that the "Seven Letters" were written some time before the rest of the Apocalypse, in part because they lack, to his eye, the element of conflict with the Roman state that distinguishes the visions. Charles regards Rev 3:10 as a redactional addition of the Seer when editing the visions (1:89). The current assumption among North American commentators is that Revelation is a unified work; see Mounce, 83–84; Boring, 85–86; and Thompson, "Literary Unity."

[10]See Boring, 85–86.

[11]Thompson, *Revelation* 193–97, applies Peter Berger's conception of a "cognitive minority" as "a group formed around a body of deviant 'knowledge' " (see Peter L. Berger, *A Rumor of Angels. Modern Society and the Rediscovery of the Supernatural* [Garden City NY: Anchor Books/Doubleday, 1970, ©1969] 6–7, 17–18) to the social location of the Book of Revelation. Thompson's conclusion that John *and* his audience constitute such a "cognitive minority" within both the larger Christian community and Roman society should be nuanced by the apparent divisions within the implied audience of Revelation. John and his circle of prophets are a "cognitive minority" within the Christian community.

[12]See Luke 7:4–5; Acts 10:1–2; 17:12; 24:22; Rom 13:1–7; 1 Thess 4:12; 1 Tim 2:1–2; 3:7; Tit 3:1; 1 Pet 2:17. For a recent critique of Dibelius's construction of "bourgeois Christianity" in the Pastoral Epistles, see Reggie M. Kidd, *Wealth and Beneficence in the Pastoral Epistles: A "bourgeois" form of early*

worldview must be preceded by acceptance of the authority of text and author. In the narrative of the Apocalypse, the messages are a transitional stage between the introduction, which creates a congruence in time and space between narrator and implied audience "on the Lord's day," and the visions, which are described from the perspective of God's heavenly throne room. John leads up to the cosmic barrage of the visions fairly carefully. Rev 1:1–20 establishes the authority of text and narrator and describes the narrative situation. Christ, not the narrator, then speaks in the messages, characterizing each church along a narrow, dualistic axis; condemning John's opponents; and hinting of both the rewards and punishments to come. In the seven messages, only Rev 3:10 foreshadows the scope of the disasters to be portrayed in the visions. This carefully constructed buildup in Revelation 1–3 leads into the overwhelming display God's power in Revelation 4–5 and, beginning in 6:1, visions of cosmic judgment, death, and destruction. The transitional messages combine two perspectives; Christ comes down to earth before John ascends to heaven. Most important for the rhetorical force of these messages, the paraenesis is delivered by Jesus Christ rather than John.[13] The moral exhortation of the seven messages comes from one whom the early Christian communities worshiped as their risen Lord.

The seven messages in Revelation 2–3 are highly stylized and have a regular structure with several repeated elements.[14] Various outlines have been proposed, the most valuable of which recognize that these are not actual letters but prophetic proclamations within the larger epistolary framework of Revelation.[15] Rather than having an epistolary structure,

---

Christianity? SBLDS 122 (Atlanta: Scholars Press, 1990).

[13]See Aune, "Social Matrix," 18.

[14]Aune, "Intertextuality and the Genre of the Apocalypse," 148–49, has suggested that the language in these messages is set in an intentionally higher style but with very scanty evidence: the more frequent use of the particles ἀλλά and δέ in the messages and the apparent reduction in paratactic style, with fewer sentences beginning with καί in Revelation 2–3 (20.5%) than in the rest of the Apocalypse (73.8%). Such statistical comparisons are potentially misleading without more rigid control; for instance, how do the messages compare to Rev 1:1–20; the other speeches of Christ; or the speech of God from the throne in Rev 21:5–8?

[15]The idea of Charles, 1:37, 43–47, that the letters were composed and sent at an earlier date and then reedited into the final version of the Apocalypse has fallen out of favor among scholars. Kirby, "Rhetorical Situations," argues that

these messages have formal and structural similarities to ancient royal or imperial edicts.[16] The association of these messages with imperial edicts strengthens the political imagery introduced in Rev 1:1–20, which I discussed in the previous chapter.[17] The messages also have a strong prophetic content, recognized by a number of scholars.[18] As with the oracle in Rev 1:7, the use of familiar prophetic forms was an integral part of the rhetorical strategy to establish John's character (*ēthos*) and authority. John intended the churches to hear these messages as Christ speaking through him prophetically so that Christ, not John, was heard addressing the particular situation of each community.

A variety of schemes have been suggested to describe the regular form of the seven messages. Each message has an opening section, a body, and a concluding section; these have been subdivided into four to eight parts.[19] After the address of the church and the command to write,

---

these are in fact letters, following the lead of Ramsay, *Letters to the Seven Churches*, and Hemer, *Letters to the Seven Churches of Asia*. The weaknesses in his position have been ably discussed by Aune, "Form and Function of the Proclamations," 194–97 and n. 46. The recent commentaries of Boring and Harrington describe Revelation 2–3 as messages while Roloff prefers "circular letters." See also L. Hartman, "Form and Message"; Kraft, 49–54; and Karrer, *Johannesoffenbrung als Brief*, 159–65.

[16]See Aune, 126–29; and "Form and Function of the Proclamations," 183, 198–203.

[17]See esp. Aune, "Form and Function of the Proclamations," 204.

[18]Boring, 85; Ferdinand Hahn, "Die Sendschreiben der Johannesapokalypse: Ein Beitrag zur Bestimmung prophetischer Redeformer," *Tradition und Glaube: Das frühe Christentum in seiner Umwelt*, ed. G. Jeremias, H.-W. Kuhn, and H. Steggemann (Göttingen: Vandenhoeck & Ruprecht, 1971) 357–94; Ulrich B. Müller, *Prophetie und Predigt im Neuen Testament: Formgeschichteliche Untersuchungen zur urchristlichen Prophetie* (Gütersloh, 1975) 47–104. Aune, *Prophecy in Early Christianity*, 326, and "Form and Function of the Proclamations," 197–98, offers the unwieldy form "parenetic salvation-judgment oracle" to describe the messages. I also question the exegetical value of identifying the messages as "*a mixed genre created by the author*" (commentary, 119, Aune's italics).

[19]For instance, Aune discerns four different structural features in the opening of each proclamation: (1) the *adscriptio*, the name or address of each church; (2) the command to write (γράψον); (3) the "thus says" formula (τάδε λέγει, NRSV "these are the words"); which leads into (4) the Christological predications, "of him who. . . . " While four opening units may be discerned formally,

each message has a formulaic, and intentionally archaic "thus says"
(τάδε λέγει), followed by a Christological description, "the one who
(etc.)." There are significant variations in these Christological predications, the only variation in the opening of the messages.[20] The body of
each message is generally divided into two parts. The first part describes
the situation in each church and includes the "οἶδα-clause," usually "I
know your works" (οἶδά σου τὰ ἔργα) but somewhat different in
the messages to Smyrna and Pergamum (Rev 2:9, 13).[21] In the second
part of the body, often after the οἶδα-clause but sometimes intermingled
with it, Christ issues an exhortation for each church.[22] These two units are
the meat of each message and difficult to distinguish from one another
precisely.[23] It is a mistake to read the οἶδα-clauses as a mere "statement
of facts," like the *narratio* or διήγησις in a deliberative or judicial
oration. To interpret these sections as narrations is to read them as
descriptions of "that which is" (Rev 1:19) without critically examining
their rhetoric. The seven οἶδα-clauses are in fact highly charged
statements of praise or blame for each community based on the church's
adherence to the author's ideology or toleration of dissenting views. As
rhetorical characterizations of each church, they are as important as the
threats and promises that follow in each message. The concluding section
of each message has two parts: a proclamation formula, "let anyone who

---

rhetorically they would have functioned as one opening unit. Boring, 86–90, also
sees eight parts which are similar to Aune's but with different names and
functions.

[20]Roloff, 41, divides the opening section into the command to write and a
messenger formula. Aune notes that variation in particles in the *adscriptio*
suggests the author was purposefully varying his style here; note also that the
fiction of addressing each angel is not held throughout the letters (Rev 2:10, 13,
20–25; 3:4).

[21]Called "οἶδα-Abschnitt" by Hahn, "Sendschreiben," 370–77; "narration"
by Kirby; *narratio* by Aune; "divine knowledge" by Boring. Roloff and
Harrington describe only one central section.

[22]Kirby "proposition"; Aune "arrangement" or *dispositio*; Boring "body."

[23]Aune sees some overlap of the two features in the proclamation to Sardis,
in which the *narratio* consists of Rev 3:1b, 4, and the *dispositio* of 3:2–4. In the
proclamation to Laodicea, Rev 3:16 starts the *dispositio* but 3:17, "for you say
'I am rich,' " may be read as part of the *narratio* since it is part of the basis for
Christ's rejection of the Laodicean attitude. Such complications support the
outlines of Roloff and Harrington, who discern one central section.

has an ear listen," an echo of the Synoptic parables; and a promise of victory, "to the one who conquers I will give (etc.)."[24]

The variations in the Christological formula in the opening of each message call attention to how this section shapes each proclamation and how it characterizes each church. These Christological passages contain direct literary references to Rev 1:4–20. Christ uses John's exact words when addressing the seven churches. Christ describes himself to the Ephesians (Rev 2:1) with the same words that John used to describe his opening vision: "these are the words of him who holds the seven stars in his right hand [see 1:16], who walks among the seven golden lampstands" (see 1:12–13).[25] This third reference to the golden lampstands in Revelation (1:13, 1:20, 2:1) occupies the important first position in the seven messages and emphasizes the positive aspects of wealth imagery in Revelation. Gold imagery frames the seven messages. The messages from Christ begin with the golden lampstands and end with gold for sale in the message to Laodicea. In the message to Sardis (3:1), Christ lifts a phrase from the epistolary greeting in 1:4 to describe himself: "these are the words of him who has the seven spirits of God and the seven stars." This is entirely plausible in narrative time, since John would have heard the messages from Christ before composing the epistolary prescript to all seven churches. And yet this intratextuality also shows the literary artifice evident in John's careful constructions throughout the Apocalypse.

Smyrna

The Christological predications provide an entry point into the two most important messages for the discussion of wealth imagery. Death and life, not poverty and wealth, are the most prominent literary features of the message to the Smyrnans, bracketing both the exhortation on poverty and wealth and the warning of persecution by the Jews. In 2:8, when beginning the message to Smyrna, Christ quotes himself from 1:18: "these are the words of the first and the last, who was dead and came to life." The scene to which this quotation refers is replete with life and death imagery. When John first sees Christ on Patmos, he falls at his feet as though dead

---

[24]"Proclamation formula" and "promise of victory" are Aune's terms; Roloff and Boring describe essentially the same two parts. Kirby combines them in an "epilogue."

[25]In the message to Thyatira (3:18), Christ uses the words from John's description in 1:14–15.

(1:17). Christ tells John not to fear, for he is "the first and the last, and the living one. I was dead, and see, I am alive forever and ever; and I have the keys of Death and of Hades" (1:18). The life-and-death motif continues in the message to Smyrna. In the conclusion of the message, Christ exhorts them to be "faithful until death" and they will receive the "crown of life" (2:10). Christ thus calls upon the Smyrnans to emulate the paradox of life through death that he has exemplified as the "firstborn of the dead" (1:5) and the lamb who was slain (5:6). The promise of victory to the Smyrnans, which comes after the proclamation formula in this message, concludes the rhetorical amplification of the theme of death and life with a reference to the final judgment described in Rev 20:11–15: "whoever conquers will not be harmed by the second death (2:11)."

The theme of poverty and wealth in the message to Smyrna shows the same paradoxical expression as the dominant life-through-death motif: "I know your affliction and your poverty [πτωχείαν], even though you are rich [πλούσιος]" (2:9). Christ was dead but comes to life; the Smyrnans are poor but rich. The Smyrnans are also promised a crown if they remain faithful until death (2:10; cf. 3:11). Crowns or wreaths (στέφανοι) in the Apocalypse are generally gold (4:4; 4:10; 9:7; 14:14); this is a promise of honor for the Smyrnans in their poverty and affliction.[26] Christ does not promise the Smyrnans wealth after death (although the crown of life suggests a future reward) but claims they are rich *now*. But why does Christ say that they are rich? The clue to the Smyrnan's wealth is Christ himself; he wears gold and appears among golden lampstands that signify the seven churches of Asia. The Smyrnans acknowledge a wealthy Lord and are, like the other churches, described as a lamp of gold. And they are rich in deeds, in suffering and endurance. Christ mentions the church's "affliction" (θλῖψις) and the "slander" (βλασφημία) caused by "those who say that they are Jews and are not, but are a synagogue of Satan" (2:9).[27] The sequence in this message suggests that Christ bestows wealth upon the Smyrnans for their fight with the Jews, which they are apparently losing.[28] Some of them will be

---

[26]See Stevenson, "Conceptual Background to Golden Crown Imagery"; Aune, 172–75.

[27]The punctuation in the NRSV, which ignores the second καί in Rev 2:9, implies that the afflictions of the Smyrnans are not related to the Jews. According to the Greek, however, 2:9 should be read as one sentence.

[28]Roloff, 47–48, stresses both the death/life leitmotif and the struggle with Jews in this message.

cast into prison.[29] The split between Christians and Jews which resulted in Jewish Christians being expelled from the synagogue probably preceded Revelation by ten or fifteen years.[30] The two references to the Jews in Revelation both include the phrase "the synagogue of Satan" (2:9, 3:9), strongly suggesting that the expulsion of the Christians from the synagogue was still a live issue in the churches of Asia.[31]

Although the Apocalypse portrays many afflictions, the word θλῖψις occurs only five times. The narrator John shares afflictions with his implied audience (1:9); the Smyrnans suffer afflictions (2:9, 10); and Christ promises afflictions for the prophet "Jezebel" and her students (2:22). The fifth occurrence is Rev. 7:14, in the context of John's vision of an unnumbered crowd before the Lamb, clothed in white. The elder identifies this throng as those "who have come out of the great ordeal [ἐκ τῆς θλίψεως τῆς μεγάλης]; they have washed their robes and made them white in the blood of the Lamb." Death by martyrdom is clearly implied. Praise and ascriptions of wealth in deeds go to those who endure afflictions, including endurance unto death. The "blood of the lamb," in which this throng washes their robes, clearly implies literal death. But John and

---

[29]Swete, 31, expresses a traditional view that their poverty was because Christians were drawn from "lower classes"; the demands of the faith brought poverty; and their property had been pillaged by pagan or, in this case, Jewish mobs.

[30]That is, if we accept a date in the early 80s CE for the Gospel of John and ca. 95 CE for Revelation. See J. Louis Martyn, *History and Theology in the Fourth Gospel*, 2nd ed. (Nashville: Abingdon, 1968) 15–62, on the two-level drama describing the life of Jesus and the early church being expelled from the Jewish synagogue in John 9; and David K. Rensberger, *Johannine Faith and Liberating Community* (Philadelphia: Westminster, 1988) 15–51. On the development of the synagogue in formative Judaism, see Howard Clark Kee, "The Transformation of the Synagogue after 70 C.E.: Its Import for Early Christianity," *NTS* 36 (1990): 1–24.

[31]B. M. Newman, *Rediscovering the Book of Revelation* (Valley Forge PA: Judson Press, 1968), 29–55, argues that the entire book of Revelation was written against a Gnostic libertine group and thus "those who call themselves Jews" are really a Jewish Gnostic group while Helmut Koester, "GNOMAI DIAPHORAI: The Origin and Nature of Diversification in the History of Early Christianity," in *Trajectories through Early Christianity*, ed. J. M. Robinson and H. Koester (Philadelphia: Fortress, 1971) 148–49, contends that "those who call themselves Jews" were really Nicolaitans. See Schüssler Fiorenza, *Justice and Judgment*, 118, that the Jews and the Nicolaitans should not be identified with one another.

the Smyrnans, both of whom have endured afflictions, are not dead yet. The afflictions of the Smyrnans also include slander and imprisonment. They are promised the "crown of life," but this promise comes not from their poverty but depends on their endurance of suffering at the hand of "Jews" and a spell in prison (2:9–10, note the future δώσω). Christ does not call the Smyrnans to repent (μετανοέω; cf. Rev 2:5, 16, 21–22; 3:3, 19). They are, however, called to change their mind about poverty and wealth, since they are really "rich." Christ does not dwell further on their poverty or wealth, nor does he draw any explicit connections between their poverty and the slander from the Jews. It is because of their suffering, not their poverty, that the Smyrnans rank high in Christ's characterization of the seven churches and are therefore called rich.

All the churches are connected to heaven's wealth by their identification as the seven golden lampstands by Christ (1:20). The message to Smyrna is much more specific about how a church gains access to God's wealth; that is, by suffering and endurance. Only the Smyrnans and the Philadelphians, who are also in a struggle with the Jews and who are praised for their endurance, receive no censure from Christ. To the Philadelphians, Christ promises that the Jews will "bow down before your feet" and that they will be spared from trials about to come on account of their "patient endurance" (ὑπομονή) in their struggle with the Jews (3:9–10). There are wealth motifs in the message to Philadelphia as well. They are told to "hold fast to what you have, so that no one may seize your crown" (3:10) and are promised citizenship in the New Jerusalem (3:12), a clear reference to the most opulent vision in the Apocalypse.[32]

The wealth imagery in the message to Smyrna has a clear rhetorical effect for the Christology of the Apocalypse. When Christ says that, in their poverty, the Smyrnans are truly rich, his words echo the philosophical *topos* of "true wealth" that we traced in chapter 3. While a similar

---

[32]The clause "I will make you pillar in the temple of my God" (ποιήσω αὐτον στῦλον ἐν τῷ ναῷ τοῦ θεοῦ) causes some difficulty. Rev 21:22 states that there will be no temple in the New Jerusalem; but see Mounce, 121, on the fluidity of apocalyptic language. Traditional interpretations of the pillar include reference to pillars in Solomon's temple or to the custom in the imperial cult of a priest erecting a pillar in the temple precincts with his name on it. Richard H. Wilkinson, "The ΣΤΥΛΟΣ of Revelation 3:12 and Ancient Coronation Rites," *JBL* 107 (1987): 498–501, finds an analogy in ancient Near Eastern coronation rites, placing this verse in the context of the extensive kingship imagery in Revelation.

moral position was expressed in the Cynic Epistles, Christ's long robe and golden belt would have been derided by a Cynic philosopher and would have marked him rather as a Stoic, like Lucian's Kantharos.[33] The message to Smyrna does not resemble Cynic philosophy so much as the aristocratic Stoicism that would be appropriate for a philosopher-king.[34] The opening vision of the Apocalypse has already characterized Christ as regal and wealthy. This message adds the characteristics of the aristocratic moral philosopher to the portrait of Christ. When a speaker pulls out the philosophical commonplace to say that the poor are "truly rich," some specific moral quality is usually implied. Philo, for instance, in "Every Good Person is Free" (*Omnis probus liber sit*), claims that the "poor" are free of attachments to physical things (and therefore not actually physically poor) and so are able to concentrate on inward, spiritual virtues. The virtues that bring wealth to the Smyrnans are struggle and patient endurance. Revelation shares the expression of this motif with 2 Corinthians and the *Testament of Job*,[35] both of which equate true wealth with suffering and endurance. What distinguishes Revelation from Paul's Cynic version of this motif in 2 Cor 4:7–6:10 is the enormous wealth of the one who makes the promise in the Apocalypse. There are no corresponding visions of wealth in the letters of Paul. The *Testament of Job*, however, offers a close parallel to Revelation since both texts include the promise of earthly as well as heavenly "true wealth." Job has a visionary experience of heaven's "true wealth" in a city (*T. Job* 18:6–7) and is rewarded by God with earthly wealth at the end of his trials (*T. Job* 44:1–45:3; 53:1–5).

Finally, the imagery of wealth in the message to Smyrna functions as part of John's heresiological rhetoric. To be "truly rich," according to Philo, is to be concerned with spiritual rather than material things (*Omn. prob. lib.* 17). To be "truly rich," according to the Apocalypse, is to participate in struggles against the Jewish synagogue. While Revelation tries to portray a world of dualistic choices between good and evil, it is clear that John is battling on at least three fronts: Rome, the Jews, and other Christian teachers, who probably formed two or three groups themselves.[36] All three enemies are united by John's rhetoric under

---

[33]See Ps.-Crates 26; Luc. *Fug.* 31.

[34]See Musonius Rufus *Frag.* 8.

[35]See *T. Job* 1:3; 26:3; 33:1–9; 36:4–5.

[36]It is not immediately clear that all the Christian teachers and opponents are united against John and his circle of prophets. Schüssler Fiorenza, *Justice and*

Satan's name: the "synagogue of Satan" in 2:9 and 3:9; the "throne of Satan" in 2:13, a reference either to the first imperial temple in Asia or to a large altar to Zeus and all the gods which overlooked the city;[37] and "the deep things of Satan" in 2:24 as a name for "Jezebel's" teaching. These account for five of the eight occurrences of "Satan" in the Apocalypse (see also 12:9; 20:2, 7); in the subsequent visions, "devil" (διάβολος) and especially "serpent" (δράκων) occur more frequently.[38] The three occurrences of "Satan" make a potent cluster in the seven messages. John's heresiological technique is to unite these three very different groups rhetorically under one banner as a satanic opposition to his construction of the one, true faith. Revelation attempts to persuade its audience to adopt a negative point of view against all of these opponents as if they were united under Satan against John.[39] There is a clear connection between the ideology of the Apocalypse and the use of wealth imagery in the rhetoric against the Jews in the message to Smyrna, a connection supported by the message to Philadelphia. By bestowing heaven's wealth to the Smyrnans, Christ, in the noble guise of an aristocratic philosopher, offers the highest reward of the Apocalypse for this conflict with the Jews.

Laodicea

The antithetical counterpart to the message to Smyrna is the message to Laodicea. Here, as in the message to Smyrna, the scripting of Christ as a philosopher is the key to understanding the many puzzles in the message. This message holds an important position as last of the seven and is directed to the entire audience of the Apocalypse as much as to

---

Judgment, 114–32, maintains that the Nicolaitans are a Gnostic group and compares them to Paul's enthusiast opponents in Corinth, but Aune, "Social Matrix," 29, argues that John and his circle and Jezebel and the Nicolaitans can be seen as fighting over the center of the Christian communities in Asia.

[37]See Ramsay, *Letters to the Seven Churches*, 205–16. According to Price, *Rituals and Power*, imperial temples and sanctuaries were common in Asia and present in all seven cities of Revelation (see xvii–xxvi, 56–58, 135–46). Price chooses Ephesus as an example where the allegiance to the emperor was "writ large" in the city's architecture.

[38]See διάβολος, 2:10; 12:9, 12; 20:2, 10; δράκων, 12:3, 4, 7, 7, 9, 13, 16, 17; 13:2, 4, 11; 16:13; 20:2.

[39]Garrett, "God of This World," argues that Paul charges his opponents in Corinth with alliance to Satan.

one church; only the first message to Ephesus carries as much rhetorical force.[40] More than any other message, including Smyrna's, this message focuses on wealth. But the opening line of the message evokes the theme of faithful endurance and suffering, including death. In the Christological predication in 3:14, Christ again quotes John's epistolary prescript: "these are the words of the Amen, the faithful and true witness, the origin of God's creation."[41] This opening of the message to Laodicea is an echo of Rev 1:5, in which John sends grace and peace to the seven churches "from Jesus Christ, the faithful witness, the firstborn of the dead [πρωτότοκος τῶν νεκρῶν], and the ruler of the kings of the earth." Rev 3:14 develops the life-through-death motif that is prominent in the messages to Smyrna and Sardis. Christ as witness (μάρτυς) suggests death by giving one's life as witness; he is firstborn of the dead because of his witness by death. This language calls attention to the major issue in the message to Laodicea; this church is not portrayed as a faithful and true witness to the faith. The Christological predication in 3:14 places the idea of witness in a political context. The phrase "the origin of God's creation" (ἡ ἀρχή τῆς κτίσεως) evokes the political theme of the proem, where Christ is called the ruler (ἄρχων) of the kings of the earth (Rev 1:5). This play on words (*paronomasia*) on *archōn* and *archē* in Rev 1:5 and 3:14 grounds Christ's political authority over the kings of the earth in his cosmic authority as the beginning or origin of creation (see also Rev 22:13).[42]

After making subtle reference to the theme of endurance and suffering, Christ goes on the attack. Rev 3:15–16 is surely one of the

---

[40]Ramsay, *Letters to the Seven Churches*, 318–19, proposed that Rev 3:19–22 should be read as the epilogue to the seven messages. While Mounce, 127–28, argues against this position, others have read at least 3:21–22 as summary or epilogue for all seven messages as well as the message to Laodicea. See Roloff, 65–66; and Bauckham, *Climax of Prophecy*, 6.

[41]"Amen" appears in doxological or benedictional forms (e.g., Rev 1:6–7, 5:14, 7:12) but as a title is unique here. Lou H. Silberman, "Farewell to O AMHN," *JBL* 82 (1963): 213–15, suggests a Hebrew antecedent in which ὁ ἀμήν is a faulty transliteration of אמון, architect or master worker, a reference to Prov 8:30. G. K. Beale, "The Old Testament Background of Rev 3.14," *NTS* 42 (1996): 133–52, points to interpretation in terms of Rev 1:5 and Isa 65:16.

[42]These motifs in Rev 1:5 and Rev 3:14 raise the possibility of intertextual references in Revelation to the Christ hymn in Col 1:15–23; see Royalty, "Dwelling on Visions."

most enigmatic passages in the Apocalypse.[43] The Laodiceans, according to Christ, are neither cold nor hot but lukewarm and therefore will be spewed forth from his mouth. This is not an auspicious opening for the Laodicean church. In the British scholarly tradition of finding "local references" to explain the imagery in the seven messages, the metaphor has been explained in terms of hot springs and cold water aqueducts in the area of Laodicea.[44] But the metaphor fits the ideology of the Apocalypse quite well without resorting to springs and aqueducts. The implied author wants strong commitment from the churches; therefore, Christ desires the Laodiceans to be "hot." Fire appears as destructive imagery in the visions,[45] but in the immediate context of the messages is a positive image (1:14–15; 2:18), particularly the "fiery gold" Christ offers to sell to this church (3:18). And while it seems unlikely that John wanted the church to be cold to his views, the sharp division between hot and cold and the rejection of lukewarm Christianity fits the dualistic worldview of the Apocalypse.[46] Those who completely reject the message of the Apocalypse fit into the neat categories described by the text and can be summarily dealt with by death and destruction. The lukewarm attitude of the Laodiceans challenges John's polarized worldview. This is a church of uncommitted fence-sitters, and wealthy ones at that. They have not rejected John's forceful message for another teacher's but neither have they rejected John's opponents. The dualistic worldview of the Apocalypse helps to explain Rev 3:15–16, but we need to push further into the message in order to understand the rhetoric of the message more fully.

Whatever the Laodiceans are or are not doing, Christ's indictment is related to their boasting over their wealth: "for [ὅτι] you say, 'I am rich, I have prospered, and I need nothing' " (3:17).[47] The Laodiceans'

---

[43]See Charles 1:95, on "the startling declaration that the absolute rejection of religion (iii.15) [would be] preferable to the Laodicean profession of it." This puzzlement can be seen in the textual traditions, where 3:15b is excluded by A. There is, however, agreement of C and ℵ for including this phrase.

[44]See M. J. S. Rudwick and E. M. B. Green, "The Laodicean Lukewarmness" *ExpTim* 69 (1957–1958): 176–78; and Mounce, 125.

[45]See Rev 8:5–8; 9:17–18; 11:5; 14:10; 16:8; 17:16; 18:8; 19:20; 20:9–10, 14–15; 21:8.

[46]See Roloff, 64: "When the church exposes such indecision, it thereby demonstrates that it has not yet grasped the substance of this message."

[47]Kirby's and Aune's division of the messages into narrative and proposition

boasting has been taken to refer to "spiritual" riches, along the line of the Corinthian enthusiasts (see esp. 1 Cor 4:8), as well as to actual material wealth.[48] Commentators have gone so far as to connect a "Laodicean heresy" with the Nicolaitans and other opponents of John, falling yet again under the spell of John's heresiological rhetoric that tries to connect all of his opponents in one diabolical opposition. A number of arguments can be made against the idea that the Laodiceans were "strong" spiritual enthusiasts and for the idea that the wealth imagery refers to material wealth. First, the characterization of the church as "lukewarm" suggests lack of commitment rather than strong adherence to spiritual enthusiasm. Second, the Nicolaitans and Jezebel and her followers are in fact condemned in Revelation for "libertine" behavior similar to the "strong" in Corinth, such as eating idol meat and alternative sexual practices, but there is no indication that these moral issues are at stake in the controversy with the Laodiceans. Third, wealth and poverty were already raised as issues in the message to Smyrna. The language of wealth introduced in 3:17 (πλούσιος, πλουτέω, πτωχός) continues in 3:18 (χρυσίον, πλουτέω), with the addition of commercial imagery (ἀγοράζω). This amplification of wealth language points to actual material wealth, most likely wealth derived from commerce, as the issue here. The independent attitude of the Laodiceans—"I have need of nothing"—stems from reliance on wealth rather than spiritual gifts. This message characterizes the Laodiceans as a church unconcerned with, even ignoring, the moral and theological controversies that have split other congregations.

Whereas Christ found wealth in the Smyrnans' poverty, he claims that the wealthy Laodiceans are really poor. We have seen that, in the message to Smyrna, Christ exhorts the Christian churches on poverty and

---

or *narratio* and *dispositio* along the lines of judicial or deliberative rhetoric breaks down in the message to the Laodiceans. Here, there are at least two narrative sections (vv. 15 and 17); 3:16 is part of the *dispositio*, according to Aune's criterion of the futuristic present μέλλω. The next formal marker of the *dispositio* is in 3:19, leaving 3:18 unaccounted for, since it immediately follows a narrative description in 3:17 but has no imperatives, futures, or futuristic presents such as βάλλω, δίδω, or μέλλω.

[48]For the interpretation in terms of "enthusiasts" such as those referred to in 1 Cor 4:8, see Bousset, 270–71; Schüssler Fiorenza, *Justice and Judgment*, 119; Müller, 136; Roloff, 64–65; and Boring, 94–97; for the view that the Laodiceans were actually wealthy, see Swete, 61 (who hedges somewhat on spiritual or material boasting); Charles 1:96; Mounce, 126; Caird, 57; Harrington, 75.

true wealth as a Stoic moral philosopher might. The Laodiceans' reliance on their wealth also suggests the discourse of the moral philosophers. We found that Christ sounded very much like a Stoic philosopher when exhorting the Smyrnans; the comparison to the Stoics is again helpful for understanding how the message to the Laodiceans would have been heard. One ancient diatribe on wealth contains a particularly striking parallel to the message to Laodicea in Revelation. This diatribe is an exchange between Epictetus and a Roman *Corrector*, or bailiff, a senatorial official with extensive administrative powers, over social duties (*Epict. Diss.* 3.7).[49] The *Corrector* is an Epicurean and Epictetus uses Socratic reasoning to stand the Epicurean doctrine of pleasure on its head. His argument is that Epicurean conduct is not consistent with its teachings; otherwise, Epicureans would engage in any number of immoral acts merely because they were pleasurable (3.7.15–18).[50] At one point, when Epictetus has pressed him fairly hard on the idea of subordinating pleasure for social duties, the Roman official replies: "But I am rich and need nothing" ('Αλλ' ἐγὼ πλούσιός εἰμι καὶ οὐδενὸς χρεία μοί ἐστιν, Arr. *Epict. Diss.* 3.7.29). The reply of the *Corrector* is striking, both in the context of the argument with Epictetus and as a parallel to the words of Christ in Rev 3:17 (λέγεις ὅτι πλούσιός εἰμι καὶ πεπλούτηκα καὶ οὐδὲν χρείαν ἔχω). The *Corrector* brandishes his own wealth and power to counter Epictetus's radical Stoic claim that pleasure should be subordinated to duty. The Laodiceans, in Christ's sardonic quotation, turn to material wealth to counter John's claim for radical obedience to his apocalyptic-prophetic version of Christianity.

While we do not need to maintain that John knew or was quoting Epictetus, this provides a closer parallel in words, context, and function for Rev 3:17 than other suggestions.[51] The thematic similarities to this one diatribe of Epictetus point to the genre itself. Rev 3:14–22 bears a

---

[49]On Epictetus and the diatribe form, see Stowers, *Diatribe and Paul's Letter to the Romans*, 53–58, 75–110; and S. L. Radt, "Zu Epiktets *Diatriben*," *Mnemosyne* 43 (1990): 364–73. Epictetus is scornful of other philosophies besides true Cynics and Stoics, particularly the Epicureans and the Peripatetics; see Arr. *Epict. Diss.* 2.19.20–21.

[50]Epictetus includes here a dig at Stoics "who talk of the noble and do the base."

[51]Such as the "free and direct rendering" of Hos 12:9 (Charles 1:96); cf. *1 Enoch* 97:8–9; Aune, 258.

number of similarities in tone, form, and content to the Stoic diatribe.[52] The diatribe developed in the philosophical school setting where the teacher used the Socratic method of "censure" (ἐλεγτικός) and "persuasion" (προτρεπτικός).[53] The diatribe is marked by its dialogical character in which the teacher addresses a real or imaginary interlocutor who raises hypothetical objections and draws false conclusions. Prominent literary features of the diatribe also include the use of the particle ἀλλά; vice lists; and ironic or hortatory imperatives.[54] The literary features of the diatribe inform our understanding of how the message to the Laodiceans would have been heard. The implied author maintains the fiction of addressing the seven churches through their angels in the second-person singular in all seven messages.[55] But only in the message to Laodicea does Christ quote and then address an interlocutor. The sardonic quotation of the Laodicean "angel" is the most prominent feature that marks this message as a diatribe.[56] The angel/interlocutor advances a false conclusion by claiming that "I am rich, I have prospered, and I need nothing." Christ dismisses this conclusion as erroneous in the manner of the Stoic diatribe. Christ's indicting response, "but do you not know" (οὐκ οἶδας), employs "an expression implying lack of percep-

---

[52]Stowers, *Diatribe*, reexamines the conclusions reached by Bultmann, *Der Stil der paulinischen Predigt*, based on research subsequent to Bultmann's dissertation and his own research of the primary sources. See also the highly critical review by Stowers in *JBL* 108 (1989): 538–42, of Thomas Schmeller, *Paulus und die "Diatribe": Eine vergleichende Stilinterpretation*, NTAbh n.s. 19 (Münster: Aschendorff, 1987); Stanley E. Porter, "The Argument of Romans 5: Can a Rhetorical Question Make a Difference?" *JBL* 110 (1991): 655–77; and Duane F. Watson, "James 2 in Light of Greco-Roman Schemes of Argumentation" *NTS* 39 (1993): 94–121.

[53]See Stowers, *Diatribe and Paul's Letter to the Romans*, 57, 76; and Arr. *Epict. Diss.* 2.26.4; 3.21.19.

[54]See Stowers, *Diatribe*, 85–93, and David E. Aune, *The New Testament in its Literary Environment* (Philadelphia: Westminster, 1987) 200–202, on the formal features of the diatribe.

[55]The fiction of addressing an angel in the second-person singular breaks down in Rev 2:10; 2:13; 2:15; 2:24; 3:4.

[56]See Stowers, *Diatribe*, 76, on the centrality of the dialogical character of the diatribe. See Philo, *Omn. prob. lib.* 1–2 [445–47]; Arr. *Epict. Diss.* 2.9.17, 19; 2.21.11–12; 2.22.4–10; 3.9.15–18; 4.1.61–75; 4.6.18–22; Plut. *Mor.* 525C; Rom 2:1, 4, 17; 3:1; 11:19; Sen. *Ep.* 7.5; 24.14.

tion" typical of diatribes.[57] Christ completes his indictment of the Laodiceans' perceptions by adding that "you are wretched, pitiable, poor, blind, naked." These terms function as the vice list that often appears in diatribes (Arr. *Epict. Diss.* 4.9.5–6; Rom 2:8, 21–23).

It would be as difficult to prove that John had no knowledge of the diatribe form as to prove that he knew it. Furthermore, the use of the diatribe in Romans and James shows that it had been used as a form of discourse in early Christianity. Given John's authorial and literary skills, we should hesitate to underestimate his rhetorical abilities. Nonetheless, the thematic and formal parallels between the message to Laodicea and the Stoic diatribe have no exegetical bite unless I can show that these parallels explain how the rhetoric of the message would have functioned in its social context. The interpretive issues in Rev 3:14–22 are considerably different from those raised in the study of the diatribe in Romans. Unlike Paul and the Romans, John knew these churches well. The evidence of the messages, moreover, suggests that John had "real" opponents to deal with.[58] A Stoic diatribe form would be particularly fitting for a message which expresses a typical Stoic philosophical *topos*, reliance on externals such as wealth. The diatribe had a pedagogical rather than polemical function and was often used for general paraenesis.[59] It is important to note that Christ does not portray the Laodicean church as opponents but rather as uncommitted. Christ wants to "reprove and discipline" the Laodiceans (or educate, ἐλέγχω καὶ παιδεύω, Rev 3:19), whom he loves; therefore, he calls them to repent. Repentance rather than condemnation is the goal (3:20); this is not a church which has gone beyond the theological or ideological pale. Christ the moral philosopher does not condemn the church but rebukes them, disciplines

---

[57]See Stowers, *Diatribe* 89; other typical expressions include οὐκ οἶσθα, ἀγνοεῖς, οὐχ ὁρᾷς, and *non vides*. The sentence could be translated as a question in Revelation: "you say that . . . but do you not know that [καὶ οὐκ οἶδας ὅτι] you are wretched, pitiable, poor, blind, and naked?"

[58]The existence or nonexistence of opponents of Paul in Rome is one of the issues in the so-called "Romans debate." See Stowers, *Diatribe*, esp. 1–5, 22–26, 152–54; Karl P. Donfried, ed., *The Romans Debate* (Minneapolis: Augsburg, 1977; rev. ed.: Peabody MA: Hendrickson, 1991). The interpretive issues in the function of the diatribe in Romans include the relation of the letter to Paul's preaching style; the composition of the Roman community; and the polemical or pedagogical use of the diatribal features in Romans.

[59]See Stowers, *Diatribe*, 75–78; Aune, *Literary Environment*, 200–202.

them, and educates them. The diatribe, with its pedagogical function, fits this agenda well.

Comparison of the message to the Laodiceans to the Stoic diatribe offers a context for the ironic tone of the message as well as suggesting parallels for the message's content, form, and function. The tone of Rev 3:14–22 is not as polemical or harsh as the tone of messages attacking Christian and Jewish opponents (cf. Rev 2:16, 22–23; 3:9). The rebuke of the Laodiceans is, however, sarcastic. Sarcasm was another typical feature of the diatribe. The sardonic quotation of the Laodicean interlocutor-angel helps to explain the enigmatic wish that the Laodiceans were either cold or hot. The opening descriptive narration, which we found so puzzling, is highly ironic: "would that you were hot or cold!" (RSV). The Greek of Rev 3:15 has more force than the NRSV's laconic "I wish that you were hot or cold." Such ironic imperatives were typical in diatribes.[60] In Rev 3:18, Christ mocks the source of the Laodiceans' wealth. Commentators have long taken the three articles for sale in Rev 3:18 as ironic references to the major industries of Laodicea.[61] Christ's sarcastic counsel to buy goods from him (the παρ' ἐμοῦ is emphatic)[62]shows that the wealth of the Laodiceans almost certainly derived from commerce; the Laodiceans are already buying from somebody else with the hope of reselling for profit. The subtext here for the audience, of course, is the low status of merchants and commerce. Christ, taking the studied pose of a Stoic philosopher, draws an implicit comparison between the commercially derived wealth of the Laodicean church and the true wealth of heaven, to which the Christians of Asia gain access by endurance and suffering (Rev 2:9).

The three items for sale (3:18), which certainly refer to the commercial source of Laodicean wealth, have powerful intratextual connections

---

[60]The aorist participle ὄφελον is not an imperative or a hortatory subjunctive, but it expresses the highly ironic and unattainable wish that the Laodiceans be hot or cold.

[61]The tradition goes back to Ramsay, *Letters to the Seven Churches*, 303–17 (orig. ed., 1904: 413–30); see Mounce, 123–26; Harrington, 75. The frequent references by commentators such as Mounce to the wealth of Laodicea, which was reportedly able to rebuild itself after the major earthquake of 60 CE, gives the false impression that everyone in Laodicea would have been rich, ignoring the steep pyramid of wealth and poverty in antiquity; see MacMullen, *Roman Social Relations*, 48–51.

[62]So Charles 1:97.

to the theme of endurance and suffering as well, a theme we noted already in the Christological predication in 3:14. The first item for sale is gold refined by fire (χρυσίον πεπυρωμένον ἐκ πυρός). The one selling fired gold is wearing gold himself (1:13). Fire figures most prominently as an image of destruction and punishment.[63] Fire is also associated with heavenly beings; John describes Christ's feet as appearing like bronze burnished by fire (πεπυρωμένης, 1:15).[64] Given the emphasis on vision in the message to Laodicea, the three passages that describe Christ as having eyes like a flame of fire (1:14, 2:18, 19:12) lend significance to the fiery gold Christ tenders to this lukewarm church. If they were already hot (ζεστός) they would have no fear of the fires that will destroy the earth and its inhabitants. Gold refined by fire echoes biblical metaphors of endurance (Jer 6:27–30; Zech 13:9; Mal 3:3; 1 Pet 1:7) as well as the gold worn by the speaker Christ. But the extent of wealth imagery in the Apocalypse applied to Christ, heaven, and the New Jerusalem far exceeds any parallel text connecting suffering and true heavenly wealth. In *Ps. Sol.* 17:43, the words of the Messiah are *purer* than the finest gold. "Fired gold" and suffering are closely connected in 1 Peter. The author of this epistle exhorts his audience to rejoice even if they are suffering trials (πειρασμοί), "so that the genuineness of your faith—being more precious than gold that, though perishable, is tested by fire—may be found to result in praise and glory and honor when Jesus Christ is revealed" (1 Pet 1:7). The verse has notorious exegetical difficulties, but whether it is the faith of the audience or the testing of that faith that is referred to here, it is *more* valuable than gold tested by fire (see 1 Pet 1:18).[65] Thus, it provides more of a contrast than parallel to Rev 3:18. For where 1 Peter explicitly contrasts the "imperishable, undefiled, and unfading" heavenly inheritance to earthly riches such as refined gold (1 Pet 1:3–4), Christ offers gold refined by fire for sale to the Laodiceans.[66]

---

[63]See Rev 8:5–8; 9:17–18; 11:5; 14:10; 16:8; 17:16; 18:8; 19:20; 20:9–10, 14–15; 21:8.

[64]Cf. Rev 4:5, 8:5, 14:18

[65]1 Peter also refers to Rome as Babylon (5:13). Troy W. Martin, *Metaphor and Composition in 1 Peter*, SBLDS 131 (Atlanta: Scholars Press, 1992), 47–70, suggests an equivalence between inheritance and glory, δόξα, that may be significant for the interpretation of Rev 21:24 (see discussion in chap. 7).

[66]*Mart. Polycarp* 15.2 may show the influence of the interpretation of Rev 3:18 as death by martyrdom.

The second product that Christ offers for sale, white garments (ἱμάτια λευκά), has connotations of suffering and death by martyrdom. White almost always describes something divine or heavenly in the visions.[67] In the fifth seal (Rev 6:9–11), a white robe (στολή) is given to reward or to pacify each of the martyrs whom John sees waiting under the altar in heaven, crying out for justice and retribution for their death.[68] John has a vision of an unnumbered crowd made up of those who "have washed their robes and made them white in the blood of the Lamb" (7:14). Clothing functions as a metaphor in Revelation for moral condition. Christ, the elders, and angels from heaven wear white and gold; the harlot of Babylon is in purple and scarlet. Two of the seven beatitudes in Revelation mention garments (16:15 and 22:14).[69] The first of these occurs in the pouring out of the sixth plague, 16:12–16, in which the kings from the east cross the Euphrates for the battle of Har-Maggedon. This blessing is also a warning to be alert and to keep one's garments (ἱμάτια) lest Christ's return catch one naked, an echo of the message to Laodicea.[70] The second beatitude which contains clothing imagery occurs in the final warnings of the text. The blessing in 22:14 upon those who wash their robes (στολάι) hints at martyrdom (cf. 7:9–13). It is not completely clear, however, that buying white garments means to die as a martyr. In the message to Sardis, Christ says that, while the church as a group is "dead," there are a few who have not soiled their garments (ἱμάτια) and who therefore will walk with him "in white garments, because they are holy" (3:4). Christ promises the one who conquers white garments as well as a name to be confessed before God and the angels (3:5). The church at Sardis is "dead," but those who have not soiled their garments are not physically dead yet.

---

[67]See 2:17, 4:4, 14:14, 19:11, 19:14, 20:11; the identity of the white horse and rider, 6:2, is not clear (see n. 12, chap. 6).

[68]The word στολή, robe, found in 6:11, had a slightly narrower meaning than ἱμάτιον, garment, used in 3:18.

[69]On the seven beatitudes, see W. Bieder, "Die sieben Seligpreisungen in der Offenbarung des Johannes," *TZBas* 10 (1984): 13–30; and Virgil P. Cruz, "The Beatitudes of the Apocalypse: Eschatology and Ethics," in *Perspectives on Christology: Essays in Honor of Paul K. Jewett*, ed. M. Shuster and R. Muller (Grand Rapids MI: Zondervan, 1991) 269–83.

[70]On echoes of Synoptic passages, see Louis A. Vos, *The Synoptic Traditions in the Apocalypse* (Kampen: J. H. Kok, 1965) 75–85.

The third article that Christ offers the Laodicean, eye salve, is directed to the audience as much as one church. These seven messages and the visions that follow are meant to change the way the audience sees their social world. The reversal of apparent wealth and poverty in the messages in the messages to Smyrna and Laodicea is one example of the type of change in vision that the Apocalypse tries to effect in its audience. Christ relabels the apparent social-economic situation of the two communities. He knows the poverty of the Smyrnans, but they are really rich; the Laodiceans claim to be wealthy, but are really poor. The text robs wealth and poverty of their common sense meanings and remaps their meaning in terms of the narrative world of the Apocalypse. To buy salve from Christ is to buy into the ideology of John's Apocalypse and gain true vision.

In Rev 3:20, the final line of the body of the message to Laodicea, Christ says that "I am standing at the door, knocking; if you hear my voice and open the door, I will come in to you and eat with you, and you with me." The door is a narrative bridge to the door that opens in heaven, inaugurating the visions (4:1). There is also a tradition of the eschatological messianic banquet (Isa 25:6–8; 62:1–9; Mic 4:1–4; Zech 8:20–23; *1 Enoch* 62:14; Matt 8:11). But there is a further social dimension to this verse. Christ here takes the stance of the wealthy and considerably higher-status patron joining his clients for a dinner party. Lucian's writings are full of satire of the desire for an invitation to dine and of the poor fare a low-status guest receives once there.[71] Part of the irony of the *Cena Trimalchionis* is that the narrator is freeborn and of higher status than his host. To dine with Christ, the son of the wealthy patron of the churches, would be perceived as a status-raising action. The conclusion of the message (Rev 3:21) promises the audience thrones around the throne of God (3:21), where the elders sit with golden crowns and white robes (4:4), a final reference to the heavenly wealth attainable for those who support the author in his struggles within the Christian communities.

Form, tone, and motifs in the messages to Smyrna and Laodicea evoke comparisons between Christ in the Apocalypse and a moral philosopher in antiquity. The use of the diatribal features in the message to the Laodiceans completes the author's characterization of Christ as a moral philosopher in the seven messages. The general paraenesis of this diatribe is addressed to the audience of the Apocalypse as much as to one

---

[71]See *Gall.* 9–11; *Nigr.* 22–23, 33; *Merc. Cond.* 14–18, 27; and *Laps.*

church in the Lycus valley of Asia. All seven of the churches would have demonstrated a variety of social levels of poverty and moderate wealth, even if Smyrna and Laodicea were particularly concentrated one way or another. More important, wealth has been introduced in Rev 1:12–16 as a motif for the description of heaven and will become even more prominent starting in Rev 4:1. Since the vision of the heavenly throne room immediately follows the message to Laodicea, the author explores the issues of wealth most fully for the entire audience in this message. The diatribal features are a signal to the audience that Christ speaks as a moral philosopher when discussing true wealth and gold refined by fire. The establishment of Christ's character is crucial for the comparison of the wealth of Babylon and the New Jerusalem. Without this moral authority, the wealth of heaven would not appear to be quite so pure. Once Christ has spoken in the guise of a moral philosopher of true wealth and fired gold, the gold and jewels of heaven acquire added luster.

Summary and Conclusion

I identified three ideological implications of the message to Smyrna. First, when addressing the *topos* of wealth, Christ speaks as a Stoic philosopher might, devaluing wealth and extolling the virtue of poverty while wearing his long white robes and golden sash. This aristocratic philosophical position strengthens the royal imagery introduced in Rev 1:1–20.[72] Second, Christ offers the Smyrnan church "true wealth" as a reward for their endurance of sufferings at the hand of the Jews. While this message shares the theme of heavenly wealth acquired by endurance of suffering with texts such as 2 Corinthians, the wealth described for the audience of the Apocalypse is far more extensive than in other texts, which generally lack any description of heaven's wealth. Third, the reward for opposition to the Jews in this message connects the imagery of wealth to the heresiological technique of the Apocalypse, by which all of John's opponents are united under Satan's banner.

The characterization of Christ as an aristocratic philosopher is developed further in the message to Laodicea, in which Christ mocks the Laodicean's reliance on wealth and the commercial source of that wealth. The Laodicean church has not taken a strong position against the authority of John and his prophetic circle. The content and form of the

---

[72]See the discussion of the political motifs in Rev 1:1–20 in chap. 4, pp. 141–43.

message, which parallels the content and form of a Stoic diatribe, and the persona of the messenger, that of an aristocratic Stoic philosopher, accentuate its goal to reprove and educate but not condemn this church. As in the message to Smyrnan, the implied author uses motifs and allusions to show that the true wealth of heaven is attainable only by those who struggle, suffer, and endure. But whereas other texts such as 1 Peter contrast perishable earthly gold to faith refined by suffering, Christ offers heavenly gold refined by fire for sale to the Laodiceans, showing again the more graphic expression of heaven's wealth in Revelation than in other texts. The scripting of Christ as a moral philosopher in the messages to Smyrna and Laodicea prepares the audience for the extensive description of opposing cities and their wealth in the visions from the heavenly throne room.

The Destruction of Babylon

The Two Cities

The Apocalypse moves toward the great climax of destruction and renewal in the description and comparison (*ekphrasis* and *synkrisis*) of Babylon and the heavenly Jerusalem. This contrast between Babylon and the New Jerusalem is made quite explicitly in the Apocalypse. The descriptions of the two cities in Rev 17:1–18:24 and 21:9–22:5 are set in clear contrast to each other.[1] The wealth imagery of the Apocalypse comes to a climax in these two passages as well. In contrasting the two cities, John takes up a biblical theme from prophets such as Isaiah and Jeremiah. Babylon continued to function as theological and ideological metaphors in Second Temple Judaism long after it had ceased to be a political threat to the Jewish people. The notion of a restored or New Jerusalem as a symbol of hope began with Second Isaiah and remained a powerful image for disenfranchised Jewish groups such as the Qumran community. The power of this idea remained strong in Jewish apocalyptic texts after the destruction of the city by the Romans in 70 CE.[2]

John's comparison of the cities is also a fitting theme for philosophical discourse and epideictic rhetoric. Sophists praised and scolded cities; Lucian compared Athens and Rome. Seneca wrote of humanity's dual citizenship:

> Let us grasp the idea that there are two commonwealths [*res publicas*]
> —the one a vast and truly common state, which embraces alike gods
> and men, in which we look neither to this corner of earth nor to that,
> but measure the bounds of our citizenship [*civitatis*] by the path of the

---

[1] Noted by several commentators, e.g. Charles 2:155; Swete, 283; see also Bauckham, *Climax of Prophecy*, 2–22. See the outline by Boring, who titles 4:1–18:24 "Judgment of the Great City" and 19:1–22:1 "God Redeems the Holy City."

[2] See Stone, "Reactions to the Destruction of the Second Temple," on *2 Baruch* and *4 Ezra*.

sun; the other, the one to which we have been assigned by the accident
of birth. This will be the commonwealth of the Athenians or of the
Carthaginians, or of any other city that belongs, not to all, but to some
particular race of men. Some yield service to both commonwealths at
the same time—to the greater and to the lesser—some only to the
lesser, some only to the greater.[3]

The notion of dual citizenship, both political and theological, was part of
the philosophical and religious climate in which the Apocalypse of John
was read. Revelation, addressed to congregations in seven prominent
cities in Asia, is evidence of the urban setting of early Christianity and
the importance of civic metaphors in moral discourse.[4] Even in the characterization of the seven churches, the Apocalypse creates the notion of
the *polis* as moral as well as political place. Then, the text changes the
context of civic identity for its audience from the seven cities of Asia to
the two great cities of Babylon and Jerusalem, theological metaphors for
damnation and salvation and the ideological focal points of the Apocalypse.

The Wealth of Heaven

When approaching the Babylon section of the Apocalypse (Rev
17:1–18:22), it is important to note that extensive visions of the wealth
of heaven come before the description of the fall of this other wealthy
city. The author gradually displays the wealth of heaven for the audience.
The Apocalypse begins with a display of Christ's wealth (1:12–16)
followed by philosophical pronouncements to the churches on true wealth
and "bad" wealth derived from commerce (2:8–11; 3:14–22).[5] It continues
with the vision of God's throne and court in Revelation 4–5, an example
of *ekphrasis*, the vivid description typical of epideictic rhetoric. The
narrator's attention in this vision is seized by the throne of God and God
seated on the throne (4:2). God shines with the brilliance of jasper and
carnelian and God's throne has the radiance of emeralds (4:3). Twenty-

---

[3]*On Leisure (De otio)* 4.1; cited by James Dougherty, "Exiles in the Earthly
City: The Heritage of Saint Augustine," in *Civitas: Religious Interpretations of
the City*, ed. Peter S. Hawkins, Scholars Press Studies in the Humanities (Atlanta:
Scholars Press, 1986) 105.

[4]See the remarks by Peter S. Hawkins, "Introduction," and Wayne A. Meeks,
"St. Paul of the Cities," in Hawkins, *Civitas*, xi–xix, 15–23.

[5]As discussed in chaps. 4 and 5.

four elders, wearing white garments and golden crowns, surround the throne of God (4:4, 10). When the elders prostrate themselves before the Lamb, they pay honor with lyres and golden bowls of incense (5:8). The *ekphrasis* of the heavenly throne room in Rev 4:5–11 includes traditional motifs from Jewish throne visions and theophanies, such as thunder and lightning, the four living creatures, and the *trisagion*, "Holy, holy, holy," from Isa 6:3. The description of the heavenly throne room that John sends to the churches in Asia contains many traditional Jewish elements.[6] As I demonstrated in chapter 2, the combined effect is more opulent than any other prophetic or apocalyptic vision of God's throne or heaven.

Wealth is one aspect of divine power revealed in the vision of the heavenly throne room in 4:2–11 and the subsequent narrative of the Lamb and the scroll in 5:1–14.[7] Rev 4:2–5:14 also intensifies the royal-political imagery that was introduced for the audience in Rev 1:1–20. The throne room narrative includes five hymns or doxologies.[8] The hymns in Rev 4:2–5:14 express this royal-political motif most strongly.[9] Two hymns are directed to God; two to Christ; and one to both "the one seated on the throne and to the Lamb." God is the Almighty (ὁ παντοκράτωρ, 4:8), worthy to receive glory and honor and power (4:11). The royal-political and wealth language applies most directly to Christ. The third hymn, to Christ, describes the significance of his death in strongly political terms:

---

[6]See Rowland, *Open Heaven*, 222–26; and Hurtado, "Revelation 4–5."

[7]See W. C. van Unnik, "'Worthy is the Lamb: The Background of Apoc 5," in *Mélanges bibliques en hommage au R. P. Béda Rigaux*, ed. A. Descamps and A. de Halleux (Gembloux: Ducolot, 1970) 445–61.

[8]Other hymnic passages include Rev 7:9–17; 8:1–5; 11:15–18; 12:10–12; 14:15, 17; 15:2–8; 16:4–7; 19:1–8. On form critical issues, see Reinhard Deichgräber, *Gotteshymnus und Christushymnus in der frühen Christenheit* (Göttingen: Vandenhoeck & Ruprecht, 1967) 44–59, who regards the hymns as literary compositions of the author rather than records of early Christian liturgy; and Klaus-Peter Jörns, *Das hymnische Evangelium* (Gütersloh: Gerd Mohn, 1971) 19, 168–78. The distinction between hymn and doxology is not critical for my exegesis; therefore, I shall use the broader term "hymn" for these passages. While the liturgical elements in the Apocalypse are not accurate records of early Christian practice, the heavenly worship scenes correspond to the Christian assembly, the intended setting for the reading of the text (1:1–3, 9). See Rowland, *The Open Heaven*, 424–46; Aune, 314–17; idem. "Roman Imperial Court," 14–20; idem., "Problem of Genre," 89–96; and Thompson, *Revelation*, 53–73.

[9]Aune, "Roman Imperial Court," 22; Thompson, *Revelation*, 64–66.

"You ransomed [ἠγόρασας] saints from every tribe and language and people and nation; you have made them to be a kingdom and priests [βασιλείαν καὶ ἱερεῖς] serving our God, and they will reign on earth" (καὶ βασιλεύσουσιν ἐπὶ τῆς γῆς, 5:9–10; cf. 1:6). The act of ransoming or purchasing saints by Christ (ἀγοράζω), an act set in the geopolitical context of "every tribe and language and people and nation," recalls for the audience the patron-slave language from the proem in Rev 1:1–20. Because of Christ's action, the saints will reign on earth in place of Caesar.[10] The amplification of wealth and political imagery climaxes in the fourth hymn, also to Christ: "Worthy is the Lamb that was slaughtered to receive power and wealth and wisdom and might and honor and glory and blessing" (Rev 5:12). This is the only doxology that ascribes wealth (πλοῦτος) to Christ in the Apocalypse (cf. Rev 4:9, 11; 5:13; 7:12).[11] The fifth hymn, uttered by "every creature in heaven and on earth and under the earth and in the sea, and all that is in them," attributes blessing, honor, glory, and might to God and to the Lamb. The wealth of God displayed in the vision of the heavenly throne room is a powerful backdrop for these resounding expressions of the political compass of God's sovereignty and Christ's death. The entire scene characterizes God and Christ as wealthy, powerful monarchs.

The gold and jewels that decorate Christ's garments, God's throne, and the elders and angels in heaven are the most prominent wealth motifs in Revelation before the visions of Babylon and the New Jerusalem. Gold and wealth are consistently parts of John's descriptions of heaven. These visions of the heavenly throne room intensify the positive correspondence

---

[10]Schüssler Fiorenza, *Justice and Judgment*, 74–76, emphasizes the eschatological reservation expressed in Rev 5:9–10 against a spiritualistic-enthusiastic understanding of salvation. Her study of the political and socioeconomic language in Rev 1:5–6 and 5:9–10 does not place this imagery in the context of wealth imagery in the Apocalypse nor the context of ideological struggles within the Christian churches.

[11]First Chr 29:11–12 is probably a source for Rev 5:12. See Bousset, 305; Swete, 83; Charles 1:149. John has again avoided an allusion to Solomon, the merchant-king, even while using Temple imagery, for the allusion in Rev 5:12 is to a speech by David. Lohse, *Colossians and Philemon*, 75, notes that the words πλοῦτος, wealth, and δόξα, glory, are found frequently together in the LXX; see Gen 31:16; 3 Kgs 3:13; 1 Chr 29:28; Esth 1:4; 10:2; Ps 111:3; Prov 3:16; 8:18; 22:4; Sir 24:17; *Ps. Sol.* 1:4; also Rom 9:23; Phil 4:19; Eph 1:18; 3:16; Col 1:27; 2:2.

between wealth and the divine established with Christ's attire in Rev 1:12–16 and the identification of the churches as golden lampstands in Rev 1:20. The elaboration of wealth imagery in the vision of the heavenly throne room (4:1–11) climaxes in the doxology in 5:12. Subsequent visions in Rev 8:1–5, 14:14–16, and 15:2–8 keep the wealth of heaven in the foreground for the audience before the wealth of Babylon ever appears. After the seventh seal is opened, an angel takes a golden censer to the golden altar before God's throne (8:3). The "Son of Man" appears on a white cloud, wearing a golden crown and bearing a sharp sickle (14:14). The seven angels with the seven plagues emerge from the temple wearing golden belts, carrying the plagues in golden bowls (15:6–7). This strong and positive association of wealth and heaven provides the narrative context for the next large complex of wealth imagery, the description of the harlot of Babylon and the woes and laments over the fall of the city of Babylon (Revelation 17–18).

One passage before the Babylon section also indicates a surprisingly callous attitude by this wealthy God toward the poor in the Apocalypse. The seven seals in 6:1–17 and continuing in 8:1–2 are the first series of disasters in the Apocalypse. The seals are crucial plot devices to move the action from heaven back to earth after the vision of the heavenly throne room, as John sees the results on earth of the Lamb opening the seals in heaven. The first four of the seven seals are the "Four Horsemen of the Apocalypse" (6:1–8). While scholars have studied the background of these four horses and riders, the function of this unit within the narrative of the Apocalypse has not received as much attention as the historical referent of each color or weapon.[12] The opening of the third seal (6:5–6) introduces a black horse and a rider carrying a balance. This rider brings famine, signaled by high prices; John hears a voice among the four living creatures: "A quart of wheat for a *denarius*, and three quarts of barley for a *denarius*, but do not damage the oil and wine!"

---

[12]See Swete, 84–89; Bousset, 307ff.; and esp. Charles 1:154–61, who summarizes the positions taken up to his time. The generally accepted scheme of interpretation is that the first horse (white) and rider refer to the Parthian empire; the second (red) to war; the third (black) to various local famines; and the fourth (pale green) to disease. See Kerkeslager, "Apollo, Greco-Roman Prophecy, and the Rider on the White Horse," who, attempting to solve the problem of repetition of meaning of the white and red horses (Rev 9:17; 19:11), advances the theory that the white horse and rider refer to pagan prophets.

(6:6).[13] These prices are very high: a day's wage barely covers a day's worth of food.[14] Two points are clear about this disaster. First, like every other plague and disaster within the Apocalypse, this famine is firmly under the control of heaven. A heavenly voice sets prices for basic commodities and excludes other items from the famine.[15] Second, the prices for wheat and barley would impact the lives of the poor, who could ill afford such high prices, much more than the rich.[16] The only other occurrence of the words for oil ($\check{\epsilon}\lambda\alpha\iota o\nu$) or wine ($o\hat{\iota}\nu o\varsigma$) in Revelation is in the list of luxury items in the merchants' cargo (Rev 18:13). The third seal is the only disaster described in the Apocalypse that discriminates on socio-economic grounds; the pattern elsewhere is either not to discriminate or to divide the inhabitants of the earth on the basis of religious loyalty to God or Satan and the beasts. For instance, the fourth seal brings death to a quarter of the earth, with no mention of socio-economic division (6:7–8). The sixth seal draws deliberate attention to the universal nature of this particular calamity: "Then the kings of the earth and the magnates and the generals and the rich and the powerful, and everyone, slave and free, hid in the caves and among the rocks and the mountains" (6:15; cf. 13:16, 19:18). Although Revelation 18 focuses on kings, wealthy merchants, and sailors, the destruction of the city includes musicians, craftspeople, brides and bridegrooms (18:22–23), and everyone who does not heed the heavenly call to abandon the city (18:4).

---

[13]Adolf Harnack, *TLZ* 22 (1902): 591–92, first advanced the theory that Rev 6:6 refers to Domitian's edict of 92 CE that vineyards in the provinces should be cut down; see Suet. *Dom.* 7. Charles 1:168, notes the Jewish expectation found in *b. Soṭa* 49b that a scarcity of grain and plenitude of wine will proceed the coming of the Messiah.

[14]The high prices can be shown from the rider's kit, the function of the seals as disasters; and the occurrence of oil and wine in the merchant's cargo list. For historical data, see Charles 1:168, that a day's wage barely covered a day's food; and Roloff, 87, that the prices in Rev 6:6 are approximately ten times the prices at the time. But Swete, 88, understands the heavenly voice to be *prohibiting* high prices in a time of scarcity, thus in effect eliminating the disaster of the third seal.

[15]Compare the heavenly control of disasters in Rev 7:1–4, where the four angels holding back the winds have been given power to harm earth and sea while the fifth angel checks their power until the sealing of God's slaves; 9:1–6, the specific instructions given to the locusts; 14:17–20, the chain of command among the angels and the precise measurement of the blood.

[16]See Roloff, 87; Boring, 122.

Thus, in the narrative world of the Apocalypse, God shows no partiality to the poor or oppressed when sending disasters from heaven. When social groups are described, as in Rev 6:15, 13:16 and 19:18, the emphasis tends to be on the universality of the punishment rather than any special concern for the poor. While this does not necessarily mean that God, in the Apocalypse, has a bias *against* the poor, God shows no special concern for economic justice either.[17] The reassurance offered to the Smyrnans is the only passage that suggests such a concern, but as noted in the previous chapter it is not poverty but the endurance of afflictions that makes this "poor" church truly "rich." The allegiances symbolized by the seal of God and the mark of the Beast, not wealth or poverty, are the only token of distinction in the plagues and calamities. The exception is the third seal, which affects the poor more than the wealthy. There are no passages in Revelation that express special concern for the poor, widows, orphans, the traditional recipients of charity, to counterbalance the bias against the poor in Rev 6:6–6. This absence is remarkable in the context of ancient Jewish and Christian literature. It is an absence made all the more striking by the wealth of heaven in the Apocalypse and is important to keep in mind when the forces of heaven destroy the wealthy city of Babylon.

The Mark of the Beast

Before Revelation 17–18, the only association of Satan and wealth in the Apocalypse is the control of buying and selling by means of the mark of the beast (13:16–18). The mark appears in John's vision of the two beasts (13:1–18), whose power stems from the dragon Satan (12:9; 13:4). In 12:18–13:18, John describes a vision of these beasts being given complete mastery over all social, political, and religious activity on earth.[18] While

---

[17]*Contra* Yarbro Collins, who has argued that "Those who have power and wealth in the present are portrayed as idolatrous and murderous, or at best as lukewarm, while the truly faithful are expected to be poor" ("Revelation 18," 202; see also "Political Perspective," 252–54); and Bauckham, "Economic Critique," who argues that Revelation critiques Rome's economic exploitation.

[18]Commentators have taken the passive verb ἐδόθη in 13:5–7 as an occurrence of the "divine passive," carrying the sense that *God* has given the Beast this power (Swete, 165; Caird, 167; Mounce, 254; Roloff, 157); furthermore, the power of the Beast is limited to 42 months. The first Beast, however, draws his original power from the serpent Satan, 13:2, who has just been

it is accurate to call the first beast the "political" power and the second beast the "religious" power,[19] these two concepts are intricately related here as they are throughout the narrative world of the Apocalypse. The beast from the sea, a fantastic hybrid animal who mimics the Lamb of God (13:1–10), slanders God's saints and makes war against them.[20] His political power inspires awe and worship for himself and his master, Satan (13:3b–4). The beast from the land organizes the worship of the image of the first beast; social and political power stem from his religious authority (13:11–18). The control of the two beasts progresses carefully through every sphere of human existence on earth: political, military, religious, and finally economic. The second beast controls the inhabitants of the earth by means of a mark (χάραγμα) on everyone's right hand or forehead (13:16). No one is able to buy or sell unless they have the mark of the beast or know its number, 666 (13:17–18). The list in 13:16 emphasizes the universality of the beasts' control via the mark: everyone is marked, small and great, free and slave, rich (πλούσιος) and poor (πτωχός).

As with the four horses and riders, attention has focused on the historical referent of the "mark of the beast" in 13:16 outside of the text. The mark could refer to Roman coins, imperial seals, Jewish *tephillin*, and slaves' tattoos.[21] The function of the mark within the text, however,

---

defeated in his effort to capture the child (12:17).

[19]So Boring, 160–61.

[20]Rev 13:3 and 17:11, 16 have been the focus of commentary in terms of the influence of the *Nero redivivus* myth on Revelation. See Wilhelm Bousset, *Der Antichrist in der Überlieferung des Judentums, des neuen Testaments und der alten Kirche: Ein Beitrag zur Auslegung der Apokalypse* (repr.: Hildesheim: Georg Olms, 1983; orig.: Göttingen: Vandenhoeck & Ruprecht, 1895); idem., "Antichrist" in *Encyclopaedia of Religion and Ethics*, ed. James Hastings et al. (Edinburgh: T.&T. Clark; New York: Scribners, 1979–1981) 1:578–81; and Bousset (commentary), 410–19; also Charles 1:350; Yarbro Collins, *Combat Myth*, 174–86; and Bauckham, *Climax of Prophecy*, 384–452.

[21]Charles, 1:362–63 and 363n.1, sums up these four options. He argues that the mark does not parody the sealing of the faithful in Rev. 7:3 and favors the idea that the mark parodies "orthodox Jews" who wore tephillin (φυλακτήρια, Matt 23:5) "on the left hand and on the head." Bousset, 427–28, rejects a reference to coins but assumes a wider apocalyptic tradition concerning buying and selling under the Antichrist. Caird, 173, interprets the mark as Roman coins although he remarks that Roman sanctions against an illegal religion were always judicial and never economic. Ramsay, *Letters to the Seven Churches*, 79–80,

is fairly clear and does not require a historical referent.[22] The mark of the beast mimics the seal of God (7:3) just as the first Beast mimics the Lamb, from the numbers of heads to the healed wound. This is another expression of the "mirroring motif" or "polemical parallelism," the structural device of Revelation discussed in chapter 4. The seal of God and the mark of the Beast are signs of religious loyalty, the "dualism of decision," in the narrative world of the Apocalypse.[23] Disaster often comes indiscriminately to the inhabitants of the earth in John's visions. But some catastrophes are parceled out according to which side people have chosen, God or Satan. Those who accept the mark of the beast may continue to buy and sell (13:17), but they will be singled out by God and the angels for torment by fire, sulphur, sores, and the lake of fire (14:9,11; 16:2; 19:20; 20:4). The visions of the Apocalypse also portray the consequences of remaining loyal by wearing the seal of God. The saints of God are conquered by the first Beast (13:7) and are killed by the second beast for refusing to worship the image of the first beast (13:15).[24] The 144,000 who cannot buy or sell (ἀγοράσαι ἢ πωλῆσαι, 13:17) are "bought" by God, (see ἀγοράζω in 14:3–4; cf. 5:9).[25] The loyalty of those who refuse the mark of the beast is rewarded by allowing them to reign with Christ for a thousand years (20:4). The mark of the beast

---

postulates that there was an official certificate of loyalty for complying with imperial religion. Soldiers sometimes branded themselves with the name of their general and mercenaries and slaves, especially Temple slaves, with the stamp of the emperor (see Müller, 255). See 3 Macc 2:27–30, where Ptolemy attempts to punish the Jews by excluding them from worship unless they follow other cultic sacrifices by registering them in a census and by branding them with a pagan symbol. Some Jews, however, continued to practice and "gave their money as a ransom for their life" (*OTP* 2:520, trans. H. Anderson). For a recent attempt to explain the mark with historical referents, see Edwin A. Judge, "The Mark of the Beast, Revelation 13:16" *TynBul* 42 (1991): 158–60.

[22]The narrative function, recognized by Swete, 173–6, has gained adherents among more recent commentators such as Mounce, 262; and Boring, 160–64.

[23]See Boring, 161.

[24]Death comes both to the "slaves of God" and "saints" who are sealed by God and to "those who dwell on the earth" who accept the mark of the Beast. See the ideological critical perspective of Pippin, "Eros and the End." On martyrdom in Revelation, see Yarbro Collins, "Political Perspective."

[25]Schüssler Fiorenza, *Justice and Judgment*, 73–74, draws attention to the commercial language in Rev 5:9.

resonates in the narrative world of the Apocalypse with significance that a reference to Roman coins alone does not encompass.

Until fairly recently, few scholars of Revelation challenged John's construction of reality in this chapter, even though it jars with so many texts, including Christian, describing life in Asia around 100 CE. Commentators have generally assumed that John describes a situation in which some sort of emperor worship is required in order to participate in commerce. The "information" offered in Rev 13:16–18 has been taken as a call for economic withdrawal from the cities of Asia or the prohibition of handling coins.[26] The search for the true reference for "666" should stop at John's apocalyptic pen. The connection between Emperor worship, military power, persecution of Christians, and commerce can only be found in Revelation 13. Just as John tries to associate his three main opponents—the Romans, the Jews, and rival Christian teachers—with Satan in the seven messages, here in Revelation 13 he tries to connect all aspects of social life in a satanic conspiracy theory. Where modern apocalyptic theorists issue alarmist bulletins over shortwave radio, John sent apocalyptic visions by prophetic letter.

The question remains, though, why John would construct *this* type of conspiracy-theory. Whether or not the mark refers to Roman coins, it gives the beasts control of trade in the narrative world of the Apocalypse. The research of chapter 3 offers an important perspective on the satanic control of commerce in this passage. John leaves to the Romans, under Satan's control, the banal occupation of trade. The 144,000 who are sealed by God have access to heaven's established wealth and have no need to participate in commerce. The vision of their selection (7:1–8) precedes the vision of the two beasts and the satanic control of commerce in Rev 13:1–18. Rev 13:16–18 creates anxiety (a type of *pathos*) in the audience, who would be understandably concerned about their ability to engage in day-to-day buying and selling without compromising their faith. Such anxiety has social as well as theological roots, for the Apocalypse takes a very negative view of the low-status occupation of trade. Revelation 13 associates Satan and Babylon/Rome with the disreputable occupation of commerce, just as Christ mocked the Laodiceans for

---

[26]Yarbro Collins interprets the mark as coins and argues that 13:16–18 is a call for economic boycott (see "Revelation 18," 202; "Political Perspective," 252–54). But note Charles's sage comment: "this interpretation does not explain the stamping of the marks on the right hand and brow" (1:363).

their commercial activity. The description of the fall of Babylon will spell out this conspiratorial association in much greater detail.

Babylon

Two short passages introduce the name and announce the fall of Babylon before Revelation 17–18 describes the fate of the city in detail. The first is the proleptic cry of the angel in Rev 14:8: "Fallen, fallen is Babylon the great [ἡ μεγάλη]! She has made all nations drink of the wine of the wrath of her fornication."[27] Fornication (πορνεία [*porneia*]) fore-shadows one of the dominant characteristics of Babylon in Revelation 17–18. The second announcement of the fall of Babylon also comes in the narrative context of cosmic judgment (cosmic judgment is such a regular feature of the visions that this may be a tautological statement). The third series of sevens, the seven plagues in golden bowls, runs from Rev 15:1–16:21. When the seventh angel pours out the seventh golden bowl, thunder, earthquakes and fire break out upon the earth; "The great city [ἡ πόλις ἡ μεγάλη] was split into three parts, and the cities of the nations fell. God remembered great Babylon and gave her the wine-cup of the fury of his wrath" (Rev 16:19). Here again, as in Rev 14:8, we find both wine and wrath, which anticipate major motifs of Revelation 17–18. This passage also connects the destruction of Babylon to the over-all scheme of destruction in the seven seals, trumpets and bowls in Revelation 6–16.[28]

There might be some confusion for the audience exactly which "great city" Rev 16:19 refers to, Babylon or Jerusalem, since another passage in Revelation describes "the great city [τῆς πόλεως τῆς μεγάλης] that is prophetically [πνευματικῶς] called Sodom and Egypt, where also

---

[27]See Charles 2:14–15, on the difficulty in the phrase "wine of the wrath of her fornication" (ἐκ τοῦ οἴνου τοῦ θυμοῦ τῆς πορνείας αὐτῆς). There are no text variants in 14:8 but several when the phrase recurs in 18:3. While "wrath" likely refers to the wrath of God, which comes with drinking the wine of Babylon's fornication, there is no reason to assume an interpolation.

[28]The connection of Rev 17:1–19:10 to 16:17–20 is a major point for Ruiz, *Ezekiel in the Apocalypse*; see 230–289. The point is somewhat labored, as the connection is fairly obvious, and does not relate to the use of Ezekiel in Revelation. Overemphasizing 16:17–20 as the introduction, moreover, runs the risk of slighting the parallelism of 17:1–3 and 21:9–10 and the *synkrisis* of the two great cities.

their Lord was crucified" (Rev 11:8). This earlier passage is a reference
to Jerusalem while 16:19 refers to Babylon, as the end of the verse makes
clear: "God remembered great Babylon and gave her the wine-cup of the
fury of his wrath." The imagery of the wine-cup of God's wrath appears
with Babylon's name in 14:8 and 18:2 and is echoed in 17:4–5. A small
number of scholars have interpreted Babylon in Revelation as Jerusalem
rather than Rome.[29] The identification of Babylon and Rome in Revelation is clear from literary and social-historical evidence; no other city in
95 CE sat upon seven hills and ruled the world (Rev 17:9, 18). The prophecy in Rev 11:1–13 is based on an earlier Jewish or Christian prophecy
about the war with the Romans in 66–70 CE and the destruction of Jerusalem.[30] In its present narrative and rhetorical context, it reminds the
audience of the destruction of the real Jerusalem by Rome, which is cast
in Revelation as Babylon. The reference to the crucifixion of Jesus in
11:8 fixes the identification of this great city as Jerusalem. The historical
Jerusalem in Rev 11:8 is not to be identified with the heavenly New Jerusalem, which comes down from heaven after the destruction of Babylon
and Satan's forces. There is an actual temple in Revelation 11:1–2, as
opposed to explicit exclusion of a temple in the New Jerusalem (21:22).
This earthly temple that was destroyed by the Romans helps set the
context for the invective against Babylon/Rome in Revelation 17–18.

The Harlot (Revelation 17)

In Revelation 17, after the two proleptic passages announcing the
judgment of the city, the narrator describes his first vision of Babylon.
The Babylon section of the Apocalypse runs from 17:1 to 18:24.[31] This
section begins with a general introduction to the major themes of the
Babylon section by the guiding angel (*angelus interprens*): "Come, I will
show you the judgment of the great whore who is seated on many waters,
with whom the kings of the earth have committed fornication, and with

---

[29]See the commentary of J. Massyngberde Ford, *Revelation*, AB 38 (Garden
City NY: Doubleday, 1975) esp. 282–307. This idea has not been well received
and was retracted by Ford at the SBL annual meeting in Philadelphia, 18 November 1995. For the well-received notion that Babylon in Revelation is Rome, see
Yarbro Collins, "Revelation 18," 185n.1; and "Political Perspective," 241.

[30]See Charles 1:269–92; Roloff, 128–31; Boring, 142–48.

[31]And arguably to 19:10, by means of a typical interlocking structure; see the
discussion below.

the wine of whose fornication the inhabitants of the earth have become drunk" (17:1–2).[32] This introduction by the angel recalls for the audience the proleptic cry of the angel in Rev 14:8 and recurs as a refrain throughout the Babylon section (17:18; 18:3, 9), emphasizing the major themes of the Babylon section: harlotry, fornication, illicit relations with the "kings of the earth," and leading the people of the earth astray. The angel who guides the narrator from here to the end of the Apocalypse is one of the seven who has poured out the seven last plagues from their golden bowls (15:5–16:21).[33] All seven of these angels wear bright linen (λίνον καθαρὸν λαμπρόν) and golden sashes (ζώνας χρυσᾶς, 15:6), like the Human One in 1:12. John's guiding angel is thus dressed properly to show John both the garish wealth of Babylon and its destruction and the pure wealth of the New Jerusalem.

In John's first vision of Babylon, the city becomes a harlot by metonymy (17:3–6).[34] He describes the scarlet beast on which the harlot sits; it has ten heads and seven horns and is "full of blasphemous names" (17:3). But it is the harlot which holds the narrator's attention. The *ekphrasis* of John's vision of the harlot foregrounds wealth imagery: "The woman was clothed in purple and scarlet, and adorned with gold and jewels and pearls, holding in her hand a golden cup full of abominations and the impurities of her fornication" (17:4).[35] The writing on her forehead (ἐπὶ τὸ μέτωπον), which might have suggested the tattoo worn by prostitutes, recalls also the mark of the beast on the forehead or hand (13:16; 14:19).[36] This writing identifies her for narrator and

---

[32]The awkward NRSV translation does not show that the relative construction breaks off with the second clause, which Charles identifies as both good Hebrew and good Greek (2.63); see BDF §469. This clause might stand better in English as an independent sentence: " . . . with whom the kings of the earth have committed fornication. The inhabitants of the earth have become drunk from the wine of her fornication."

[33]See Hansgüter Reichelt, *Angelus interpres-Texte in der Johannes-Apokalypse*, Europäische Hochschulschriften 23:507 (Frankfurt: Peter Lang, 1994).

[34]See Schüssler Fiorenza, 95–96; "the female imagery of Revelation . . . would be completely misconstrued if it were understood as referring to the actual behavior of individual women" (96).

[35]Aune, "Intertextuality," 158, characterizes this passage as the *ekphrasis* of a tableau.

[36]On the tattoo worn on the forehead by Roman prostitutes, see Charles 2:64; Aune, *HarperCollins Study Bible*, 2329; contra this view, see Roloff, 197.

audience as not only harlot but "mother of whores" and of the "abominations" (βδελυγμάτα) of the earth as well (17:5). The description of the
harlot ends with a third condemnatory statement, that the woman was
drunk with the blood of saints and martyrs (17:6), further increasing the
pathos of this vision.

This vision of the harlot contains the first explicit wealth imagery
associated with Satan or Babylon in the Apocalypse. Her luxurious attire
is a challenge to the wealth of heaven. No character to this point in
Revelation has displayed so much wealth as the harlot. Whereas the
heavenly forces are decorated with gold and jewels, the harlot also wears
purple, scarlet, and pearls. A number of rhetorical moves distinguish the
wealth of heaven already viewed by the narrator and the audience from
the wealth of the harlot Babylon displayed in Rev 17:3–6. Christ, the 24
elders around the throne, and the angels who serve at the altar in heaven
are clothed in white (1:14; 4:4; 19:11, 14). White clothing is also a
positive image in the messages and for the saints and martyrs in heaven
(3:4–5; 6:11; 7:9, 13–14). Martyrs' garments turn white in the holy blood
of persecution (7:13–14; cf. 19:13), but the same blood stains the harlot.
Her scarlet garments, and the beast on which she sits, are dyed red with
the blood of saints and witnesses to Jesus. Purple, a prominent luxury
good in antiquity and a distinguishing mark of the Roman senatorial
aristocracy, is only associated in Revelation with Babylon (17:4; 18:12,
16), even though it was associated with the Hebrew cult.[37] The second
way the wealth of heaven and Babylon are distinguished for the audience
is by means of the motif of harlotry (*porneia*). The majority of the twenty
porn- words in Revelation are in the Babylon section (17:1–19:10).[38]
Before John views the harlot, *porneia* and cognates are associated with
John's Christian opponents; these opponents' approval of eating meat
from the pagan temple, which "Christ" clearly considers to be idolatrous
(2:14, 20, 21); and the worship of idols (9:21). The association of idolatry
and sexual immorality was well established in Jewish and early Christian

---

[37]In the cult: Exod 28:1–39; 35:20–29; 39:8–14; 1QM 7:8–10; *T.Levi* 8:1–11;
Josephus *J.W.* 5 §§184–226; as a symbol of wealth, luxury, and decadence: Jer
10:1–10; *Sib. Or.* 3.657–668; Hor. *Ep.* 1.17.1–32; Juv. *Sat.* 3.81; *Ps. Melissa
Letter to Kleareta*; Luc. *Nigr.* 3–7.
[38]In addition to πόρνη (harlot), πορνεία, πόρνος, πορνεύω; Rev 17:1,
2, 2, 4, 5, 15, 16; 18:3, 3, 9; 19:2, 2. Rev 14:8 also associates Babylon and
πορνεία.

tradition before the Apocalypse.[39] The association of the harlot of Babylon and wealth implies that her gold, jewels, and pearls were payments from the kings of the earth for sexual favors. The harlot's wealth is derived from a trade, one which Cicero would have certainly included among "those catering to sensual pleasures" and therefore vulgar for the gentle-born (Cic. *De off.* 1.150).

The implied author of Revelation extends the connotations of fornication with the great harlot Babylon to include not only idolatry but commerce as well. This connection is most explicit in Revelation 18 but is alluded to in 17:2. The idea of portraying a city as a harlot comes from the Hebrew Bible. Jerusalem is frequently referred to as a harlot by the Hebrew prophets. In Isa 47:1–15, a passage used in Rev 18:4–8, Babylon is described as a fallen queen and slave-courtesan. Rev 17:2, however, probably echoes the Tyre oracle in Isa 23:17, foreshadowing the application of the Ezekiel oracle on Tyre to Babylon in Revelation 18.[40] The echo of Isaiah in Rev 17:2 is subtle and would have been obscure for anyone unfamiliar with the Hebrew scriptures and meaningless for those only knowledgeable in the LXX. The MT version of Isa 23:17 emphasizes the harlotry of Tyre (אתנן "gift" or "harlot's pay"; זנה "prostitute") while the LXX focuses on the commercial activity of the city without any mention of harlotry.[41] The question arises, however, whether the audience would have understood these allusions. Rev 17:1–6 alone contains allusions to Isa 23:17; Jer 25:15; Jer 51:7; Jer 51:13; and Nah 3:4.[42] None of these allusions are, of course, acknowledged in Revelation, and it is

---

[39]See Caird, 212; and Phyllis Bird, "'To Play the Harlot': An Inquiry into an Old Testament Metaphor," in *Gender and Difference in Ancient Israel*, ed. P. L. Day (Minneapolis: Augsburg Fortress, 1989) 75–94, who focuses on the governing metaphor of Hosea 1–3. The metaphorical use of זנה in Hosea identified by Bird evoke two images of dishonor in Israelite culture: the prostitute and the promiscuous daughter or wife. See also Exod 16:36; 23:2; 32:6; Judg 2:17; 8:33; 8:27; Deut 31:11; Isa 1:21; Jer 2:2; Ezek 16:36; 23:2; 1 Cor 10:6–8; and the rabbinic literature cited by Wayne A. Meeks, "'And Rose up to Play': Midrash and Paraenesis in 1 Corinthians 10:1–22," *JSNT* 16 (1982): 64–78.

[40]See the discussion in chap. 2, p. 62.

[41]The LXX of Isa 23:17 reads καὶ ἔσται ἐμπόριον πάσαις ταῖς βασιλείαις τῆς οἰκουμένης.

[42]NA[26] notes a weak reference to Ezek 28:13 as well, apparently on the occurrence of λίθοι τίμιοι in both verses.

not clear that John intended his audience to understand them as allusions.[43] The different reading for Isa 23:17 in the LXX and MT highlights
the difficulties the audience would have had. John plucks different
images—harlot, cup, kings of the earth—from different prophetic
passages, not giving any one Hebrew oracle particular primacy. The
allusions and echoes discerned by scholars would not have been
accessible to John's audience.

While there is no guarantee that the Asian audience would have heard
Rev 17:2 as a reference to commerce, we can be more sure that the harlot
described in Rev 17:4 would have been perceived as tawdry. This is the
most garish use of wealth imagery in Revelation. John marvels at this
vision, which is an unusual intrusion by the narrator.[44] The harlot of
Babylon in her gilded attire can be compared with Fortunata and Scintilla,
who wear several pounds of gold apiece (*Sat.* 67). This is not to say that
Rev 17:1–6 is an allusion to Petronius's *Satyricon*. Appearance was
important in antiquity, however, whether harlot or merchant's wife,
senator or philosopher. The ways the audiences heard this text would
have been influenced by social life in Ephesus and Smyrna rather than by
the intensive exegesis of the Hebrew Bible that the author must have
gone through. John takes imagery from the Old Testament and uses it in
his invective in a social context where it acquires new meanings
associated with aristocratic disdain of commercial wealth as well as moral
disdain of prostitution and sexual immorality.

---

[43]Against Caird, 11; and Fekkes, *Isaiah and Prophetic Traditions*, 289–90.
The lack of any citation formula in Revelation is notable when compared to other
early Christian literature; see Moyise, *Old Testament in Revelation*, 11–23.

[44]There are relatively few narrated reactions as compared to authorial interpretive intrusions into the narrative; compare such reactions in 1:17, 5:4,
7:13–15; 19:10 to interpretations by the omniscient implied author such as
11:4–14; 12:9; 14:12; 15:1–2; 20:5–6. On the seer's reaction, see Ruiz, *Ezekiel
in the Apocalypse*, 338–40; and Steven Thompson, *The Apocalypse and Semitic
Syntax* (Cambridge: Cambridge University Press, 1985) 12. According to Ruiz,
Revelation 17 contains a "high concentration of hermeneutical imperatives" (338,
where "hermeneutical imperatives" are defined as specific exhortations to the
audience "which focus and direct the attention of the interpreter" [336; see
190–225]). These "hermeneutical imperatives" are μυστήριον (17:5, 7; see
1:20; 10:7); forms of θαυμάζω (17:6, 7, 8; see 13:3); and the call for wisdom,
σοφία (17:9; see 13:9–10, 18).

The explanation of the vision of the harlot evokes the political theology of the Apocalypse. As in the throne room narrative in Revelation 4–5, so here wealth and political imagery go together, but in Revelation 17 the wealth belongs to heaven's enemy, the gold-encrusted harlot astride the scarlet beast. While the angel promises in 17:7 to tell John the "mystery" of the harlot, he does not mention her again until 17:18, after the lengthy interpretation of the beast, its head, and its horns.[45] This explication ignores some aspects of John's vision; interprets motifs that are not in the vision; and focuses mostly on the political symbolism of the heads and horns of the scarlet beast (17:9–14, 16).[46] The scarlet beast upon which the harlot sits has the same number of heads and horns as the beast from the sea (Rev 13:1). The angel describes these heads and horns as two groups of kings (17:10–12).[47] In a reversal of the delegation of authority from Satan to the two beasts (13:4, 12),[48] the angel says that these kings "are united in yielding their power and authority to the beast" (17:13). These kings, according to the angel, will make war on the Lamb but the Lamb will conquer them (17:14). The angel makes explicit here for the audience that the beast upon which the harlot sits, the same as the beast from the sea, parallels the lamb who was slain (5:6), who has seven horns (5:1). In typical polemical parallelism, the author now sets the "kings of the earth," and their wealth, against Christ, *archōn* of the kings of the earth (1:5), and the wealth of heaven.[49]

---

[45]On this gap, see Charles 2:66–75, and Pippin's dramatically different feminist-ideological interpretation, "Eros and the End."

[46]The angel explains "the waters that you saw" (17:15) but the narrator never mentions seeing any waters; the angel himself mentions them in his introduction in 17:1. Babylon the great harlot "sits upon many waters," an allusion to Jer 51:13 (28:13): "You who live by mighty waters, rich in treasures, your end has come, the thread of your life is cut." The Hebrew word for treasure, אוֹצָר, carries the connotations of wealth in a palace or temple (Jer 15:13; 1 Kings 7:51) or cosmic wealth, such as the treasure of Yahweh in heaven (Deut 28:12). See William L. Holladay, *A Concise Hebrew and Aramaic Lexicon of the Old Testament* (Grand Rapids: Eerdmans; Leiden: E. J. Brill, 1988) s.v. אוֹצָר, 7.

[47]The possible associations between these kings and Roman emperors have been neatly summarized by Aune in a table in *The HarperCollins Study Bible*, 2330. See Ruiz, *Ezekiel in the Apocalypse*, 341–42n.87, for bibliography on Revelation and the Roman emperors; see also Ste. Croix, *Class Struggle in the Ancient Greek World*, 394–402.

[48]The passives in 13:5–8 suggest that this is all under God's control.

[49]These "kings of the earth" are introduced in 6:15, where they are destroyed

The vision of the gold-encrusted harlot and the explanation of this vision's "mystery" by the angel begin to tie together a number of negative motifs that are part of the author's ideological arsenal: wealth, commerce, and *porneia* with Roman authority and Greco-Roman culture. At the end of chapter 17, the angel identifies the harlot as "the great city that rules over the kings of the earth" (17:18), which segues into the visions and auditions of the destruction of this great harlot-city in Revelation 18.

The City (Revelation 18)

Wealth imagery in the vision of the great harlot in Rev 17:1–6 is but a prelude to the extended description of the tremendous commercial wealth of the city and its destruction in Rev 18:1–24. The strength and extent of the condemnation of Rome's wealth in Revelation 18 have become the focal point for commentators when discussing wealth and the Apocalypse.[50] We are at the heart of the matter for analyzing the ideological function of wealth imagery in the Apocalypse. It is in this passage that the author's rhetorical strategies become most evident for distinguishing the good wealth of heaven from the evil wealth of Babylon.

Use of the Hebrew Bible

When considering the use of biblical sources in Revelation 18:1–24, we are faced with the same question as when studying the harlot: how much does analysis of John's sources help us to understand how the text would have been heard? My expressed interests lie more in how John's language would have functioned in social-historical context than John's intent when composing the Apocalypse. Jan Fekkes's careful and detailed study of the

---

with everyone else by the great earthquake of the sixth seal. The kingdom of the beast is associated with the kingdoms of the earth in the disasters inaugurated by the fifth and sixth bowls (16:10–16). The fifth angel pours his bowl on the "throne of the beast" and plunges the kingdom into darkness and agony. The sixth bowl prepares the way for the "kings of the east," usually identified as the Parthians, and calls forth three demonic spirits from the satanic trinity that assemble the kings of the world for battle at Har-mageddon. They are destroyed in battle by Christ, in his incarnation as the "faithful and true" rider (19:17–21).

[50]See D. H. Lawrence, *Apocalypse*, quoted at the head of chap. 1; Yarbro Collins in "Revelation 18," "Political Perspective," and esp. *Crisis and Catharsis*; and Bauckham "Economic Critique"; and the discussion of methodological issues in chap. 1.

use of the Hebrew Bible in Revelation sets out to challenge "the common
assumption that John is not consciously interpreting the OT, but simply
using it as a language and image base." His focus is, in fact, authorial
intent, as the term "conscious interpretation" indicates. As Fekkes
demonstrates and we have seen in this study, John uses OT passages with
similar "setting and purpose" when composing the Apocalypse.[51] The
elements of the vision of Christ on Patmos come from OT visions; the
motifs in Revelation 18 are from passages describing Babylon and Tyre
in the Hebrew Bible; and the glories in Revelation 21–22 are borrowed
from passages describing the restoration of Jerusalem. The implied author
of Revelation does indeed select and apply Isaiah passages according to
subject, as Fekkes argues. But this is not an effective rebuttal to the
"common assumption" of scholars such as Schüssler Fiorenza or Vos,
with whom Fekkes takes issue.[52] As is the case with Ruiz, who studies
the use of Ezekiel in Rev 16:19–19:10, Fekkes takes too narrow a view
of the text and thus misses both the rhetorical strategies at work and the
ways the text could have been heard in social-historical context. The
security officers at Jurassic Park counted only the dinosaurs they expected
to find and so did not know that the ancient reptiles were breeding on the
island. Fekkes cleans and sorts the text by focusing on Isaiah so that he
loses sight of the rest of the "dinosaurs" in the Apocalypse: the bewildering, chaotic use of the OT from the *audience's* perspective.

This point is particularly apt for study of Revelation 18, although the
same could be said for any wealth passage in Revelation. I have already
noted the difficulty the audience would have faced in discerning the
multiple allusions in Rev 17:1–6. John does indeed draw from oracles
against Babylon in the Hebrew Bible in Revelation 18. He also applies
oracles against Tyre to Babylon/Rome, which calls to mind Bloomian
misprision more than the rabbinic categories Fekkes offers as analogous.[53]
John also applies OT passages describing the destruction of *Jerusalem*
from Jeremiah to his description of the destruction of Babylon. At least
twice, these are clear allusions: Jer 22:8 in Rev 18:18 and Jer 25:10 in
Rev 18:22, as well as echoes of other passages such as Jer 19:9–13;

---

[51]See Fekkes, *Isaiah and Prophetic Traditions*, 102–103, 281–90.
[52]See Fekkes, *Isaiah and Prophetic Traditions*, 286, citing Schüssler
Fiorenza, *Justice and Judgment*, 135–36; Vos, *Synoptic Traditions*, 51–52.
[53]See Bloom, *Anxiety of Influence*, 5–45; *The Revelation of St. John the
Divine*, 1–5.

22:6–9; 25:9–11,17; 26:6, 9; and 44:2–3.[54] It is difficult to find parts of Revelation 18 that contain allusions to only one OT passage.[55] As we saw in chapter 2, the author draws primarily from Isaiah 47, Jeremiah 50–51, and Ezekiel 26–28, but there is no discernible order to John's use of the OT outside of his own rhetorical framework. The cry of the angel in Rev 14:8 that announces the fall of Babylon, repeated in 18:2, uses bits and pieces from Isa 21:9, Isa 13:21–22; Jer 51:8; and Dan 4:27. Rev 18:4–8 and 18:20–24, the two passages which frame the laments of the kings, merchants, and seafarers, are constituted substantially of allusions to Jeremiah, although Isa 47:7–9 forms the basis of Rev 18:7–8. The cry of the second angel for the people to come out of Babylon in Rev 18:4 echoes Jer 51:45. In Rev 18:6, the second heavenly voice uses the words of Jer 50:29 when calling for the city to receive a double portion of her own works. The call to rejoice in Rev 18:20 and the figure of a stone thrown into the water as a symbol of the destruction of the city are adapted from Jer 51:48 and 51:63. The central laments in 18:9–19, their cast of characters, and their descriptions of the merchants' cargo are based on Ezekiel 26–27. Finally, the end of *Babylon's* cultural life described in Rev 18:21–24 uses imagery from Jer 25:10 that describes the desolation of *Jerusalem*. These allusions to the Hebrew prophets come so thick and fast and in such a bewildering order that, aside from thematic similarities, the audience would be hard pressed to recognize any biblical passage at all.

John does use the Hebrew scriptures as a thesaurus for his imagery—with a specific rhetorical result. The sources are completely replaced by the final product; John's Babylon overshadows all precursors. Revelation 18 sounds like "biblical" language because it is just that—phrases, words and images taken from the Hebrew scriptures and crafted into a new, highly rhetorical *psogos* or invective against Babylon/Rome. This is not exegesis, as Fekkes claims, along the lines of the Qumran pesharim or Florilegium. The Qumran pesharim are expositions of one prophetic book in light of the community's situation. While the Florilegium (4QFlor) interprets passages from a number of different

---

[54]Fekkes, *Isaiah and Prophetic Traditions*, 87–88, does not include the reference to Jer 22:8 in Rev 18:18 but does list the reference to Ezek 27:32, a Tyre passage, in Rev 18:18b. When accounting for the reference to Jer 25:10 in Rev 18:22, Fekkes writes that this is a reference in Jeremiah to the "nations," although all passages listed in Jeremiah clearly apply to Jerusalem and Judah.

[55]So also Ruiz, *Ezekiel in the Apocalypse*, 407, on Rev 18:1–8.

biblical books, the structure of the text includes quotation or citation formulas that clearly distinguish lemma from interpretation for the audience. Commentators frequently point out that *Sib. Or.* 3.356–8 and 5.168–174 also use Isaiah 47 in attacking Rome. The allusion to Isaiah 47 in *Sibylline Oracles* 3 and 5 is the only OT allusion in both sibylline passages, whereas John has included this allusion with literally dozens of others.

The strong interest among scholars in John's use of the OT comes from the overwhelming evidence that the Apocalypse is soaked with scriptural references. While these references do have general thematic similarities with the original passages, there are too many for the audience to discern any clear *exegetical* technique aside from their thematic similarities. The garb of the Human One in Rev 1:12 refers to no one particular passage but to several. Revelation 18 does not highlight one prophetic passage against Babylon but all of them—as well as passages against Tyre and Jerusalem. The Apocalypse exhorts its audience to hear the words of *this* book (Rev 1:3; 22:7, 10–11, 18–19). The overwhelming allusiveness of Revelation 18, as with the other wealth passages, turns us not to the text's sources for understanding but to the rhetorical construction of the text itself.

Outline of Rev 18:1–24

Reading for the rhetoric of Revelation 18 requires that we first understand the outline or arrangement of the passage. In Rev 17:18, the guiding angel identifies the great harlot as "the great city that rules over the kings of the earth," explicitly tying 17:1–18 to 18:1–24 for the audience. Rev 18:1–24 consists of a lament over this city. The lament over Babylon in Rev 18:1–24 comprises three speeches, as follows:

1. Speech of the First Angel from Heaven, 18:1–3
2. Speech of a Heavenly Voice, 18:4–20
   a. Announcement of Judgment, 18:4–8
   b. Three Laments
      i. Kings, 18:9–10
      ii. Merchants, 18:11–17
      iii. Seafarers, 18:18–19
   c. Call to Rejoice, 18:20
3. Speech of the Mighty Angel, 18:21–24

The arrangement of the lament shows the rhetorical nature of Revelation 18. The audience hears a series of three speeches upon the occasion of the destruction of Babylon, a proper situation for epideictic rhetoric. The boundaries of each speech are clearly marked. John, the narrator, had been carried away from the heavenly throne room by an angel in the spirit to a place in the wilderness, where he saw the great harlot (17:3ff). Now, in 18:1–2, he sees an angel coming down from heaven and crying out the first speech in a mighty voice (ἐν ἰσχυρᾷ φωνῇ, 18:2). After this first speech, John hears another voice from heaven (ἄλλην φωνήν, 18:4). This speech includes the three dirges or laments of the kings, merchants and seafarers, and continues to 18:20. A mighty angel then throws a stone into the sea and gives the final lament for the city (18:21). A new section begins in Rev 19:1, again clearly marked for the audience (μετὰ ταῦτα ἤκουσα; cf. Rev 18:1 μετὰ ταῦτα εἶδον). Rev 19:1–10 is an audition that begins with heavenly rejoicing for God's judgment of the "great whore who corrupted the earth with her fornication" (19:2). Rev 19:1–10 includes a reaction to the destruction of Babylon and can be connected to 18:1–24.[56] Rev 19:1–10, however, is a heavenly throne room scene that introduces the bride of Christ, who is identified as the New Jerusalem in 21:2.[57] It is thus a transitional section, presenting a number of new themes.[58]

The central speech in 18:4–20 presents some difficulty for understanding the lament. As the outline above shows, this speech falls into three sections (marked a, b, and c), but within and between these sections

---

[56]Ruiz includes the seventh seal and marks the boundaries of his study in 16:17–19:10. Yarbro Collins sees the "Babylon appendix" running from 17:1–19:10, followed by seven unnumbered visions in 19:11–21:8 and the "Jerusalem appendix" in 21:9–22:5. Bauckham has ably pointed out the problems with Yarbro Collins's division (see chap. 4, n. 17); note also that the description of the New Jerusalem begins properly in 21:2. Bauckham divides the sections into Babylon, 17:1–19:10; transition from Babylon to the New Jerusalem, 19:11–21:8; and the New Jerusalem, 21:9–22:5. Rev 19:1–10, however, is clearly transitional, even if one allows that it concludes the Babylon section; the bride is introduced in 19:7–8. Boring also discerns seven unnumbered visions following the destruction of Babylon, but he places 19:1–10 at the head of this section rather than the conclusion of the Babylon section (17:1–18:24, which are part of a major division running from 4:1–18:24, "God Judges the 'Great City' "); the seven unnumbered visions then run from 19:11–22:5, thereby including Yarbro Collins's "appendix."

[57]See Boring, 191–94; and Aune, *HarperCollins Study Bible*, 2332.

[58]See the discussion of Rev 19:1–10 below, in chap. 7, pp. 211–14.

there are radical shifts of tense, voice, and point of view.[59] This heavenly voice begins by calling for "my people" to leave the city, grounding the command in a summary of Babylon's sins and God's judgment (18:4–5). The voice then turns to the heavenly host, calling for vengeance against Babylon (18:6–7). While all the imperatives in Rev 18:4–7 have the same form, it is unlikely that the heavenly voice instructs the people themselves to take vengeance upon the city.[60] In Revelation 18, as in the rest of the Apocalypse, God and the heavenly forces control events and take action while people on earth passively watch and wait.[61] The heavenly voice shifts to the indicative in Rev 18:8 in the pronouncement of judgment. It then takes up ironic laments in the role of the city's former allies: kings, merchants and sailors (18:9–19). These are not the kings or merchants speaking themselves but the heavenly voice, describing the scene and then ironically lamenting the city. The direct address to Babylon in 18:14, using second person singular, interrupts the rendition of the merchants' lament.[62] Rev 18:14 is a direct taunt from heaven directed against the wealthy commercial city. The heavenly voice concludes by directing "heaven," in a second-person singular imperative, to rejoice (18:20), along with the saints, apostles, and prophets, at the destruction of the city.

---

[59]E.g., the shift in audience of the plural imperatives in 18:4–7, discussed below; the use of the future tense in the lament of the kings in 18:9–10 followed by present tense for the merchants in 18:11, returning to future in 18:15; and then aorist and imperfect for the seafarers in 18:17–18; the shift to second person singular in 18:14, with shifts in this verse from the aorist ἀπῆλθεν to future εὑρήσουσιν; and the second-person singular middle imperative εὐφραίνου in 18:20, in contrast to the plural imperatives which opened the speech.

[60]Rev 18:4–7 includes of a series of second-person plural imperatives: ἐξέλθατε, "come out"; ἀπόδοτε, "render"; διπλώσατε, "repay"; κεράσατε, "mix"; and δότε, "give."

[61]As Yarbro Collins shows in "Political Perspective," the ideology of Revelation follows the passive approach exemplified by Daniel rather than the active approach in Maccabees or the Zealot tradition. See Rev 6:9–12, where the martyrs are instructed to wait; or 14:1–4, where the 144,000 are revealed as those who "have been redeemed," (ἠγοράσθησαν, passive voice) by God. The destruction of Babylon is clearly engineered by God and the heavenly forces (14:8; 16:17–20; 17:14, 17; 18:8, 20–21); the people of God have no role.

[62]See Charles, 2:105–13, who rearranges 18:21-24 completely, adding 18:14 and 18:20 and calling 18:23e "meaningless"; see also Bousset, 485; Lohmeyer, 151; Kraft, 235. Yarbro Collins, "Taunt Song," 194–95, makes a sound argument for reading 18:14 in its present location as part of the central section.

The key to understanding the speech is recognizing that it is given by one heavenly voice.[63] Candidates for this heavenly voice include God, an angel, or one of the other members of the throne room such as an elder, but a strong case can be made that this is the voice of Christ.[64] Christ would have the authority to summon "my people" from the city; order a double punishment for Babylon from the heavenly forces; and pronounce judgment on the city. So, of course, would God. But God does not speak in the Apocalypse until 21:5–8; if this extended speech in Revelation 18 over Babylon were by God, it would steal much of the rhetorical thunder of that passage.[65] The speech refers to God, moreover, in the third person (18:8, 20). The other two speakers in Revelation 18 are explicitly identified as angels (18:1, 21), as is usually the case in the Apocalypse when an angel speaks.[66] The direct address to Babylon in 18:14 and the call to heaven to rejoice in 18:20 suggest that the speaker is Christ. Christ is referred to as a voice first in 1:11–12 and again in 4:1.[67] "Voice" in Revelation 18 stands for Christ by synecdoche. The audience would have already heard Christ identified as a voice in the opening proem and the beginning of the heavenly visions. More significantly, Christ has already given speeches on wealth. The messages in Revelation 2–3 carefully establish Christ's authority to speak about pure and impure wealth by characterizing Christ as a moral philosopher. Rev 18:4–20 is a speech about the wealth of Babylon and its destruction. As with the messages,

---

[63]So recognized by Lohmeyer, 147; Caird, 228; Yarbro Collins, "Revelation 18," 193, who effectively argues against the divisions in the chapter proposed by Charles, 2:87–95; Bauckham, "Economic Critique," *Climax of Prophecy*, 340–41.

[64]Charles, 2:97, and Allo, 290, hold that it is Christ; Bousset, 482, that it could be Christ or God; Mounce, 324, and Roloff, 205, identify this voice as an angel. Yarbro Collins, "Taunt Song," 193, prefers to leave the issue open since the voice quotes scripture in 18:4. As we have seen, Christ quotes the proem of Revelation when speaking to the seven churches in Asia so clearly, in the narrative world of the Apocalypse, he could quote Jeremiah as well.

[65]See the discussion of Rev 21:5–8 below, in chap. 7, pp. 220–24.

[66]For instance Rev 5:11; 7:2; 10:3–5 (in contrast to "a voice from heaven"); 14:7, 8, 14–20 (where an angel gives instructions to the Son of Man); 16:5; 17:1–18; 19:9–10; 21:9.

[67]In 10:4 and 10:8, the instructions given by "a voice from heaven" parallel the instructions given by Christ to write in 1:19 and 22:10, suggesting that this too is the voice of Christ; see also 14:13. The voice in 22:10–11 is most likely Christ, even though an angel speaks in 22:9, since it is clearly Christ in 22:12–13.

so here the implied author uses his most authoritative character to speak at length about wealth. For there is a tricky rhetorical task to be performed. The city that is to be destroyed has a number of similarities in wealth and power to the heavenly throne room and to the New Jerusalem, which will replace Babylon. Proper words must be spoken on this occasion to separate for the audience the wealth of heaven from the wealth of Satan.

While the phrasing, diction and individual units of the speech show its biblical sources, Christ's speech also suggests the monody, "an emotional lament, not entirely unlike some passages in the prophets, usually on the death of a person or the destruction of a city."[68] According to Menander Rhetor, in his second treatise on epideictic rhetoric (2.16), the purpose of the monody is "to lament and express pity" (θρηνεῖν καὶ κατοικτίζεσθαι [434.19]).[69] He writes that a monody should fall into three "periods" (χρόνοι) covering the present, past, and future. Menander discusses the monody only in terms of a person, but Aelius Aristides delivered a famous monody on Smyrna in 178 CE, after that city was destroyed by an earthquake. Composed in the short, rhythmic cola of the style called "Asiatic" by the sophists, this monody also falls into three sections: the destruction of Smyrna; the former state of the city; and a threnody.[70] In the central section on the city's past, Aristides describes the former glories of Smyrna:

> Was mankind satiated for all their intercourse and association? What other city for them came close? The springs, theaters, avenues, and streets both covered and open to the air! The beautiful and splendid market place! The streets named for gold and sacred rites, at every square each like a market place! The harbors longing for the embrace of their city most dear! The indescribable beauty of the gymnasiums! The grace of the temples and the precincts! Where in the earth did you sink! The monuments of the seacoast! All those dreams! What springs

---

[68]Kennedy, *Rhetorical Criticism*, 76. In a personal correspondence (19 April 1993), David E. Aune suggested the parallels between Revelation 18 and Greek ritual laments, referencing Aesch. *Pers.* 249–52; Antip. Sid. *Pal. Anth.*9.151; and Ael. Aris. *Or.* 18.

[69]See D. A. Russell and N. G. Wilson, ed. and trans., *Menander Rhetor* (Oxford: Clarendon, 1981) 200–207, 347–47. As a lament, the monody provides a better comparison than the *paramythētikos* or consolatory speech; or the *epitaphios* or funeral speech.

[70]See Behr, *Complete Works* 2.58.

of tears are sufficient for so great an evil? What concerts and sympho-
nies of all the choruses will be enough to bewail the city of fair
choruses, much-hymned and thrice-desired by mankind? The fall of
Asia! (*Or.* 18.6–7)[71]

The comparison between Revelation 18 and the monody tells us more
about how the passage might have been heard by the Asian audience than
what John had in mind during its composition. The monody was to be
short, no more than 150 lines, since "mourners do not tolerate long delays
or lengthy speeches at times of misfortune or unhappiness" (Menander
Rhetor 2.16 [437.1–4]). The three speeches of Rev 18:1–24, as outlined
above, describe the present, past, and future of Babylon, although the correspondence is likely coincidental. A monody was, strictly speaking, "one
voice," and there are three speakers in Revelation 18, with one of them,
Christ ironically speaking for a chorus of kings, merchants, and sailors.

Rev 18:1–24 could have been heard as prophetic lament or epideictic
speech. The power of the rhetoric of Revelation is that it evokes two
great traditions, the language and forms of the Hebrew prophets and the
style of Greek epideictic rhetoric. The indictment of the city in Revelation
18 is a powerful *psogos* against Babylon as well as an oracle against the
nations. While source criticism reveals John's debt to scriptural traditions,
the urban Asian setting of the Apocalypse suggests sophistic performance
as well. It is difficult to imagine that John's knowledge of rhetorical theory approached his scriptural erudition, but both author and audience
would have had some grasp of public rhetoric. In either case, the lament
is delivered with considerable irony. Recognition of the irony is important
since commentators such as G. B. Caird have seen admiration for Babylon and "infinite pathos" in the passage.[72] Whatever glories are described
in the laments of the merchants or sailors or the speech of the mighty
angel are mediated by the harsh descriptions of Babylon's sins: sexual
profligacy, commercial wealth, sorcery, and bloodthirsty persecution.

The Invective against Babylon

The destruction of a city was a proper setting for epideictic rhetoric. As
a rhetorical composition, Rev 18:1–24 shows balance, focus, and above
all amplification (αὔξησις or *auxēsis*, Lat. *amplificatio*) of its main

---

[71]Ibid., 2.8.
[72]See Caird, 227.

topics, the sexual immorality and commercial wealth of the city. The narrative and rhetorical center of the chapter is the speech of Christ in 18:4–20. The two shorter speeches which enclose 18:4–20 add to the rhetorical force and clarity of the chapter. The speech of the first angel in 18:2b–3 functions as the proem for the entire chapter by presenting the major themes of the invective against Babylon. The audience would have recognized part of this speech, for it uses as its frame their first introduction to Babylon, the allusive two-part cry from 14:8, "Fallen, Fallen is Babylon the great." The angel adds a graphic description of Babylon's impure condition between "Fallen, fallen" and "for all the nations have drunk," portraying the city as demonic and thrice-foul (18:2). Rev 18:3 then recites the litany of Babylon's fornication with the nations and the kings of the earth, continuing the themes of the vision of the harlot in 17:1–18. The angel speaking here has "great authority" from heaven (ἐξουσία μεγάλη, 18:1), a polemical contrast to the power and authority exchanged between beast and kings (δύναμις καὶ ἐξουσία, 17:12–13). Finally, the angel introduces a significant new reason for the fall of the city, trade. Babylon has fallen because "the merchants of the earth have grown rich from the power of her luxury" (18:3). Rev 18:2–3 is a summary (κεφάλαιον [*kephalaion*]) of the charges against Babylon. The themes from the proem are repeated in the third speech of the chapter (18:23c–24), addressed now directly to the fallen city, to insure that the audience gets the rhetorical point. This speech is the epilogue or *peroratio* for the invective against Babylon. The "mighty angel" emphasizes Babylon's commercial wealth: "for your merchants were the magnates of the earth, and all nations were deceived by your sorcery [φαρμακεία]" (18:23cd). "Sorcery" here is a nice twist, since the audience would expect *porneia* again (cf. 17:2; 18:3). The *porneia* of the harlot shows up in 19:2, but "sorcery" calls to mind the deceits of Satan and the beasts in Revelation 13 as well as the "dwelling place of demons" and "haunt of every foul spirit" in 18:2.

The central speech of Christ in 18:4–20 is framed by proem and epilogue that emphasize the commercial wealth, excessive luxury, sorcery, and sexual immorality of the city. The first part of Christ's speech in 18:4–5, a direct address to the people of God, mentions neither wealth nor fornication directly. But the context of the vision in 17:1–18 and the proem in 18:2–3 shape Christ's words so that the audience could hear ironic references to these overpowering motifs. The "sins heaped high as heaven" (18:5) include Babylon's wealth, ill-gotten and tawdry in the Apocalypse, heaped in piles around the harlot/city, reaching to heaven but not matching the pure wealth of God's throne room. When Christ calls on the heavenly forces to "mix a double draught for her in the cup she mixed" (Rev 18:6), the cup in which Babylon's punishment is to be mixed is the golden cup of impurities and fornication (17:4). Babylon glorified herself and "lived luxuriously" (ἐστρηνίασεν, 18:7) because the merchants of the earth "have grown rich from the power [στρήνους] of her luxury" (18:3). References to "legitimate" social positions for a woman, widow and queen (18:7), are ironic references to the scripting of Babylon as a harlot.

The irony in 18:4–8 prepares the audience for the mock-laments of the kings, merchants, and sailors, in which Christ takes on the voice of Babylon's clients who mourn her destruction. The fire called down from heaven by Christ (18:8) sets the narrative context for these laments, as each group stands back and mourns the burning city. Each lament includes three parallel features, with the threnody of the merchants somewhat expanded.[73] First, the group is described by means of its relationship to Babylon. The kings fornicated and "luxuriated" (στρενιάω, 18:9) with Babylon. The merchants and sailors are identified as those who grew rich from her (πλουτέω, 18:15, 19). Second, there is a description of the reaction of the group to the destruction. The merchants cry and mourn; they stand at a distance "in fear of her torment" (18:15; cf. 18:9, 18). Third, there is the "woe" itself. Each group utters the same first line, "Alas, alas, the great city" (οὐαὶ οὐαί, ἡ πόλις ἡ μεγάλη; 18:10, 16, 19).[74] Both the merchants and the sailors have a longer second line than the kings, which emphasizes the wealth they received from Babylon. The woe of the merchants describes their good customer Babylon, clothed in their wares, looking very much like the vision of the woman seated on the scarlet beast in Rev 17:4, with the addition here of fine linen (βύσσινος). The six items in the woe are all included in the list of the merchants' cargo in Rev 18:12–13. The final line of their woe continues the emphasis on πλοῦτος: "For in one hour all this wealth has been laid waste!" The sailors describe how they grew

---

[73]Yarbro Collins, "Taunt Song," 194, labels these laments "announcements of judgment" based on the perspective of the author, intended readers, and book as a whole, but this misses the irony of the laments. Compare Swete, 231, who calls them by the Greek *thrēnos*.

[74]On the construction of the woe, see Charles, 2:101, who notes Luke 6:25; and LXX constructions in Isa 5:8, 11, 20, 21, 22; Hab 2:6, 12, 19; Zeph 2:5; and Amos 5:18.

rich from their trade on the sea, ending with a line similar to that of the kings (18:19b; cf. 18:9b). The change in verb tenses among the three laments, from future to present to aorist, marks a change in narrative perspective for the audience as the destruction of Babylon moves from future promise to past reality.[75]

These laments in 18:9–19 emphasize above all else Babylon's commercial power and her desire for wealth. The lament of the kings, 18:9–10, is the shortest of the three. The motif of the kings of the earth and their fornication with the city was developed with a clear political interpretation by the guiding angel in Revelation 17, as we discussed above.[76] In the context of Christ's speech in Revelation 18, the kings set the form of the lament for "the great city," whose judgment comes now in "one hour" rather than a single day (18:10; cf. 18:8). This form is taken up and modified by the next two groups in ways that emphasize Babylon's commercial might. No reason is given for why the kings "weep and mourn," although we can assume that, unaware that their judgment is coming soon (see 19:17–21), they will miss the opportunity for fornication and enjoying the luxury of Babylon. The second two laments, of the merchants and seafarers, focus entirely on Babylon/Rome's commercial activity. These laments highlight not so much the articles of wealth as the activity of trade.[77] The merchants weep and mourn "because no one buys their cargo anymore" (18:12). Similarly, the seafarers and "all whose trade was on the sea" weep because they have lost the opportunity to practice their occupation; "all who had ships at sea grew rich by her wealth" (18:19). The relationship between the merchants and seafarers and Babylon was based entirely on commerce and trade. Their appearance as characters and the content of their laments does not include any reference to fornication, sorcery, or oppression but only develops the motif of the Babylon's commercial wealth.

The cargo list in 18:12–13 has generally been interpreted either as an adaption from Ezek 27:12–22 or as a list of articles of Roman trade in the first two centuries CE.[78] While Ezekiel 26–27 provided many themes

---

[75]See Yarbro Collins, "Taunt-Song," 195–96.

[76]See above, pp. 193–94.

[77]Bauckham, "Economic Critique," *Climax of Prophecy*, 342, stresses the emphasis on the cargo list but not the activity of commerce itself.

[78]Bousset, 484–85, offers a few Greco-Roman references but Swete, 232–35, provides a fuller analysis of the organization of the list and the costliness of each item; see also Charles, 2:103–105. While Yarbro Collins, "Revelation 18"

and ideas for Revelation 18, comparison of John's list with Ezekiel's does not advance our understanding of the function of 18:12–13 in context or its rhetorical effect on the audience. Most of the 28 items in Rev 18:12–13 are found in Ezek 27:12–22, which contains 40 items, but they have been rearranged and changed so that there is no longer any significant resemblance between the two lists.[79] The implied author of Revelation adds several items which are not actually in Ezekiel: pearls (μαργαρίται) where Ezekiel already has gold, silver and precious stones; and silk (σιρικός) where Ezekiel already has linen and purple. More significantly, John changes the format of the list. The lament in Ezekiel 27 lists the city or country which supplied each item with a description of the item itself, conveying a sense of sorrow at the fall of Tyre and highlighting the trade with the other cities. John borrows the actual items but changes the list to a strict list of goods, organized by category by order of value from highest to lowest: metal and jewels; cloth; material for buildings or ware; spices; food, livestock, and slaves. More important than the appearance of these items in Ezekiel is their appearance elsewhere in Revelation. While the merchants' cargo is not completely replicated in visions of heaven, several items which do appear in that list also appear in visions of the throne room: gold (1:13; 4:4; 8:3; 14:14; 15:6–7); jewels (4:3; 21:11,19); pearls (21:21); fine linen (βύσσινος, 19:8, 14); and incense (5:8; 8:3–4). One luxury item appears on angels in heaven, linen, (λίνον, with gold in 15:6) which is not part of the cargo. The replication of wealth imagery in both descriptions of heaven and Babylon highlights the implied author's problem—how to distinguish the "good wealth" of God from the "bad wealth" of Babylon/Rome—and the rhetorical solution, the association of Babylon with commerce.

The items which the implied author of Revelation adds to Ezekiel's list were also traded in the early Empire.[80] Some of the items in the list would have been familiar to the Christians of Asia Minor, who lived in

---

confines her study to form-critical analysis, Bauckham, "Economic Critique," *Climax of Prophecy*, 352–66, provides fresh research on the list, concluding that the list includes many of the costliest items imported by Rome.

[79]So also Bauckham, "Economic Critique," *Climax of Prophecy*, 350–51, who prefers the realities of "concrete history" and Roman trade to the list in Ezekiel as an explanatory device.

[80]See Swete, 232–35; Bauckham, "Economic Critique," *Climax of Prophecy*, 350–66.

or near major ports such as Ephesus and Smyrna. Many luxury items listed in Rev 18:12–13 were produced in Spain, Gaul, North Africa, or the far East. But analysis of each item does not explain the function of the list as a whole.[81] The sheer comprehensiveness of the list demonstrates the rhetorical techniques of *amplificatio* and *variatio*, amplification of a topic with a variety of diction and technique. Above all, the list in Rev 18:12–13 suggests the bragging of the noveaux riches. We noted in chapter 3 several occurrences of lists of wealth and possessions in the context of the critique of new, commercial wealth.[82] The interjection of Christ in 18:14, marked by a shift to second-person singular, draws attention to the pleasure Babylon/Rome had in acquiring these extensive luxury goods through the commercial network of the city.[83]

In addition to associating Babylon/Rome with luxury items—several of which are found in heaven and the New Jerusalem—the laments in Revelation 18 associate the city with merchant-traders and sailors. These threnodies are uttered by those who made Rome's traffic possible. Small-scale trade and wholesaling at a high margin were both on Cicero's list of "sordid" occupations; merchants received a particularly stern appraisal from Ben Sira. Merchants and shippers had very low status relative to their wealth in the cities of the Greek East.[84] Anyone with a ship (recall Trimalchio) could have made a profit dealing with Rome because commerce was the key to the new wealth of the city. Again, John's rewriting of the Hebrew Bible highlights this point. Although he uses

---

[81]Bauckham's "concrete historical" analysis in "Economic Critique" of the list in Revelation 18 requires that he place every item in social and economic historical context in order to demonstrate that the items are among the costliest luxury goods traded in the Roman Empire. By trying to show that John has constructed an "accurate" critique of the Roman economic system, Bauckham treats an essentially moral issue as an issue of economic history.

[82]See the list of production from Trimalchio's estates in (which range from Italy to Africa, *Sat.* 48), *Sat.* 38; the lists of his or his wife's extensive gold, silver, and jewels (*Sat.* 30–33; 38; 50; 53; 67); and the list of signs of wealth in Luc. *Gall.* 14 that accrued to Simon(ides): scarlet and purple dyed garments (ἀλούργημα, ὑσγινοβαφής); household slaves (οἰκετεία); carriages (ζεῦγος); golden cups (χρυσῆ ἔκπωμα); and ivory-legged tables (ἐλεφαντόπους τράπεζα).

[83]So Bauckham, "Economic Critique," *Climax of Prophecy*, 368.

[84]See the discussion in chap. 3; note esp. Pleket, "Urban elites and business," 139–41.

Ezekiel as one of his main scriptural sources, John does not include several characters from Ezekiel 26–27: warriors; rowers; caulkers, ship workers, and other craftspeople; and inhabitants. The only characters who appear in Revelation from Ezekiel's oracles are the kings of the earth and those engaged in commerce, underscoring for the audience the association of Babylon/Rome with the degrading, sordid activity of trade. Babylon and heaven are decorated with the same luxury goods but only Babylon engages in trade.

The criticism of Rome's immorality, taste for luxury, and commercial excesses so carefully constructed by the implied author in Revelation 18 has many similarities with the critique of Rome in contemporary moralists and satirists.[85] The critique can be found in the writings of upper-class Romans as well as eastern Greeks.[86] We uncovered the oblique criticism of the Roman obsession with trade and wealth in Aristides' speech ostensibly praising the empire, "Regarding Rome."[87] A more blatant attack on Rome can be found in the writings of Lucian:

> "It is they," he said [speaking of the wealthy in Rome], "who buy expensive dainties and let wine flow freely at dinners in an atmosphere of saffron and perfumes, who glut themselves with roses in midwinter, loving their rarity and unreasonableness and despising what is season-able and natural [*kata phusin*] because of its cheapness; it is they who drink myrrh." And that was the point in which he criticised them especially, that they do not even know how to give play to their desires, but transgress in them and obliterate the boundary-lines, on all sides surrendering their souls to luxury. (Luc. *Nigr.* 31)

Nigrinus's philosophical critique of Rome, like Christ's in Revelation 18, is presented as an epideictic display of invective against the city of Rome, which Nigrinus compares rhetorically to Athens.[88] Christ's dirge or

---

[85]Bauckham, "Economic Critique," *Climax of Prophecy*, 368, attempts to distance John's thoroughgoing critique from Roman upper-class moralists. His Roman sources (chiefly Pliny the Elder, but also Tacitus, Seneca, Martial, Juvenal, and Petronius) bring moral constraints to bear on their attitude towards these items, as Bauckham recognizes; in my analysis here, John and these other moralists share the same perspective on Roman trade.

[86]See chap. 3; see also Pliny *HN* 9.104–105 [53]; 9.117–124 [58–60; 33.37–42 [10–12]; Mart. 3.82; Juv. *Sat.* 3 *passim*; Suet. *Nero* 11; 30–32.

[87]See the discussion in chap. 3, pp. 115–20.

[88]See chap. 3, pp. 120–23; also Dio *Or.* 7.8–10, 103–104.

monody over the fallen city in Rev 18:9–19 plays the same themes in a highly ironic fashion to an eastern Greek audience and prepares for *synkrisis* with the New Jerusalem.

The insatiable appetite of Babylon for wealth and luxury portrayed in Revelation 18 is a symptom of complete depravity. This is a city whose moral perversity has run wild (see στρῆνος, 18:3, and στρενιάω, 18:7, 9). John describes the city of Babylon as a drunk harlot, sated with sex and wine and intoxicated by her power and the adulation of kings (18:3, 7–10). The luxuries that the city has acquired by trade still do not reach as high as the city's sins, which are "heaped high as heaven" (18:5). Such sin and depravity cannot stand against the wrath of heaven in the narrative world of the Apocalypse. As predicted (14:8, 16:19), the city is destroyed. In 18:20, the heavenly voice of Christ issues a final victory cry to heaven, saints, apostles and prophets, to rejoice in God's judgment over the fallen enemy. Amidst the rejoicing of the hosts of heaven, an angel casts a heavy stone into the sea to mark its fall (18:21). The long description of the city's judgment and destruction ends with a summation of Babylon's abominations (18:23–24): commercial wealth, "for your merchants were the magnates of the earth"; magic and political intrigue, "and all nations were deceived by your sorcery"; and persecution of the church, "in you was found the blood of prophets and of saints, and of all who have been slaughtered on earth." With the destruction of Babylon, the marriage of the Lamb and the bride of Christ is now ready.

Conclusions: Wealth and Sex

With the extensive use of wealth imagery in Revelation, it is necessary for the implied author to distinguish between good and bad wealth. The characterization of Babylon/Rome's wealth as commercially derived is necessary to differentiate the gold, jewels and fine linen of the Harlot from the wealth of the Human One, the heavenly throne room, and the New Jerusalem. Association with commerce casts Babylon's wealth as lower status than heaven's. The *ekphrasis* of the vision of the harlot in 17:1–6 and the speeches in Rev 18:2–24 clearly display the evil and immorality of Babylon/Rome by describing the fornication, sorcery, bloody persecution, and commerce of the city. These are the hallmarks of the moral portrait of Babylon in Revelation. Not only do these chapters present the evil wealth of Babylon, they provide a stark contrast to the glorious and pure wealth of heaven. My analysis of Revelation 17–18 has shown the extent of this rhetorical strategy.

In his construction of a demonic opposition, John tars all the opposition with the same brushes: fornication, trade, Satan. The harlot Babylon rides a scarlet beast with seven heads and ten horns (17:3), the same beast that takes authority from the dragon (13:1–4), "that ancient serpent, who is called the Devil and Satan" (12:9). Babylon is thus clearly satanic; so too are those who call themselves Jews (2:9; 3:9). Revelation 17–18 develops at great length the notion of Babylon's fornication with the kings of the earth and the nations as a political challenge to the Lamb. So too "Jezebel" beguiles "Christ's" slaves to "practice fornication" (πορνεῦσαι, 2:20). The message to Thyatira characterizes this prophet in sexual imagery just as the vision of Babylon emphasizes *porneia*. "Christ" threatens to throw "Jezebel" upon a bed (of sickness) and to kill her students, with whom she practices adultery (2:22–23). Some in Pergamum have also taken up "the teaching of Balaam" and "eat food sacrificed to idols and practice fornication" (πορνεῦσαι, 2:14), a moral taint the implied author attempts to pass on to the "Nicolaitans" as well. John attacks Roman wealth and power by appealing to the Greek disdain for new wealth derived from commerce. Trade links the wealthy and independent Laodiceans to this unholy moral trinity of fornication, commerce, and Satan. The thematic links between the attack on Babylon/Rome and the polemic against John's opponents in the seven churches show how the ideology of wealth in Revelation functions in two contexts, within the Christian church and between the church and Rome. John heightens the wealth, power and status of his visions of God, and therefore the authority of his revelation among the Christian communities of Asia Minor, not only by describing the heavenly throne room and New Jerusalem with images of wealth and luxury but also by attacking Rome's wealth. As much as John's visions build up his God against Rome, they also build up John against his opponents.

The New Jerusalem

John's vision of the New Jerusalem has become such an entrenched part of Western culture—for instance, the "pearly gates" of heaven—that we are especially challenged in trying to act as ethnographers and hear the words as the original audience might have heard them. Our task is more complicated since the vision of the New Jerusalem falls within an established tradition that the restored city would be opulent, as we saw in chapter 2. Although the author has concentrated wealth motifs in Revelation 21–22 so that it is an even more opulent vision than many of its literary predecessors, the New Jerusalem in Revelation still fits within a tradition whereas other wealth passages in the Apocalypse do not. Nonetheless, when we set this vision in its narrative and rhetorical context, particularly in the context of the explicit contrast to the vision of the destruction of Babylon, we will see the complex theological and ideological functions of the wealth imagery. For it is here, on the golden streets of the heavenly city, that the imagery and ideology of wealth in the Apocalypse of John come to a rhetorical climax.

The Marriage of the Lamb (Revelation 19:1–10)

As I noted in the previous chapter, it is difficult to place Rev 19:1–10 with either the preceding Babylon scene or the subsequent scenes of judgment. This passage concludes the Babylon section and also introduces a number of important themes for the vision New Jerusalem. Rev 19:1–10 is one of the most entrenched transitional passages in the Apocalypse, interwoven and interlocked with other speeches and visions, making it difficult to separate it from what precedes and follows. The heavenly host responds to the final destruction of Babylon with a series of hymns that lead the audience from the destruction of Babylon to the marriage of Christ and the New Jerusalem (19:1–8). These hymns, like those in Revelation 4–5, magnify God's power, glory, and kingship (19:1b, 6b).[1] The first two "hallelujah choruses" in this section comment directly on the destruction of Babylon (19:1–2, 3). The heavenly multitude expresses delight in the judgment and fiery destruction of the city, recalling the sins

---

[1]See the discussion of the hymns in Rev 4–5 in chap. 6, pp. 179–80.

of the destroyed city (19:2–3). They remember Babylon's *porneia* and
bloody persecution of God's slaves, but not the fallen city's wealth. After
this heavenly reaction to the destruction of Babylon, the third chorus by
the heavenly multitude introduces the bride of the Lamb: "Hallelujah! For
the Lord our God the Almighty reigns. Let us rejoice and exult and give
him the glory, for the marriage of the Lamb [ὁ γάμος τοῦ ἀρνίου]
has come, and his bride [γυνή] has made herself ready" (19:7; see also
19:9).[2] The sequence of these hymns, which move from the destruction
of Babylon to the marriage of the Lamb, is important. In the narrative
context of the Apocalypse, the marriage of the lamb takes place because
Babylon was destroyed. While in the final speech over Babylon the
mighty angel says that "the voice of bridegroom and bride will be heard
in you no more" (18:23), a heavenly wedding of Christ and the church
now replaces the destroyed earthly weddings.

Although four different judgment scenes come between the heavenly
rejoicing for the marriage of the lamb in 19:6–10 and the vision of a new
creation in Rev 21:1–8, the implied author makes sure that the appearance
of the heavenly city is connected to the destruction of the satanic one.
Wedding imagery links the transitional Rev 19:1–10 to the description of
the New Jerusalem in Revelation 21 as well as to the destruction of
Babylon in Revelation 18. When John first sees the city, he describes it
as appearing like "a bride adorned for her husband" (ὡς νύμφην τῷ
ἀνδρὶ αὐτῆς, 21:2). The metonymic trope linking heavenly city and
bride also links Babylon and the New Jerusalem. This repetition of the
bride metaphor from 19:6–10 in 21:2 invites comparison by the audience
between the New Jerusalem and Babylon as opposing cities of good and
evil. One city is a harlot, the other a heavenly bride. City replaces bride
by metonymy, but the idea that the New Jerusalem *is* a bride never
completely disappears (see νύμφη, 21:2, 9; 22:17).[3] The bridal trope in

---

[2]Fekkes, "Revelation 19–21 and Isaian Nuptial Imagery," has argued that the
influence of Isa 61:10 should be seen in Rev 19:6–8 as well as Rev 21:2b, where
it is usually noted by commentators.

[3]Fekkes, "Revelation 19–21 and Isaian Nuptial Imagery," attempts to connect
his sound redactional analysis on the sources used by the implied author in the
so-called "bridal construct" of Rev 19:7–9; 21:2; and 21:9, 18–21 to the function
of the bridal metaphor in Revelation. The two questions are neither related nor
dependent upon one another, and the argument of his third section (283–87)
collapses. Fekkes tries to move from authorial intention, as demonstrated by
redaction and source criticism, to "thematic development" in Revelation without

Rev 21:1 prepares the audience for the wealth of the New Jerusalem, since bridal attire could reasonably be expected to be costly and luxurious.[4]

Finally, the marriage of the Lamb section in 19:1–10 focuses the audience's attention on the ideology of wealth in the Apocalypse. The bride of the lamb is "clothed with fine linen, bright and pure" (βύσσινον λαμπρὸν καθαρόν, 19:8).[5] This is the only wealth motif in 19:1–10, but its juxtaposition with the destruction of Babylon's wealth is a daring challenge to the audience to compare the wealth of heaven with the wealth of Satan. The same luxury item is an attribute of the demonic and divine within 28 verses. The bride's attire is contrasted explicitly with that of the harlot Babylon, who wore purple and scarlet and purchased fine linen (βύσσινος) from the merchants (17:4; 18:12). The clothing metaphor in 19:8 reminds the audience of the personal, moral cost of "pure" wealth. The bride's linen is bright and pure while the harlot's was purple and scarlet, stained with the blood of saints and martyrs. Furthermore, the bride's luxurious garments are described as "the righteous deeds of the saints" (19:8). Although it is not clear who says this in the passage, we do not need to read this as a gloss, for the juxtaposition of satanic and heavenly wealth requires some sort of explanation for the audience.[6] These garments have been cleaned for a price, the price

---

providing sufficient evidence for how this imagery would have been heard. While some listeners familiar with Jewish literature might have recognized allusions to either Isa 54:11 or Tob 13:16–18, neither of which contain any marriage imagery, it is unlikely that auditors (with the possible exception of members the author's inner circle) could follow the redactional chain uncovered by Fekkes. The argument that Rev 21:18–21 is part of the "bridal construct" must be made on narrative and rhetorical grounds rather than on the basis of authorial intention or redaction or source criticism. The only link between 21:18–21 and 21:2 is the repetition of the verb κοσμέω. As I argue below, the city motif is dominant both in the text and in the social world of the urban Christian audience.

[4]See Fekkes, "Revelation 19–21 and Isaian Nuptial Imagery," 284–85. Fekkes notes as parallels *Joseph and Aseneth* 18:5–6; Pliny, *Ep.* 5.16; *T. Jud.* 13:5 *Herm. Vis.* 4.2.1–2; and various O.T. passages. I would quibble with the references to the *Testament of Judah*, which is more apt as a comparison for Rev 17:1–6; and the *Shepherd of Hermas*, which contains no wealth imagery. See also Plut. *Mor.* 144F–155D; Hierocles *On Duties* 4.21.22–24.

[5]The armies of heaven appear in the next scene wearing "fine linen, white and pure" (βύσσινον λευκὸν καθαρόν, 19:14).

[6]Charles, 2:128, sees this as a later gloss.

of the blood of prophets and saints slaughtered by Babylon (18:24). The phrase "righteous deeds of the saints" connotes martyrdom; the saints' blood turns their linen garments metaphorically and ideologically pure. Christ appears as "Faithful and True" on a white horse, wearing a robe dipped in blood (19:13), the blood in which "those who have come out of the great ordeal" have washed their robes and made them white (7:14). This metaphor challenges the audience, moreover, to imagine themselves also as clothing the bride with their own righteous deeds.[7]

These righteous deeds suggest endurance and struggle. The angel who has shown John the judgment of Babylon charges the narrator: "Write this: Blessed are those who are invited to the marriage supper [δεῖπνον] of the Lamb" (19:9). This is the fourth of the seven beatitudes in the Apocalypse, which have focused on suffering and endurance (see 14:12–13; 16:15). While a gruesome invitation to supper follows soon upon this invitation (19:17–18),[8] another significant invitation, by Christ in the message to Laodicea, has preceded this one: "If you hear my voice and open the door, I will come in to you and eat [δειπνήσω] with you, and you with me" (3:20). This is an invitation by Christ to the Asian churches to dine with their wealthy patron and concludes the diatribe on true wealth in the message to Laodicea (3:14–22).[9] The angel's second invitation to dine, after the marriage-hymn to the Lamb, is a call to stand firm against Babylon to the point of death and shapes the rhetoric of the first invitation by Christ. The refining process for the gold that Christ offers for sale to the Laodiceans (Rev 3:18) is the same as the cleansing process for the bride's bright wedding garments (19:8), namely, the endurance of suffering.

The New Jerusalem

In 21:1, the narrator describes a vision of a totally new creation in which heaven and earth are replaced and the sea, the primordial symbol of chaos, is no more.[10] He sees the "holy city " of the New Jerusalem descend from heaven, adorned as a bride. While the physical description

---

[7]On the idea that the audience would consider themselves to be the bride, see Harrington, 187–88, and Isa 54:5; 2 Cor 11:2; Eph 5:23–24.

[8]See Boring, 193.

[9]See the discussion of this passage in chap. 5, pp. 174-75.

[10]On the sea as a symbol of chaos, see Bousset, 508; Charles 2:205; Yarbro Collins, *Combat Myth*, 226–27.

of the city awaits the invitation of the angel in 21:9, John immediately hears, upon the descent of the city, two important speeches describing the moral character of the city (Rev 21:3–4, 5–8). The order of the description of the New Jerusalem in Revelation breaches usual epideictic arrangement. Geographical *ekphrasis* generally preceded discussion of topics such as politics or morality in speeches about cities.[11] John was probably not working from classical rhetorical theory, but the arrangement of the New Jerusalem speeches does show a clear rhetorical purpose. Since the primary point of comparison for the New Jerusalem is Babylon, the order of description of the heavenly city parallels the order of polemic against its evil earthly counterpart. Extensive moral condemnation of Babylon in 18:2–8 precedes the description of the city's destroyed wealth and culture (18:9–24). So also the description of the moral character of the New Jerusalem precedes the *ekphrasis* of the physical city, including its wealth. The two topics are combined in each description, of course, since wealth imagery in the Apocalypse is part of the moral and ideological rhetoric of Revelation. Wealth imagery functions to define the moral character of each city.

City or Community?

Discussion of the "physical city" of the New Jerusalem raises an important interpretive issue for the exegesis of Revelation 21–22. Although most commentators recognize that the New Jerusalem is a city, a tradition of allegorical interpretation has maintained that John does not describe a city but rather the ideal Christian community.[12] This interpretation began most likely in Alexandria as part of the allegorical hermeneutic that kept Revelation in the Christian canon despite so many theological and political problems with the text. As Dawson has shown, nonliteral readings reveal more about tensions within the interpretive communities of later readers than the situation of the original audience of a text.[13] For instance, Clement relates his allegorical interpretation of jewels in the heavenly city (Rev 21:19–21) to Christian women in Alexandria wearing

---

[11]See Menander Rhetor, 346.26–367.8. The order is found typically in the speeches of Aelius Aristides, which are used as models by Menander.

[12]Humphrey, *The Ladies and the Cities*, 103–11, argues that the woman clothed with the sun in Revelation 12 is transformed into the New Jerusalem in Revelation 21.

[13]See Dawson, *Allegorical Readers*, 235–40; and chap. 1, pp. 2–3 and n. 3.

jewels.[14] The allegorical interpretation of the New Jerusalem as "symbol of the saints" has recently been put forward as a plausible "historical-referential" interpretation for the original audience of Revelation.[15] While a response to every allegorical interpretation of Revelation is hardly necessary, the claim that the New Jerusalem would have been heard by its original audience as a symbol of the Christian saints rather than a description their future dwelling place needs to be refuted in order to establish the proper social-historical interpretive context for this passage. In classic allegory, all nonliteral readings began with a literal reading. In the case of the original audience of Revelation, we should allow full expression for the spatial language of the text since "city" was such a rich and powerful concept in antiquity.

Four main points may be cited in favor of understanding the New Jerusalem as a city rather than as a symbol of the Christian community. The first is the social setting of the audience. Christianity in the first century was centered in the cities, and both language and metaphor in Revelation fit this urban context. John sends the Apocalypse to seven Christian communities identified by *city* (cf. the provinces used in 1 Pet 1:1). The second argument comes from a narrative-rhetorical reading of the text.[16] Not only is the New Jerusalem identified as a *polis* or city repeatedly (12 times in 21:1–22:19), it is set in contrast to another city, Babylon, which is destroyed by God and the heavenly forces and ironically mourned by Christ and the angels. The Apocalypse tries to convince its urban audience to turn away from one great city, Babylon/Rome, toward the New Jerusalem, the city of God. Any allegorical reading of the New Jerusalem as the saints would have to include a

---

[14]See Clem. *Paed.* 2.12, 119.1–3; see also Orig. *Contra Celsum* 8.19–20 on the jewels in Isa 54:11–14.

[15]Gundry, "The New Jerusalem," 255. Although claiming a "historical-referential" context for his interpretation, Gundry completely ignores the social setting of early Christianity. See also W. Thüsing, "Die Vision des 'Neuen Jerusalem' (Apk 21, 1–22, 5) als Verheissung und Gottesverkündigun," *TTZ* (1968): 17–34; T. Holtz, *Die Christologie der Apokalypse des Johnannes*, TU 85; (Berlin: Akademie, 1962) 191–95; J. M. Ford, "The Heavenly Jerusalem and Orthodox Judaism," in *Donum gentilicium: New Testament Studies in Honour of David Daube*, ed. E. Bammel, C. K. Barrett, and W. D. Davies (Oxford: Clarendon, 1978) 215–26; and Roloff, 233.

[16]Gundry, "The New Jerusalem," relies exclusively on narrative-critical evidence for his "historical-referential" interpretation.

symbolic reading of Babylon as only the people of Rome or evil people rather than the city and empire of Rome. Revelation hardly admits such a reading (see 16:19; 17:9, 18). A third point stems from John's historical and literary sources. Babylon and Jerusalem *were* real cities. The destruction of Jerusalem by the Romans in 70 CE was probably fresh in the author's mind (see Rev 11:1–14) and, possibly, in the minds of some hearers of the Apocalypse. The sources used by John from Isaiah, Jeremiah, and Ezekiel applied to the historically real cities of Jerusalem, Tyre, and Babylon. To be sure, the destruction and restoration of these cities acquired great theological significance in Jewish and Christian thought, but to admit symbolic or theological significance for a text does not require that we adopt an exclusively allegorical or nonliteral reading. Gundry's assertion that "John wanted his Christian readers . . . to see in the New Jerusalem, not their future dwelling place, but . . . their future selves and state" is particularly surprising in light of this long-established Jewish tradition of theological discourse about Jerusalem and Babylon.[17]

A fourth observation suggesting that the original audience would have construed the description of the New Jerusalem in a spatial sense comes from study of Greco-Roman discourse about cities. The speeches describing the moral and theological character of the New Jerusalem do not signify that the New Jerusalem is a symbolic state of the community rather than an actual city. From Aristotle to Aristides, discussion of the real or ideal *polis* included discussion of moral character as well as physical characteristics. When Dio Chrysostom addressed the Rhodians or Alexandrians, he focused more on civic vice than civic beauty. After describing the harbor and geographical situation of Alexandria (*Or.* 32.36), Dio draws a pointed comparison between the physical and moral virtues of a city:

> Perhaps these words of mine are pleasing to your ears, and you fancy that you are being praised by me . . . but I was praising water and soil and harbours and places and everything except yourselves. For where have I said that you are sensible and temperate and just [φρόνιμοι καὶ σώφρονες καὶ δίκαιοι]? For when we praise human beings, it should be for their good discipline, gentleness, concord, civic order [κόσμος πολιτείας], for heeding those who give good counsel, and

---

[17]Quotation from Gundry, "The New Jerusalem," 364. See Robert R. Wilson, "The City in the Old Testament," *Civitas*, 3–13; and Jonathan Z. Smith, "Jerusalem: The City as Place," *Civitas*, 25–38.

for not being always in search of pleasures. But arrivals and departures of vessels, and superiority in size of population, in merchandise, and in ships, are fit subjects for praise in the case of a fair, a harbour, or a marketplace, but not of a city. *(Or.* 32.37)

Dio offers a closely contemporary parallel for discussing the ideal *polis* in moral as well as physical terms. Where Dio sees order (κόσμος) as part of this ideal, John describes a city that is adorned with physical and moral beauty (κοσμέω, Rev 21:2, 19, which means "order, arrange" as well as "adorn, embellish"). Dio looks for citizens who are just (δίκαοι); John clothes the bride of the lamb with the righteousness (δικαίωμα) of the saints (Rev 19:8). Dio contrasts an orderly, peaceful, and gentle city with one seeking pleasures, just as John sets the pleasure-seeking Babylon against the moral and physical purity of the New Jerusalem. In drawing these comparisons, I am not attempting to deny that John's language has biblical roots but to demonstrate how this language would have been heard by a Greco-Roman audience in urban Asia, who could well have been more familiar with sophistic encomium than with the Hebrew Bible or Greek Septuagint. The moral characteristics of the New Jerusalem presented in Revelation 21–22 also belong to the domain of civic discourse.

Speeches from the Throne

By showing the limitations of a nonspatial reading of John's vision of the New Jerusalem, I have set the proper interpretive context for reading Revelation 21–22. The city that descends from heaven is presented as the future dwelling for loyal Christians and contrasted with the evil city of Babylon/Rome. Where immorality and commercial wealth characterized Babylon/Rome, moral purity and noble wealth characterize the New Jerusalem. The description of the New Jerusalem opens with two speeches praising and characterizing the city: the address by "a loud voice from the throne," probably the voice of Christ,[18] in Rev 21:3–4 and the speech by God, identified periphrastically as "the one who was seated on the throne," in 21:5–8.[19] The first speech focuses on the ideology of endur-

---

[18]On the synecdoche "voice" for "Christ," see chap. 6, pp. 200–201, and Rev 1:11, 12; 4:1; 10:4, 8; 16:17; 18:4; 19:5, all of which could plausibly be construed either as the voice of Christ (so Bousset, who calls this the voice of the "Lamb") or an "Angel of the Presence" (Swete, 244, 277).

[19]Roloff, 234–35, describes a chiastic structure in which the speech of the

ance and martyrdom. The "loud voice" introduces the city to the audience, using the powerful theological language of the *Shekinah* or tabernacle of God: "See, the home [σκηνή] of God is among mortals. He will dwell [σκηνώσει] with them as their God; they will be his peoples, and God himself will be with them and be their God" (21:3).[20] In Rev 21:3, the author uses language from the Hebrew Bible to forge a contract between the ruler of the New Jerusalem, who occupies the throne, and its inhabitants.[21] The slaves of God will dwell with their wealthy patron in this glorious city. This voice from the throne then repeats the words of the elder in Rev 7:17, which themselves are a paraphrase of Isa 25:8: "he will wipe every tear from their eyes" (Rev 21:4). It is a surprising intratextual reference (why would Christ quote the elder?) with intertextual overtones of Isaiah's prophecy of the eschatological feast and restoration of God's people (Isa 25:6–10). While the Isaiah reference is appropriate for the joyous celebration of the descent of the New Jerusalem after the final destruction of Satan (see Rev 20:7–10), the intratextual allusion reminds the audience of the price of citizenship in this heavenly city. The speech of the elder in Rev 7:14–17, which ends with "God will wipe away every tear from their eyes," describes the martyrs before the throne of God who have "washed their robes and made them white in the blood of the Lamb" (Rev 7:14). The promise that death will be no more in 21:4 applies to those who conquer and endure. This is the case with the other great promises of the

---

"voice" in 21:3–4 describes the city of 21:2 while the speech of God describes the new creation of 21:1 (he does not explicitly identify the figure as chiastic). Many commentators identify 21:1–22:5 as the New Jerusalem section (Swete, Boring, Bousset, Caird), while a number (Yarbro Collins, Bauckham, Harrington) break off 21:1–8 for various structural reasons, despite the introduction of the city in 21:2.

[20]See Lev 26:11–12; Ezek 37:27; Zech 2:14; Swete, 278; Caird, 263–64; the change to plural "peoples" from the O.T. singular has textual support (‫א‬ A 2053. 2062 and others), signifying that the promises of the O.T. do not apply only to one nation or people. The addition of "and be their God" (αὐτῶν θεός) lacks the support of ‫א‬ but has an authoritative combination of uncial and minuscules (A 2053. 2062).

[21]Fekkes, "Revelation 19–21 and Isaian Nuptial Imagery," 283, makes the tenuous claim that this covenant promise "is ultimately patterned after Near Eastern marriage contracts." The source is more likely Ezek 37:27, which immediately precedes the discourse on Gog and Magog (Ezekiel 38–39; cf. Rev 20:8).

Apocalypse, such as the ends of the seven messages, the speech of the elder quoted here in 21:4, God's subsequent speech in 21:5–8 and the epilogue of the Apocalypse in 22:8–21. The question is whether the rhetoric of endurance is directed only against Babylon/Rome or also against those Christians who oppose John and whom John opposes. I am arguing that the message applies to all struggles faced by John's followers, be they struggles with Greco-Roman culture or with John's Christian opponents.

The conclusion of this first speech from the throne continues the focus on martyrdom by means of a series of complicated word plays (*paronomasia*) on the word "death," θάνατος: "Death will be no more; mourning and crying and pain will be no more, for the first things have passed away" (21:4). According to Rev 20:14, "Death and Hades" were thrown into the lake of fire, which is "the second death." "Death will be no more" (Rev 21:4), then, as the "first things" have passed away (21:1) in the wake of the "first resurrection" (20:5), which precedes the final judgment of the "second death" (20:14). The cessation of death and pain apply only to those who have met the theological and ideological standards of the Apocalypse. Those outside the city (22:15) are subject to the second death (21:8; cf. 2:11), the lake of fire which continues to burn in the new creation announced in Rev 21:1.

The speech by God in Rev 21:5–8 is the climactic point of the entire Apocalypse.[22] Suspense has been building since John first described God and the heavenly throne room in Rev 4:1–11; God finally addresses the audience directly from the throne for the first time.[23] As the rhetorical climax, this speech is one of the most important expressions of the theology and ideology of the Apocalypse. Indeed, this speech by God shows that ideology *is* the core theological message of the Apocalypse, for God reveals here to the audience that opposition to the Romans and John's Christian opponents is at the heart of the churches' relationship with God. This important point can only be shown by working through the speech in detail.

Three narratorial comments (καὶ εἶπεν, καὶ λέγει, καὶ εἶπεν) divide the speech into three parts of two short lines followed by

---

[22]Hellholm, "The Problem of Apocalyptic Genre" and Aune, "The Problem of Genre" use quite different methods to come to this same conclusion.

[23]So also Swete, 279. According to Boring, 215, and Roloff, 236, after 1:8, this is the second and last time; Mounce, 373, holds that God also speaks in 16:1, 17.

a third longer part.[24] God's speech begins with an allusion to Isa 43:18–19, "See, I am making all things new" (Rev 21:5), an allusion which also appears in Paul's letters (2 Cor 5:17; Gal 6:15; see Eph 2:15; 2 Pet 3:13). As part of early Christian tradition, it was probably familiar to the audience. Rhetorically, this opening line recapitulates the thought expressed in Rev 21:1 and 21:4 and is a *kephalaion* or summary statement of God's speech. It serves notice to the audience that the speech will explain to the audience the essence of the new creation. The second line of God's speech is a reaffirmation for the audience of the faithfulness and trustworthiness of the text they are hearing. God directs the seer to write down what is said, for "these words are trustworthy and true" (21:5). Rev 21:5 functions as an ethical proof, underscoring the narrator's credibility and reliability.[25] Commands from heaven for the narrator to write have been issued before (1:11, 19; 14:13; and 19:9). Three times "these words," that is the text being read in the Christian assemblies, are characterized as "trustworthy and true" (πιστοὶ καὶ ἀληθινόι; 19:9 [only ἀληθινόι]; 21:5; 22:6).[26] In the narrative world of the Apocalypse the commands from heaven instruct the narrator how to proceed and endorse his prophecy to the audience as "trustworthy and true," but in critical perspective we see intrusions by the implied author in order to cloak his text with divine authority. The Apocalypse ends with specific warnings against ignoring or changing the text (22:10, 18–19). The claim to authority in the Apocalypse is a point the audience should not, and could not, miss; thus it receives a prominent place in God's speech from the throne.

God assures the audience of the authority of the narrator as well as the text with the opening line of the third part of the speech: "It is done! I am the Alpha and the Omega, the beginning [ἀρχή] and the end" (Rev 21:6). This line repeats the prophetic utterance from Rev 1:8 and functions as a divine recognition from the throne of God of the prophetic power of the narrator.[27] God then promises "water to the thirsty," an allu-

---

[24]While Swete, 279, holds that the tense changes show different speakers, Mounce, 373, argues that they remain the same.

[25]See the discussion of ethical and pathetical proofs in chap. 4, pp. 132–33.

[26]Christ rides down from heaven to conquer as "Faithful and True" (πιστὸς καὶ ἀληθινός, 19:11; cf 3:7, 14), wielding in effect the power of the text against the beasts and the kings of the earth.

[27]See also Rev 3:14; Col 1:18; and the discussion of ἀρχή in chap. 5, p. 165. The phrase "I am the Alpha and the Omega" recurs in Rev 22:13.

sion to Isa 55:1, a passage which describes the restoration of Jerusalem's fortunes. The application of this prophecy to Christian eschatological hope was probably familiar to the audience as part of early Christian tradition (John 4:13–14; 6:35; 7:37; Rev 7:16). The audience will soon learn that the river of the water of life flows from the throne of God through the middle of the New Jerusalem's golden street (Rev 22:1). God then makes a second promise to "those who conquer" that they will inherit "these things" (ὁ νικῶν κληρονομήσει ταῦτα, Rev 21:7).[28] This is a clear reference back to the promise by Christ to "those who conquer" at the end of each of the seven messages in Revelation 2–3.[29] While the verb "conquer" (νικάω) appears in the visions of Revelation 4–22 as well as the messages, its use as a refrain at the end of the seven messages clearly identifies "those who conquer" as members of the churches who have successfully struggled and endured according to the terms set out in John's Apocalypse.[30] This reference in Rev 21:7 to the messages in Rev 2:1–3:22 connects the rhetorical situation of God's speech, which describes cosmic changes, to the local situation of the seven churches in Asia. The inheritance of those who conquer—that is, "these things" in God's speech—is the New Jerusalem itself, with all its wealth and splendor as well as the water of life and absence of death and pain. Christ's words of assurance to the poor Smyrnans, "I know your affliction and your poverty, even though you are rich" (2:9), become now a promise to all the churches when God describes the New Jerusalem as their heavenly inheritance. The verb κληρονομέω, to inherit, has special significance. It is used regularly in the Synoptics and Paul to describe access to the kingdom of God or God's promises (Matt 5:5; 19:29; 25:34;

---

[28]Plurals in the NRSV translation are used to make the language more inclusive.

[29]Rev 2:7, 11, 17, 26; 3:5, 12, 21.

[30]Aside from the seven messages, the act of conquering in Revelation is under God's control. Rev 5:5; 12:11; 15:2; and 17:14 refer to conquering either by the Lamb or the Lamb's followers. The first horse and rider conquers (6:2) but he is released under heaven's control. The beast from the bottomless pit conquers the two witnesses (11:7) and the beast from the sea conquers God's saints (13:7), but again this beast "is allowed to" conquer (ἐδόθη αὐτῷ . . . νικῆσαι). The passive in 13:7 suggests divine control and shades the interpretation of 11:7. While divine authority is not clearly given to the beast from the bottomless pit in 11:7, the narrative of this passage (11:1–14) suggests the unfolding of a divine plan under God's authority.

Mark 10:17; Rom 8:17; 1 Cor 15:50; Gal 4:7; 1 Pet 1:3–7).[31] But, it is also significant that inheritance was the most respectable way to gain a fortune and raise one's status in antiquity.[32] The Christians inherit landed property, a city of gold and jewels. "Those who conquer" gain not only heavenly wealth but *respectable* heavenly wealth through respectable means.

Not all, however, will be inheritors of this wealth. Although the NRSV translation is "those who conquer," the Greek is a promise in the *singular* to inherit "these things" and to be a child (Gr. υἱός) of God. The promise is not made to all the Christians in Asia, or even in John's audience. The exclusivity of this inheritance is driven home when God concludes the speech with a comprehensive vice list of those who will be excluded from the New Jerusalem and thrown into the second death of the fiery lake: "the cowardly, the faithless, the polluted, the murderers, the fornicators, the sorcerers, the idolaters, and all liars" (Rev 21:8; cf. 22:15). Vice lists were common in moral-philosophical tradition and were well attested in the Pauline tradition.[33] Furthermore, several Pauline passages use a vice list to illustrate who will or will not inherit the kingdom of God and therefore are particularly significant comparisons for Rev 21:8 (1 Cor 6:9–10; Gal 5:19–21; Eph 5:3–5).[34] But there is not much overlap with these Pauline vice lists in God's speech; the implied author has constructed here a specific, polemical message rather than merely borrowed a traditional motif.[35] The vice list in Rev 21:8, like the promise to "those who conquer" in 21:7, does have a number of links with the seven

---

[31]See J. Weiss, 104; *TDNT* 3:767–85, s.v. κληρονομέω.

[32]See Ludwig Friedländer, *Roman Life and Manners under the Early Empire*, 4 vols. (London: Routledge; New York: E. P. Dutton, 1913) 1:212–16; 4:404–405; MacMullen, *Roman Social Relations*, 101–102, 190; Dio *Or.* 45.47; Luc. *Timon* 20–22; *Gall.* 12, 13–15; *Histr. Conscr.* 20; *Tox.* 22; *Tyr.* 6; *Dial. Necr.* 11.3.

[33]See Malherbe, *Moral Exhortation*, 138–41, who identifies the functions for vice lists as characterization; supplements to precepts; illustrations; paraenetic antitheses; protreptics; and polemics; see Rom 1:29–31; Gal 5:19–23; Col 3:5, 8; 1 Tim 1:9–10; 6:4; 2 Tim 3:2–4; Tit 3:3; 1 Pet 4:3.

[34]1 Cor 6:9–10 and Gal 5:19–21 use a form of the verb κληρονομέω and Eph 5:3–5 uses the noun κληρονομία, "inheritance."

[35]The words in common are εἰδωλολάτρης (1 Cor 6:9; Gal 5:20 [εἰδωλολατρία]; Eph 5:5, where it is defined as πλεονέκτης, greedy); πόρνοι (1 Cor 6:9; Eph 5:5); and φαρμακεία (Gal 5:20).

messages in Revelation 2–3. The list contains terms used elsewhere to describe John's opponents and vices associated with Babylon: "the polluted" (ἐβδελυγμένοι; cf. βδελύγματα, 17:4–5); "the fornicators" (πόρνοι; cf. πορνεία, πορνεύω, 2:14, 20; chaps. 17–18 passim); "sorcerers" (φάρμακοι; cf. φαρμακεία, 18:23); "idolaters" (εἰδωλολάτραι; cf. εἰδωλόθυτα, 2:14, 20); and "all liars" (πάντες οἱ ψευδεῖς; cf. ψευδεῖς, 2:2).[36] God's speech from the throne in 21:5–8 concludes with a very harsh polemic against John's opponents. This is another example of the author's heresiological strategy of tarring all opponents with the same brush in order to construct one satanic opposition out of otherwise disparate groups.[37] More importantly, this vice list shows how the author contextualizes the ideology of the Apocalypse in the Asian churches.

The two speeches introducing the New Jerusalem begin with glorious promises of a home for God among humankind; the end of pain and death; and the water of life. They end with a harsh attack on John's opponents, both Christian and pagan. By concluding the speech of God with this vice list, John shows that opposition to his enemies is the heart of the relationship of the Christian communities with God, at least as this relationship is constructed in the Apocalypse.[38] The ideology of the Apocalypse is its central theological message. A second vice list in the epilogue underscores this point. The seventh beatitude, in the epilogue of the Apocalypse, pronounces blessings upon those with clean garments who may enter the New Jerusalem ("the city," ἡ πόλις) by the gates (22:14).[39] Outside this city, however, are "dogs and sorcerers and fornicators and murderers and idolaters, and everyone who loves and practices falsehood" (22:15), a repetition of four of the vices from God's

---

[36]See also the list in Rev 9:20–21, which links the worship of idols (εἴδωλα) with murder (φόνος), sorcery (φαρμακεία), fornication (πορνεία), and theft (κλέμμα).

[37]Discussed in chap. 5 (see 163–64, 175–76) in terms of the use of Satan in messages and elsewhere; in chap. 6 (see 209–10) in terms of wealth and sex.

[38]According to Schüssler Fiorenza, *Priester für Gott*, 373–75, Rev 5:10, 20:4–6, and 22:3–5 express an "eschatological reservation" in opposition to John's "gnosticizing" opponents. She thus connects, in a different manner, the promise of the New Jerusalem to the ideology of the Apocalypse.

[39]On white garments, cf. 19:14 and see above, "The Marriage of the Lamb," pp. 211–14. The speaker in 22:14–15 is most likely Christ, since Christ speaks in 22:12–13 and 22:16; but the identity of the voices in the epilogue is conjecture.

speech in 21:8.[40] These vice lists specifically exclude John's opponents from the inheritance of the New Jerusalem, thereby denying them access to eternal heavenly wealth through socially acceptable means. All will not inherit the New Jerusalem. The point is made quite forcefully for the audience in the closing chapters of the Apocalypse; the list of those excluded from the heavenly city is repeated twice. Any hint of inclusivity in the visions of redemption is shattered by this climactic pronouncement from the throne of God.[41]

Tour of the City

The New Jerusalem has been properly introduced and characterized, according to the conventions of epideictic rhetoric, before the angel begins John's tour. The audience knows that the city is part of a new heaven and earth; that it is beautiful and opulent, adorned as a bride on her wedding day; that it is a place where God the *pantokratōr* dwells and death and pain will no longer exist; and that it is a city of moral purity. The immoral opposition has been excluded from the New Jerusalem and sentenced to everlasting death. This city, God has told them, is the inheritance for "those who conquer," for the faithful members of the Christian church who have struggled and endured. Finally, the bride appears, and with much more luxurious attire than just fine linen (see 19:8). The angel takes John to a high mountain in the spirit where he can view and describe the city (Rev 21:9–10).[42] Pure wealth is a more prominent part of John's vision of the New Jerusalem (21:1–22:5) than of any other of the displays of heavenly wealth that precede it in the book of Revelation. The narrator's tour of the heavenly city by the angel falls into three main sections: an introduction and overview (21:9–14); a detailed physical description and *amplificatio* of the city's wealth

---

[40]Namely sorcerers, *pornoi*, idolaters, and liars. Murderers (οἱ φονεῖς) recall murder (φόνος) in 9:21.

[41]*Contra* Thüsing, "Die Vision des 'Neuen Jerusalem' "; Schüssler Fiorenza, *Priester für Gott*, 359; Boring, 213–31.

[42]This passage closely parallels 17:1–3 and thus sets the New Jerusalem in direct comparison to Babylon. Charles, 2:144–57, maintains that, since John describes the descent of the New Jerusalem in both 21:2 and 21:10, there must be two cities, one for the millennial kingdom and one for the new earth (see Charles's comment on the significance of καινή, 2:157). His exegesis becomes increasingly unreliable for Rev 20–22 due to his excessive editing and rearranging of the text.

(21:15–21); and a description of social life in the new city (21:22–22:5). This tour will show the audience how different the pure, aristocratic wealth of heaven is from the tawdry, commercial wealth of Babylon. Rev 22:6–7, which parallels the end of the "Marriage of the Lamb" section in 19:9–10, concludes the New Jerusalem section before the epilogue to the Apocalypse (22:8–21).

The wealth of the New Jerusalem is carefully revealed and amplified in this three-part structure. The overview of the city in Rev 21:9–14 has only one line attributing wealth, but it is John's first impression: "it has the glory of God and a radiance like a very rare jewel, like jasper, clear as crystal" (21:1). Further description of the city's wealth awaits, but the overall effect of the vision of the New Jerusalem emphasizes the jewel-like radiance of the city. This line echoes the first description of the glories of heaven in the Apocalypse. Each of the elements in Rev 21:1 is part of the description of the heavenly throne room in Rev 4:1–11, recalling for the audience that other vision: glory (δόξα, 4:9, 11); jasper (λίθος ἰάσπις, 4:3); and crystal (κρύσταλλος, 4:6). The narrator next gives an overview of the layout and architectural details of the city: the high wall with twelve gates; the position of the gates; and the twelve foundations of the wall.[43] The wall, which is mentioned six times in 21:12–19, is the central architectural feature of the city.[44] Although the gates of the city are never shut (21:25), it is this wall that separates those inside from those outside (see 22:14–15), protecting the exclusive city from ideological assault. Along with its twelve gates, which are inscribed with the names of the twelve tribes of Israel as in Ezek 48:30–35, the wall has twelve foundations (θεμέλιοι; 21:14). The "names of the twelve apostles of the Lamb" are inscribed on the twelve foundations, a metaphor for the foundation of the Christian church itself. The urban audience of the Apocalypse would be accustomed to seeing the names of emperors, proconsuls, and established aristocrats, with their titles and accomplishments, in public inscriptions in their own cities. The twelve

---

[43]John seems to be working from Ezek 48:30–35, which describes twelve gates in the New Jerusalem, one for each tribe; see Swete, 286; Bousset, 513. Rev 21:13–14 lists them ENSW, which appears to be an intentional change ; Ezekiel is NESW; Num 2:3 is ESWN.

[44]So William W. Reader, "The Twelve Jewels of Revelation 21:19–20: Tradition History and Modern Interpretations" *JBL* 100 (1981): 433; Fekkes, "Revelation 19–21 and Isaian Nuptial Imagery," 275.

tribes of Israel and the twelve apostles replace the Greco-Roman aristocracy in the inscriptions of the New Jerusalem.[45]

The catalogue of wealth in the New Jerusalem in Rev 21:15–21, which follows the overview of the city, is the most concentrated and detailed amplification of heaven's wealth. Indeed, it is the most concentrated and detailed amplification of *any* wealth imagery in the Apocalypse. Each descriptive detail in this passage magnifies the extent of the city's wealth. The guiding angel has a golden measuring rod (21:15); in Ezekiel this was a plain reed rather than gold (Ezek 40:3–5). The enormous size of the city and its wall revealed by the angel's measurements (Rev 21:16–17) increases the effect of the wealth imagery on the audience because so much more gold, jewels, and pearls would be required to decorate it.[46] The "structure" or "material" (ἐνδώμησις) of the wall is jasper (ἴασπις, 21:18), hence the first appearance of the city's radiance from the high mountain (21:11; see 21:1).[47] The entire city is "pure gold, clear as glass" (21:18). Even in context, this is hyperbole, but hyperbole was an acceptable rhetorical trope. Josephus described the view of Herod's temple from a distance similarly.[48] If the city itself is made of gold, it follows naturally that "the street" of the city is also pure gold (21:21), referring to the main thoroughfare of the city, through which the river of life flows (22:2).[49] As was the case with God's speech from the throne, so also this vision is directed to the situation of the

---

[45]The names on the gates and foundations lend weight to the hypothesis that the number for the twenty-four elders around the throne of God (Rev 4:4) derives from such a combination of twelve tribes and twelve apostles.

[46]See Swete, 289: "It must indeed be confessed that these measurements exceed the wildest fancies of the Jewish writers." See Michael Topham, "The dimensions of the New Jerusalem," *ExpTim* 100 (1989): 417–19, on the size of the city. Boring, 221–22, contends that the enormous size and open gates are symbols of the "radical inclusiveness" of the New Jerusalem. His theological reading filters out the strong ideology of the text.

[47]The translation of ἐνδώμησις is problematic and made more difficult by a variant reading of ἐνδόμησις in the Majority texts. See Swete, 290; Charles 2:164; and esp. Fekkes, "Revelation 19–21 and Isaian Nuptial Imagery," 275–77 and nn. 14–16. The ἐνδώμησις is certainly to be distinguished from the θεμέλιοι and may be understood as either material or structure for exegetical purposes here. The NRSV merely supplies "wall."

[48]See Jos. *J.W.* 5 §§222–23.

[49]On διαυγής to clarify further καθαρός, see Swete, 294.

seven churches. The enormous wealth of the New Jerusalem shown to
John by the angel places Christ's admonition to the Laodiceans (Rev
3:14–22) in a new context. The wealth of the Laodiceans is really poverty
in comparison to the wealth of the New Jerusalem. The amount of gold
in John's description of the New Jerusalem recalls for the audience
Christ's offer to *sell* "gold refined by fire" to the Laodiceans. We noted
in Chapter 5 that this offer was ironic, in the typical style of the Stoic
diatribe, since Christ mocked the commercially derived wealth of this
church. The offer now becomes doubly ironic for the audience, because
if they endure and conquer such pure gold is part of their *inheritance* in
the New Jerusalem, a much more socially acceptable way to make a
fortune than through commerce.

The magnification or rhetorical *amplificatio* of the wealth of the city
has its most detailed element in the adornments for the twelve gates and
twelve foundations. The twelve gates, over which an angel stands and on
which the names of the tribes of Israel are inscribed (21:12), are made
from a single pearl (21:21). Gates of pearl in the New Jerusalem are also
found in rabbinic traditions that may have developed from interpretations
of "gates of jewels" in Isa 54:12b.[50] While a pearl forms the city's twelve
gates, each of the city's twelve foundations (θεμέλιοι), which are
inscribed with the names of the twelve apostles, have a different jewel for
decoration (Rev 21:19–20). Scholars have been unable to decide on the
source for this list of the twelve jewels.[51] Commentators usually begin

---

[50]See *b. Sanh.* 100a; *b. B. Bat.* 75a; Bousset, 516; Swete, 294; Charles 2:170.
See also Fekkes, "Revelation 19–21 and Isaian Nuptial Imagery," 277–80
(=*Isaiah and Prophetic Traditions*, 241–44), who follows up on the suggestion
of Caird, 276–77, that John takes the Heb אקדח in Isa 54:12b, a hapax legomenon
usually translated as precious stone or beryl, to mean "pearls" by way of the
Aram. קדח, "to bore." This is the interpretation taken in the haggadic exegesis
of R. Johanan in *b. B. Bat.* 75a. The LXX for Isa 54:12b is λίθοι κρυστάλλου,
"crystal gems," and Tob 13:17 is σάπφειρος καὶ σμάραγδος, "sapphires and
emeralds," both of which apparently interpret אקדח by way of Heb. קדח, "to
kindle."

[51]On the jewels see J. Massyngberde Ford, "The Jewel of Discernment," *BZ*
n.s. 11 (1967): 109–16; for overviews of the history of research in this century
and extensive parallels in Jewish literature (biblical, Hellenistic, rabbinic, and
medieval), see Una Jart, "The Precious Stones in the Revelation of St. John
xxi.18–21," *ST* 24 (1970): 150–81; and Reader, "The Twelve Jewels of
Revelation 21:19–20," 433–57. A number of commentators on Revelation—

with the list of twelve jewels in the high priest's breast piece in Exod 28:17–20. The list of twelve gems in Rev 21:19–20 does not completely agree, however, with the list in Exodus, neither the MT nor LXX.[52] The introduction to John's list, "the foundations of the wall of the city are adorned with every jewel," shows the influence of Ezek 28:13: "You were in Eden, the garden of God; every precious stone was your covering." But the list in the MT of Ezek 28:13 has only nine stones rather than twelve.[53] Most commentators also posit some connection with the twelve signs of the zodiac.[54] While the original audience may have associated the number twelve or the jewels with the zodiac, magic,[55] or

---

Bousset, Swete, Charles, Farrer—have put forward complicated theories which are dismissed by Jart or, with more vehemence, by Reader.

[52]Bousset, 515, began the scholarly game by peremptorily rearranging the list without any apparent justification. Reader, "The Twelve Jewels of Revelation 21:19–20," provides charts of the gem lists in Rev 21:19–20; MT Exod 28:17–20 and Exod 39:10–13; MT Ezek 28:13; LXX Exod 28:17–20, Exod 39:10–13, and Ezek 28:13, which preserve a traditional Greek list different from the MT; Philo *Leg. Alleg.* 1:81–82; Jos. *J.W.* 5 §234; Jos. *Ant.* 3 §168; *Tg. Neof., Tg. Ps.-J.,* and *Tg. Onq.* for Exod 28:17–2, 39:10–13, and Ezek 28:13; *Tg. Ps.-J.* Num 2:3, 10, 18, 25; *Tg. Ket.* Cant 5:14; *Sam. Tg.* Exod. 28:17–20; *Exod. Rab.* 38:8 (96c); and *Bib. Ant.* 26:10–11.

[53]Fekkes, "Revelation 19–21 and Isaian Nuptial Imagery," 277, sees the influence *first* of Ezek 28:13 *then* Exod 28:17–20 because of the close correspondence in the introductions to the two lists. This is a clear violation of his own thesis that John's use of the O.T. shows careful attention to the original function of the O.T. verse. This is the foundation of his *Isaiah and Prophetic Traditions* (the point is repeated there, 241), appearing first in "Revelation 19–21 and Isaian Nuptial Imagery," 272–73, when he objects to the proposal of Kraft, 263, that the marriage imagery in Ezekiel 16 is used to describe the New Jerusalem in Rev 21:2. While Fekkes claims that a negative portrayal of Jerusalem in Ezekiel could not have been used by John to describe the New Jerusalem, he nonetheless chooses a lament over the king of Tyre, who was cast down by God for pride, profanation, and iniquity, as the primary influence in the description of the New Jerusalem.

[54]See Farrer, *A Rebirth of Images,* 216–44, and explanatory chart on the endpaper. Charles, 2:165–68, using unsubstantiated sources put forward in the seventeenth century, claims that the gems are a *reversed* list of the signs of the zodiac and therefore are meant to be a repudiation of speculations on the city of the gods; he is followed by Caird, 274–77. But see T. F. Glasson, "The Order of Jewels in Revelation XXI, 19–20: A Theory Eliminated," *JTS* 26 (1975): 95–100.

[55]Gems are mentioned relatively infrequently in the magical papyri (e.g.,

both, the "sources" for the twelve gates and foundations of the wall are given quite explicitly in Rev 21:12–14, the twelve tribes and the twelve apostles. John is writing within a well-established tradition of wealth in the New Jerusalem (Isa 54:11; Tob 13:17–18; 5QNJ) and needs twelve gems, since he has placed the city on the foundation of the twelve apostles. There is no need to attribute any more significance to the different jewels than to the jasper, crystal, pearls, or gold that also adorn the city.[56] The point of the twelve jewels is rhetorical. The description of the New Jerusalem is the climax of the extensive motif in the Apocalypse of heaven's wealth. All of the jewels and the pearls that adorn the New Jerusalem were quite costly in antiquity.[57] The jewels, crystal, gold, and pearls of the New Jerusalem show that this city is very wealthy, wealthier even than the destroyed city of Babylon.

The quality of that wealth is as important as the quantity; the main contrast between Babylon and the New Jerusalem is a moral one. As we saw, the two speeches of Christ and God in Rev 21:3–8 focused on the moral character of the heavenly city. The third section describing the New Jerusalem, 21:22–22:5, also centers on its moral nature, chiefly by describing its social life. Wealth imagery is not explicitly part of this section, in contrast to the *amplificatio* of wealth imagery in the catalogue (21:15–21). Worship is the first and most important aspect of social life described; control of worship was also the lynchpin of Satan's control over all aspects of social life on earth in Revelation 13. God and the Lamb dwell in the city and replace the temple (21:22), so that the slaves of these wealthy patrons might worship them directly (22:3–4).[58] Again,

---

PGM 1.67, 144; 5.213–303, 447–58; *PDM* 12.6–20); presumably they would be beyond the means of many practitioners of magic or their clients. See Morton Smith, "Relations between Magical Papyri and Magical Gems," *Papyrological Bruxellensia* 18 (1979): 129–36; and Hans Bonnet, *Reallexikon der ägyptischen Religionsgeschichte* (Berlin: de Gruyter, 1952) 427–29, s.v. "Löwe."

[56]Reader, "The Twelve Jewels of Revelation 21:19–20," proposes Pseudo-Philo's *Biblical Antiquities* as the best parallel to Rev 21:19–20, but his thesis is not fully developed and is hampered by his effective rebuttal of all other proposals (see his positive conclusion based on negative evidence, 445) and his recognition of the rhetorical placement and function of the jewels. Thus there is no clear reason for his objection to my line of interpretation, for which he takes Kraft, 271–72, as typical.

[57]See Pliny *HN* 9.106–124; *HN* 32; Jart, "Precious Stones in Revelation."

[58]On the social importance of slavery, see the discussion in chap. 4 (pp.

as with all of heaven's wealth imagery in Revelation, there are no allusions to Solomon's opulent temple since Solomon was a great merchant-king. After religious life, the author describes the political life of the New Jerusalem. The "glory of God" that is the light for the city attracts the nations and the "kings of the earth," who fornicated with the harlot and lamented the destruction of Babylon. Ostensibly destroyed by "Faithful and True" in 19:17–21, these kings make their final appearance in Rev 21:24. The kings who fornicated with Babylon and enjoyed that city's luxury (17:2; 18:3, 9) now bring their glory (δόξα) into the New Jerusalem (21:24). The gates are always open so that kings and nations can bring in their glory and honor to the heavenly city (cf. Isa 60:11).[59]

But open gates do not signify a truly open city. Most important for John, the New Jerusalem will be morally and ideologically pure. Nothing unclean or accursed will enter through these open gates (21:27; see 22:3). The idea that nothing unclean will enter Jerusalem comes from the Hebrew Bible (see Isa 35:8; 52:1), but the implied author makes this notion polemical rather than positive by referring to his Christian opposition in the Asian churches as the "unclean." As noted above, the terms in Rev 21:27, such as "unclean," "abomination," and "falsehood," refer back to polemical passages directed against Babylon/Rome and John's Christian opponents.[60] Only those whose names have been written into the Lamb's book of life will be able to enter the New Jerusalem. This special group has enjoyed special privileges already in the disaster visions of the Apocalypse (see 13:8; 17:8). According to Rev 20:15, those whose names are not written in this book will be thrown into the lake of fire, effectively keeping them off the golden streets. The promise of Rev 21:27 that "nothing unclean" will enter the New Jerusalem is really a threat against "anyone who practices falsehood or abominations," a reference to John's opponents such as "Jezebel" and the "Nicolaitans." The emphasis in Rev 21:27 on the book of life and its "registered members" was anticipated in the messages. Christ exhorts the church in Sardis to conquer and not be blotted out of the book of life (3:5). In chapter 5, I identified the church in Sardis as a battleground church which did not clearly follow John or one of his opponents. The description of

---

136–39) and Martin, *Slavery as Salvation*, 2–49.

[59]The NRSV supplies "people" as a the subject of οἴσουσιν in Rev 21:26 but the kings and nations of 21:24 are a more likely subject for the third-person plural verb.

[60]See above, pp. 223–25.

the New Jerusalem in 21:22–22:5 shows that registry in the lamb's book of life, which determines citizenship in the New Jerusalem and thus eligibility for this wealthy inheritance, requires adherence to John's ideology and authority.

There is no explicit wealth imagery in Rev 21:22–22:5, but there are some notable absences. Analysis of these gaps involves a shift from rhetorical criticism to exploration of authorial intent by examining John's sources in more detail. But this particular side trip reveals the degree to which the author has kept references to commercially derived wealth from tainting the pure gold of the New Jerusalem. Rev 21:24–26 is constructed, in a careful if convoluted fashion, from images found in the description of the restored Jerusalem in Isa 60:1–22. The motifs from Isaiah used here in Revelation include light imagery; the perpetually open gates; and nations and kings flocking to the restored city.[61] Isaiah's prophecy of these nations coming to the New Jerusalem includes a refrain of the "wealth of the nations" (חיל גוים) in the MT of the Hebrew Bible, the text followed by the NRSV (Isa 60:5, 60:11, 61:6, cf. Isa 45:15). The LXX differs from the Hebrew text:[62]

> Isa 60:5 "the wealth [πλοῦτος] of the sea and of nations and peoples will turn to you"
>
> Isa 60:11 "so that they may import [εἰσαγαγεῖν] the power of the nations to you, leading their kings"
>
> Isa 61:6 "you shall receive the power of the nations and in their wealth [πλοῦτος] be admired"

John borrows the concept of nations and kings coming to Jerusalem from Isaiah but does not have them bring any wealth into the city, only "glory."[63] There are clear rhetorical reasons for the change in Revelation. The wealth of the nations or kings of the earth will not come in to taint the pure gold of the New Jerusalem, for this was the sort of commercial

---

[61]See the discussion in chap. 2, pp. 72–73.

[62]Isa 60:5 μεταβαλεῖ εἰς σὲ πλοῦτος θαλάσσης καὶ ἐθνῶν καὶ λαῶν; Isa 60:11 εἰσαγαγεῖν πρὸς σὲ δύναμιν ἐθνῶν καὶ βασιλεῖς ἀγομένους; Isa 61:6 ἰσχὺν ἐθνῶν κατέδεσθε καὶ ἐν τῷ πλούτῳ αὐτῶν θαυμασθήσεσθε.

[63]Isa 60:13, "the glory (כבוד, δόξα) of Lebanon shall come to you," may have suggested the substitution (cf. glory of Lord in Isa 60:1, 2, 19, 21; 61:3). Fekkes, *Isaiah and Prophetic Traditions*, p. 270 n. 127, suggests possibilities of interchange between חיל, "wealth," and כבוד, "glory" and "abundance, riches."

wealth associated with the destroyed city of Babylon. The LXX passages, moreover, suggest commercial activity ("wealth of sea and nations," "import"). The author of the Apocalypse thus preserves the wealth of the New Jerusalem from any association with commerce. Most, if not all, of the audience would have missed the change from Isaiah's prophecy. But it would have been clear to all that the wealth of the New Jerusalem, unlike that of Babylon, does not derive from commerce with kings and nations but is a pure inheritance for conquering, faithful Christians.[64]

Sources of Wealth

This last point, which relies on exegesis of the subtleties of the text of Revelation and the mind of the author, highlights the importance of keeping the wealth imagery in the Apocalypse in its rhetorical context. It is important that Babylon and the New Jerusalem are set in contrast to each other, for without the wealth of Babylon, the wealth of heaven and the New Jerusalem would look decidedly different. Two wealthy cities are described for the audience, a satanic haunt of demons, merchants, and fornicating kings, and the glorious, landed inheritance of faithful Christians. I have focused throughout this study on the sources of wealth in the Apocalypse, both literary sources and commercial sources. Heaven is the source of the wealth revealed to John in his visions of Christ and the heavenly throne room, the wealth promised to the Smyrnans for their faithfulness through afflictions and tribulations, and the wealth that adorns the New Jerusalem. The audience would almost certainly have already had some expectations for the wealth of heaven and the glorious adornments of the New Jerusalem. Some of these expectations could have come from familiarity with John's literary sources in Revelation 21–22, such as Isaiah or Tobit. The audience might also have been familiar with a number of other traditions, including descriptions of the real or ideal Jewish Temple; Jewish, Christian, or Stoic discussions of the eternal and imperishable wealth of heaven; and Jewish and Greco-Roman conceptions of paradise. But significant differences between Revelation and these

---

[64]Swete, 297, recognizes the association of these verses with the wealth motif in the destruction of Babylon: "As Rome in her time attracted the merchandise of the world (xviii.11ff.) so in days to come all that is best in human life will flow into the City of God"; so also Fekkes, *Isaiah and Prophetic Traditions*, 270–71. Charles, 2:172–73, sees an independent translation by John from the Hebrew. Caird, 269, 279, translates δόξα as "treasures."

other traditions show us clearly how Revelation's presentation of heavenly wealth has been rhetorically constructed for ideological and polemical purposes.

Commentators have typically discerned three traditional Jewish motifs in Rev 21:9–22:5: the ancient notion of the heavenly city of the gods; the garden of paradise; and the new or restored Jerusalem.[65] Of these three, only Jerusalem traditions contain significant wealth motifs. The religiohistorical tradition of the heavenly city lies behind John's more ancient sources, such as Isaiah, and is not of primary importance for rhetorical criticism of the Apocalypse. As we have seen, a number of the wealth motifs in John's vision come from or are shared by Jewish descriptions of the restored city of Jerusalem. But there are several apocalyptic passages that describe the future or restored Jerusalem without any wealth imagery whatsoever.[66] The author of Revelation takes a position within the "wealthy" or Isaian side of the tradition for the description of the New Jerusalem, in contrast to many of his apocalyptic colleagues. The author goes further than any other text by adding cultic and temple imagery to the vision of the New Jerusalem. The descriptions of tabernacle, furniture, and priestly vestments in Exodus 25–28, which are based on a heavenly prototype (Exod 25:9) would suggest that the dwelling place of God should be a rich and opulent place. With the exception of Ezekiel 40–48, descriptions of the temple in Jewish tradition are also quite lavish.[67] By combining cultic, temple and New Jerusalem traditions, John creates a vision of the New Jerusalem that is more extravagantly wealthy than those of his predecessors or apocalyptic contemporaries.

John also combines traditional imagery for the New Jerusalem with imagery of the Garden of Eden.[68] The river of life and the healing fruits of the tree of life in Rev 22:1–2 reflect the tradition of agricultural bounty and the absence of pain that mark the blessed realm of paradise. In the Jewish tradition, wealth motifs are not a major part of the descrip-

---

[65]See Charles 2:157–61; Lohmeyer, 171; Schüssler Fiorenza, *Priester für Gott* 348–49; Roloff, 233.

[66]See the discussion of wealth in the New Jerusalem in chap. 2, pp. 72–76. "Wealthy" Jerusalem texts include Isa 45:13–14; 54:11–12; 60:1–22; Tob 13:16–18; and 5QNJ; texts without wealth motifs in the New Jerusalem include Bar 4:5–5:9; *1 Enoch* 10:18–20; 11:1; 24.4–26.2; *2 Apoc Bar* 4:2–6; 73:2–7; 74; 4 Ezra 7:26; 8:52; 10:27, 54; 13:36; and *Psalms of Solomon* 17.

[67]See chap. 2, pp. 76–78.

[68]See Gen 2:10; Psa 46:4; Ezek 47:1–12; Zech 14:8; *1 Enoch* 26:1–3.

tion of the garden of paradise.[69] Expulsion from paradise precipitates the need for garments, farming, and most importantly the working of gold and silver and the use of money.[70] The Greek tradition, however, shows a greater expectation of wealth in the "blessed isle" than do the Jewish descriptions of the garden. Lucian, in *A True Story*, parodies this expectation:

> Thereupon our garlands [στεφάνων] fell away of themselves, and we were set free and taken into the city and to the table of the blessed. The city itself is all of gold [πᾶσα χρυσῆ] and the wall around it of emerald [σμαφάγδινον]. It has seven gates, all of single planks of cinnamon. The foundations [ἔδαφος, not θεμέλιοι] of the city and the ground within its walls are ivory. There are temples of all the gods, built of beryl [βηρύλλου λίθου], and in them great monolithic altars of amethyst [ἀμεθύστινοι], on which they make their great burnt-offerings. Around the city runs a river of the finest myrrh, a hundred royal cubits wide and five deep, so that one can swim in it comfortably. For baths they have large houses of glass, warmed by burning cinnamon; instead of water there is hot dew in the tubs. For clothing they use delicate purple spider webs. (*VH* 2.11–12)[71]

The scholiast believes that Lucian is parodying the New Jerusalem of Revelation itself. Since Lucian had some knowledge of Christianity, it is an intriguing question (seven gates? foundations?), but there are in fact numerous Greek literary traditions of the "blessed isle" (μακάρων νῆσος), where the golden fruit of the Hesperides were kept, being parodied here.[72] While the wealth imagery in Revelation 21–22 can be

---

[69]See *1 Enoch* 24:1–6, where the tree of life is surrounded by seven mountains of precious stones; 25:3–4; and esp. 32:1–6, the "garden of righteousness"; 4 Ezra 3:6; 8:52, where the tree of life and a city are found together, with no wealth motifs; *T. Levi* 18; *Jub.* 2:5–7 ("in Eden, in luxury"); *Apoc. Mos.* 40:2, in which God instructs the archangels to bring cloths of linen and silk from "Paradise in the third heaven" to cover Adam's body (only linen in *Life of Adam and Eve [Vita]* 48:1), but no other wealth motifs describing the garden; *2 Enoch* 8.

[70]See *1 Enoch* 10; the same tradition is found in the Greek myths of the Golden Age and Prometheus; see Hes. *Op.* 42–105, 109–26; *Theog.* 507–616.

[71]Cited by Jart, "Precious Stones in Revelation," from Wettstein's commentary on Revelation.

[72]See PW 14.2.628–32, s.v. Μακάρων νῆσος; Hom. *Od.* 4.561–68; Hes. *Op.* 168–74; *Theog.* 215; Pl. *Phdr.* 249a; *Grg.* 523a; 524a; Philost. *VA* 5.3; Bompaire, *Lucien écrivain*, 661–63.

traced to Jewish literature, John's description of wealth in the New Jerusalem would have met the expectations of a Greek audience for wealth and luxury in the heavenly realm. The Greek sources for this tradition, however, do not set life on the blessed isle in rhetorical contrast to a luxurious, commercial city destroyed by God's forces.

Treasures in Heaven

Perhaps most important for how the descriptions of the wealth of heaven in Revelation could have been heard by the first audience is the idea of "heavenly wealth" as an eternal and incorruptible reward for the righteous. This motif was well developed in ancient Jewish and Christian literature and is related to the broader philosophical concept of "true wealth."[73] The theme appears in texts close to the time and place of Revelation. Expressions of this concept invariably have a strong ethical dimension. The moral appeal in these passages is that "heavenly wealth" is permanent and incorruptible whereas earthly gold and possessions are corruptible and perishable. Thus by being righteous, doing good works, having faith in the gospel—however these moral and theological goals are construed in the various texts—the believer gains access to a more valuable reward than if that person sought earthly compensation. "Do not store up for yourselves treasures on earth [θησαροὺς ἐπὶ τῆς γῆς], where moth and rust consume and where thieves break in and steal; but store up for yourselves treasures in heaven [θησαροὺς ἐν οὐρανῷ], where neither moth nor rust consumes and where thieves do not break in and steal" (Matt 6:19–20). Matthew includes this saying in the Sermon on the Mount, a deliberative speech in which Jesus describes how to live, with a number of other ethical examples. The saying of Jesus in Matthew expresses a similar philosophical idea as the Cynic claim that true wealth is found in hardships and self-denial. Jesus describes "heavenly wealth" as a reward for the righteous for doing good deeds. In 1 Tim 6:17–19, "those who in the present age are rich" (τοῖς πλουσίοις ἐν τῷ νῦν αἰῶνι) are advised to be "rich in good works" (πλουτεῖν ἐν ἔργοις καλοῖς) in order to store up "the treasure of a good foundation [θεμέλιον] for the future." The harshest attack on earthly wealth in the NT, Jas 5:1–3, describes more graphically the effect of Jesus' moth and rust on perishable earthly wealth (cf. Luke 6:24). Of particular significance in comparison to Revelation are texts which describe eternal,

---

[73]See the discussion in chap. 3, pp. 93–97.

heavenly wealth as a reward for the endurance of suffering. The "treasure in clay jars" revealed to Paul by God gives him strength to endure hardships (2 Cor 4:7–12; cf. 5:1–5). Thus he claims that, like the Cynic sage, he is "making many rich" despite his poverty, "having nothing, yet possessing everything" (2 Cor 6:10).[74] The appeal to the permanence of "heavenly wealth" is even more explicit in 1 Peter, in which the author claims that Christians have been given a "new birth" into "an inheritance [κληρονομίαν] that is imperishable, undefiled, and unfading, kept in heaven for you" (1 Pet 1:3–4).

The distinguishing element between Revelation and these other early Christian texts which appeal to heavenly wealth is that Revelation describes that wealth in excessive, earthly detail while the other texts do not. Second Corinthians, 1 Timothy, and James do not describe wealth at all. Nor is this heavenly wealth described in any detail in Matthew, as it is in Revelation, but is referred to as "eternal life" (Matt 19:16–30; cf. 25:29–30). 1 Peter does not portray the inheritance in visions of gold and jewels but explicitly contrasts heavenly wealth to earthly gold (1 Pet 1:7).[75] In 1 Peter, heavenly wealth is of an entirely different nature from earthly wealth—it is imperishable and incorruptible. In Revelation, heavenly wealth is different from earthly wealth only in that it is *proper* wealth. The *Testament of Job* includes detailed descriptions of Job's earthly wealth, which was lost when Satan was turned loose on him (*T. Job* 8:1–2; chs. 9–13; 15:7–9).[76] After Job patiently endures his trials, the Lord returns double of his former possessions to him (*T. Job* 44:1–7). The wealth motifs in the *Testament of Job* parallel those in Revelation. But there are significant differences as well. The appeals to the eternal, unchanging nature of heavenly wealth are quite explicit in the *Testament of Job*. In one telling passage set in the midst of his most painful trials (*T. Job* 18:1–7), Job envisions his heavenly reward as a wealthy city; he is willing to discard all of his possessions in order to enter that city. For Job, his earthly wealth is nothing compared to the eternal throne he will have in heaven as a reward for his patient endurance: "My throne is in

---

[74]See Fitzgerald, *Cracks in an Earthen Vessel*, 166–79, 184–201; Garrett, "The God of This World," 101–104.

[75]See also above, chap. 5, pp. 172–73.

[76]In the *Testament of Job*, Job, interestingly enough, is never associated directly with trade. Job's wealth is primarily agricultural; he finances others in trade but never engages in trade himself.

the holy land and its splendor is in the *unchangeable* world" (*T. Job* 33:5, my emphasis; cf. 26:3; 36:4–5).

The expectations for heavenly wealth found in texts such as Matthew, 2 Corinthians, or the *Testament of Job* would have influenced how the audience understood the promises of the Apocalypse. This theme appears in Revelation along with the aristocratic disdain of wealth derived from commerce and the Stoic notion of "true wealth." These themes are concentrated just as wealth motifs in passages from the Hebrew scriptures are concentrated in John's visions. But the function of wealth imagery in the Apocalypse is significantly different from other texts which appeal to heaven's "true wealth." The amount of wealth in Revelation far outweighs any other text. Whereas other texts contrast earthly wealth with heavenly wealth, the Apocalypse describes heavenly wealth in opulent, excessively "earthly" detail. No other text presents so much heavenly wealth for the audience to see as their reward nor does any other text blur the line between literal and metaphorical senses of the wealth imagery as the Apocalypse does. It is not completely clear in the Apocalypse that the wealth imagery stands for something else. The Apocalypse, moreover, never makes explicit appeals to the imperishable nature of heavenly wealth, as does the *Testament of Job*. Earthly wealth, whether of the Laodiceans or Babylon, is not corruptible but rather commercially derived. In no other text are two types of wealth set in such polemically sharp opposition as they are in Revelation. John presents his audience with two diametrically opposed cities, which contain essentially the same luxury goods and wealth. Rather than constructing a contrast between perishable and eternal wealth, the Apocalypse places wealth in a different set of rhetorical contrasts: pure/impure, moral/immoral, and old, aristocratic wealth/new, commercial wealth.

Summary and Conclusion

We have seen in this chapter how the *ekphrasis* of the New Jerusalem develops and emphasizes a number of themes in the Apocalypse. The figure of the "marriage of the lamb," which immediately follows the destruction of Babylon, prepares the audience for the wealth imagery in the New Jerusalem and provides one of the links between the two passages. Other literary and stylistic devices set Babylon and the New Jerusalem in explicit rhetorical contrast, or *synkrisis*. The description of the New Jerusalem should be read as a description of a city, not of an ideal for the community. Speeches from the throne, including an important summary by God, characterize the moral and ideological purity of the inheritance of the Christians. This sets the stage for extensive description of the size and opulent adornment of the city of pure gold. The purity of the New Jerusalem is expressed in several ways: the city is morally pure; ideologically pure; adorned with pure gold and jewels; and pure from any association with commerce.

By comparing Revelation 21–22 to other texts, we have seen how the New Jerusalem concentrates a number of wealth motifs. In Revelation, as in 1 Peter or the *Testament of Job*, heavenly wealth is a reward for those who adhere to the moral exhortations of the text. But the other ancient Jewish or Christian texts that feature the motif of true or heavenly wealth include a more explicit appeal to the unchanging nature of heaven's wealth and lack the full description of heaven's wealth found in Revelation. We have also seen the ideological function of wealth imagery in the description of the New Jerusalem and in the Apocalypse. The wealth of the New Jerusalem is eternal and uncorrupted; it is also ideologically pure. And the wealth of Babylon, which functions in the Apocalypse as "earthly wealth," is associated with a cluster of impure motifs: Satan, fornication, commerce. Christians earn access to New Jerusalem by steadfastly enduring the trials and tribulations of the faith. But, even more so, they gain access by contesting the authority of Rome, the Jews, and especially John's Christian opponents. The pure, eternal wealth of heaven is a reward for those who have faithfully endured according to the ideological standards of the Apocalypse.

Summary and Conclusions

Summary

I set out in this study to solve a problem based on the bewildering array of wealth imagery in the Apocalypse. The poor Smyrnans, who are praised by Christ, are really rich. The wealthy Laodiceans, who are censured by Christ, are really poor. Christ himself appears to John on Patmos dressed in gold; his golden attire is typical of the court of the heavenly throne room. God's throne is bejeweled and the angels and elders who serve God have golden crowns, belts, and bowls. The most powerful expressions of these confusing wealth motifs are the descriptions of the opulent cities of Babylon and the New Jerusalem, which are set in clear opposition to one another. The same luxury items—gold, jewels, pearls, and fine cloth—adorn each city and its inhabitants. And yet Babylon is destroyed by God for its excessive sins while the New Jerusalem is the pristine reward for the saints of God who have conquered and endured.

How would this wealth imagery have been heard and understood by a first-century audience in the cities of Asia Minor? I formulated two hypotheses in chapter 1 to guide the search for an answer to this question. The first hypothesis is that struggle and conflict within and among the Christian communities of Asia marks the social setting of the Apocalypse. The proper ideological stance toward the dominant Greco-Roman culture and the Roman authorities was one issue in this struggle; alienation from the Jewish synagogue was another. But the actual conflict that precipitated the "crisis of the Apocalypse" was not conflict with the Romans or the Jews. Rather, it was conflict within the Christian churches over the authority of John and his circle of prophets against the authority of other Christian teachers, apostles, and prophets. My second hypothesis followed directly from the first: the function of the Apocalypse relates to this social setting. The Apocalypse was sent to the churches in Asia to heighten the sense of crisis in the Christian communities in order to influence the power struggle within the churches by enhancing the authority of the author. If these hypotheses were correct, I would be able to discover how this wealth imagery would have functioned rhetorically to support the ideological agenda of the Apocalypse.

I needed a great deal more information to begin to answer this question. I began in chapter 2 by comparing the wealth motifs in the Apocalypse to motifs in the books of the Hebrew prophets and in other Jewish literature. This survey yielded two conclusive results. First, study of Revelation's sources in the Hebrew Bible revealed the extent to which the author of the Apocalypse had selected and concentrated wealth imagery from his prophetic sources. The visions in Revelation contain significantly more wealth motifs than their biblical sources or any Second Temple Jewish texts. I was able to conclude that the visions of the Apocalypse were "wealthier" than any of their sources or contemporaries. Second, I demonstrated that the extensiveness of the use of the Hebrew Bible in Revelation—layer upon layer of allusion and echo—raised serious doubts about whether the audience would have understood the extent of the allusions or recognized John's sources. One sentence in Revelation might have four or more scriptural referents. Even a competent reader might not hear most of these echoes, a conclusion made more plausible by the difficulties of modern scholars in sorting through the allusions.

This second conclusion led to the next phase of the study. John had manipulated his text so that the biblical pieces made up an entirely new set of visions. Study of the author's sources showed the extent of wealth imagery in Revelation; it revealed little about how the audience would have understood that imagery. In chapter 3 I turned to the social context of urban Asia Minor to study the ways in which wealth motifs appeared in Greco-Roman philosophy, literature, and inscriptions. I found considerable correspondence between the different functions of wealth imagery in the narrative world of Revelation and the functions of wealth motifs in the social world of the audience.

The exploration of the Jewish sources and Greco-Roman context for Revelation in chapters 2 and 3 paved the way for exegetical answers to the question of how the imagery of wealth in the Apocalypse would have functioned rhetorically as part of the ideology of the text. My exegetical findings may be summarized in four main points.

First, the introduction (Rev 1:1–20) challenges Roman authority and power by casting God and Christ as the wealthy patrons of the Christian communities with more power and status than Caesar. Second, Christ is characterized as an aristocratic moral philosopher when he addresses the churches of Smyrna and Laodicea on the topics of wealth and poverty. Christ awards "true wealth" to the Smyrnans because of their endurance in the opposition to the Jews. Christ censures and rebukes the Laodiceans, encouraging them to support John and his prophetic circle in the power struggles within the Christian churches. Third, the salient features of the moral portrait of Babylon/Rome in Revelation, fornication and commercial wealth, undercut Rome's political power by lowering the status of the earthly city relative to the powers of the heavenly court. The characterization of Babylon/Rome's wealth as commercially derived differentiates the wealth of the harlot from the wealth of heaven. Fourth, the New Jerusalem is a morally and ideologically pure inheritance for "conquering" Christians. The grand vision of the New Jerusalem refers back to the situation of the seven churches and the "crisis" at hand. The city is a high-status dwelling for those who support the author and oppose other Christian teachers and prophets. The New Jerusalem is very wealthy and very exclusive.

Conclusion: Wealth, Status, and Ideology

Beyond analysis of its imagery and ideology of wealth, this study has produced three important findings for the study of the Apocalypse. First, I have shown the importance of rhetorical criticism in understanding how the text would have been heard by its original audience. Second, I have shown that the intricate and even excessive use of the Hebrew Bible in Revelation casts doubt on the value of source-critical study for understanding how the text would have been heard by this audience. In order to understand Revelation in its social-historical context, we have to move beyond a preoccupation with the author's sources and background. Furthermore, I have suggested that the implied author's use of the Bible deconstructs the authority of his prophetic sources through a series of strong misreadings. Third, I have demonstrated the importance of the heresiological agenda in Revelation. The heresiological rhetoric of the Apocalypse tars all of John's opposition with the same set of brushes: commercial wealth, Satan, sorcery, sex. The rhetorical strategy of this heresiological construction is to categorize all of John's opponents, Roman, Jewish, and Christian, as part of a unified, satanic opposition. Valuable research remains to be done on the development of heresiological polemics in Revelation and other late-first-century and early-second-century CE Christian texts from Asia Minor.

These three points have been made in the course of the major focus of this study, the function of the wealth imagery of the Apocalypse in its social setting. As discussed in chapter 1, three interpretations have been traditionally presented for wealth imagery in the Apocalypse, but none of these do justice to the complexity of the motifs in the narrative world of the text. The traditional notion in Jewish and Christian literature of true, heavenly wealth as eternal and unchanging might explain the wealth imagery in the messages to Smyrna and Laodicea, in the vision of Christ on Patmos, and perhaps in the visions of the heavenly throne room. But this interpretation does not account for the vehement attack on Babylon/Rome's commercial wealth in Revelation 18 nor for the excessive description of the wealth of the New Jerusalem. A second line of interpretation sees in Revelation's critique of Babylon a Marxist critique of the Roman economic system, with its attendant oppression and injustices. Those who take this approach would construe Revelation 18 as a cry against Roman control of the marketplace and the means of production. My study has shown that this view does not correspond to ancient conceptions of the economy nor to the ways in which ancient Greeks and Romans talked about wealth. Nor does this Marxist view explain how wealth imagery functions positively in the praise of heaven and the New Jerusalem. A third interpretation, epitomized in the quotation from D. H. Lawrence at the head of chapter 1, would explain the wealth imagery in terms of resentment of Roman wealth and power by poor Christians. But advances in social-historical and sociological study of early Christianity have shown that the Christian communities were not composed only of the poor and lower class. Furthermore, the way wealth imagery is used to praise and blame in Revelation is too complex to be explained merely by resentment.

The visions of Revelation do attack Roman wealth and power, but in ways that are more complex than theories of psychological resentment or Marxist critique might suggest. Rather, the author uses traditional motifs of heavenly wealth, the temple, and the New Jerusalem in conjunction with eastern Greek disdain for Rome's commercial wealth and cultural inferiority. The intentional rhetorical contrast between Babylon and New Jerusalem is crucial for understanding the social function of the language. In his attack on Rome, the author uses imagery of wealth that would have been perceived as low status. The Apocalypse strips Babylon of any status its wealth might suggest by casting the city as a commercial power. The court of God and the city of the New Jerusalem, in contrast, have both wealth and status. The author's rhetorical moves have profound theological and ideological consequences. First, the imagery of wealth in Revelation functions to legitimate the power of God and Christ against the power of Rome. Whether or not they were officially oppressed, Christians were a minority group subject to perceived oppression in Greco-Roman culture. Revelation supports Christians in Greco-Roman society by challenging the claims of Rome and asserting the identity of Christ as Lord and God as *pantokratōr*. Second, the rhetoric of wealth legitimates the authority of the author within the Christian communities. In Revelation, John makes the Christian church the battleground for his fight with Rome. When attacking Rome, the author also attacks other Christian teachers, apostles, and prophets whom John claims are allied with Rome and Satan. Thus, John uses wealth images and motifs that convey higher status to support both the Christians against the Romans and his prophetic circle against other Christian leaders and groups. John projects onto heaven and Babylon not lower-class resentments but the moral, theological, and ideological struggles of the Christian communities. This ideological function of wealth imagery has been well demonstrated in this study.

In its attack on Roman wealth, Revelation takes the view from above. God, Christ, the New Jerusalem, and John and his fellow slaves all occupy a high-status position while the Roman, Jewish, and Christian opposition have the lower-status position. My contention that the implied author of Revelation uses status "hot buttons" to advance his theological and ideological agenda does not require that I prove that the audience was entirely high or low status or even mixed status. If the members of the churches of Asia were a mixed-status group with a high degree of status inconsistency, such as freed slaves or merchants and artisans, the use of wealth imagery in the Apocalypse would have been particularly effective. But people and groups with high status, such as Cicero or C. Vibius Salutaris, used similar language to maintain or enhance their position in society. The attitudes of the dominant aristocracy would have been accepted by groups without power in society as well. The deprecation of Babylon/Rome's wealth and the glories of the New Jerusalem would have resonated with lower-status Christians. The appeal of God's wealth in contrast to Babylon's wealth would have worked up and down the social ladder.

The function of wealth imagery in the Apocalypse, therefore, parallels the function of wealth in maintaining or increasing status in aristocratic Greco-Roman culture. This use of wealth in the text mimics the way wealth supported the dominant culture that the Apocalypse attacks. The descriptions of Christ and the heavenly throne room borrowed from the Roman and Hellenistic court ceremony. The description of the New Jerusalem borrows from Hellenistic conceptions of the ideal city. The symbols of status and power from Greco-Roman culture play a prominent role in a text which purports to attack that culture. Moral issues such as eating meat from the temple or the portrayal of Roman functionaries as satanic beasts would suggest that Greco-Roman culture is the enemy. Deeper analysis has shown, however, that it is not the culture but power itself that is the issue at stake in the Apocalypse.

In conclusion, this study has shown that opposition to the dominant culture in the Apocalypse is not an attempt to redeem that culture but rather an attempt to replace it with a Christianized version of the same thing. The powerful combination of the imagery of wealth and its effects on status from Greco-Roman culture expressed in Revelation entangles the text in that culture. The text creates a new culture of power that mimics the dominant ideology; only the names and labels are changed. Revelation replaces Rome with the New Jerusalem and Caesar's court with God's, but the underlying power structures are essentially the same. The point of this rhetoric is not the redemption of the world or even of the Christian community but the establishment of a new theocratic empire. Ultimately, Revelation constructs a theology in which ideological judgment is the heart of the Gospel message. The good news proclaimed is that the faithful slaves who have endured have a place in the golden city and that their evil opponents do not. For those who oppose this ideology, the text offers judgment with no justice, crisis without catharsis.

Bibliography

I. Primary Sources, Texts, and Translations

Aelius Aristides. *P. Aelii Aristidis opera quae exstant omnia.* Edited by Frederick Walther Lenz and Charles A. Behr. Volume 1, *Orationes I–XVI.* One volume in four parts. Leiden: E. J. Brill, 1976.

_____. *Aelii Aristidis Smyrnaei quae supersunt omnia.* Edited by Bruno Keil. Volume 2, *Orationes XVII–LIII.* Berlin: Weidmann, 1958.

_____. *Panathenaic Oration and In Defence of Oratory.* Translated by C. A. Behr. LCL. Cambridge MA: Harvard University Press; London: William Heinemann, 1973.

Apocalypsis Henochi Graece. Edited by Matthew Black. PVTG 3. Leiden: E. J. Brill, 1970.

Aristides. *P. Aelius Aristides: The Complete Works.* Two volumes. Translated by Charles A. Behr. Leiden: E. J. Brill, 1986.

Aristotle. *The Art of Rhetoric.* Translated by J. H. Freese. LCL. 1926.

Biblica hebraica stuttgartensia. Edited by Karl Elliger and Wilhelm Rudolph. Stuttgart: Deutsche Bibelstiftung, 1967–1977, 1983.

Cicero. *De officiis.* Translated by Walter Miller. LCL. 1913.

Clement of Alexandria. Volume 1, *Protrepticus und Paedagogus.* Third edition. Edited by Otto Stählin and Ursula Treu. GCS 12. Berlin: Akademie-Verlag, 1972.

_____. *The Exhortation to the Greeks, The Rich Man's Salvation, To the Newly Baptized.* Translated by G. W. Butterworth. LCL. 1919.

Cynic Epistles, The. A Study Edition. Edited by Abraham J. Malherbe. SBLSBS 12. Missoula MT: Scholars Press for SBL, 1977.

Dead Sea Scrolls in English, The. Third edition. Edited and translated by Geza Vermes. Sheffield UK: JSOT Press, 1987.

Dead Sea Scrolls of St Mark's Monastery, The. Edited by Millar Burrows, J. C. Trever, and W. H. Brownlee. Volume 1, *The Isaiah Manuscript and the Habbakuk Commentary.* New Haven CT: ASOR, 1950.

Dio Chrysostom. Five volumes. Translated by J. W. Cohoon and H. L. Crosby. LCL. 1932–1951.

_____. *Orations VII, XII and XXXVI.* Edited and translated by D. A. Russell. Cambridge: Cambridge University Press, 1992.

Diogenes Laertius. *Lives of Eminent Philosophers.* Two volumes. Translated by R. D. Hicks. LCL. 1938.

Enoch, 1 (Ethiopic Apocalypse of). Translated by E. Isaac. In *The Old Testament Pseudepigrapha*, edited by James H. Charlesworth, 1:5–89. Garden City NY: Doubleday, 1983.

Enoch, The Books of. Aramaic Fragments from Qumrân Cave 4. Edited by J. T. Milik with Matthew Black. Oxford: Clarendon/Oxford University Press, 1976.

Enoch or 1 Enoch, The Book of. Translated by R. H. Charles. Oxford: Clarendon/Oxford University Press, 1912.

Enoch or I Enoch, The Book of: A New English Edition. Edited and translated by Matthew Black in consultation with James C. Vanderkam and with an appendix on the "Astronomical" Chapters (72–82) by Otto Neugebauer. SVTP 7. Leiden: E. J. Brill, 1985.

Epictetus. *The Discourses as Reported by Arrian, The Manual, and Fragments*. Two volumes. Translated by W. A. Oldfather. LCL. 1925–1928.

Eusebius. *The Ecclesiastical History*. Two volumes. Translated by Kirsopp Lake and J. E. L. Oulton. LCL. 1926–1932.

Greek Magical Papyri in Translation, The, Including the Demotic Spells. Edited by Hans Dieter Betz. Chicago: University of Chicago Press, 1986.

HarperCollins Study Bible, New Revised Standard Version, with the Apocryphal/Deuterocanonical Books. Edited by Wayne A. Meeks et al., with the Society of Biblical Literature. New York: HarperCollins Publishers, 1993.

Hesiod, The Homeric Hymns, and Homerica. Translated by H. G. Evelyn-White. LCL. 1914.

Horace. *Satires, Epistles, and Ars Poetica*. Translated by H. R. Fairclough. LCL. 1932.

Horgan, Maurya P. *Pesharim: Qumran Interpretations of Biblical Books*. CBQMS 8. Washington DC: Catholic Biblical Association of America, 1979.

Josephus. Ten volumes. Translated by H. St. J. Thackeray et al. LCL. 1926–1965.

Knibb, Michael A. *The Qumran Community*. Cambridge Commentaries on Writings of the Jewish and Christian World 200 BC to AD 200. Cambridge: Cambridge University Press, 1987.

Lucian. Eight volumes. Translated by A. M. Harmon et al. LCL. 1913–1967.

Menander Rhetor. Edited and translated by D. A. Russell and N. G. Wilson. Oxford: Clarendon/Oxford University Press, 1981.

Musonius Rufus: The Roman Socrates. Edited and translated by Cora E. Lutz. In *YCS* 10:3–147. New Haven CT: Yale University Press, 1947.

Novum Testamentum Graece. Twenty-sixth edition. Edited by Kurt Aland et al. Stuttgart: Deutsche Bibelgesellschaft, 1979.

Old Testament Pseudepigrapha, The. Two volumes. Edited by James H. Charlesworth. Garden City NY: Doubleday, 1983, 1985.

Philo. Twelve volumes. Translated by F. H. Colson, G. H. Whitaker, and R. Marcus. LCL. 1929–1962.

Philostratus. *Lives of the Sophists*. Translated by W. C. Wright. LCL. 1921.

_____. *The Life of Apollonius of Tyana, The Epistles of Apollonius*, and *The Treatise of Eusebius*. Two volumes. Translated by F. C. Conybeare. LCL. 1912.

Pliny the Elder. *Natural History*. Ten volumes. Translated by H. Rackham. LCL. 1938.

Pliny (the Younger). *Letters*. Two volumes. Translated by W. Melmoth and W. M. L. Hutchinson. LCL. 1958.

Plutarch. *Moralia*. Sixteen volumes. Translated by F. C. Babbitt et al. LCL. 1927–1969.

_____. *Lives*. Eleven volumes. Translated by B. Perrin. LCL. 1914–1926.

Psalms of Solomon, The. Translated by R. B. Wright. In *The Old Testament Pseudepigrapha*, edited by James H. Charlesworth, 2:639–70. Garden City NY: Doubleday, 1985.

Quintillian. *Institutio Oratoria*. Four volumes. Translated by H. E. Butler. LCL. 1920.

Seneca. *Epistulae Morales*. Three volumes. Translated by R. M. Gummere. LCL. 1917–1925.

Seneca. *Moral Essays*. Three volumes. Translated by J. W. Basore. LCL. 1928–1935.

Septuaginta. Id est Vetus Testamentum graece iuxta LXX interpretes. Two volumes (in one). Edited by Alfred Rahlfs. Repr.: Stuttgart: Deutsche Bibelgesellschaft, 1979; =1935.

Sibyllina, Die Oracula. Edited by Johannes Geffcken. GCS 8. Leipzig: J. C. Hinrichs'sche, 1902.

Sibylline Oracles, The. Translated by John J. Collins. In *The Old Testament Pseudepigrapha*, edited by James H. Charlesworth, 1:317–472. Garden City NY: Doubleday, 1983.

Songs of the Sabbath Sacrifice. A Critical Edition. Edited and translated by Carol A. Newsom. HSS. Atlanta: Scholars Press, 1985.

Tacitus. *The Histories and the Annals*. Five volumes. Translated by R. M. Ogilvie et al. LCL. 1925–1970.

Testament of Job, The, according to the SV Text. Edited and translated by Robert A. Kraft et al. SBLTT 5. SBL Pseudepigrapha Series 4. Missoula MT: Scholars Press, 1974.

3 Maccabees. Translated by H. Anderson. In *The Old Testament Pseudepigrapha*, edited by James H. Charlesworth, 2:509–30. Garden City NY: Doubleday, 1985.

II.   Commentaries on Revelation

Allo, Ernest Bernard. *L'Apocalypse*. Third edition. Paris: J. Gabalda, 1933.

Aune, David. *Revelation*. WBC 52A. Dallas: Word Publishers, 1997.

Beasley-Murray, G. R. *The Book of Revelation*. NCB. London: Oliphants, 1974.

Boring, M. Eugene. *Revelation*. IBC. Louisville KY: John Knox, 1989.

Bousset, Wilhelm. *Die Offenbarung Johannis*. Fifth edition. MeyerK. Göttingen: Vandenhoeck & Ruprecht, 1896.

Caird, G. B. *A Commentary on the Revelation of St. John the Divine*. Second edition. London: A. & C. Black, 1984; [1]1966.

Charles, R. H. *A Critical and Exegetical Commentary on the Revelation of St. John*. Two volumes. ICC. Repr.: Edinburgh: T. & T. Clark; New York: Charles Scribner's Sons, 1985 =1920.

Fiorenza, Elisabeth Schüssler. *Revelation: Vision of a Just World*. Proclamation. Minneapolis: Augsburg/Fortress, 1991.

Ford, J. Massyngberde. *Revelation. Introduction, Translation, and Commentary*. AB 38. Garden City NY: Doubleday, 1975.

Harrington, Wilfrid J. *Revelation*. Sacra Pagina 16. Collegeville MN: Liturgical/Michael Glazier, 1993.

Garrow, A. J. P. *Revelation*. New Testament Readings. London and New York: Routledge, 1997.

Kraft, Heinrich. *Die Offenbarung des Johannes*. HNT 16a. Tübingen: J. C. B. Mohr (Paul Siebeck), 1974.

Lohse, Eduard. *Die Offenbarung des Johannes*. NTD 11. Göttingen: Vandenhoeck & Ruprecht, 1971.

Lohmeyer, Ernst. *Die Offenbarung des Johannes*. Second edition. HNT 16. Tübingen: J. C. B. Mohr (Paul Siebeck), 1953.

Mounce, Robert H. *The Book of Revelation*. NICNT. Grand Rapids: Eerdmans, 1977.

Müller, Ulrich B. *Die Offenbarung des Johannes*. Gütersloh and Würzburg: Gütersloher and Echter, 1984.

Prigent, Pierre. *L'Apocalypse de Saint Jean*. CNT 14. Paris: Delachaux and Niestlé, 1981.

Roloff, Jürgen . *Revelation: A Continental Commentary*. Minneapolis: Fortress Press, 1993. German orig.: Zurich: Theologischer Verlag Zürich, 1984.

Swete, Henry Barclay. *The Apocalypse of St. John. The Greek Text with Introduction, Notes, and Indexes*. Third edition. London: MacMillan and Co., 1911; [2]1907; [1]1906.

Weiss, Johannes. *Die Offenbarung des Johannes: Ein Beitrag zur Literatur- und Religionsgeschichte*. FRLANT 3. Göttingen: Vandenhoeck & Ruprecht, 1904.

III. Secondary Sources

Aalen, Sverre. "St Luke's Gospel and the Last Chapters of I Enoch." *NTS* 13 (1966): 1–13.

Aldridge, Alan. "Negotiating Status: Social Scientists and Anglican Clergy." *Journal of Contemporary Ethnography* 22 (1993): 97–112.

Anderson, Graham. *The Second Sophistic: A Cultural Phenomenon in the Roman Empire*. London and New York: Routledge, 1993.

_____. *Lucian: Theme and Variation in the Second Sophistic*. Mnemosyne Supp. 41. Leiden: E. J. Brill, 1976.

Arnold, J. Phillip. "The Davidean Dilemma—To Obey God or Man?" In *From the Ashes: Making Sense of Waco*, edited by James R. Lewis, 23–31. Lanhmam MD: Rowman & Littlefield, 1994.

Attridge, H. W. "Josephus and His Works." In *Jewish Writings of the Second Temple Period*, edited by M. E. Stone, 185–232. CRINT2.2. Assen and Philadelphia: Van Gorcum and Fortress, 1984.

Auerbach, Erich. *Mimesis: The Representation of Reality in Western Literature.* Princeton NJ: Princeton University Press, 1953, 1974.

Aune, David E. "The Apocalypse of John and Graeco-Roman Revelatory Magic." *NTS* 33 (1987): 481–501.

_____. "The Apocalypse of John and the Problem of Genre." *Semeia* 36 (1986): 65–96.

_____. "The Form and Function of the Proclamations to the Seven Churches (Rev 2–3)." *NTS* 36 (1990): 182–204.

_____. "The Influence of the Roman Imperial Court Ceremonial on the Apocalypse of John." *BR* 28 (1983): 5–26.

_____. "Intertextuality and the Genre of Apocalypse." *SBLSP* (1991): 142–60.

_____. *The New Testament in its Literary Environment.* Library of Early Christianity 8. Philadelphia: Westminster Press, 1987.

_____. *Prophecy in Early Christianity and the Ancient Mediterranean World.* Grand Rapids MI: Eerdmans, 1983.

_____. "The Prophetic Circle of John of Patmos and the Exegesis of Revelation 22.16." *JSNT* 37 (1989): 103–16.

_____. "The Social Matrix of the Apocalypse of John." *BR* 26 (1981): 16–32.

Ausbüttel, Frank M. *Untersuchungen zu den Vereinen im Westen des römischen Reiches.* FAS 11. Frankfurt: Michael Lassleben, 1982.

Bakhtin, M. M. *The Dialogic Imagination.* Austin and London: University of Texas Press, 1981.

Baldwin, Barry. "Lucian as Social Satirist." *CQ* n.s. 11 (1961): 199–208.

Bandstra, Andrew J. "'A Kingship and Priests': Inaugurated Eschatology in the Apocalypse." *Calvin Theological Journal* 27 (1992): 10–25.

Barnett, Paul. "Polemical Parallelism: Some Further Reflections on the Apocalypse." *JSNT* 35 (1989): 111–20.

Barr David L. "The Apocalypse as a Symbolic Transformation of the World: A Literary Analysis." *Int* 38 (1984): 39–50.

_____. "Towards an Ethical Reading of The Apocalypse: Reflections on John's Use of Power, Violence, and Misogyny." *SBLSP* (1997): 358–73.

Barr, James. "Biblical Theology." In *The Interpreter's Dictionary of the Bible*, Supplementary Volume, edited by Keith Crim et al., 104–11. Nashville: Abingdon Press, 1976.

Barrett, C. K. "Gnosis and the Apocalypse of John." In *The New Testament and Gnosis. Essays in Honour of Robert McL. Wilson*, edited by A. H. B. Logan and A. J. M. Wedderburn, 125–37. Edinburgh: T. & T, Clark, 1983.

Bartsch, Shadi. *Actors in the Audience: Theatricality and Doublespeak from Nero to Hadrian.* Cambridge MA and London: Harvard University Press, 1994.

Bauckham, Richard. *The Bible in Politics: How to Read the Bible Politically.* London: SPCK, 1989.

_____. *The Climax of Prophecy: Studies on the Book of Revelation.* Edinburgh: T. & T. Clark, 1993.

_____. "The Economic Critique of Rome in Revelation 18." In *Images of Empire*, edited by L. Alexander, 47–90. JSOTSup 122. Sheffield UK: JSOT, 1991. Repr.: In *Climax of Prophecy*, 338–83. Edinburgh: T. & T. Clark, 1993.

_____. "The Rich Man and Lazarus: The Parable and the Parallels." *NTS* 37 (1991): 225–46.

Bauer, Walter. *A Greek-English Lexicon of the New Testament and Other Early Christian Literature.* Second edition. Translated and revised by W. F. Arndt, F. W. Gingrich, and F. W. Danker. Chicago: University of Chicago Press, 1979.

Beale, G. K. "The Old Testament Background of Rev 3.14." *NTS* 42 (1996): 133–52.

_____. *The Use of Daniel in Jewish Apocalyptic Literature and in the Revelation of St. John.* Lanham MD and London: University Press of America, 1984.

Beasley-Murray, G. R. "The Interpretation of Daniel 7." *CBQ* 45 (1983): 44–58.

Beck, Roger. "Encolpius at the Cena." *Phoenix* 29 (1975): 271–83.

_____. "The Satyricon: Satire, Narrator, and Antecedents." *Museum Helvetica* 39 (1982): 206–14.

Behr, C. A. *Aelius Aristides and the Sacred Tales.* Amsterdam: Adolf M. Hakkert, 1968.

Berger, Peter L. and Thomas Luckmann. *The Social Construction of Reality: A Treatise in the Sociology of Knowledge.* New York: Doubleday, 1966.

Berger, Peter L. *A Rumor of Angels. Modern Society and the Rediscovery of the Supernatural.* Garden City NY: Anchor Books, 1970, ©1969.

Betz, H. D. "Jesus and the Cynics: Survey and Analysis of Hypothesis." *JR* 74 (1994): 453–75.

_____, editor. *Plutarch's Ethical Writings and Early Christian Literature.* Leiden: E. J. Brill, 1978.

Bieder, W. "Die sieben Seligpreisungen in der Offenbarung des Johannes." *TZBas* 10 (1984): 13–30.

Bird, Phyllis. "'To Play the Harlot': An Inquiry into an Old Testament Metaphor." In *Gender and Difference in Ancient Israel*, edited by P. L. Day, 75–94. Minneapolis: Augsburg/Fortress, 1989.

Bitzer, Lloyd F. "The Rhetorical Situation." *Philosophy and Rhetoric* 1 (1968): 1–14.

Black, Matthew. "The Throne-Theophany Prophetic Commission and the 'Son of Man.'" In *Jews, Greeks, and Christians: Religious Cultures in Late Antiquity. Essays in Honor of William David Davies*, edited by R. Hammerton-Kelley and R. Scroggs, 57–73. SJLA 21. Leiden: E. J. Brill, 1976.

Blass, F., and A. Debrunner. *A Greek Grammar of the New Testament and Other Christian Literature.* Translated and revised by R. W. Funk. Chicago: University of Chicago Press, 1961.

Bloom, Harold, editor. *The Revelation of St. John the Divine.* New York, New Haven, and Philadelphia: Chelsea House, 1988.

Bloomer, W. Martin. *Latinity and Literary Society at Rome.* Philadelphia : University of Pennsylvania Press, 1997.

Bompaire, J. *Lucien écrivain: Imitation et Création.* Bibliothèque des Ecoles Françaises d'Athènes et de Rome 190. Paris: E. de Boccard, 1958.

Bonner, C. *Studies in Magical Amulets Chiefly Graeco-Egyptian.* Ann Arbor: University of Michigan Press, 1950.

Bonnet, Hans. *Reallexikon der ägyptischen Religionsgeschichte.* Berlin: de Gruyter, 1952.

Booth, Wayne. *The Rhetoric of Fiction.* Second edition. Chicago and London: University of Chicago Press, 1983.

Borgen, Peder. "Polemic in the Book of Revelation." In *Anti-Semitism and Early Christianity: Issues of Polemic and Faith,* edited by C. A. Evans and D. A. Hagner, 199–211. Minneapolis: Augsburg/Fortress, 1993.

Boring, M. Eugene. "Narrative Christology in the Apocalypse." *CBQ* 54 (1992): 702–23.

————. *Sayings of the Risen Jesus: Christian Prophecy in the Synoptic Tradition* Cambridge: Cambridge University Press, 1982.

Boulluec, Alain Le. *La notion d'hérésie dans la littérature grecque IIe-IIIe siècles: Tome I, De Justin à Irénée.* Paris: Etudes Augustiniennes, 1985.

Bousset, Wilhelm. *Der Antichrist in der Überlieferung des Judentums, des neuen Testaments und der alten Kirche: Ein Beitrag zur Auslegung der Apocalypse.* Repr.: Hildesheim: Georg Olms, 1983. Orig.: Göttingen: Vandenhoeck & Ruprecht, 1895.

————. "Antichrist." In *Encyclopaedia of Religion and Ethics,* edited by James Hastings et al., 1:578–81. Edinburgh: T. &T. Clark; New York: Scribners, 1979–1981.

Bowersock, G. W. *Greek Sophists in the Roman Empire.* Oxford: Clarendon/Oxford University Press, 1969.

Bowersock, G. W., editor. *Approaches to the Second Sophistic: Papers Presented at the 105th Annual Meeting of The American Philological Association.* University Park PA: American Philological Association, 1974.

Bowie, E. L. "Greeks and their Past in the Second Sophistic." In *Studies in Ancient Society,* edited by M. I. Finley, 166–209. London and Boston: Routledge and Kegan Paul, 1974.

————. "The Importance of Sophists." In *YCS* 27:29–59. New Haven CT: Yale University Press, 1982.

Broughton, T. R. S. "Roman Asia Minor." In *An Economic Survey of Ancient Rome,* edited by Tenney Frank, 4:499–918. Repr.: New York: Octagon Books, 1975; orig.: Baltimore: Johns Hopkins University Press, 1938.

Brown, Raymond. *The Death of the Messiah. From Gethsemane to the Grave. A Commentary on the Passion Narratives in the Four Gospels.* Two volumes. AB Reference Library. New York: Doubleday, 1994.

Brown, Francis, S. R. Driver, and C. A. Briggs. *A Hebrew and English Lexicon of the Old Testament.* Corrected reprint: Oxford: Clarendon/Oxford University Press, 1975; orig. 1907.

Brueggemann, Walter. "At the Mercy of Babylon: A Subversive Rereading of the Empire." *JBL* 110 (1991): 1–14.

Brunt, P. A. "Aspects of the Social Thought of Dio Chrysostom and of the Stoics." *Proceedings of the Cambridge Philological Society* n.s. 19 (1973): 9–34.

_____. "From Epictetus to Arrian." *Athenaeum* 55 (1977): 19–48.

Buchanan, G. W. "Jesus and the Upper Class." *NovT* 7 (1964–1965): 195–209.

Bultmann, Rudolf. *Der Stil der paulinischen Predigt und die kynische-stoische Diatribe* FRLANT 13. Göttingen: Vandenhoeck & Ruprecht, 1984.

Burkett, Delbert. *The Son of Man in the Gospel Tradition.* JSNTSup 56. Sheffield UK: Sheffield Academic Press, 1991.

Callewaert, C. "Les persécutions contre les Chrétiens dans la politique religieuse de l'Etat romain." *Revue des questions historiques* 82 (1907).

Canfield, L. H. *The Early Persecutions of the Christians.* New York: Columbia University Press, 1913.

Casey, Maurice. "The Use of Term 'Son of Man' in the Similitudes of Enoch." *JSJ* 7 (1976): 11-29.

_____. *The Son of Man: The Interpretation and Influence of Daniel 7.* London: SPCK, 1979.

_____. "Idiom and Translation: Some Aspects of the Son of Man Problem." *NTS* 41 (1995): 164–82.

Clements, R. E. *Isaiah 1–39.* Grand Rapids MI: Eerdmans; London: Marshall, Morgan, and Scott, 1980.

Cohen, Shaye D. *Josephus in Galilee and Rome: His Vita and Development as a Historian.* Columbia Studies in the Classical Tradition 7. Leiden: E. J. Brill, 1979.

Cohn, Norman. *The Pursuit of the Millennium: Revolutionary Millenarians and Mystical Anarchists of the Middle Ages.* Revised edition. Oxford: Oxford University Press, 1970.

Collins, Adela Yarbro. *Crisis and Catharsis: The Power of the Apocalypse.* Philadelphia: Westminster Press, 1984.

_____. *The Combat Myth in the Book of Revelation.* Missoula MT: Scholars Press for the Harvard Theological Review, 1976.

_____. "Feminine Symbolism in the Book of Revelation." *Biblical Interpretation* 1 (1993): 21–33.

_____. "Introduction: Early Christian Apocalypticism." *Semeia* 36 (1986): 1–11.

_____. "The Origin of the Designation of Jesus as the 'Son of Man.' " *HTR* 80 (1987): 391–407.

_____. "The Political Perspective of the Revelation to John." *JBL* 96 (1977): 241–256.

_____. "Revelation 18: Taunt-Song or Dirge?" In *L'Apocalypse johannique et l'Apocalyptique dans le Noveau Testament,* edited by J. Lambrecht, 185–204. BETL 53. Leuven: J. Duculot, 1980.

_____. Review of *The Book of Revelation: Apocalypse and Empire,* by Leonard Thompson. *JBL* 110 (1991): 748–50.

Collins, John J. *The Apocalyptic Imagination: An Introduction to the Jewish Matrix of Christianity.* New York: Crossroad, 1992.

_____. *Apocalypticism in the Dead Sea Scrolls.* London: Routledge, 1997.

_____. *Daniel*. Hermeneia. Minneapolis: Augsburg/Fortress, 1993.

_____. "Introduction: Towards the Morphology of a Genre." *Semeia* 14 (1979): 1–19.

_____. *The Scepter and the Star: The Messiahs of the Dead Sea Scrolls and Other Ancient Literature*. AB Reference Library. New York: Doubleday, 1995.

_____. *The Sibylline Oracles of Egyptian Judaism*. SBLDS 13. Missoula MT: Scholars, 1974.

_____. "The Son of Man in First-Century Judaism." *NTS* 38 (1992): 448–66.

_____. "Testaments." In *Jewish Writings of the Second Temple Period*, edited by Michael E. Stone, 349–54. CRINT2.2. Assen: Van Gorcum; Philadelphia: Fortress Press, 1984.

Countryman, L. William. *The Rich Christian in the Church of the Early Empire: Contradictions and Accommodations*. New York and Toronto: Edwin Mellen, 1980.

Cranfield, C. E. B. *The Gospel according to St. Mark*. CGTC. Cambridge: Cambridge University Press, 1959.

Cross, Frank M. *Canaanite Myth and Epic*. Cambridge MA: Harvard University Press, 1973.

Cruz, Virgil P. "The Beatitudes of the Apocalypse: Eschatology and Ethics." In *Perspectives on Christology: Essays in Honor of Paul K. Jewett*, edited by M. Shuster and R. Muller, 269–83. Grand Rapids MI: Zondervan, 1991.

D'Arms, John. *Commerce and Social Standing in Ancient Rome*. Cambridge: Harvard University Press, 1981.

Dalton, William J. *Christ's Proclamation to the Spirits: A Study of 1 Peter 3:18–4:6*. Second edition. AnBib 23. Rome: Editrice Pontificio Istituo Biblico, 1989.

Davis, Ellen F. *Swallowing the Scroll: Textuality and the Dynamics of Discourse in Ezekiel's Prophecy*. JSOTSup 78. Sheffield UK: Almond, 1989.

Dawson, David. *Allegorical Readers and Cultural Revision in Ancient Alexandria*. Berkeley, Los Angeles, and London: University of California Press, 1992.

Deichgräber, Reinhard. *Gotteshymnus und Christushymnus in der frühen Christenheit*. Göttingen: Vandenhoeck & Ruprecht, 1967.

deSilva, David. "The Revelation to John: A Case Study in Apocalyptic Propaganda and the Maintenance of Sectarian Identity." *Sociological Analysis* 53 (1992): 375–95.

Diefenbach, Manfred. "Die 'Offenbarung des Johannes' offenbart, daß der Seher Johannes die antike Rhetoriklehre kennt." *Biblische Notizen* 73 (1994): 50–57.

Dill, Samuel. *Roman Society from Nero to Marcus Aurelius*. New York: MacMillan, 1905.

Dimant, Devorah. "The Biography of Enoch and the Books of Enoch." *VT* 33 (1983): 14–29.

Donfried, Karl P., editor. *The Romans Debate*. Minneapolis: Augsburg, 1977. Revised edition. Peabody MA: Hendrickson, 1991.

Dougherty, James. "Exiles in the Earthly City: The Heritage of Saint Augustine." In *Civitas: Religious Interpretations of the City*, edited by Peter S. Hawkins, 105–21. Atlanta: Scholars Press, 1986.

Downing, F. Gerald. "Cynics and Early Christianity." In *Le Cynisme ancien et ses prolongements. Actes du colloque international du CNRS*, edited by Marie-Odile Goulet-Cazé and Richard Goulet, 281–304. Paris: Presses Universitaires de France, 1993.

Draper, Jonathan A. "The Development of 'the Sign of the Son of Man' in the Jesus tradition." *NTS* 39 (1993): 1–22.

Dudley, Donald R. *A History of Cynicism.* London: Methuen & Co., 1937.

Duncan-Jones, Richard. *The Economy of the Roman Empire: Quantitative Studies.* Second edition. Cambridge: Cambridge University Press, 1974, 1982.

Eagleton, Terry. *Literary Theory: An Introduction.* Minneapolis: University of Minnesota Press, 1983.

Eco, Umberto. *The Role of the Reader: Explorations in the Semiotics of Texts.* Bloomington and London: Indiana University Press, 1979.

Ellul, Jacques. *Apocalypse: The Book of Revelation.* Translated by G. W. Schreiner. New York: Crossroad/Seabury, 1977.

Farrer, Austin. *A Rebirth of Images: The Making of St John's Apocalypse.* Boston: Beacon; London: Westminster, Dacre; orig. Glasgow UK: University Press, 1949.

Fekkes, Jan III. "'His Bride has Prepared Herself': Revelation 19–21 and Isaian Nuptial Imagery." *JBL* 109 (1990): 269–87.

_____. *Isaiah and Prophetic Traditions in the Book of Revelation.* JSNTSup 93. Sheffield: JSOT Press, 1994.

Feldman, Louis H. "A Selective Critical Bibliography of Josephus." In *Josephus, the Bible, and History*, edited by L. H. Feldman and G. Hata, 330–448. Detroit: Wayne State University Press, 1988.

Ferguson, John. "Seneca the Man." In *Neronians and Flavians: Silver Latin I*, edited by D. R. Dudley, 1–23. London and Boston: Routledge & Kegan Paul, 1972.

Finley, M. I. *The Ancient Economy.* Sather Classical Lectures 43. Berkeley and Los Angeles: University of California Press, 1985.

Finley, M. I., editor. *Studies in Ancient Society.* London and Boston: Routledge and Kegan Paul, 1974.

Fiorenza, Elisabeth Schüssler. *The Book of Revelation: Justice and Judgment.* Philadelphia: Fortress Press, 1984.

_____. *Priester für Gott: Studien zum Herrschafts- und Priestermotiv in der Apokalypse.* NTAbh n.s. 7. Münster: Aschendorff, 1972.

_____. "Reading Revelation 17–18." Paper presented at the annual meeting of the Society of Biblical Literature, San Francisco, November 1997.

Fitzgerald, John J. *Cracks in an Earthen Vessel: An Examination of the Catalogues of Hardships in the Corinthian Correspondence.* SBLDS 99. Atlanta: Scholars Press, 1988.

Ford, J. Massyngberde. "The Heavenly Jerusalem and Orthodox Judaism." In *Donum gentilicium: New Testament Studies in Honour of David Daube*, edited by E. Bammel, C. K. Barrett, and W. D. Davies, 215–26. Oxford: Clarendon/Oxford University Press, 1978.

_____. "The Jewel of Discernment." *BZ* n.s. 11 (1967): 109–16.

Frank, Tenney, editor. *An Economic Survey of Ancient Rome.* Four volumes. New York: Octagon Books, 1975. Orig.: Baltimore: Johns Hopkins University Press, 1938.

Frei, Hans. *The Eclipse of Biblical Narrative.* New Haven: Yale University Press, 1974.

Friedländer, Ludwig. *Roman Life and Manners under the Early Empire.* Four volumes. Translated by J. H. Freese and A. B. Gough. London: Routledge; New York: E. P. Dutton, 1913.

Friesen, Steven J. *Twice Neokoros: Ephesus, Asia and the Cult of the Flavian Imperial Family.* Religions in the Graeco-Roman World (formerly EPRO) 116. Leiden, New York, and Köln: E. J. Brill, 1993.

Frischer, Bernard. *The Sculpted Word: Epicureanism and Philosophical Recruitment in Ancient Greece.* Berkeley: University of California Press, 1982.

Frum, David. "Welcome, Noveaux Riches." *New York Times.* 14 August 1995.

Fuchs, Harold. *Der geistige Widerstand gegen Rom in der antiken Welt.* Second edition. Berlin: Walter de Gruyter, 1964; ¹1938.

Furnish, Victor P. *II Corinthians.* AB 32A. New York: Doubleday, 1984.

Gager, John. *Kingdom and Community: The Social World of Early Christianity.* Englewood Cliffs NJ: Prentice-Hall, 1975.

Garnsey, Peter. "Aspects of the Decline of the Urban Aristocracy in the Empire." *ANRW* 2/1:229–52.

_____. Review of *Commerce and Social Standing in Ancient Rome,* by John D'Arms. *CPh* 79 (1984): 85–88.

_____. "Slaves in Business." *Roma* 1 (1982): 105–108.

Garrett, Susan R. "Chaos or Community? The Social World of the Book of Revelation." Master's thesis, Princeton Theological Seminary, 1983.

_____. *The Demise of the Devil: Magic and the Demonic in Luke's Writings.* Minneapolis: Augsburg/Fortress, 1989.

_____. "The God of This World and the Affliction of Paul: 2 Cor 4:1–12." In *Greeks, Romans, and Christians: Essays in Honor of Abraham J. Malherbe,* edited by David L. Balch, Everett Ferguson, and Wayne A. Meeks, 99–117. Minneapolis: Fortress Press, 1990.

_____. "Revelation." In *The Women's Bible Commentary,* edited by Carol A. Newsom and Sharon H. Ringe, 377–82. Louisville: Westminster/John Knox; London: SPCK, 1992.

_____. "Sociology of Early Christianity." In *The Anchor Bible Dictionary,* edited by David Noel Freedman et al., 6:89–99. New York: Doubleday, 1992.

_____. "The 'Weaker Sex' in the *Testament of Job*." *JBL* 112 (1993): 55–70.

Gasper, Joseph W. *Social Ideas in the Wisdom Literature of the Old Testament.* Catholic University of America Studies in Sacred Theology second series 8. Washington DC: Catholic University of America Press, 1947.

Geertz, Clifford. *The Interpretation of Cultures.* New York: Basic Books, Harper Torchbooks, 1973.

George, Peter. "Style and Character in the Satyricon." *Arion* 5 (1966): 336–58.

The Streets of Heaven

Gill, Christopher. "The Sexual Episodes in the Satyricon." *CP* 68 (1973): 172–85.

Glasson, T. F. "The Order of Jewels in Revelation XXI, 19–20: A Theory Eliminated." *JTS* 26 (1975): 95–100.

Gleason, Maud W. *Making Men: Sophists and Self-Presentation in Ancient Rome.* Princeton: Princeton University Press, 1994.

Goulder, Michael. "Colossians and Barbelo." *NTS* 41 (1995): 601–19.

Goulet-Cazé, Marie-Oudile. *L'ascèse cynique: Un commentaire de Diogène Laërce VI 70-71.* Paris: J. Vrin, 1986.

———. "Le cynisme à l'époque impériale." *ANRW* 2/36/4:2721–2833.

———, and Richard Goulet, editors. *Le Cynisme ancien et ses prolongements. Actes du colloque international du CNRS.* Paris: Presses Universitaires de France, 1993.

Grassl, Herbert. *Sozialökonomische Vorstellungen in der kaiserzeitlichen griechischen Literatur (1.–3. Jh. N. Chr.).* Historia 41. Weisbaden: Franz Steiner, 1982.

Gray, John. *I & II Kings: A Commentary.* Second edition. OTL. Philadelphia: Westminster Press, 1970.

Greenberg, Moshe. "The Design and Themes of Ezekiel's Program of Restoration." *Int* 38 (1984): 181–208.

———. *Ezekiel 1-20.* AB 22. New York: Doubleday, 1983.

Greenfield, J. C., and Michael E. Stone. "The Enochic Pentateuch and the Date of the Similitudes." *HTR* 79 (1977): 51–65.

Gressman, H. *Vom reichen Mann und armen Lazarus: eine literargeschichtliche Studie.* Abhandlungen der königlich preussischen Akademie der Wissenschaften: Philosophisch-historische Klasse 7. Berlin: Verlag der königlich Adademie der Wissenschaft, 1918.

Griffin, Miriam T. *Seneca: A Philosopher in Politics.* Oxford: Clarendon/Oxford University Press, 1976.

Gundry, Robert H. "The New Jerusalem: People as Place, Not Place for People." *NovT* 29 (1987): 254–64.

Haas, Cees. "Job's Perseverance in the Testament of Job." In *Studies on the Testament of Job,* edited by Michael A. Knibb and Pieter W. van der Horst, 117–54. SNTSMS 66. Cambridge: Cambridge University Press, 1989.

Hahn, Ferdinand. "Die Sendschreiben der Johannesapokalypse: Ein Beitrag zur Bestimmung prophetischer Redeformer." In *Tradition und Glaube: Das frühe Christentum in seiner Umwelt,* edited by G. Jeremias, H.-W. Kuhn, and H. Steggemann, 357–94. Göttingen: Vandenhoeck & Ruprecht, 1971.

Hall, Robert G. "Living Creatures in the Midst of the Throne: Another Look at Revelation 4.6." *NTS* 36 (1990): 609–13.

Halperin, David. *The Faces of the Chariot: Early Jewish Responses to Ezekiel's Vision.* Texte und Studien zum antiken Judentum 16. Tübingen: J. C. B. Mohr (Paul Siebeck), 1988.

Hammond, N. G. L., and H. H. Scullard, editors. *The Oxford Classical Dictionary.* Second edition. Oxford: Clarendon/Oxford University Press, 1970.

Hanson, Paul D. *The Dawn of Apocalyptic.* Philadelphia: Fortress Press, 1975.

_____. "Jewish Apocalyptic against Its Near Eastern Environment." *RB* 78 (1971): 38–51.

_____. "Rebellion in Heaven, Azazel, and Euhemeristic Heroes in 1 Enoch 6–11." *JBL* 96 (1977): 195–233.

Hare, Douglas R. A. *The Son of Man Tradition.* Minneapolis: Fortress Press, 1990.

Hartman, L. "Form and Message. A Preliminary Discussion of 'Partial Texts' in Rev 1–3 and 22,6ff." In *L'Apocalypse johannique et l'Apocalyptique dans le Noveau Testament,* edited by J. Lambrecht, 129–49. BETL 53. Leuven: J. Duculot, 1980.

Hawkins, Peter S., editor. *Civitas: Religious Interpretations of the City.* Scholars Press Studies in the Humanities. Atlanta: Scholars Press, 1986.

Hays, Richard B. *Echoes of Scripture in the Letters of Paul.* New Haven CT and London: Yale University Press, 1989.

_____. *The Faith of Jesus Christ: An Investigation into the Narrative Substructure of Galatians 3:1–4:11.* SBLDS 56. Chico CA: Scholars Press, 1983.

Head, Barclay V. *Historia numorum: A Manual of Greek Numismatics.* Oxford: Clarendon/Oxford University Press, 1911. Repr.: Chicago: Argonaut, 1967.

Heiligenthal, Roman. "Wer waren die 'Nikolaiten'? Ein Beitrag zur Theologiegeschichte des frühen Christentums." *ZNW* 82 (1991): 133–37.

Hellholm, David, editor. *Apocalypticism in the Mediterranean World and the Near East.* Tubingen: J. C. B. Mohr (Paul Siebeck), 1983.

_____. "The Problem of Apocalyptic Genre and the Apocalypse of John." *Semeia* 36 (1986): 13–64.

Helm, R. "Lukianos." *PW* 13.2 (1927): 1725–77.

Hemer, Colin J. *The Letters to the Seven Churches of Asia in their Local Setting.* JSNTSup 11. Sheffield UK: JSOT Press, 1986.

Hengel, Martin. *Property and Riches in the Early Church: Aspects of a Social History of Early Christianity.* Philadelphia: Fortress Press, 1974.

Hershbell, Jackson P. "Plutarch and Stoicism." *ANRW* II/36/5 (1992): 3336–52.

Hicks, E. L., editor. *The Collection of Ancient Greek Inscriptions in the British Museum. Part Three: Priene, Iasous, and Ephesos.* Oxford: Clarendon/Oxford University Press, 1890.

Himmelfarb, Martha. *Ascent to Heaven in Jewish and Christian Apocalypses.* New York and Oxford: Oxford University Press, 1993.

_____. *Tours of Hell: An Apocalyptic Form in Jewish and Christian Literature.* Philadelphia: University of Pennsylvania Press, 1983.

Hirsch, E. D., Jr. *Validity in Interpretation.* New Haven CT: Yale University Press, 1967.

Hock, Ronald F. "Lazarus and Micyllus: Greco-Roman Backgrounds to Luke 16:19–31." *JBL* 106 (1987): 447–63.

_____. "Simon the Shoemaker as an Ideal Cynic." *GRBS* 17 (1976): 41–53.

_____. *The Social Context of Paul's Ministry: Tentmaking and Apostleship.* Philadelphia: Fortress Press, 1980.

Holladay, William L. *A Concise Hebrew and Aramaic Lexicon of the Old Testament.* Grand Rapids and Leiden: Eerdmans and E. J. Brill, 1988.

_____. *Jeremiah: A Commentary on the Book of the Prophet Jeremiah.* Two volumes. Hermeneia. Minneapolis: Fortress Press, 1986, 1989.

Holtz, T. *Die Christologie der Apokalypse des Johannes.* TU 85. Berlin: Akademie, 1962.

Hooker, M. D. "Were There False Teachers at Colossae?" In *Christ and Spirit,* 315–31. Festschrift C. F. D. Moule. Cambridge: Cambridge University Press, 1973.

Horn, Friederich Wilhelm. "Zwischen der Synagoge des Satans und dem neuen Jerusalem: Die christlich-jüdische Standortbestimmung in der Apokalypse des Johannes." *ZRGG* 46 (1994): 143–62.

Humphrey, Edith McEwan. *The Ladies and the Cities: Transformation and Apocalyptic Identity in Joseph and Aseneth, 4 Ezra, the Apocalypse and The Shepherd of Hermas.* JSPSup 17. Sheffield UK: Sheffield Academic Press, 1995.

Hurtado, L. W. "Revelation 4–5 in the Light of Jewish Apocalyptic Analogies." *JSNT* 25 (1985): 105–24.

Inwood, Brad. *Ethics and Human Action in Early Stoicism.* Oxford: Clarendon, 1985.

Iser, Wolfgang. *The Act of Reading: A Theory of Aesthetic Response.* Baltimore and London: Johns Hopkins University Press, 1978.

Jameson, Frederic R. *The Political Unconscious: Narrative as a Socially Symbolic Act.* Ithaca NY: Cornell University Press, 1982.

Jaquette, James L. "Life and Death, *adiaphora,* and Paul's Rhetorical Strategy." *NovT* 38 (1996): 30–54.

_____. "Paul, Epictetus, and Others on Indifference to Status." *CBQ* 56 (1994): 68–80.

Jart, Una. "The Precious Stones in the Revelation of St. John xxi.18–21." *ST* 24 (1970): 150–58.

Johnson, Luke T. *The Literary Function of Possessions in Luke-Acts.* SBLDS 39. Scholars Press, 1977.

_____. "The New Testament's Anti-Jewish Slander and the Conventions of Ancient Rhetoric." *JBL* 101 (1989): 419–41.

Jones, C. P. *Culture and Society in Lucian.* Cambridge MA: Harvard University Press, 1986.

_____. *The Roman World of Dio Chrysostom.* Cambridge MA: Harvard University Press, 1978.

Jones, Brian W. *The Emperor Domitian.* London : Routledge, 1992.

Jörns, Klaus-Peter. *Das hymnische Evangelium.* Gütersloh: Gerd Mohn, 1971.

Judge, Edwin A. "The Mark of the Beast, Revelation 13:16." *TynBul* 42 (1991): 158–60.

Kaiser, Otto. *Isaiah 1–12: A Commentary.* Second edition. OTL. Philadelphia: Westminster Press, 1983.

_____. *Isaiah 13–39: A Commentary.* OTL. Philadelphia: Westminster Press, 1974.

Karrer, Martin. *Die Johannesoffenbarung als Brief: Studien zu ihre literarischen, historischen und theologischen Ort.* FRLANT 140. Göttingen: Vandenhoeck & Ruprecht, 1986.

Kee, Howard Clark. "The Transformation of the Synagogue after 70 C.E.: Its Import for Early Christianity." *NTS* 36 (1990): 1–24.

Kennedy, George A. *Greek Rhetoric under Christian Emperors.* Princeton NJ: Princeton University Press, 1983.

_____. *New Testament Interpretation through Rhetorical Criticism.* Chapel Hill and London: University of North Carolina Press, 1984.

Kerkeslager, Allen. "Apollo, Greco-Roman Prophecy, and the Rider on the White Horse in Rev 6:2." *JBL* 112 (1993): 116–21.

Kermode, Frank. *The Sense of an Ending: Studies in the Theory of Fiction.* Oxford: Oxford University Press, 1966, 1967.

Kidd, Reggie M. *Wealth and Beneficence in the Pastoral Epistles: A "bourgeois" form of early Christianity?* SBLDS 122. Atlanta: Scholars Press, 1990.

Kirby, John T. "The Rhetorical Situations of Revelation 1-3." *NTS* 34 (1988): 197–207.

Klauser, Theodor. "Aurum Coronarium." In *Gesammelte Arbeiten zur Liturgiegeschichte, Kirchengeschichte, und christlichen Archäologie,* edited by E. Dassman, 292–309. JAC Ergänsungsband 3. Münster: Aschendorffsche, 1974.

Koester, Helmut. "GNOMAI DIAPHORAI: The Origin and Nature of Diversification in the History of Early Christianity." In *Trajectories through Early Christianity,* edited by James M. Robinson and Helmut Koester, 114–57. Philadelphia: Fortress Press, 1971.

Kraabel, A. T. "Paganism and Judaism: The Sardis Evidence." In *Paganisme, Judaïsme, Christianisme: Influences et affrontements dans le monde antique,* edited by A. Benoit, M. Philonenko, and C. Vogel, 13–33. Mélanges offerts à Marcel Simon; Paris: de Baccard, 1978.

_____. "The Diaspora Synagogue: Archaeological and Epigraphic Evidence since Sukenik." *ANRW* 2/19/1:477–510.

Kraft, Robert A. "Septuagint." In *The Interpreter's Dictionary of the Bible,* Supplementary Volume, edited by Keith Crim et al., 807–15. Nashville: Abingdon Press, 1976.

Lafaye, G., editor. *Inscriptiones Graecae ad Res Romanas Pertinentes.* Four volumes. Paris: Ernest Leroux, 1927.

Lausberg, Heinrich. *Handbuch zum literarischen Rhetorik: Ein Grundlegung der Literaturwissenschaft.* Two volumes. Munich: Max Hueber, 1960.

Lawrence, D. H. *Apocalypse and the Writings on Revelation.* Edited by M. Kalnins. Cambridge: Cambridge University Press, 1980.

Layton, Bentley. "The Significance of Basilides in Ancient Christian Thought." *Representations* 28 (1989): 135–51.

Le Bas, P., and W. H. Waddington. *Voyage archélogique en Grece et en Asie Mineure.* Three volumes. Paris, 1870.

Lenski, Gerhard E. "Status Crystallization: A Nonvertical Dimension of Social Status." In *Sociology: The Progress of a Decade,* edited by S. M. Lipset and N. Smelser, 485–94. Englewood Cliffs NJ: Prentice-Hall, 1961. Orig.: *American Sociological Review* 19 (1954): 405–13.

Lewis, James R., editor. *From the Ashes: Making Sense of Waco.* Lanham MD: Roman & Littlefield, 1994.

Liddell, Henry George, and Robert Scott. *A Greek-English Lexicon.* Ninth edition, revised by Henry Stuart Jones, Roderick McKenzie, et al. Oxford: Clarendon/Oxford University Press, 1940.

Lieberman, Saul. "On Sins and their Punishments." In *Texts and Studies,* 33–48. New York: Ktav, 1974.

Lipset, Seymour. "Social Class." In *International Encyclopedia of the Social Sciences,* edited by David L. Sills, 15:296–31. New York: MacMillan and Free Press, 1968.

Lohse, Eduard. *Colossians and Philemon.* Hermeneia. Philadelphia: Fortress Press, 1971.

Long, A. A. *Hellenistic Philosophy.* Second edition. Berkeley and Los Angeles: University of California Press, 1986.

MacMullen, Ramsay. *Enemies of the Roman Order: Treason, Unrest, and Alienation in the Empire.* Cambridge MA: Harvard University Press, 1966.

_____. *Roman Social Relations, 50 B.C. to A.D. 284.* New Haven CT: Yale University Press, 1974.

Magie, David. *Roman Rule in Asia Minor: To the End of the Third Century after Christ.* Two volumes. Princeton NJ: Princeton University Press, 1950.

Maier, Gerhard. *Die Johannesoffenbarung und die Kirche.* WUNT 25. Tübingen: J. C. B. Mohr (Paul Siebeck), 1981.

Malherbe, Abraham J. "Cynics." In *The Interpreter's Dictionary of the Bible,* Supplementary Volume, edited by Keith Crim et al., 201–203. Nashville: Abingdon Press, 1976.

_____. "Gentle as a Nurse: The Cynic Background to I Thess ii." *NovT* 12 (1970): 203–17.

_____. *Moral Exhortation: A Greco-Roman Sourcebook.* Library of Early Christianity 4. Philadelphia: Westminster Press, 1986.

_____. "Self-definition Among Epicureans and Cynics." In *Jewish and Christian Self-Definition. Volume Three: Self-Definition in the Greco-Roman World,* edited by Ben F. Meyer and E. P. Sanders, 46–59. Philadelphia: Fortress Press, 1982.

_____. *Social Aspects of Early Christianity.* Second edition. Philadelphia: Fortress Press, 1983.

Martens, John W. "Romans 2.14–16: A Stoic Reading." *NTS* 40 (1994): 55–67.

Martin, Troy W. *Metaphor and Composition in 1 Peter.* SBLDS 131. Atlanta: Scholars Press, 1992.

Martin, Dale B. *Slavery as Salvation: The Metaphor of Slavery in Pauline Christianity.* New Haven CT and London: Yale University Press, 1990.

_____. "Tongues of Angels and Other Status Indicators." *JAAR* 59 (1991): 547–89.

_____. Review of *Echoes of Scripture in the Letters of Paul,* by Richard B. Hays. *Modern Theology* 7 (1991): 291–92.

Martin-Achard, R. "Esaïe 47 et la tradition prophétique sur Babylone." In *Prophecy: Essays Presented to Georg Fohrer on his Sixty-Fifth Birthday,* edited by J. A. Emerton, 83–105. BZAW 150. Berlin: de Gruyter, 1980.

Martyn, J. Louis. *History and Theology in the Fourth Gospel.* Second edition. Nashville: Abingdon Press, 1968.

Maxfield, Valerie A. *The Military Decorations of the Roman Army*. Berkeley and Los Angeles: University of California Press, 1981.

McMurtry, Larry. "Return to Waco." *The New Republic*. 7 June 1993, 16–19.

Meeks, Wayne A. *The First Urban Christians: The Social World of the Apostle Paul*. New Haven CT: Yale University Press, 1983.

————. "A Hermeneutics of Social Embodiment." *HTR* 79 (1986): 176–86.

————. *The Moral World of the First Christians*. Library of Early Christianity 6. Philadelphia: Westminster Press, 1986.

————. "'And Rose up to Play': Midrash and Paraenesis in 1 Corinthians 10:1–22." *JSNT* 16 (1982): 64–78.

————. "St. Paul of the Cities." In *Civitas: Religious Interpretations of the City*, edited by Peter S. Hawkins, 15–23. Atlanta: Scholars Press, 1986.

Meijer, Fik and Onno van Nijf. *Trade, Transport and Society in the Ancient World*. London: Routledge, 1992.

Michaels, J. Ramsay. "Revelation 1.19 and the Narrative Voices of the Apocalypse." *NTS* 37 (1991): 604–20.

Millar, Fergus. *The Emperor in the Roman World, 31 BC–AD 337*. Ithaca: Cornell University Press, 1977.

Milner, Murray Jr. "Status and Sacredness: Worship and Salvation as Forms of Status Transformation." *JSSR* 33 (1994): 99–109.

Minear, Paul. *I Saw a New Earth: an Introduction to the Visions of the Apocalypse*. Washington DC: Corpus Books, 1968.

Momigliano, A. "M. I. Rostovtzeff." In *Studies in Historiography*, 91–104. London: Weidenfeld and Nicolson, 1966. Orig.: *The Cambridge Journal* 7 (1954): 334–46.

————. "Some Preliminary Remarks on the 'Religious Opposition' to the Roman Empire." In *On Pagans, Jews, and Christians*, 120–41. Middletown CT: Wesleyan University Press, 1987.

Moore, Carey A. "Tobit." In *The Anchor Bible Dictionary*, edited by David Noel Freedman et al., 6:585–54. New York: Doubleday, 1992.

Moore, Stephen D. "Are the Gospels Unified Narratives?" *SBLSP* (1987): 443–58.

————. "The Beatific Vision as a Posing Exhibition: Revelation's Hyper-masculine Deity." *JSNT* 60 (1995): 27–55.

Morray-Jones, C. R. A. "Paradise Revisited (2 Cor 12:1–12): The Jewish Mystical Background of Paul's Apostolate." *HTR* 86 (1993): 177–217, 265–92.

————. "Transformational Mysticism in the Apocalyptic-Merkabah Tradition." *JJS* 43 (1992): 1–31.

Moyise, Steve. *The Old Testament in the Book of Revelation*. JSNTSup 115. Sheffield UK: Sheffield Academic Press, 1995.

Müller, Ulrich B. *Prophetie und Predigt im Neuen Testament: Formgeschichte-liche Untersuchungen zur urchristlichen Prophetie*. Studien zum Neuen Testament 10. Gütersloh: Gütersloh Verlagshaus Mohn, 1975.

————. *Zur frühchristlichen Theologiegeschichte: Judenchristentum und Paulinismus in Kleinasien an der Wende vom ersten zum zweiten Jahrhundert n. Chr.* Gütersloh: Gütersloh Verlagshaus Mohn, 1976.

Mussies, G. *The Morphology of Koine Greek as Used in the Apocalypse of John.* NovTSup 27. Leiden: E. J. Brill, 1971.

Newman, B. M. *Rediscovering the Book of Revelation.* Valley Forge PA: Judson Press, 1968.

Newsom, Carol A. "The Development of *1 Enoch* 6-19: Cosmology and Judgment." *CBQ* 42 (1980): 310–29.

Nickelsburg, George W. E. "Apocalyptic and Myth in 1 Enoch 6–11." *JBL* 96 (1977): 383–405.

_____. *Jewish Literature Between the Bible and the Mishnah: A Historical and Literary Introduction.* Philadelphia: Fortress Press, 1981.

_____. "Riches, the Rich, and God's Judgment in 1 Enoch 92-105 and the Gospel according to Luke." *NTS* 25 (1979): 324–44.

Niditch, Susan. "Ezekiel 40–48 in a Visionary Context." *CBQ* 48 (1986): 208–24.

O'Neil, Edward. "De cupidatate divitiarum (Moralia 523C–528B)." In *Plutarch's Ethical Writings and Early Christian Literature,* edited by Hans Dieter Betz, 289–362. SCHNT 4. Leiden: E. J. Brill, 1978.

Osiek, Carolyn. *Rich and Poor in the Shepherd of Hermas: An Exegetical-Social Investigation.* CBQMS 15. Washington DC: Catholic Biblical Association of America, 1983.

Pascal, Roy. "Narrative Fictions and Reality: A Comment on Frank Kermode's *The Sense of an Ending.*" *Novel* 11 (1977): 40–50.

Paulien, Jon. *Decoding Revelation's Trumpets: Literary Allusions and Interpretations of Revelation 8:7–12. AUSS* 11. Berrien Springs MI: Andrews University Press, 1988.

Perrin, Norman. "Mark 14:62: The End Product of a Christian Pesher Tradition?" In *A Modern Pilgrimage in New Testament Christology,* 10–22. Philadelphia: Fortress Press, 1974.

Petersen, Norman. *Rediscovering Paul: Philemon and the Sociology of Paul's Narrative World.* Philadelphia: Fortress Press, 1985.

Pfister, F. "Epiphanie." *PWSup* 277–323.

Pippin, Tina. *Death and Desire: The Rhetoric of Gender in the Apocalypse of John.* Louisville: Westminster/John Knox, 1993.

_____. "Eros and the End: Reading for Gender in the Apocalypse of John." *Semeia* 59 (1992): 193–210.

Pleket, H. "Urban elites and business in the Greek part of the Roman Empire." In *Trade in the Ancient Economy* edited by P. Garnsey, K. Hopkins, and C. R. Whittaker, 131–44. Berkeley: University of California Press, 1983.

Porter, Stanley E. "The Argument of Romans 5: Can a Rhetorical Question Make a Difference?" *JBL* 110 (1991): 655–77.

Price, S. R. F. *Rituals and Power: The Roman imperial cult in Asia Minor.* Cambridge: Cambridge University Press, 1984.

Radt, S. L. "Zu Epiktets *Diatriben.*" *Mnemosyne* 43 (1990): 364–73.

Ramsay, William Mitchell. *The Letters to the Seven Churches of Asia and Their Place in the Plan of the Apocalypse.* Edited by Mark W. Wilson. Peabody MA: Hendrickson Publishers, 1994. Repr.: Minneapolis: James Family Pub.

Co., 1978. Orig.: London: Hodder & Stoughton, 1904; New York: A. C. Armstrong, 1904.

Reader, William W. "The Twelve Jewels of Revelation 21:19–20: Tradition History and Modern Interpretations." *JBL* 100 (1981): 433–57.

Reichelt, Hansgüter. *Angelus interpres-Texte in der Johannes-Apokalypse.* Europäische Hochschulschriften 23:507. Frankfurt: Peter Lang, 1994.

Rensberger, David K. *Johannine Faith and Liberating Community.* Philadelphia: Westminster Press, 1988.

Richlin, Amy. *The Garden of Priapus: Sexuality and Aggression in Roman Humor.* Revised edition. New Haven CT: Yale University Press, 1992.

Rist, John M. "Seneca and Stoic Orthodoxy." *ANRW* II/36/3 (1989): 1994–95.

Rogers, Guy M. *The Sacred Identity of Ephesos: Foundation Myths of a Roman City.* London and New York: Routledge, 1991.

Rose, Kenneth. "Time and Place in the Satyricon." *TAPA* 93 (1962): 402–409.

Rostovtzeff, M. *The Social and Economic History of the Roman Empire.* Two volumes. Second edition, revised by P. M. Fraser. Oxford: Clarendon/Oxford University Press, 1957.

Rowland, Christopher. C. "Apocalyptic, the Poor, and the Gospel of Matthew." *JTS* n.s. 45 (1994): 504–18.

_____. *The Open Heaven: A Study of Apocalyptic in Judaism and Early Christianity.* New York: Crossroad, 1982.

Royalty, Robert M., Jr. "The Streets of Heaven: The Imagery and Ideology of Wealth in the Apocalypse of John." Ph.D. diss., Yale University, 1995. Abstract in *Dissertations Abstracts International* 57-01A.

_____. "The Rhetoric of Revelation." *SBLSP* (1997): 596–617.

_____. "Dwelling on Visions: On the Nature of the so-called 'Colossians Heresy.'" Paper presented at the annual meeting of the Society of Biblical Literature, San Francisco, November 1997.

Rudberg, Gunnar. "Zu den Sendschreiben der Johannes-Apokalypse." *Eranos* 11 (1911): 170–79.

Rudwick, M. J. S. and E. M. B. Green. "The Laodicean Lukewarmness." *ExpTim* 69 (1957–8): 176–78.

Ruiz, Jean-Pierre. *Ezekiel in the Apocalypse: The Transformation of Prophetic Language in Revelation 16,17–19,10.* Europäische Hochschulschriften 23:376. Frankfurt: Peter Lang, 1989.

Sandbach, Francis Henry. *The Stoics.* Second edition. Bristol UK: Bristol; London: G. Duckworth; Indianapolis: Hackett, 1989.

Sanders, J. T. "The Transition from the Opening Epistolary Thanksgiving to the Body in the Letters of the Pauline Corpus." *JBL* 81 (1962): 348–62.

Schmidt, Thomas E. *Hostility to Wealth in the Synoptic Gospels.* JSNTSup 15. Sheffield UK: JSOT Press, 1987.

Schmithals, Walter. "The *Corpus Paulinum* and Gnosis." In *The New Testament and Gnosis. Essays in Honour of Robert McL. Wilson,* edited by A. H. B. Logan and A. J. M. Wedderburn, 107–24. Edinburgh: T. & T. Clark, 1983.

Schoedel, William R. *Ignatius of Antioch.* Hermeneia. Philadelphia: Fortress Press, 1985.

Scholem, Gershom G. *Jewish Gnosticism, Merkabah Mysticism, and Talmudic Tradition*. Second edition. New York: Jewish Theological Seminary, 1965.

Schubert, Paul. *Form and Function of the Pauline Thanksgivings*. Berlin: Alfred Töplemann, 1939.

Schütz, John. Introduction to *The Social Setting of Pauline Christianity*, by Gerd Theissen. Philadelphia: Fortress Press, 1982.

Scobie, Charles H. H. "Local References in the Letters to the Seven Churches." *NTS* 39 (1993): 606–24.

Sherwin-White, A. N. E. "Early Persecutions and Roman Law Again." *JTS* n.s. 3 (1952): 199–213.

————. "Why Were the Early Christians Persecuted? An Amendment." In *Studies in Ancient Society*, edited by M. I. Finley, 250–55. London and Boston: Routledge and Kegan Paul, 1974.

Silberman, Lou H. "Farewell to O AMHN." *JBL* 82 (1963): 213–15.

Slater, Thomas B. "*Homoion huion anthropou* in Rev. 1.13 and 14.14." *BT* 44 (1993): 359–60.

————. "One Like a Son of Man in First-Century CE Judaism." *NTS* 41 (1995): 183–98.

Smith, Christopher R. "The Structure of the Book of Revelation in Light of Apocalyptic Literary Conventions." *NovT* 36 (1994): 373–93.

Smith, Morton. "Relations between Magical Papyri and Magical Gems." *Papyrological Bruxellensia* 18 (1979): 129–36.

Smith, Jonathan Z. "Jerusalem: The City as Place." In *Civitas: Religious Interpretations of the City*, edited by Peter S. Hawkins, 25–38. Atlanta: Scholars Press, 1986.

————. "Wisdom and Apocalyptic." In *Visionaries and their Apocalypses*, edited by Paul D. Hanson, 101–20. IRT 4. Philadelphia: Fortress Press; London: SPCK, 1983.

Smyth, Herbert Weir. *Greek Grammar*. Revised by Gordon M. Messing. Cambridge: Harvard University Press, 1984; orig. 1916, 1920.

Spittler, Russell P. "The Testament of Job: Research and Interpretation." In *Studies on the Testament of Job*, edited by Michael A. Knibb and Pieter W. van der Horst, 7–32. SNTSMS 66. Cambridge: Cambridge University Press, 1989.

Staden, Heinrich von. "Hairesis and Heresy: The Case of the 'haireseis iatrikai.'" In *Jewish and Christian Self-Definition: Self-Definition in the Greco-Roman World*, edited by Ben F. Meyer and E. P. Sanders, 3:76–100. London: SCM, 1982.

Ste. Croix, G. E. M. de. *The Class Struggle in the Ancient Greek World*. Ithaca NY: Cornell University Press, 1981.

————. "Why Were the Christians Persecuted?" *Past and Present* 26 (1963): 6–38. Repr.: In *Studies in Ancient Society*, edited by M. I. Finley, 210–49. London and Boston: Routledge and Kegan Paul, 1974.

————. "Why Were the Christians Persecuted?—A Rejoinder." *Past and Present* 27 (1964): 28–33. Repr.: In *Studies in Ancient Society*, edited by M. I. Finley, 256–62. London and Boston: Routledge and Kegan Paul, 1974.

Stendhal, Krister. "Biblical Theology." In *The Interpreter's Dictionary of the Bible*, edited by George Arthur Buttrick et al. A–D:418–32. Nashville: Abingdon Press, 1962.

Stevenson, Gregory M. "Conceptual Background to Golden Crown Imagery in the Apocalypse of John (4:4, 10. 14:14)." *JBL* 114 (1995): 259–60.

Stone, Michael E. "Apocalyptic Literature." In *Jewish Writings of the Second Temple Period*, edited by M. E. Stone, 383–441. CRINT2.2. Assen: Van Gorcum; Philadelphia: Fortress Press, 1984.

_____. "The Book of Enoch and Judaism in the Third Century, B.C.E." *CBQ* 40 (1978): 479–92.

_____. "Enoch, Aramaic Levi and Sectarian Origins." *JSJ* 19 (1988): 159–70.

_____. *Fourth Ezra*. Hermeneia. Minneapolis: Augsburg/Fortress, 1990.

_____. "Reactions to Destructions of the Second Temple: Theology, Perception and Conversion." *JSJ* 12 (1981): 195–204.

_____. *Scriptures, Sects and Visions: A Profile of Judaism from Ezra to the Jewish Revolts*. Philadelphia: Fortress Press, 1980.

Stone, Michael E., editor. *Jewish Writings of the Second Temple Period*. CRINT2.2. Assen: Van Gorcum; Philadelphia: Fortress Press, 1984.

Stowers, Stanley K. *The Diatribe and Paul's Letter to the Romans*. SBLDS 57. Chico, CA: Scholars Press, 1981.

_____. *Letter Writing in Greco-Roman Antiquity*. Library of Early Christianity 5. Philadelphia: Westminster Press, 1986.

_____. *A Rereading of Romans: Justice, Jews, and Gentiles*. New Haven: Yale University Press, 1994.

_____. Review of *Paulus und die "Diatribe": Eine vergleichende Stilinterpretation*, by Thomas Schmeller. *JBL* 108 (1989): 538–42.

Strand, Kenneth. "The 'Spotlight-On-Last-Events' Sections in the Book of Revelation." *AUSS* 27 (1989): 201–21.

Sullivan, J. P. "On Translating Petronius." In *Neronians and Flavians: Silver Latin I*, edited by D. R. Dudley, 155–83. London and Boston: Routledge & Kegan Paul, 1972.

Sundberg, A. C. Jr. "Canon of the NT." In *The Interpreter's Dictionary of the Bible*, Supplementary Volume, edited by Keith Crim et al., 136–40. Nashville: Abingdon Press, 1976.

Tabor, James D. "The Waco Tragedy: An Autobiographical Account of One Attempt to Avert Disaster." In *From the Ashes: Making Sense of Waco*, edited by James R. Lewis, 13–21. Lanhmam MD: Rowman & Littlefield, 1994.

_____. "Religious Discourse and Failed Negotiations: The Dynamics of Biblical Apocalypticism in Waco." In *Armageddon in Waco*, edited by Stuart A. Wright, 263–81. Chicago: University of Chicago Press, 1995.

_____ and Eugene V. Gallagher. *Why Waco? Cults and the Battle for Religious Freedom in America*. Berkeley: University of California Press, 1995.

Taylor, Vincent. *The Gospel according to Mark*. London: MacMillan & Co., 1952.

Theissen, Gerd. *The Social Setting of Pauline Christianity*. Translated by John Schütz. Philadelphia: Fortress Press, 1982.

Thompson, Leonard. *The Book of Revelation: Apocalypse and Empire.* New York: Oxford University Press, 1990.

————. "The Literary Unity of the Book of Revelation." In *Mappings of the Biblical Terrain: The Bible as Text (= Bucknell Review* 33/2), edited by V. L. Tollers and J. Maier, 347–63. Lewisburg PA: Bucknell University Press; London and Toronto: Associated University Presses, 1990.

Thompson, Steven. *The Apocalypse and Semitic Syntax.* Cambridge: Cambridge University Press, 1985.

Thüsing, W. "Die Vision des 'Neuen Jerusalem' (Apk 21, 1–22, 5) als Verheissung und Gottesverkündigun." *TTZ* (1968): 17–34.

Topham, Michael. "The Dimensions of the New Jerusalem." *ExpTim* 100 (1989): 417–19.

Treggiari, Susan. *Roman Freedmen During the Late Republic.* Oxford: Clarendon/Oxford University Press, 1969.

Trites, Allison A. "Μάρτυς and Martyrdom in the Apocalypse: A Semantic Study." *NovT* 15 (1973): 72–80.

Tuell, Steven Shawn. *The Law of the Temple in Ezekiel 40–48.* HSM 49. Atlanta: Scholars Press, 1992.

Unnik, W. C. van. "'Worthy Is the Lamb: The Background of Apoc 5." In *Mélanges bibliques en hommage au R. P. Béda Rigaux*, edited by A. Descamps and A. de Halleux, 445–61. Gembloux: Ducolot, 1970.

Vanni, Ugo. "Liturgical Dialogue as a Literary Form in the Book of Revelation." *NTS* 37 (1991): 348–72.

Vermaseren, M. J. editor. *Die orientalischen Religionen im Römerreich.* EPRO 93. Leiden: Brill, 1981.

Veyne, Paul. "Le 'je' dans le Satiricon." *REL* 42 (1964): 301–24.

————. "Vie de Trimalcion." *Annales (ESC)* 16 (1961): 214–15.

Vos, Louis A. *The Synoptic Traditions in the Apocalypse.* Kampen: J. H. Kok, 1965.

Wainright, Arthur W. *Mysterious Apocalypse: Interpreting the Book of Revelation.* Nashville: Abingdon Press, 1993.

Wald, Kenneth D., Dennis E. Owen, and Samuel S. Hill, Jr. "Evangelical Politics and Status Issues." *JSSR* 28 (1989): 1–16.

Watson, Duane F. "James 2 in Light of Greco-Roman Schemes of Argumentation." *NTS* 39 (1993): 94–121.

Watts, James W. "Text and Redaction in Jeremiah's Oracles Against the Nations." *CBQ* 54 (1992): 432–47.

Weiss, H.-F. "Gnostische Motive und antignostische Polemik im Kolossser- und im Epheser-brief." In *Gnosis und Neues Testament*, edited by K.-W. Tröger, 311–24. Gütersloh: Mohn, 1973.

Westermann, Claus. *Isaiah 40–66: A Commentary.* OTL. Philadelphia: Westminster Press, 1969.

Wheeler, Sondra Ely. *Wealth as Peril and Obligation: The New Testament on Possessions.* Grand Rapids MI: Eerdmans, 1995.

White, Hayden. *Tropics of Discourse: Essays in Cultural Criticism.* Baltimore and London: Johns Hopkins University Press, 1978.

White, Nicholas P. "Stoic Values." *The Monist* 73 (1990): 42–58.

Wilkinson, Richard H. "The ΣΤΥΛΟΣ of Revelation 3:12 and Ancient Coronation Rites." *JBL* 107 (1987): 498–501.

Wilson, Robert R. "The City in the Old Testament." In *Civitas: Religious Interpretations of the City*, edited by Peter S. Hawkins, 3–13. Atlanta: Scholars Press, 1986.

Wisse, Frederik. "The Epistle of Jude in the History of Heresiology." In *Essays on the Nag Hammadi Texts in Honour of Alexander Böhlig*, edited by M. Krause, 133–43. Leiden: E. J. Brill, 1972.

Yadin, Yigael. *The Scroll of the War of the Sons of Light against the Sons of Darkness*. Oxford: Oxford University Press, 1962.

_____. *The Temple Scroll*. Jerusalem: Israel Exploration Society, 1983.

Zimmerli, Walther. *Ezekiel*. Two volumes. Hermeneia. Philadelphia: Fortress Press, 1979 and 1983.

Indexes

Index of Modern Authors

Subject Index

in Revelation, 187-88, 195-97, 211-39
Restoration of , 72-76, 80, 195, 234
Wealth of, 73, 80, 211
Jesus,
as Cynic, 88n.20, 236
as wealthy, 96n.46
miracles of, 132
Jews, 35n.107, in Sardis, 35; *see also*
Christianity, early, and Jews
Jezebel, 28, 29n.85, 31-33, 161, 164, 164n.36,
167, 210, 231
in 1 Kings, 47n.21
John of Patmos, 17-18, 30, 134n.25, 138, 152,
153, 218, 220
as prophet, 17-18, 134n.26, 143, 146
Justin Martyr, 36, 83

Kata phusin (according to nature), 84-87, 89-90,
208
Kings of the earth, 141-42, 148-49, 182, 189,
193-94n.49, 199, 204-205
Koresh, David, 12

Laodicea, 19, 26, 68n.85, 96, 97n. 48, 110n.102,
112-13, 123, 152-53, 158n.23, 242-43
Attitude toward wealth, 88-89, 164-76, 210,
228
Letter writing, in early Christianity, 17
Literary criticism, 6-11, 31-32
Living creatures, four, 49-50
Lucian, 85n.10, 92-93, 112, 112n.107, 120-23,
174, 177, 208-209, 235
Luxury items, 95, in Rome, 121-23, 206-207

Magic, in Revelation, 149n.62, 229, 229-30n.55
Marcus Aurelius, 112
Mark of the Beast, 183-87
Martyrdom, 141, 161-62, 165, 173, 190, 213-14,
219-20
Meat offered to idols, eating of, 30-32, 128, 167,
190, 246
Menander Rhetor, 116n.119, 201-202, 215n.11
Merchants, 102-107, 109-11, 118, 171, 182,
198-99, 202-208, 231
in Hebrew Bible, 63-64, 64n.73
Messages to the Seven Churches, 28-33, 151-59,
222
Form, 154-59
Function, 155-57
Micaiah ben-Imlah, 49n.29
Millenarianism, 1-2,
Moneylending (*faeneratores*), 22-23, 103n.72

Monody, 201-202, 209
Musonius Rufus, 83, 86

Narrative world. *See* Revelation, narrative world
Narrative criticism, 9-10; *see also* Revelation,
narrative world
Nepos, 2
Nero, 15n.42, 16n.43, 34, 68-69, 68n.87, 69n.90,
99, 99n.59, 113n.111
New Age, Jewish images of, 71-72, 75-76, 234-
36
New Criticism, 6n.14, 9n. 23
New Jerusalem, 30, 71-72, 127, 129, 177-78
as city, 215-18
Temple in, 76, 230-31, 234
Wealth of, 4, 24, 71, 80, 175, 189, 201, 209-
10, 218, 222-23, 225-39
Nicolaitans, 28, 29n.85, 30-31, 161n.31,
164n.36, 167, 231
Number of the Beast ("666"), 184, 186

Outlines of Revelation. *See* Revelation, structure

Panegyric. *See* Encomium
Papias, 2
Pastoral Epistles, 33-34
Patmos, 34, 145
Patron, God and Christ as, 138-40, 143, 174,
180, 214, 230, 242, 245
Paul, 17, 19, 33n.96, 95-96, 139-40, 140n.38,
142-44, 153, 221, 223, 237
Perceived crisis, 13
Pergamum, 31, 81, 152, 210
Peristaseis (hardships), 82, 85, 96n.47
Persecution, 144, 160-62; *see also* Christianity,
early, persecution
Philadelphia, 110n.102
Philo, 90n.27, 93-94, 163
Philosophy, 28, 31, 120-23, 223, 242
and appearance, 87-88, 88nn.20-22
and wealth, 82-97, 103, 123-24,
Philostratus, 112n.104, 113-14
Plebiscitum Claudianum, 106n.84
Pliny, 13, 22, 35
Plutarch, 92
Porneia (fornication), 32-33, 187, 189-91, 203-
204, 209-10, 243
Poststructuralism, 6-7, 7n.16
Poverty, 85, 87, 152, 160-62, 167-68, 174, 182-
83, 222, 228, 242
Proofs, rhetorical, 132-33, 135-36, 144, 157, 221
Prophecy, 17-18, 28, 142-43, 157, 221-22

Index of Ancient Sources

The Index of Ancient Sources is arranged as follows: (a) Hebrew Bible (Old Testament), in canonical order; (b) Apocrypha, Pseudepigrapha, etc., in alphabetical order; (c) New Testament, in canonical order; (d) Early Christian Literature, in alphabetical order; (e) Greek and Latin Texts, in alphabetical order; and (f) Rabbinic Literature, in alphabetical order.

(a) Hebrew Bible

(b) Apocrypha, Dead Sea Scrolls, Pseudepigrapha, and other Ancient Jewish Writings

(c) New Testament

(d) Early Christian Literature

(e) Greek and Latin Texts

(f) Rabbinic Literature

The Streets of Heaven.
The Ideology of Wealth in the Apocalypse of John.
by Robert M. Royalty, Jr.

Mercer University Press, 6316 Peake Road, Macon, Georgia 31210-3960 USA
Isbn 0-86554-609-6. Catalog and warehouse pick number: MUP/H465.
Text and interior design, composition, and layout by Edmon L. Rowell, Jr.
Cover and dust jacket design and layout by Jim Burt.
Dust jacket illustration: *The Last Judgment* (detail), by Fra Angelico (Guido di Pietro,
    ca. 1400–1450. Tempera on panel. Museo di San Marco, Florence.
Camera-ready pages composed on a Gateway 2000 (and an AOpen BG45-AP5VM)
    via dos WordPerfect 5.1 and WordPerfect for Windows 5.1/5.2
        (with WordPerfect 6.1 and Corel WP 7) and printed on a LaserMaster 1000.
Text fonts: TimesNewRomanPS 11/13; ATECH Hebrew and Greek.
    Display font: TimesNewRomanPS bf.
Printed and bound by McNaughton & Gunn, Inc., Saline, Michigan 48176,
    via offset lithography on 55# Writers Natural 360ppi.
Smyth sewn and cased into Arrestox A 44000 (blue linen) cloth,
    with one-hit gold foil stamping on spine and c. 4.
Dust jacket printed four-color process on 80# Gloss and film laminated.
[September/October 1998 / 2M]

100598elr